CW01496084

Silences and Divided Memories

European Anthropology in Translation
Published in Association with the Society for the Anthropology of Europe
(SAE), a Section of the American Anthropological Association (AAA)

General Editor: **Nicolette Makovicky**, University of Oxford

This series introduces English-language versions of significant works
on the Anthropology of Europe that were originally published in other
languages. These include books produced recently by a new generation
of scholars as well as older works that have not previously appeared in
English.

*For a full volume listing, please see the series page on our website:
https://www.berghahnbooks.com/series/european-anthropology-in-translation*

Silences and Divided Memories

The Exodus and Its Legacy in Postwar Istrian Society

Katja Hrobat Virloget

Translated by Marko Petrović

berghahn
NEW YORK • OXFORD
www.berghahnbooks.com

Published in 2023 by
Berghahn Books
www.berghahnbooks.com

English-language edition
© 2023 Berghahn Books

Translated by Marko Petrović

Library of Congress Cataloging in Publication Data

Names: Hrobat Virloget, Katja, author. | Petrović, Marko, translator.
Title: Silences and divided memories : the exodus and its legacy in post-war Istrian
 society / Katja Hrobat Virloget ; translated by Marko Petrović.
Other titles: V tišini spomina. English | Exodus and its legacy in post-war Istrian society
Description: English-language edition. | New York : Berghahn, 2023. | Series:
 European anthropology in translation ; volume 12 | Original title: V tišini
 spomina: "eksodus" in Istra. | Includes bibliographical references and index.
Identifiers: LCCN 2023007748 (print) | LCCN 2023007749 (ebook) |
 ISBN 9781805390381 (hardback) | ISBN 9781805390398 (ebook)
Subjects: LCSH: Collective memory—Istria (Croatia and Slovenia) | Italians—Istria
 (Croatia and Slovenia)—History—20th century. | Istria (Croatia and
 Slovenia)—Emigration and immigration—History—20th century. | Istria
 (Croatia and Slovenia)—Ethnic identity—History—20th century. | Istria
 (Croatia and Slovenia)—Ethnic relations—History—20th century.
Classification: LCC DR1350.I78 H7613 2023 (print) | LCC DR1350.I78 (ebook) |
 DDC 305.80094972—dc23/eng/20230417
LC record available at https://lccn.loc.gov/2023007748
LC ebook record available at https://lccn.loc.gov/2023007749

British Library Cataloguing-in-Publication Data

A catalogue record for this book is available from the British Library

ISBN 978-1-80539-038-1 hardback
978-1-80539-039-8 ebook

https://doi.org/10.3167/9781805390381

We were at war, and we continued being at war, simply because of the eternal question of whether we were Italians, Croats, or Slovenes, although in reality we were all of mixed origin.

—Fulvio Tomizza, *Boljše življenje*

That's how it is in history, my old man, where people and borders are mixed up, is it not? And it's the people that suffer then, and just as you were mocked and called "šćavo" while under Italy, so he too, and also you later, were called Italians; in Yugoslavia before the war, they called him a wop, frog-hunter, cat-eater, you see . . .

—Milan Rakovac, *"Riva i druži" ili, caco su nassa dizza*

Contents

Illustrations

Map

Figures

Acknowledgments

First of all, I would like to thank all the interlocutors I quote in this book using fictitious names, which is a shame because they should be seen. However, this is still such a sensitive topic, it is better to protect people with anonymity. Another thing that bothers me is my critical analysis. As a researcher, I have the unpleasant task of being on both sides of the fence: on the one hand, I try to give a voice to people who have been silenced, but on the other hand, I must critically analyze the feelings voiced from a scientific distance. And this is where I must apologize to all my interlocutors who saw in me the possibility of gaining a voice, but I then had to subject this voice to critical analysis. I apologize if I have offended anyone by doing this. As a researcher I can empower the marginalized, but I must also fulfill the thankless role of detached critic. Maybe this will make my writing unpleasant for some people.

Whatever the case may be, I am grateful to all my interlocutors, both those mentioned in the book and those not mentioned. To all of you who lent me your tears and your emotions, to all who spoke freely, to all who felt they had said too much and then regretted it, to all who found it embarrassing or simply fun evoking memories, and to all who helped me contact the interlocutors. This book would not exist without you.

Thanks to Aleksej Kalc, who has supported me all these years and included me in research projects, thereby enabling me to carry out research and publish this book and other publications.

Special thanks for all the moral support and professional discussions goes to Mateja Habinc, Petra Kavrečič, and Neža Čebron Lipovec. Neža particularly encouraged me to study this silenced topic. There are also many other friends who supported me all along. Thanks to my reviewers Mila Orlić, Mojca Ramšak, and Marta Verginella for her comments.

I would also like to thank my two translators—Marko Petrović for the English and Lucia Gaja Scuteri for the Italian—for all their efforts (summary translated by Nives Mahne Čehovin, copy edited by Murray Bales); the editors Martina Kafol and Alina Carli for helping find photographs, their editorial work, for promoting the book, and for all our discussions; and the journalist Stefano Lusa for being the first to make the book known in the media.

Finally, my family was most understanding, patiently putting up with all my absences due to both books—the Slovenian and English versions. Thank you, Samuel, my son, Baptiste, my husband, and Milena, my mother.

The monograph was financially supported by the Slovenian Research Agency (SRA).

The research results of this book derive from several SRA research projects: Migration control in the Slovenian area from the times of Austria-Hungary to independent Slovenia, led by Aleksej Kalc (J6–8250; 2020-2023); postodoctoral project, The burden of the past. Co-existence in the (Slovenian) Coastal region in light of the formation of post-war Yugoslavia, led by Katja Hrobat Virloget (Z6-4317; 2012-2014), Migration and social transformation in a comparative perspective: the case of Western Slovenia after WWII, led by Aleksej Kalc (J6-3143; 2021-2024), and Urban Futures: Imagining and Activating Possibilities in Unsettled Times, led by Saša Poljak Istenič (J6-2578; 2020-2023). Thanks to the Faculty of Humanities, University of Primorska, Koper/Capodistria, Slovenia, for its support.

Introduction

Problems and Frameworks of Memory in Ethnological Research

My grandma often told me the story of how in World War II a German saved her home village of Kastelec, situated on the southern edge of the Karst, from being burned down. While they were busy sewing red stars, a German soldier suddenly entered the house. There was a moment of deathly silence. He stepped to the table and swept all the stars from under the sewing machine so that they fell behind the table. At that moment other German soldiers entered the room, had a quick look round, and departed. The German soldier, who in Slovene eyes was an occupier and aggressor, was never seen again, but they knew he had saved them from being killed and probably also prevented the village from being burned down. This is how a former partisan courier taught me as a young girl to "see the people" behind all kinds of stereotypes and also gave me the strength to undertake this difficult research.

This book talks about the memories of the people who stayed in Istria as well as those who came after the exodus. I deliberately use the term "exodus," although it is controversial, and despite being reproached by most Slovenian historians who strictly refer to these movements as post-war migrations or emigration. The controversy surrounding the term reflects the different national discourses that exist when interpreting the past. Each nation defends its own parallel version of history and the reasons for the migrations, so different numbers of migrants are cited and different appellations are used (Verginella 2000; Ballinger 2003: 42–45).[1] While Italians and migrants call themselves *esuli*, which means refugees or exiles (Ballinger 2003), the predominant term in Slovenian and Croatian discourse is *optant*. This stems from the legal right to opt for Italian citizenship (based on the Treaty of Peace with Italy, signed in Paris on February 1947 and the London Memorandum in 1954), which entailed an obligation to move to Italy (Volk 2003: 47–50; Gombač 2005: 65; Pupo 2015). While Italian historians talk about the Italian exodus (Pupo 2015), Slovenian and Croatian researchers emphasize that the migrations included Italians, Slovenes, Croats, and both voluntary and forced migrants. There are also interpretations arguing that wartime and postwar migrations from Istria to Italy across the new national border better suit the criteria of regional emigration than international migration (Gombač 2005). As a counterbalance to the exodus, Croatian historians have even introduced the concept of the "first exodus," during which between 50,000 and 100,000 Croats and Slovenes are said to have left Istria and were Italianized by fascist violence (Strčić 2001; Dota 2010: 91, 103–6). Due to long-standing accusations of performing one-sided research because I do not include fascism in my investigations of the exodus, I have grown accustomed to mentioning the migrations of Slovenes and Croats on account of fascist violence before speaking about the exodus. I use the term "exodus" without any political or mythological connotations, without referring to a "mononational" process (Ballinger 2003: 7), which is often the case with Italian researchers, despite the fact that this is a very complex migration phenomenon. It is simply a term that is best known by the general public. Some Slovenian researchers use it (Volk 2003; Kalc 2019), and it is most frequently used in international literature. However, by using this term I do not pretend that the process was not monumental, after all it almost wiped out an entire ethnic community from a specific territory. By using it, I also question the so greatly extolled "free choice" or option, although in a legal sense it did exist.

My research into the memories of the so-called exodus began after I moved from Ljubljana to Piran/Pirano to begin a new job.[2] In summer the town was full of tourists, people hustling and bustling, shops and restaurants open, while in the winter it was like a ghost town where you hardly met anyone on the streets, only the odd local here and there, a number of them lost to alcohol and drugs, the streets empty, and closed shutters on the flats and houses. It is true that the inhabitants of Primorska (the Slovenian Littoral region)—known as Primorci—are used to this winter emptiness, but when I compared it with life in Brittany, which I was also familiar with, I felt something was not right. As far as I could see in France, people on the coast really lived with the sea; you could hardly find a local who did not have a sailing boat and whose life was connected with the sea the whole year round. It was more than a kind of decoration in the summer tourist season. How is it that in Istrian towns the locals did not seem to live with the sea? It is true that throughout the Mediterranean there is a difference between the winter and the summer, which is full of life and tourists, yet in Piran I had the impression that the people living by the sea did not really live with it, at least most of them did not. A few years ago, the parish priest in Strunjan/Strugnano complained that when he wanted to revive the traditional boat pilgrimage from Piran to Strunjan on the eve of the feast of Our Lady's Assumption, he could not find enough people who actually owned boats. I remember my surprise during an interview with an elderly Italian local to determine how many Istro-Venetian dialectal words for the sea existed. This is logical as they lived with it and constantly observed it. Probably less than half of these words are known in the languages that came here following the exodus. This absence of expressions and the fact that the present-day fishermen have taken most of their maritime and fishing vocabulary from the local Istro-Venetian dialect shows that most of Istria's present-day population, the immigrants, had no connection with the sea.[3] When I began this research ten years ago, people, especially the Italian speakers, did not like to talk about the exodus. During this decade, other subjects indirectly connected with the exodus have also been studied. For example, Neža Čebron Lipovec (2018, 2019) studied ideological changes in the architecture of Istrian towns following the exodus, Suzana Todorović (2016) studied Istrian dialects, and the exodus has increasingly been mentioned in the media. Even in 2017, it was difficult to talk publicly in Slovenia about the suffering of people at the time of the exodus, and this is proven by the fact that after an interview I gave on this subject on Radio Trieste, I received a call from an Italian politician who congratulated me for this brave and sincere act.

Although prior to my research quite a number of historical studies had been done on the exodus, mostly by Italians, I still missed hearing the views of the people who had experienced this dramatic social change, that is, an ethnological view or in the vocabulary of historians "the view from the bottom up." I encountered the simple affirmation that "the people left"; yet I wondered how someone who is attached to their homeland, house, and sea can simply "go," leave everything behind and become a refugee. Was the act that cut so deeply into people's lives really based only on a voluntary decision? How can 200,000 to 300,000 people—the figures quoted for the exodus from Istria—voluntarily leave their home? And how is it that nothing is known about these migrations that brought such far-reaching social, ethnic, and economic change in Istria? Why is there nothing in school curricula, nothing in the Slovenian media, nothing except some academic literature?[4] Beginning with very simple questions, which historians with their frequently dry data focused only on politics do not bother answering, I embarked on an ethnological study that placed people, their thoughts, emotions, and views in the forefront. My study is therefore less concerned with politics although with an awareness of its grip. The aim is not to judge who was right and who was not but simply to understand the people: those who stayed and those who went. How did they experience the changes? How did they live together? What kind of relationships did they establish among themselves and toward their environment?

This study, therefore, does not deal with history but rather addresses ethnology and cultural anthropology. The basic premise is memory, which in anthropology is understood to be the "trace of the past in the present" (Lavabre 2007: 139). Another theoretical framework is provided by David Lowenthal's postmodern, constructivist paradigm, which states that the past is solely an artifact of the present (Lowenthal 1985: XVI). The past is so distant that it must be reconstructed, and it is solely an identifier in the present (Hobsbawm 1996; Fakin Bajec 2011: 27). This means the past does not exist on its own, but only in relation to the sociopolitical context of the present. The present is constantly redefining the past. Even if it is not so distant, it is always marked by the present context and historicity (Fr. l'*historicité*) (de Certeau 1987). This is why the study does not focus on reconstructing the past on the basis of memory—the work of historians—but rather investigates what people said happened and not what did happen. This leads to the question of what these representations of the past say not only about the past but also about the present. How do people remember what they experienced, what do they emphasize, what do they now consider to be important? If historians ask themselves what the (past) reality was like, anthropologists ask how people see and construct this (past) reality?[5] As anthropologists respond to postmodern critique, constructed reality is also reality. It is equally effective and materializes in the practice of people (Muršič 1999: 24). This book therefore gives a voice to the people who remained silent because their memories did not correspond with the public discourse of either. I will probably not clarify the past, but I will give it the freedom to speak through different voices and touch us in the present.

As Maurice Halbwachs first argued, a person remembers together with their community. Such remembrance is not an individual act but takes place together with other members of the group to which a person belongs. According to Halbwachs's theory, memory depends on *les cadres de la mémoire*—frameworks of memory. In his opinion, memory is like everyday life, the ordinariness of social worlds, groups, and individuals who belong to or identify themselves with groups that share common or collective memories. This collective memory is adapted to suit the needs of contemporary time and social context so memory is selected depending on the needs of the present time. Society supports what will be remembered and what will be forgotten, as will become evident when we deal with silence as the result of the collective censorship of those individual memories that do not support the collective view of the past. Individual memory is only temporary, without meaning, as memory remains collective because we always think as members of a group. And if memory is the intersection of collective influences and social networks in which the individual is active, then we are talking about Halbwachs's "multiplicity of social times," as the individual with his multiplicity of social identities is always a member of different groups—the family, religious community, social class, and more. For Maurice Halbwachs, all human thought is memory. The "present of the past" is, on the one hand, a trace of the past in the present and, on the other hand, memory of or selective reference to the past. Memory connects the individual with the community and determines their belonging. The fact that it establishes a connection between the past and the present makes it a fundamental element of identity. This is why memory is more connected with identity and the present than the past (Halbwachs 1925, 1971; Confino 1997; Fabietti and Matera 1999; Lavabre 2007; Širok 2009; Baussant 2019).

The theoretical framework of this study is based on Halbwachs's paradigm of *les cadres de la mémoire*, which explores the social conditions necessary for the production of memories, remembering and forgetting. His concept of the multiplicity of memories is particularly useful, and one of the fundamental questions is how the transition from individual memories to collective memory and vice versa occurs. This concept may be applied to the question of competitiveness, representations, conflicts, and in understanding memory as the result of the simultaneity of different, overlapping and opposing identities (Halbwachs 1971; Confino 1997; Lavabre 2007).

This study contains little of the dominant historical perception of memory, which is mostly based on the politics of memory and the paradigm of *les lieux de mémoire* (Nora 1984, 1986, 1993), where the subject being studied is the genealogy of the representation of symbols in which collective identities, public narratives of the past, and even more political (ab)use of the past are crystallized (Lavabre 2007). In this approach, memory is reduced to its ideological and political form, that is, to the subjective experience of a group that uses memory to maintain power relations. Therefore, the field of research does not cover the social and experiential - the everyday history of memory. By reducing a cultural phenomenon to its political dimension, the transmission, diffusion, and meaning of representations is neglected. A problem arises if a historian is attentive only to the visible and official memory while neglecting the reception of this memory by the people (Confino 1997). Such critique of memory by historians applies primarily to political history. As Marie-Claire Lavabre (2007) observes, unlike the sociological or anthropological perspective, memory in the hands of historians is mostly reduced to an epistemological curiosity, subject to the imperatives of proof and argument. The perception of memory through oral history is more akin to that of anthropology. Alessandro Portelli, one of the first theoreticians of oral history, draws attention to the combination of three aspects: the historical event as a fact from the past, the narrative we are listening to as a fact in the present, and the relationship between the two as a combination of the past and the present. According to Portelli, oral sources tell us not only what people did but also what they wanted to do, what they believed they were doing, and what they now think they did (Portelli 2016). The main theoretical framework of this book will not be political or historical as in so-called border studies, which focus on the political aspect of memory, but rather anthropological literature about memory, migrations and migrant societies, heritage, and so forth.

Life Stories and the Ethnographic Position

Almost ten years had to pass after the first interviews were carried out before I began writing this book. The French anthropologist and sociologist Nicole Lapierre describes a similar need to distance herself from emotionally charged memories in her book on the study of Jewish memories of the Holocaust *Le silence de la mémoire*. She writes that it was necessary to step back in order to free herself of connections with the people, so that the complex landscape of different life stories and memories could clear up. When carrying out research so close to home in a place that is fed by the shadow of drama, and where you are in touch with intimacy and keep a distance, how do you justify that you no longer call or visit the people who welcomed you into their homes? Distancing and freeing oneself therefore come with the risk that you will be considered ungrateful (Lapierre 1989: 77–78). The same was necessary in my case. Time had to pass so I could calm my emotions after the life stories I had heard and recover from the tears I had shared with the people. I had to distance myself from the Italian speakers whose painful memories had upset me,[6] especially as in the early phase of my research I felt a moral obligation to be a spokesperson for their mute memories. First I had to deal with my own stereotypical views of Italians. As a member of Slovenian society, my perception of them was burdened with the predominant stereotype of fascists responsible for over twenty years of violence against Slovenes. Now I sympathized with these Italians and dismantled the notions of the "good Slovenian" and "evil Italian" I had been taught. I faced the unpleasant consequences of our "righteous" national liberation struggle,[7] which produced thousands of migrants from Istria, and the marginalization of those "who do not belong (any more)."

Although in the beginning I kept returning to some of the narrators, naively thinking that I would learn new facts and thereby acquire a more complete picture, I reached saturation point and everything began to appear the same. I already knew everything in advance. I had to experience this satiation, when the life stories and information become repetitive and enthusiasm wanes (Lapierre 1989: 77–78). I had to survive this "cursed" part of ethnographic study in which you become a foreigner in your own research and are overcome by fatigue and boredom (Perrot 1987 in Lapierre 1989: 77), and when all the stories appear to be the same. Some time had to pass for me to establish a critical distance from all the conversations and all the people I had talked with. In truth, both sides are victims of history, some happy in their new home, others unhappy, some robbed of connections with their roots, others of their community, some ignorant, others triumphant, while some feel guilty because of the people who had to leave. Some time had to pass before I could abandon the black and white dichotomy between "victims" and "perpetrators," "victors" and "losers," "persecutors" and the "persecuted," "good" and "bad," "lies" and "truths" (Baussant and Foscarini 2017: 22–23) and before I could realize that the roles are interchangeable and unclear, and before I could stop making moral judgments. Above all, I began to see people and their individual fates set against political and historical backgrounds.

Sometimes I am asked why I need to delve into such painful, conflictual topics and would it not be better if such "undigested history" (Baskar 2002; Ballinger 2003; Rogelja and Janko Spreizer 2017: 70) were simply forgotten or swept under the carpet? As Tim Ingold (2018: 27–28) says, the goal of researchers is not only to contextualize and analyze but to show that we care about someone. By giving the people we talk to a voice, we show that we care about them and through their memories we place them in our present and put the past into context. The past is not just an object of memory. "In remembering, on the other hand, the past is not finished but active in the present" (Ingold 2018: 28).

The beginning of this ethnographic research, when I first encountered such different memories, was emotionally very difficult. I listened in tears to the pain of Italian Istrians who had become complete foreigners in their own homes, their feeling of being abandoned by the state, families, friends, acquaintances, and their feelings of marginalization, stigmatization, and collective criminalization. In the background there was the unutterable feeling of social roles being overturned, when you are no longer esteemed, important, and "civilized," but become invisible and a second-class citizen. On the other side, there are stories of oppressed people who finally freed themselves from the yoke of fascism, not only its physical violence but also its symbolic oppression that made them feel inferior and as if they were second-class citizens. Stories about the "promised land," which became "ours" after so many decades of injustice, suffering under fascism and World War II. Then there are the stories of those who came to this newly acquired part of Yugoslavia, the promised land of new opportunities, as complete foreigners, unaware of the heavy burden of history and the region's deep wounds. And the stories of the *esuli*,[8] the migrants, the story of how someone committed suicide because of the pain caused by his completely different status in the promised land of Italy, where they went from "being someone to being nothing," the stories of the *esuli*, the word with the most negative connotations, and people who were so disappointed by the "promised" land that they returned home. People who go quiet when they hear the word "exodus," people who neither want to hear nor speak about the exodus. . . . Or people who no longer want to speak with the researcher after having told her too much. And parts of painful testimonies, parts of interviews not recorded because of very intimate moments and tears. . . . Without any scientific evidence . . .

As Ruth Behar (1996: 2) wonders, what are the limits of an ethnographer's listening and note-taking when the person being interviewed opens up their heart? What are the limits of compassion and respect, which should not be surpassed, not even in the name of scientific research? Anthropologists discovered a long time ago that anthropological truth is person-specific.[9] All depends on the researcher's emotional and intellectual baggage. No two researchers ever hear the same story, the researcher never observes something that did not happen outside his presence (Behar 1996: 6–9). Both the researcher and the person who is the subject of the research are affected by conscious and unconscious psychological processes. In the process of forming ethnological knowledge, we cannot avoid the subjective experience while objective reality is illusionary; all our descriptions of the "other" are the product of our own projections, which lie deep within us and of which we are frequently not even aware (Corin 2007: 258; Leibing, McLean 2007, 19–20). The fundamental paradox of anthropology is in its fundamental method of participant observation. The anthropologist is supposed to attain the native point of view, but without actually going native. They then write down what they have heard, compare it to what they have read by Karl Marx, Max Weber, Antonio Gramsci, and Clifford Geertz and are on their way to doing anthropology (Behar 1996: 5). Unfortunately, anthropology has developed into an artificial feeling of superiority, personal testimonies being considered taboo due to depersonalized modern trends. Although the discipline developed out of the need for giving a voice to "others," the Western fantasy of studying the barbaric "others" focused on "culture" and not on the "individual." From self observation with the awareness of the complex historical and psychological picture, we have made the transition to observing ourselves—and we should be pluralistic, ahistorical, and impersonal. However, sensitivity does not mean that everything is personally acceptable, instead it is more a case of identifying with the observed person (Behar 1996: 14–16, 26).

There is no sincere interview without empathy, so every ethnological study is part of the researcher, their emotions, acceptance, facing and empathizing with the observed. This is why I have no illusions that ethnological writing (as any other) can be objective. After so many years of research, my initial naivety, struggles with my stereotypes about "others," assuming the role of spokesperson for the silenced "others"—the Italian minority—I began to establish a critical distance with which I try to view all people in history in the same, distant way, but this is probably a great disappointment for all who allowed me to enter their intimate world and expected me to become their spokesperson. In this respect, I can neither completely disappoint them nor satisfy them. Similarly to Nicole Lapierre (1989: 33), I was moved by the life stories I heard and felt a certain moral responsibility after hearing them, which lies like a shadow of burden on this study. By becoming a spokesperson, while at the same time trying to preserve the critical distance of the external observer, I am pushed into the difficult ethnological role of the researcher who disappoints everyone—all who entrusted me with some of their intimate memories, in the hope that they would perhaps be heard by society at large. Despite the fact that so much remains untold and unutterable; caught in the gestures, looks, silent pauses. ..
"The word is impossible but oblivion unbearable" (Lapierre 1989: 16), all the more so when the boundaries between the perpetrator and the victim are blurred and interchangeable, when both sides bear the burden of the past both collectively and individually.

My observational position is both a problem and an advantage. On the one hand, I can be an "external" researcher as anthropology demands. Neither I nor my family comes from Istria but from neighboring Karst. As part of the broader Primorska region, we share a common history with Istria having been part of the same littoral region in the

Austro-Hungarian Empire, as well as a common recent past under fascist Italy and a common struggle against the Italian (and later German) occupier during World War II. Trieste was historically our region's economic center, which meant that the inhabitants of the Karst and the Brkini had regular contact with Italians, who unlike in Istria were not a community that had historically been present in the region. I was far enough and also near enough to "understand" or at least try to understand the Istrians. On the other hand, I can also consider myself to be an insider observer. I attribute this to my Primorska identity, which like Istria has a political discourse based on the anti-fascist struggle, my knowledge of the Italian language due to everyday contact with Italians, and my education and current work in Koper/Capodistria, where I have a network of friends, acquaintances, and colleagues. It is thanks to this situation that I was able to come into contact with the people I interviewed, although I realize that these Istrians I spoke with consider all people like me who come from above the imaginary border above Črni Kal as "Slovene" or *forešt* (foreigner). Pier Paolo Viazzo would call such an anthropological view, that is neither "native" nor "distant," a "view from up close" or a "view from the neighborhood" (Baskar 2014: 438). Although I am neither completely "inside" nor completely "outside" in my perception, I am nevertheless more "outside" for many Istrians and will always hear the reproach: "you don't know our history" (van de Port 1999: 14)!

On Interlocutors and the Method

Due to a lack of ethnological and cultural anthropological research focusing on the exodus and its impact on Istrian society, at the beginning of my study I concentrated on understanding this phenomenon "from the bottom up," that is, from behind political narratives, focusing on the memories of the people who now live here. Most studies of so-called population movements mainly focus on the experiences of migrants, while the space left behind in the wake of mass migrations is often ignored as if life there had stopped. Attention is therefore rarely turned to the "emptied" and "newly settled" areas,[10] which are usually referred to by concepts such as contested places, pasts, and memories.

This study includes the views of not just one ethnic group, but all who now live in Istria: Slovenian and Italian Istrians, Slovenian and Italian immigrants, and immigrants from the southern republics of the former Yugoslavia, that is, from the dominant, hegemonic to the marginalized and overlooked. Most interlocutors were of Slovene or Italian ethnicity. Further research will place greater emphasis on gathering memories of people from the southern republics of the former Yugoslavia. In the anthropological framework, we talk about the multivocal approach, which is used when studying the concept of place (Rodman 1992), and in this case in connection with the perception of heritage. From the point of view of oral history, it partly resembles the method of *histoire croisée* (Werner and Zimmermann 2006; Verginella 2010; Čebron Lipovec 2018).

The study is based on transcribed interviews with fifty-three people; some interviews were carried out more than once with the same people. It is also necessary to count the numerous untranscribed interviews, during which recording was not possible. For these rare quotes from conversations, it is expressly mentioned that they are field notes. Most interviews are based on life stories that directly reflect the social and political circumstances in the past, and I tried to find out more about views on migrations and social realities. As Istria is my working environment, the research includes many everyday, random, informal conversations; many examples of participant observation; notes from many public round tables I attended on the subject of Istria, and more. Finding interlocutors was like a "snowball effect": one person recommended another and most were recommended by friends and colleagues from Istria. I could have carried on doing more interviews but there comes a point at which a limit has to be set on the research. In addition to the transcribed, unstructured interviews, a number of students carried out ethnographic research involving interviews on different subjects at the Faculty of Humanities of the University of Primorska during these ten years. There were also many informal, unrecorded conversations; the material gathered includes notes jotted down on the go, thoughts from everyday conversations in the street, at work in Koper and in Piran—basically in the course of my everyday work in Istria. I limited my research to the Slovenian part of Istria, both the urban and non-urban parts, the main reason being practicality as this is part of my everyday working environment and my social network meant it was easier to find interlocutors. On the other hand, I must mention that I also obtained many insights into the social realities of the Croatian part of Istria, from where a number of my interlocutors originate.

I also tried to obtain the views of the third side, that is, the *esuli*, the Italians who left Istria. However, with the exception of the very communicative president of a French association of emigrants from Istria and Dalmatia in Paris, I ran into an impregnable wall so I quickly gave up on the idea. The above president was surprised that the *esuli* did not want to speak to me. This is an expression of the deep, unhealed wounds and hatred for those who are supposed to have forced them in one way or another to leave, and contempt for the *sc'avi* that drove many to engage in right-wing politics.[11]

I also made use of the already published life stories of contemporary Istrians (Pahor 2007, 2011, 2014; Menih 2011) and books containing the memories of Italians who remained,[12] supplemented with the memories of those who left (Castelli 2018).[13] In addition to academic works I found that literary works by Istrian writers of Slovene, Croat, and Italian origin also provided a good introduction to the topic. They give clear evidence of the social wounds caused by the exodus, of traumas and dilemmas, immigration, new and old social relations, and more (Tomizza 1980, 1989, 2015; Rakovac 1983; Ugussi 1991; F. Juri 2010; Milani Kruljac 2011).

The interlocutors in the book are anonymous. They have been given fictitious names either because they asked for this or because of the sensitivity of the topic that remains controversial after so many decades. As Elda, an Italian interlocutor said regarding anonymity: "There's no doubt, these matters are too sensitive."[14]

This book was written to show the people's perspective and their emotions. I wish to draw attention to ordinary people caught up in the turmoil of great political upheavals, to place people at the forefront with anthropological theory serving only to shed light on these processes. Blank spaces will undoubtedly be left in our knowledge of this turbulent episode in history and its influence on present-day society. My version of the truth will probably be just one of many different versions. As Elda, an elderly Italian interlocutor commented, "But no one will tell you the truth. Even after so many years it is unpleasant for some people there to remember these things. . . . You see, she too would like to understand those people who left, and the people who came. But it will be hard for you to get to the end because no one tells anything, no one wants to tell."[15]

By studying Istria's contentious past, this book turns to self-critical reflection on an overlooked chapter of national history; focusing on national discourses; relations between the majority and the minority, a taboo topic; the relations between marginal, alternative, and dominant hegemonic memories and heritage; fluid borderland identities; place attachment; appropriations of traditions and the past; and more. These views may well shake the self-evident convictions—as they did mine—which we as members of Slovenian society have consciously and unconsciously adopted through education, the media, and everyday discourse. As the Croatian ethnologist Dunja Rihtman Auguštin (2001: 210–17) wrote, ethnologists must be like their society's conscience, it being their

Map 0.1. Positions of the border between Italy and Yugoslavia after 1945 (Made by Andrej Preložnik in Hrobat Virloget, Gousseff, and Corni 2015: 23, Figure 1).[16]

moral and even patriotic duty to be critically present, constantly alert, and ready to criticize and deconstruct political myths. Both national collective memory and national heritage are based on chosen, unforgettable achievements, making selections from the past and tradition while silencing and forgetting what would constitute a different story from another perspective. Memory and heritage are under the influence of the power and authority of those who have colonized the past and whose versions of history matter (Hall 2008: 221). Oblivion and even a historical mistake are crucial for the formation of a nation, so the development of history (and anthropology) constitute dangers for a nation (Renan 1998: 8–9; Orlić 2012: 17). The fact is that courage is needed to sincerely confront ourselves, what has been kept silent, and stereotypes about the "other," both individually or collectively. As Aleida Assmann (2007: 23), a researcher of memory, asserts, European integration will remain an empty dream until nations establish a shared consciousness as victims and perpetrators. To achieve this, "inappropriate" memories must be integrated and not erased, people must face their own memories and listen to "others" with empathy. This is also the aim of this book.

Notes

1. I will deal with the problem of national identities in the Istrian multicultural environment later.
2. The territory is officially bilingual so every toponym in Istria must be written in both languages. For the sake of simplicity, I will give both the Slovenian and Italian names of places only when they are mentioned for the first time. In direct speech, the name is given in its narrated form—either Italian or Slovenian.
3. As the linguist and Italian language specialist Suzana Todorović wrote (email, 29 October 2019), "You can only carry out a survey of fishing and maritime terms in the coastal area among autochthonous Romance-speaking Istrians." It is generally considered that the present-day Slovenian fishing industry in Istria was not originally Slovenian (Rogelja and Janko Spreizer 2017: 23).
4. Much more has been written on the Italian side.
5. I would like to thank Michéle Baussant (CNRS, Paris) and Mateja Habinc (University of Ljubljana Faculty of Arts) for thoughts expressed in discussions and Petra Kavrečič (University of Primorska) for her advice concerning oral history.
6. In order to avoid the longer term "Italian speakers" I often say Italians or Italian Istrians, although many in Istria are not defined as Italians in terms of nationality but as Slovenians and before that as Yugoslavs.
7. From a speech by the President of the National Assembly of Slovenia Milan Brglez held on 20 March 2015 in a celebration at the anti-fascist monument in Strunjan (more on this in the chapter on conflicting national memories).
8. In Italian public discourse *esuli* is the generally accepted term for migrants from Istria and Dalmatia. In Italian it means exile or refugee.
9. In this book I used the terms ethnology and cultural anthropology as different names for the same discipline as they have overcome their differences and different research emphases in the past (see Eriksen 1995: 13–15; Slavec Gradišnik 2000: 105–10).
10. As will be shown later, the exodus had different phases, but only the last one can be referred to as mass migration, which took place in both directions—into and out of the territory.
11. The distinctly contemptuous and insulting word *schiavo/sc'avo/ščavo* (also *sclavo*) has an older origin as it was already used in the early Middle Ages to designate the inhabitants of the region of Goriška, Istria, Friuli, Carniola, and Dalmatia. This word, *Sclavi* (meaning "slaves" in Italian), was the general designation for the wider Slav

linguistic and ethnic group, ignoring the differences between different Slavic languages and identities (Makuc 2015: 165–66). An example that describes the attitude
of the *esuli* toward Slovenes and Croats is the story of an *esule* from Gorizia, who
in his disappointment that Istria had become part of Yugoslavia, devoted his whole
life to proving the borders of the Romance-speaking territory, Venetian identity,
and therefore the Italian identity of his native Poreč/Parenzo in Istria. This hatred
stemming from his pain was overcome by his daughter who, to her father's chagrin,
began climbing Slovenia's mountains (Rijavec 2020: 25).

12. Istrian Italians do not like to be defined as the ones who remained (It. *rimasti*). As
Valeria says, "I never want to say that I 'remained'—I was born here, I didn't remain.
When someone talks about 'the ones who stayed' I am offended." I am sorry and
apologize to all Italians if I have offended them, but I use this word for want of
finding a better one to designate those who did not emigrate.

13. In addition to these there are also many other published memories of *esuli*, in particular a series of books entitled *Chiudere il cerchio: memorie giuliano-dalmate*, which
could be translated as Closing the Circle: Julian-Dalmatian Memories (Miletta Mattiuz and Rumici 2008).

14. The personal information of the people I spoke with is kept in my personal archive.

15. "Però la verità non te la dirà mai nessuno. Anche dopo tanti anni non è piacevole
ricordare quelle cose li, per certi . . . La vedi anche ella che vuol arrivar al capo di
'sta . . . di gente che xe andata via di gente che xe andata via, di gente che xe restada.
Ma arriverà con fatica al capo perché nessun dixi, nessun vol dir." Just to illustrate I
have given the exact words used by my interlocutors speaking in the Istro-Venetian
dialect. Unfortunately, in the text, all the speech will be translated meaning that the
book will lose the richness of the Istro-Venetian dialects.

16. Grey lines: The borders of the Venezia Giulia between 1945 and 1947 which was
divided by the Morgan line (the dashed line) in zone A (administered by the Allied forces; darker color, western part) and zone B (administered by the Yugoslav
National Army; brighter color, eastern part). The western border almost entirely
coincides with the border between Italy and the Austro-Hungarian monarchy until
1918 and the eastern border follows the border between Italy and Yugoslavia in
1941. Dotted lines: The borders of the Free Territory of Trieste (1947–1954). After
the Paris Peace Treaty (1947), zone A of the Venezia Giulia (west of Gorizia and
Monfalcone, dotted) was given to Italy, while the majority of the zone A of the
Venezia Giulia (the eastern part and the area around Pula) and the majority of zone
B went to Yugoslavia. The most disputed part of the former Venezia Giulia gained
special status and was divided into zone A (administered by Allied forces; darker
with lines, northern part) and zone B (administered by the Yugoslav National Army;
brighter with lines, southern part) of the Free Territory of Trieste. After the London
Memorandum (1954), zone A became part of Italy and zone B part of Yugoslavia.
Black lines: the present-day borders between Italy, Slovenia, Croatia, and Austria.

Chapter 1

Difficult Pasts, Silence, and Conflicts of Memory

Difficult Pasts, Contested Territory

*Population Movements and the Shifting of
National Boundaries in Istria*

As a multiethnic, multicultural, and officially bilingual Mediterranean frontier region, Istria is a prime example of a territory that has been contested for centuries and has "problematic" and mostly "undigested" histories, where people construct various "pure" and hybrid identities (Baskar 2002; Ballinger 2012; Rogelja and Janko Spreizer 2017: 34–35, 75). The first written sources mentioning the coexistence of a Romance-speaking (Istro-Venetian dialect) urban population in the Istrian coastal towns and a Slav population (speaking Slovene and Croat dialects) in the hinterland date back to the ninth century. From the thirteenth century onward, most of Istria belonged to the Republic of Venice, the Serenissima, until the nineteenth century when all of Istria came under Habsburg rule and later formed part of the Austrian Empire. In the twentieth century, the Istrians lived under five different powers, from empires to nation-states. With the rise of nationalism in the nineteenth century, social, linguistic and class differences in Istria were increasingly defined in terms of ethnic or national identity (Baskar 2002).

After World War I, Istria (the coast and interior) and the broader Primorska region (the former Austrian Littoral) became the subject of political negotiations. When in 1915 Italy entered World War I as an Allied Force, it was "promised" a large portion of the territory of Primorska if the war ended with a positive outcome for the Allied forces.

As Italy participated actively in the war and was on the "winning" side, it was granted the promised territories. Following diplomatic negotiations with the Kingdom of Serbs, Croats, and Slovenes and the Allies, the territory formally came under Italy with the Treaty of Rapallo in 1920. The aim of the Italian fascist regime (which lasted from 1922) was to completely Italianize the Slovene and Croatian speaking populations, which meant more than two decades of violent, repressive, and assimilatory politics against the Slavs. The fascist violence left a deep impression on the region's Slovene population, although it also operated against all Italians who opposed it. It began with the burning of the Slovene Cultural Centre in Trieste in 1920 and continued with the "Italianization" of schools (500 schools abolished, teachers sacked and exiled). Slovene and Croatian were banned from use in public, in education, and in churches, names were Italianized, land was confiscated, all Slovene and Croat organizations and institutions were banned (sports, cultural, youth, social, cooperatives, financial institutions, libraries, cultural centers), all Slovene and Croat press was abolished, Slovene signs were removed from shops, restaurants, and gravestones, and there were violent physical attacks by fascists, individuals suffered political persecution, political parties were banned, access to public services was limited, people were tortured and murdered (e.g., the poisoning and death of the composer Lojze Bratuž who was forced to drink machine oil). A special court to protect the Italian state was founded (1926) with the first and second trial in Trieste resulting in prison sentences and fourteen death sentences for Slovenes that were carried out. There was military occupation, massacres were perpetrated and villages were burned down, and more. The aim was to completely destroy Slovene and Croat national identity in the Julian March (Pirjevec 1982; Kacin Wohinz 1998; Pelikan 2002; Guštin and Troha 2004; Bertucelli and Orlić 2008; Kacin Wohinz and Verginella 2008).

Fascist violence in the interwar period caused around 100,000 Slovenes and Croats to escape from the Julian March at the eastern end of the Italian empire (of which Istria made up approximately a third), 70,000 of them going to Yugoslavia. Approximately 129,000 Italian migrants moved to the Julian March, mainly to urban centers. This did not completely change the population's ethnic makeup but it did break up the Slovenian middle class (Čepič and Nećak 1979; Verginella 2015: 59–60; Purini 2010: 146–75). Due to the migrations of Slovenes, Croats and German-speakers, the ethnically mixed territory of the Julian March was ethnically homogenized and Italianized. However, the decline in the non-Italian population and increase in the number of Italians registered in a census is not only due to migrations but also "ethnic bonification" through "Italianization" of the population by means of political discrimination against non-Italians, violence, and intimidation (Purini 2010: 9, 53–58, 81–88). Piero Purini (2010: 175) nevertheless finds that the fascist policy of denationalizing the Slovene and Croat population did not prove successful. Although Slovenes and Croats suffered heavy blows from a social, cultural, and economic point of view, they still remained quite strong in terms of numbers. The time leading up to and during World War II is marked by Slovene resistance to fascism and the struggle for national emancipation, which combine in the national liberation struggle. All this represents the basis of Slovene national identity (Fikfak 2009: 359).

During World War II (in 1943), Italy surrendered as an Axis power and formally joined the Allies. Yugoslavia (still a kingdom at the time) was attacked in 1941 and occupied, and it developed a strong partisan resistance movement that meant it was on the side of the Allied forces. Although Italy was an aggressor and an ally of Germany and the other Axis powers, its position changed after the end of the war and its borders were not dealt with in the same way as those of other Axis powers. As one of the victorious Allied forces, the new Yugoslav state demanded that the border between Yugoslavia and Italy be corrected, as it believed that the Treaty of Rapallo had been unjust for the Slovene and Croat national communities. It turned out, however, that the alliances crumbled after the main enemy was defeated so the postwar period was marked above all by the world being divided into the Eastern and Western Blocs.

In 1945, following long diplomatic discussions, the border in the Julian March was set on the so-called Morgan Line, which was the border between two military administrations: the Yugoslav administration in the east and the Allied Military Government in the west. The territory was not just a disputed area situated between Yugoslav and Italian demands, but was also intended to reduce the possibility of conflict between Yugoslav and Allied forces. The border question was partially resolved in 1947 with the Paris Peace Treaty, which set the border between Italy and Yugoslavia at the northern end of this contested multiethnic territory, as well as the border between Yugoslavia and the Free Territory of Trieste, founded as a temporary, sovereign state in the region. Similarly to the Julian March, the Free Territory of Trieste was also divided into two areas: Zone A being the area around Trieste, administered by the Allied Military Government, and Zone B, which included the northern part of Istria from Koper to Novigrad/Cittanova, administered by the Yugoslav People's Army. The coexistence of both zones proved unworkable, leading to the disintegration of this small state in 1954. Zone B, which included more of Istria than Zone A, was given to the

Figure 1.1. Departure, Pula/Pola, 1947 (Rovigno Historical Research Centre, Photo library, Pola, nro. inv. 3081-F-2004 (4)).

republics of Slovenia and Croatia within the former Yugoslavia, while Zone A, which encompassed Trieste with the directly adjoining Karst hinterland was joined to Italy (Pirjevec 2000; Rogoznica 2011; Troha 2019). This meant Istria become a frontier land between the Eastern and Western Blocs.

The Istrian exodus took place in this time of uncertainty, when national borders were being defined.[1] It began after World War II when this region was still a part of the Julian March (It. *Venezia-Giulia*) after the Paris Peace Treaty was signed in February 1947 and the Free Territory of Trieste was established, with Zone B in this area. It culminated with the joining of Zone B to Yugoslavia and Zone A to Italy following the London Memorandum in October 1954 (Gombač 2005: 10; Pupo 2015: 29; Kalc 2019: 146). Both international treaties allowed people to opt for Italian citizenship, meaning they then had to leave for Italy (Gombač 2005: 65; Pupo 2015). Some Italian researchers speak also of prior, illegal, preventive "exoduses," such as the flight of individuals who were most closely involved with fascism after 1943, or the preventive mass exodus of the inhabitants of Pula/Pola in Croatia in 1946 (Pupo 2015: 28–29). Meanwhile, other historians interpret the latter as an "organised emigration of the population," organized by the Italian authorities in combination with strong Italian propaganda. As there was no possibility of an actual plebiscite, the inhabitants of Pula expressed their will by means of a mass departure, which was like a plebiscite to show the city's Italian identity (Volk 2003: 45–46; Purini 2010: 250–51).

Figure 1.2. Departure, Pula/Pola, 1947 (Rovigno Historical Research Centre, Photo library, Pola, nro. inv. 3081-F-2004).

In Slovenian coastal towns, where prior to World War II around 90 percent of the population had been Italian, in 1957 Italians made up only 7.7 percent of the population in Koper, 8.15 percent in Izola/Isola, and 15.7 percent in Piran (Troha 1997: 58–59). The number of migrants to leave the whole of Istria stands between 200,000, and in the opinion of Pamela Ballinger (2003: 274), an excessive 350,000. The Yugoslav authorities filled the void that remained after the Italians had left by encouraging immigration from other parts of Slovenia and Yugoslavia, completely altering the ethnic, social, and cultural makeup of Istria (Gombač 2005: 11). According to Slovenian and Italian historians, the result of the exodus from Istria was the ethnic homogenization of contested lands in favor of annexation to either Italy or Yugoslavia: Italian denationalization of Zone B (part of Istria) and its "Yugoslavization" with the immigration of Yugoslavs, and the "Italianization" of Zone A (Trieste and its environs) with the immigration of Italians and emigration of Slovenes (Pupo 2000: 203; Volk 2003: 289–301). Mass population movements, including the "Istrian exodus," often served to colonize marginal territories, as in the case of the "repatriation" of Greek migrants from Asia Minor to the Slav areas of Macedonia, the migrations of Poles to western Poland from where Germans were expelled, and the movement of Italians from Istria and Dalmatia to Trentino-Alto-Adige, where a German minority was present (Bazin and Perron 2018: 29; Corni 2018).

I must also mention the last chapter in the history of shifting borders in Istria, when with the disintegration of Yugoslavia in 1991 this part of Istria became part of the new state of Slovenia and again a border territory between Italy and another former Yugoslav republic, Croatia, which has also been independent since 1991. The story of contested territories and borders between different national demands has therefore shifted by only a few kilometers (Rogelja and Janko Spreizer 2017).

Historians warn that the Istrian exodus must be understood outside purely nationalist frameworks as part of the much wider European historical context. The problem can partially be understood in connection with the broader social mechanisms and processes that accompanied the rise of nationalisms. At the beginning of the twentieth century, the disintegration of large multinational European empires, such as Austria-Hungary, Ottoman Turkey, and Russia, led to the creation of smaller multinational states and the politics of ethnic cleansing. Newly founded "successor states" such as Czechoslovakia, the Kingdom of Yugoslavia, Bulgaria, Turkey, Poland, Latvia, and others, dispelled thousands of minority members from their newly acquired territories. During World War II, European cities were almost entirely "cleansed" of Jews. Following the disintegration of multinational states into mononational ones, ethnic groups that remained outside the borders of the "motherland" emigrated (voluntarily or under pressure) to their respective "motherlands." In the wake of the Greco-Turkish war in the 1920s, during World War II and after, and following the recent war in the former Yugoslavia, the populations of entire regions or urban centers changed completely as people who did not correspond to the new dominant national identity had to move to the "motherland," for example, in parts of Greece, Turkey, Ukraine, Poland, Cyprus, Czechoslovakia, Yugoslavia, Russia (Karelia), and in cities, such as Kaliningrad, Gdansk, Trieste, Riga, Teplice, Nicosia, Zadar, Rijeka/Fiume, Piran, Pula, Koper, and others (Hirschon 1989; Reinisch and White 2001; Ther 2001; Várdy and Tooley 2003; Čapo Žmegač 2007). The first internationally sanctioned mass movement of population as a radical solution for minority problems took place on the basis of the Treaty of Lausanne in 1923, which determined the "exchange"[2] of Greek and Turkish minorities and led to a humanitarian catastrophe, 1.5 million migrants and 500,000 missing people. In Eastern and Central Europe, the largest population movements and ethnic cleansing occurred after World War II, dictated by Allied politics, which considered the ethnic homogenization of national territories to be the only way of preventing further violence and ensuring peace and stability. For their collective responsibility and to punish them for World War II, around 12 million Germans were expelled from Eastern and Southeastern Europe. Forced population movements most badly affected the regions populated by Germans that were annexed to different countries including Poland, Czechoslovakia, the Soviet Union, and the states of Southeastern Europe. A similar fate to that of the Germans was suffered by nations accused of collaborating with Nazism, such as the Hungarians, Slovaks, Ukrainians, and in a certain sense also Italy. They all experienced the anger of the winning side—some more, some less. As a result, in 1948, Central and Eastern Europe consisted of almost completely homogeneous nation-states for the first time in history (Ther 2001; Mazower 2010; M. Orlić 2012: 19–20; Kosmač 2017: 13–85). While in those times population movements were considered to be the solution for the problem of national minorities, they are nowadays considered human rights violations. A decisive role in bringing about a change in the perception of population movements was played by the UN's recognition of the "right to return" for Palestinians in 1974 and attention was redirected to victims in the 1980s (Bazin and Perron 2018: 16–17).

On the other hand, Pamela Ballinger (2015) proposes a different context for understanding the Istrian exodus that would not take into account only recent interpretations of postwar population movements. In these interpretations she sees the consequences of the postimperial processes of Italy's disintegration in the time of fascist rule, when the state lost its newly acquired territories in Africa and the Balkans.

Istria: A Contested Name?

Problems with the past and identity are nowadays reflected in dilemmas concerning the name Istria. There have been heated debates among experts for decades over what this area should be called (Gams 1991: 10), and it was recently the subject of two roundtables. The first one was held on 13 November 2018 in Koper, was organized by the Department of Geography of the University of Primorska's Faculty of Humanities, and had the neutral title "What would be a suitable name for the region comprising the four coastal municipalities?" The second one had a similar title, was held on 27 November 2019, and was organized by the Municipality of Koper and the Institute for Linguistic Studies at ZRS Koper.

In 1991, the geographer Ivan Gams (1991) noticed that Istria possessed an unusually large number of names: Obala (the Coast), Obalna regija (the Coastal Region), Obmorska Slovenija (Coastal Slovenia), Obmorska regija (the Coastal Region), Šavrinsko Primorje (the Šavrinje Littoral), Šavrinska brda (the Šavrinje Hills), Šavrinsko gričevje (the Šavrinje Hills), Slovenska Istra (Slovenian Istria), Istrska Slovenija (Istrian Slovenia), Koprsko (the Region of Koper), Koprsko primorje (the Koper Littoral), Koprska pokrajina (the Region of Koper), Koprsko obmorje (the Koper Littoral), Šavrinsko primorje (the Šavrinje Littoral), Primorje (the Littoral), and more. Each name is connected to different perceptions and ideologies (see also Tucovič 2012; Čebron Lipovec 2018: 47–50), and considering the relevance of the problem and the intensity of the discussion, it is clear that names conceal the unsolved challenges of problematic or "undigested" (Baskar 2002) pasts, which are controlled by various political and ideological discourses. Witnessing such dilemmas over the naming of a historical region, where not even the inhabitants can agree on a name, one gets the impression that something is seriously wrong with this "land."

Out of the many different appellations, Obala (the Coast) is quite widespread. Bojan Baskar (2002: 182–89) considers it to be the result of deliberate postwar distancing from a Venetian, that is, Italian, identity of the region that is supposedly expressed by the old name Istria. Bojan Baskar and the roundtable participants ascribed the appellation Obala to the inhabitants of internal, continental Slovenia who have a "holiday attitude" to this area (Baskar 2002: 183; Tucovič 2013: 26). At the first roundtable, a retired journalist clearly demonstrated how Istria had been renamed Obala in socialist times due to ideological demands:

> I will not put on sackcloth. We journalists were at the service of the regime, proponents of the system that rechristened this area, and renaming is also a form of taking back possession. And it is an ideological concept. Kajtimir, the famous leader who closed down Mihevčev trg . . . two people had authority, the committee president and Kajtimir as the commissar, and they introduced this concept of Obala here. [Replying to the comment that Mihevc was also responsible as an architect, the journalist commented that Ravnikar also drew plans.] For the news on Radio Koper I always left out the first word. And wrote Istria.

In the same way an older listener at the first roundtable, who was born in Istria, indignantly ascribed the term "Obala" to postwar immigrants as the name Istria was supposed to have negative connotations:

> After freedom is what we call when Slovenia gained this area, . . . they sent us foreign people, all who came were foreign, teachers, everyone; we didn't have our own intellectuals and these people, when they spoke with their relatives back home, didn't say they had come to Istria because that was considered pejorative. So they made something up and suddenly

introduced this name Obala that had been imposed from elsewhere. . . .
But this had always been Istria throughout history. . . . Who is afraid
of this name? Who is afraid of this name and is inventing Šavrinsko,
Obalno, Koprsko? Who is afraid of the name Istria? What is going to
bite them?

At the second roundtable, the representative of the committee for the
standardization of names also began his speech with the sentence "Do
not be afraid of the word 'Istria'!" And in this discussion, some people
also pointed out that the word "Istria" had a negative connotation, like
in the saying "You're as daft as an Istrian." At both public discussions,
the question of Istrian origins was posed, that is, who has the right to
call themselves Istrian. Such questions undoubtedly reflect the difficult
past, marked by mass migrations. The statement made by the mayor of
Koper, Aleš Bržan, who said that even the people living in Istria who
do not have roots there must be called Istrians, is therefore meaningful.
A similar identity dilemma was evident in a man who did not dare to
publicly declare himself an Istrian although he had been living in Koper
for seventy-five years. He said the word "Istrian" had negative connotations and that the newcomers, that is, most of the population in Istrian
towns, had an undefined identity. The following statement he made was
significant: "We must also get used to the fact that we, who have been
living here for the past few decades, are Istrians."

It is possible to observe that in contrast to the older Istrians who are
comfortable with the name Istria, the young people, especially in the
urban environments, prefer to use the name Obala (Čebron Lipovec
2018: 49). Feeling unease due to the ideological connotations of this
name, a student who also participated in the roundtable admitted that
despite wanting to identify himself as Istrian, it "simply isn't possible."

At the second roundtable, held only one year after the first, a change
could be observed when the mayor of Koper announced that the Istrian mayors had jointly agreed to use the name Istria, and that it had
replaced the name Obala in the region's most important newspaper, *Primorske novice.*

In any case, Istria is now divided between two countries, Slovenia and
Croatia, and also Italy if we count the small bit in the north, so many experts are drawing attention to the fact that by using geographically more
precise terms in accordance with regional tendencies, that is, Slovenian
Istria, we are subtly introducing mononational discourse and excluding
the non-Slovenian population, Italians more than others (Gams 1991:
9; Tucovič 2013: 25; Čebron Lipovec 2018: 49). Over two decades ago,
Ivan Gams warned that such terms are problematic, especially "in works

that discuss current social matters, as the number of prewar Istrians is smaller than the number of newcomers" (Gams 1991: 9).

Even the terms "Šavrinska brda" or "Šavrinsko gričevje" (Šavrinje Hills), which designate the southern part of "Slovenian Istria" and are derived from the name of its inhabitants, seems problematic as the "increasing numbers of newcomers from other parts of Slovenia and Yugoslavia, and Italians do not identify themselves with this population" (Gams 1991: 9). The name is interesting from the point of view of the processes of contemporary regionalization and nationalization of Istria through the invention of the Šavrinje identity in the 1990s. As Borut Brumen observes (2000, 2001), during the process in which the former Yugoslav republics of Slovenia and Croatia became independent countries, the common identity of the Istrians had been divided into the Croatian Istrian and the Slovenian Šavrin through the reciprocal creation of the "other." This "Šavrinization" of part of Istria in the 1990s was therefore a process of "Slovenization" or nationalization of the newly founded Slovenian Istria (Brumen 2000: 404), which later turned into an affirmation of rural identity as opposed to that of the coastal towns (Baskar 2002: 210; Ledinek Lozej and Rogelja 2012: 544). While in 1991 there was opposition to the name Šavrini "because of apparently negative connotations" (Gams 1991: 9)—a comment undoubtedly based on older views—the region of Šavrinija and its inhabitants the Šavrin are now sidelined in favor of the romantic idea of the suffering, heroic Šavrinka (the term for a woman from Šavrinija), a "façade erected for tourists" (Ledinek Lozej and Rogelja 2012: 544) and the "nostalgic search for lost time and an authentic lifestyle" (Ledinek Lozej and Rogelja 2012: 544). As Štelio, an Istrian of Slovene origin from the hinterland confirmed, the Šavrini hills were first written about in the 1970s. "This area . . . the Šavrini hills . . . was never written about in any book, ever. . . . At least not until about 1970." Out of political correctness and sensitivity toward the present-day inhabitants of Istria, some researchers decide to use a more neutral expression that does not exclude anyone, for example northern Istria (e.g., Čebron Lipovec 2018), however, this is also not clearly defined geographically and does not indicate national borders. In the end, all this deliberation over the most suitable name for a region, concern over political correctness, all these desired or undesired, overt or covert ideological nuances in the names of regions are only a reflection of the deep, historical wounds, unprocessed pasts, and the resulting contemporary crisis in the collective identity of different generations of people in this region, whose population has thoroughly changed, but where all the memories and knowledge connected with it have been silenced by the decades-long taboo.

In the Silence of Memory

Muted Personal Memories in the Stranglehold of Collective Memory

From the very beginning, my study of the exodus has been pervaded by an omnipresent silence that I felt in my encounters with people, a discomfort due to something unutterable, something we prefer to avoid, shy away from, especially Italians. When my friend, a member of the Italian minority, tried to find Italian interlocutors to discuss this subject with me, she was surprised when they all declined, saying that too much time had passed since the exodus. For the first time, she too became aware that she had grown up in a society in which there had been no exodus. I noticed the same phenomenon among my students who are members of the Italian minority—they know very little or nothing about the exodus.

The oral historian Luisa Passerini (2008: 224–25) defines memory as "the relationship between the present and the past, silence and the word, between the individual and the collective," it is "a narrative structured by individual and collective oblivions." We therefore cannot analyze memories without placing them in the context of silence. We have to understand its limits and references, depending on whom or on what it is based (Passerini 2008: 252–53). This begs the question: could silence over the exodus also be due to the ethnologist's "foreignness" in the community they are studying? This may be partly true, but on the other hand, as we will see later, the members of the same community are also shrouded in silence.

"People communicate in language, gesture and silence" (Lichterman 2017: 39). While in some places the silence is glaringly obvious, elsewhere it is hidden behind words. Rarely does a researcher succeed in discerning silenced memory beyond spoken words. Such was the interview with an Italian from Friuli who had such faith in the socialist system after World War II that he moved to Istria together with a few thousand workers from Monfalcone in Italy.[3] A researcher would not notice that he had omitted anything. If I had not been told previously by his son that his father would keep quiet about his father-in-law's experience of Goli Otok,[4] I would have had no idea about this, but even being aware of it, I did not dare question him on the matter. It is known that following liberation in 1956, all internees at the communist reeducation camp on Goli Otok had to keep silent about their experiences, otherwise they would be rearrested (Purini 2010: 272). A researcher may well wonder how much information was withheld in many other such apparently successful interviews. I sensed that the silence was filled with words in my interview with Amalia, an Italian interlocutor who was pressured into an interview rather than being eager to talk. The lady spent a whole week before the interview preparing for it by writing down all her thoughts in a notebook. Our conversation, if I can call it that, unfolded in such a way that she mostly read from her notes, a mixture of personal memories underpinned by "objective" historical facts: Pula during the war, the bombardments, hiding underground until the city was burned down, the ruins, the Yugoslav occupation, Allied politics, her mother's death, her uncle joining the partisans, postwar explosions and dozens of casualties, the general panic, omnipresent fear and the resulting exodus of Italians, "out of 31,000 people, 28,000 Italians left Pula alone."[5] She explained why she had written down her memories for the interview:

> Because these things hurt, people don't want to talk about this because they relive it . . . That's why I made notes yesterday because I wanted to relive these things a little, so that I wouldn't cry in public. People don't want to relive things because these are painful situations, very painful, and we are not to blame for them . . . Neither Slovenes, nor Croats, nor Italians. Things happen, history is something and . . .

When after one hour she had read through everything she had written, she broke down in tears. All her relatives joined the exodus by boat, and she remained alone with her grandparents and father, a pain she had never got over.

> In my family, that's the second most terrible thing that happened, in my family all the aunts on my mother's side of the family left. They left on 13 March 1947 on board the *Toscana*. . . . On that day my family was split in two, never to reunite [the aunts left for Italy and Argentina]. How can I put it, a family that is separated this way . . . Especially for me as they were like my mother to me [her mother had died previously], especially my grandma, but they too . . . It is terrible for a child as you lose all your sense of security, all the affection . . . This is the worst thing that happened to me personally, that's it. This is the wound that never healed, this wound.

If we try to understand this kind of silence that is filled with words yet appears to function as a "scientific," impersonal narration, we can consider it to be silence because of the traumatic experience and at the same time because of the inconsistency with the predominant memory. Andrea Smith (2006: 147–59) noticed a similar kind of silence among the *pieds-noirs* while studying the memories French immigrants in Algeria had of the Franco-Algerian War. When speaking about it, people

Figure 1.3. Pula/Pola, the Temple of Augustus following bombardment in 1945 (Rovigno Historical Research Centre, Photo library, Pola, nro. inv. 3081-F-2004 (3)).

censored and disciplined their memories, trying consciously to avoid them or structuring them in a rational, impersonal way. They resorted to these tactics in order to retain control over emotionally burdensome memories that were not compatible with the French collective memory of the war and that recalled their own personal participation in unspeakable and shameful cruelties, in something that was close to a civil war and which was not acknowledged for decades in the French collective memory.

At the time of the drastic change that broke up families, friendships, village and city communities, and demolished existing society, most of my interlocutors were still children. They internalized the trauma and never really dealt with it. Although it is not entirely comparable, Marija Jurić Pahor describes the concentration camp trauma, which is immediately dissociated from the person and pushed into the subconscious. If a memory tried to force its way into the conscious, it had to be stopped so that the trauma would not express itself with all its original strength (Jurić Pahor 2004: 38, 40–41). As Primo Levi writes, "a person who has been wounded tends to block out the memory so it does not hurt even more" (Levi [1986] 2003: 18 in Jurić Pahor 2004: 40).

Researchers studying the transmission of extremely traumatic experiences of concentration camp survivors have noticed that they do not talk about their experiences of persecution with their families but rather keep silent. Victims of extremely traumatic experiences protect themselves by keeping silent and avoid everything that reminds them of the trauma. In fact, silence is not just a form of self-protection but also a way of protecting family members (Jurić Pahor 2004: 52–53). However, even in silence "something absent is relived as massively present. Therefore, not speaking is by no means the same as not communicating; silence can be a mighty form of communication" (Jurić Pahor 2004: 53). Although taking place in silence, the intergenerational interaction between concentration camp survivors and their children is a form of communication or transmission via a system of signs and embodied memory, which is reflected in practices that make the unspeakable past present here and now. In Maurice Halbwachs's words, the transmission is performed intimately as a "lived" memory interwoven with everyday experience's social milieu (Halbwachs 2001; Wajnryb 2001; Kidron 2009: 18).

Another Italian interlocutor cried during each interview, and she later sought the help of a psychotherapist. The fair number of interviews I had with her gave me the impression that after she first spoke about the subject she needed to speak and be heard. She was not the only one in tears as I too cried when confronted with the painful emotions of collective guilt for what had been done to those who in "my" nation's perception were "the evil ones," fascists. When I asked her if people would tell me more if I was an Italian researcher, she said no. No, people have simply grown accustomed to not speaking. She also admitted to having a "lump in the throat" throughout the interviews.

In the interviews with Italian ladies, unprocessed childhood trauma is what marks memories of the exodus and the circumstances that led to it. Vittoria gave a contemporary example of how a lady in the company of elderly Italian ladies spoke about the humiliation she had experienced in school as an Italian. However, the others did not react and simply remained silent.

> After hearing this story I said nothing to the lady as the others were also silent. . . . They do not want to talk, they try to play things down. . . . They do not want to deal with this problem. Perhaps too painful. Perhaps someone persuaded them it was not so. . . . Because at the time it was happening, we were not allowed to talk about it. So we had to conceal it.

Maurice Halbwachs, an important name in anthropological and sociological memory research, said that we remember as members of a collective entity. Individual memory requires the support of community members, so it is difficult for it to endure outside the collective memory. Memories adapt to momentary needs and circumstances. To remember precisely, individual memory requires the support of the memories of members of the same community and vice versa. Collective memory cannot exist without the intertwining and meeting of individual memories. It is by remembering that a person gains a place in community and society (Brumen 2000: 25–27; Halbwachs 2001: 23–54; Širok 2009). Silence ensues when memory cannot rely on collective memory because it is intentionally adapted or unacknowledged, censored, or because it hurts too much so we rather avoid it or suppress it. Psychotherapists find that in the case of intergenerational transmission of experience of genocide, if the parents' experiences are not recognized as historical truth and if the perpetrators do not recognize their crimes, the trauma will turn into delirium and a suffocating nightmare for the next generation (Althounian 2005: xiv). Florence Dosse, the daughter of a soldier sent to war in Algeria, which was silenced for decades in the French collective memory while in families, memories were transmitted more by what was not said—the omnipresent silence. In her book *Les héritiers de silence: enfants d'appelés en Algérie* (Heirs of silence: The children of those sent to Algeria), she emphasizes the need for connecting her own family experience with national history and for making these events visible in society's deep amnesia (Dosse 1993: 12–13). Vittoria's idea that the lady had perhaps been convinced by someone that her experience of the past was not genuine conceals all the complexity of the relationship between individual and collective memory. Individual memories can enrich and support the collective memory if they are valued, but on the other hand, those individual memories that do not conform to the collective self-image or do not suit the collective view of the past are censored, rejected, stigmatized, or excluded from collective (national) discourse (Halbwachs 1925; Candau 2005: 76; Assmann 2007: 16). Not only the memory, but also the individual as the carrier of an "inappropriate" memory is thrown out of society.

We may then ask the question: if the community shares memories on which collective identity is based (Halbwachs 2001), can the community also share silence? As evidenced by the above example of collective silence and the more general silence surrounding the exodus, especially among the Istrian Italians, the answer is yes. Yes, the community can share silence as well as memories, and just like memory, it can form the basis of collective identity.

This "unspeakable pact of silence" concerning postwar emigration was obviously so much stronger while it was happening, as is shown by the example of Vittoria, who discovered the exodus decades after it occurred when reading a fictional work by the Istrian Italian writer Tomizza while studying Italian in Belgrade.

> I asked at home, I remember, in 1954, 1955, as there were forty-three of us in the first class, and every day someone went missing. I returned home and said, "Mother, he's gone, Vinicio's gone, Lucio's gone, Maria's gone, where have they gone?" "Ah, they'll come back, you'll see," she would say. I was small; we lived in isolation. But I tell you, I only discovered the exodus when I read Tomizza's books. When I was at university in Belgrade. . . . It was not spoken of.

What it means for memory to have the support of the community became very clear when silenced memories were told at the presentation of a photo-book of life stories of those that left and those that stayed (Castelli 2018) on 25 April 2019 in Piran.[6] Memories that had been silenced for a long time surfaced in public, one after another. There were many tears of emotion, some people thanked the author and other people for their testimonies, saying that a great burden had been lifted from them. There were also tears when people remembered the difficult dilemma of whether to "stay or go." The occasion is a good illustration of Halbwachs's theory (2001) of the frameworks of memory (Fr. *les cadres de la mémoire*). Individual memory survives only if it relies on collective memory.

We usually consider silence to be a "signal of psychopathologized processes of avoidance and repression, suspect processes of personal secrecy, or collective processes of political subjugation" (Kidron 2009: 6). As we will show later, the memories of the Italians who remained in Istria do not correspond with the dominant Slovenian memory, which sees the exodus as voluntary migrations, nor with the dominant Italian discourse, which considers the exodus to be the result of violence by "barbaric" Slavs and the communist system against the Italians (Ballinger 2003: 129–67; Hrobat Virloget 2015a, 2015b, 2019: 166–69, 2021; Nemec 2015: 148). In contrast with the latter, they are well aware of the causal link between the exodus and the fascist violence against Slovenes and Croats to which the dominant Italian state discourse turns a blind eye. In addition to the non-compatibility of memories and trauma, the silence may also probably be ascribed to the isolation and abandonment of the Italians in Istria, as after the exodus and the completely altered social situation in the new state of Yugoslavia, they became "the others." They were transformed from a majority, at least in the towns and cities, into a national minority. As will be shown later, after the exodus, the altered social structure, the loss of a social network, a change in the dominant language, the reversal of social status from superior to inferior, and so on meant they felt like foreigners although they were at home, and on top of all that, they were stigmatized as "fascists" (Ballinger 2003: 207–44; Hrobat Virloget 2015a: 164–72).

From a psychological point of view, the reason for being silent about the exodus could also be ascribed to the fact that mourning and expressing painful memories in the company of the winners, with the affected person on the side that lost the war, was probably considered unacceptable. The internalization of this prohibition of mourning may be a consequence of unauthorized mourning where, due to external, public expectations or prohibitions, broader society does not recognize or denies the events connected with it. Victims can only speak if the injustice has been unambiguously recognized and named (Erzar 2017: 31, 85–87). This is all the more evident in this context of the black and white, stereotypical dichotomy: Italians ("fascists") and Yugoslavs ("innocent victims") who won the war. The Italians who remained kept their pain to themselves as those who beat the fascists do not publicly recognize their right to feel like victims. In the dominant Slovenian discourse, Italians are perceived as perpetrators and fascists, or at least those who were free to leave for Italy. This also explains why so many Italians rejected the possibility of giving an interview. It is clear that the migrants have retained a deep pain and hatred for the Yugoslavs, while the Italians who remained do not believe that the representatives of the "winners" will understand their pain (Hrobat Virloget and Logar 2020).

Knowing that their memories do not conform to the dominant memory, two elderly Italian ladies, Elda and Antonella, warned me not to stir things up now by meddling with something as sensitive as the exodus:

> Elda: I'll tell you this just as I see it: stirring things up now is like throwing a bomb for which you do not know when it will explode. . . . Because you still come across pig-headed individuals.
> Antonella: You must be quiet . . . There are ears everywhere.

During the interview, Elda brought up the subject of silence on a number of occasions. "some who are older than me are probably afraid of speaking out. Let's be frank, I don't care about either side. The names can be revealed . . . And that's not good." The idea of names that must not be pronounced indicates the third type of silence, the one that stems from the struggle for power, including within one's own community. I was forewarned of this type of silence, which some were said to be turning into a trauma about the Italians as victims, by two Italian minority politicians. The father of one of them was a member of the Communist Party but as we will see in the chapter on reasons for departure, he rejected the regime's instructions to persuade Italians from Koper to leave. He thereby avoided "getting his hands dirty."

> There were also many individuals who quickly adapted to the new situation and the new politics. I will be very blunt now—I am aware that many of our parents, Italians, who lived here had very close connections with the new regime. Many of their sons would like to erase this memory and become very Italian, even victims . . . . Many fled then for different reasons: economic uncertainty, collectivization, simply because they were losing . . . And it is interesting that part of the Italian minority helped create this pressure. And this guilty conscience, I believe, is the reason why some people are silent. Quite a number of people. [Regarding a politician.] We were all in the same boat. I do not have this trauma, I have written about this and speak out about it . . . . Often, the Italian minority does not want to speak about this, because it knows it was involved in a system.

The silence and pretense of not knowing, of some Italians who collaborated with the new system and even helped exert pressure, is also mentioned by the other politician. "Unlike those who made a job out of it—those few Italians who adapted to the system and were actually even more evil. As always happens. To account for their difference, they become more Catholic than the pope."

Oral historians say silence is the result of the tense social relations that arise in rebellious movements and which, with changes in social systems and hierarchies, conceal social conflicts, shifts in power relations, and civil war in a time when there is violence among members of the same nation, community and even family (Pavone 1992; Portelli 1997; Van Boeschoten 2005: 39). In a similar way, a study of memories of World War II and the time after the war in a Slovenian Istrian village indicated many facts that people kept silent in connection with the participation of some villagers in fascist organizations. After the war and the change in ideology, they suppressed their memories and conformed to the new dominant ideology. The village converts who went from being fascist collaborators to proponents of communist ideology and were hence considered depraved by other villagers are the ones who were shrouded in silence. The reason for silence is therefore not to be found in the political system but in the relationships within the village community and the struggles for dominance or survival strategies of individuals faced with changing politics and ideologies (Rožac Darovec 2012).

Perhaps it was because of these names and the fact that too much light had been shed on "dirty" events from the time of the exodus and after it that one talkative Slovenian Istrian, my former interlocutor, who was also politically active in the socialist system, began avoiding me in the days following the interview and also angrily rejected me when I tried to call him.

Silence over the difficult postwar situation is connected not only with the Italians but also with Istrians of other ethnic identities. When the exodus was mentioned, especially the reasons for it, they too went quiet, looked around, whispered, or simply allowed the silence to speak. For example, Ante, who moved to Koper from the Croat part of Istria in 1957, told me that they frightened the Italians at night by beating on their windows (see below), but when I wanted to find out more, he went quiet (Hrobat Virloget 2015b: 540).

However, silence is not just an absence of words or a voice as the logocentric paradigm would claim (Kidron 2009: 6). Some Slovenians also find it hard to speak about the postwar situation in Istria, and their fear is reflected even after many decades in embodied memory or bodily memory practices (Kidron 2009). This is clearly shown by the example of an interview with the psychotherapist Janez Logar in which only the therapist's trained eye and body detected something that the ethnologist's listening ear failed to pick up. The interviewee had gone through incredibly difficult life experiences, from serving in both the Nazi and Yugoslav armies during World War II, to being a POW, and after the war, he was sent as a teacher to the newly annexed Istria with the aim of helping establish a Slovene school system. The man participated rationally in the conversation throughout, he chose the right words, remembered many details, was relaxed, satisfied, smiling and sometimes serious and pensive. Only the therapist's eye observed a slight moment of hesitation, some small physical gesture that even seventy years later expressed embodied fear while discussing communist spies in an Istrian village. When asked about them, the man went silent for a moment and froze. He trembled ever so slightly. Then immediately, in a second, he changed the subject of conversation. The psychotherapist Janez Logar felt fear on his own body, which the interlocutor was not aware of but expressed physically. This fear forced the man to change the subject as it is too hard to speak about subjects that are still imbued with deep fear. Psychotherapists are aware that "the body remembers" (Van der Kolk 2014; Gostečnik 2008: 251; Masero 2017: 657–68; Hrobat Virloget and Logar 2020).

Some immigrants from other former Yugoslav republics experienced the exodus themselves, while others did not because they arrived in an already "Slovenized" area. This was the most "invisible" group of people in the study. After Slovenia's declaration of independence in 1991, the immigrants from the former Yugoslavia became the new "others," experienced social marginalization and were treated as "inferior" citizens (without minority rights, some of them were literally "erased" from the population register) (Zorn and Lipovec Čebron 2008; Hrobat Virloget et al. 2016: 80, 85). As Irena Weber finds in her study of Piran (2006: 5), the breakup of Yugoslavia brought about another trauma when it activated the latent ethnic intolerance. Although they constitute the majority population in the centers of Istrian coastal towns, the memories of immigrants from the southern republics of the former Yugoslavia remain unnoticed, silent (Hrobat Virloget et al. 2016; Hrobat Virloget 2017a). They very rarely participate in public discussions or demonstrations of Istrian culture and history, which are dominated by Slovenian and Italian intellectuals (e.g., Čebron Lipovec 2015). Although my research did not focus on them at the beginning, establishing contact with them seems even more difficult. This is clearly illustrated by the example of an immigrant from Serbia who did not agree to an interview with Slovenian students, saying that he did not speak good enough Slovene, but he did agree to speak to a student who spoke his language. This clearly shows the unpleasant feelings of immigrants whose places of origin are considered inferior in the new environment (see A. Smith 2006: 138).

The son of one of the oldest immigrants from the former Yugoslav Republic of Macedonia, decided after a long silence to tell me his family's secret about how his father was given a cake shop from the authorities but he repaid its former owner, an *esule* who had been dispossessed. His decision to end the silence came from the idea that everyone involved was probably dead by now, and that the "official memory," that of historians (!), would not be too badly hurt.

> I will say something else, I don't know if I should . . . Historians probably won't take offense, no-one will . . . Most are already dead. . . [His father was given an already-equipped cake shop.] But they said to him: "If that Italian comes and demands anything from you, just call the police, we'll deal with it." My father accepted and began working. After some time, a couple of months, the Italian turned up. . . . And he stared and then broke into tears. . . . They sat down, had a chat and then he said to my father: "Sir, I am the owner of this shop. I just had to leave everything and go. I have not come to demand anything, I just came to tell you. I have documents in Italy that allow me to come and go. I came to see, you know, I built this with my bare hands." . . . My father . . . said: "You know what, I will not attain happiness running such a shop. Someone is crying over something they left behind . . . I will not be happy in such a shop. What can us two agree on, tell me the price, I don't have any money, but if you agree I will pay you in installments. Either every month or every two months. I will pay as much as you say." They reached an agreement

and then he paid installments for two or three years . . . . And they remained lifelong friends.

This heartwarming story about human kindness, which was told after
the son considered enough time had passed, and his caution in telling
the story, reminds me of *The Whisperers* by Orlando Figes (2009). He describes a form of communication in Stalinist Russia that was burdened
with people's fear of being heard. People learned to lead dual lives: information, thoughts, religious beliefs, family values, interpersonal relations
and everything that did not comply with the norms of the Soviet system
was hidden from the neighbors and even from their own children. People learned how to whisper (Figes 2009: 13). In a situation in which it is
not safe to speak and in which personal memories do not comply with
the dominant memory, silence can become the foundation, the corner-
stone of personality (Hrobat Virloget and Čebron Lipovec 2017: 66).

"Detabooization"

The "quiet detabooization" of the controversial topics of the exodus and
the *foibe*[7] did not begin in Yugoslavia until the "shy winds of liberaliza-
tion" blew into the public domain in the 1980s. The regime was also
slowly losing its grip on historiography, but it was not the historians
who were the first to mention this but the writers. The first to speak out
were the Italians who stayed in Istria (Dota 2010: 73–85). One of my
interlocutors, a politician with Italian-Croat-Slovene roots, emphasizes
that great international conflicts are fed by taboos.

> . . . because I was one of the co-founders of Group 88. This was a group
> that removed the taboo on certain topics: the *foibe*, the exodus. We dis-
> cussed this for the first time in 1988; we had a roundtable in the theater
> in Koper, which was attended by a very large number of people—a his-
> torical event, a turning point actually, for the Italian minority as well as
> for society at large, where we raised the subject of the exodus and also
> invited representatives of the *esuli*. And Hartman also came, people who
> had been members of the Communist Party, from the SZDL, the Social-
> ist Alliance, and it was quite . . . They did not know how to behave. It
> was no longer possible to suppress as it was already in the process of being
> opened. Our society, you did not go to prison because of that, but there
> was quite some annoyance, and we were under a lot of pressure . . . Well,
> and then, what did he do, Ciril Ribičič being clever, he said: "Why don't
> we broach this subject at the Central Committee at some point." And it
> happened, I think it was in 1988 . . . He invited me to come to the party's
> central committee. Kučan was there, even Hafler was there, the old ones . . .
> And I addressed them; I was not offensive, nothing, but I said it's time

we talked openly about this taboo topic. And some of them accepted, the young ones accepted—Bekeš, Ribičič, Lev Kreft, and they said "Yes, let's also talk about this!" Because if you demystify a subject, then there are no more arguments for exaggeration . . . . But OK, I strongly supported that mixed commission [the Italian-Slovenian commission].[8] It is a basis for further research, including opening one of the *foibe* and analyzing what's inside, everyone's afraid of that. Those who think there might be many corpses are afraid, and those who think there might not be any corpses are even more afraid. So, a myth is being created and on the basis of these myths this great misunderstanding between nations is continuing.

At that time the theory of the joint responsibility of the postwar authorities for the exodus first appeared in Yugoslavia. In the middle and especially toward the end of the 1980s, it is written about by writers and journalists but not by historians, so these texts are not legitimized by professionals and scientific methodology. After the break-up of Yugoslavia, the last reason for silence on diplomatic grounds—to maintain stable relations between states—disappeared. The taboo crumbled with the democratization of society and the fall of socialism, when its dogmatic fetters and the self-censorship impeding a critical approach to historiography on the war and the postwar period fell away (Dota 2010: 73–85). After the downfall of the single official memory in Yugoslavia, which was based on glorifying the antifascist and partisan struggle, forbidden memories took revenge (e.g., the *ustashe*) and history was revised. Up to that point, under the communist regime, alternative memories had been preserved within families, among migrants and the native population that had anti-Yugoslav and anti-communist views (Cipek 2009; Czerwiński 2013; Čapo Žmegač 2015b: 123–24). From the postwar period onward, Yugoslav historiography at the service of the state denied and forgot the suffering of the Italian population and its departure. At the same time, the autochthony of the Italians is being intentionally diminished, their departure is seen as a "return to the homeland," and the departure of Croats and Slovenes, both under fascism and at the time of the exodus, is being emphasized (Dota 2010: 57–72).

The fact that the "memory gap" concerning the exodus is still present today may also be attributed to the foundations of Slovene identity, especially in Primorska (the Littoral Region). This idenity is based on the national liberation struggle, the heroic resistance against fascist violence, and the fight for ethnic emancipation (Fikfak 2009: 359; Hrobat Virloget 2015a: 161). Any defamation is considered either still inappropriate or is interpreted in the context of over seventy years of conflictual political discourse, based on the opposition between "the whites and the reds" (see Čapo Žmegač 2015b). Despite the fact that after 1989 the memory of the World War II victors has been joined by the opposing memory of its losers, portrayed as victims (M. Orlić 2012: 15), political speeches that consider the dark side of one's past, such as the one given by the President of Slovenia's National Assembly Milan Brglez below, are still rarely heard in public. The general public in Slovenia hardly knows anything about the almost complete population change that took place, especially in Istrian towns, and the resulting social changes. The history curricula in Slovenian primary and high schools are also selective and postwar migrations are barely mentioned. The situation in Italian schools is a little better, because, according to my interlocutor who teaches at the Italian primary and high schools in Koper and Piran, some attention is devoted to regional history. A former headmistress of the Italian school, Vittoria, says that in the past this subject was not discussed at all in schools.

> In the Italian school, this was never discussed. Never, for as long as I was at the school. Absolutely not. . . . Teachers could not . . . Did not speak about this, it never happened. Because it always ended earlier, with 1918. History, the grammar school syllabus ended with 1918. What happened later, what we knew, what we heard in the family, fascism. We talked a lot about partisan offensives . . . Everything was up in the air. There was no furthering of knowledge, no discussion. Because this was the order that was given: not to speak. So it was a subject that was completely removed.

It is logical that Italian syllabuses ended with 1918, as the Italian collective identity was based for a long time on the winning memory of the "Great War," World War I. A myth was developed surrounding the deceased and their sacrifice (Kavrečič 2017: 157). This national myth declined after the downfall of fascism, and yet it retained a strong symbolic/ritual significance for the *esuli* who use it to glorify the memory of the love for the *patria,* which by conquering territory as far down as Dalmatia fulfilled the hopes of all Italians in the "unredeemed" lands (Ballinger 2003: 54). The history taught in Slovenian schools in Yugoslavia was also selective, and like elsewhere in the Eastern Bloc it focused on the fight against Nazism and fascism in World War II (for the similar case of Kaliningrad—former Königsberg, see Sezneva 2003: 71–72).

All over Europe repressed memories burst out in 1989 after the collapse of the bipolar political framework. While in Western Europe it was normal for reconstructions of the past to be aligned with the standards of historical scholarship, this was not necessarily the case in Eastern Bloc countries where interwoven memories of persecution and collaboration, victimization and guilt emerged. According to Aleida Assmann (2007: 16), even nowadays many of these nations are in the process of recreating old national myths or creating new ones.

A similar "memory gap" may be observed among the Czechs concerning the expulsion of the Sudeten Germans. In communist times, they were not really a taboo subject, but they were marginalized. In communist discourse, German history was connected with the bourgeoisie and the Nazi regime. The Germans were linked to capitalist exploitation, international aggression, fascism, and persecution. The argument against collective national guilt for their expulsion was that this was simply a reaction to all the distress inflicted by the Germans during the war. In this way, the state remains morally intact by emphasizing its victim role. This perception has not changed drastically even today as German history is still not integrated into Czech memory, especially not in comparison with the much more public memory of the Holocaust (Spalová 2017).

In their expulsion of Germans, the Eastern Bloc countries generally considered themselves to be the victims and did not recognize the "others" as victims. In Poland, public debate about the expulsion of Germans was not allowed in communist times, and writing was subject to censorship, so memory of this was preserved only in the privacy of family circles. Communist memory considered the acquired or "returned" territories of western Poland, from where Germans were expelled after World War II, as its great achievement, while it denied losing territory in eastern Poland, Kresy, from where most of the Polish population was "transferred" to newly acquired land in the west. Here too the memory of population movements, in particular from eastern Poland, was preserved only in the privacy of family circles. The first to speak out about the loss of land in the east and the subsequent population movements were the Polish emigrants in the west, and their voice was increasingly heard during the change in political system in the years 1989–1990 (Halicka 2018: 119–27).

Similarly, Cathie Carmichael (2002: 109–14) quotes Yugoslav discourse, which claims that after World War II, 100,000 Germans left Vojvodina "of their own accord," their fate having no connection with the victorious liberators. A study of the memories of the Germans who remained shows that the Yugoslav regime treated them roughly and accused them of collaborating with the occupier.

In the areas in which entire ethnic groups were forced to leave, history was either rewritten or silenced, and their symbols and monuments (churches, mosques, graveyards, architectural monuments, street names, signs, and more) were destroyed, erased, or altered. New historical nar-

ratives tried to excuse the expulsion *post-festum*. Following democratization, a frail stability was preserved in the hope of avoiding any demands
for restitution, compensation, right to return, or any discussions about
the role of the former government, army, and/or elite in the process of
population movements (Bazin and Perron 2018: 31).

In Italy, the public silence surrounding the exodus also ended when
alternative memories broke out in Europe. This was in the so-called
Berlusconi Era, from the beginning of the 1990s onward. Prior to that,
the exodus was politically exploited only along Italy's eastern border,
where most of the *esuli* lived and were politically active. It was used
by the far right and the Christian Democratic Party for inciting hatred of Slavs and communists. In the broader Italian collective memory,
the exodus remained only on the level of personal memories. This was
both due to postwar Italian politics, which developed an ambiguous
attitude toward the eastern border and Yugoslavia (which was growing
in political and economic strength), and the presence of *esuli* as a dis-
turbing reminder of fascism. With the rise of right-wing politics in the
Berlusconi Era, the *foibe* and the exodus were exploited to create the
impression that Berlusconi's party was the only true national and patriotic party, while its political opponents—communist politics and its
postwar historiography—were accused of keeping silent for decades the
"dark side of Italian history" and siding with Yugoslavia (1943–1945),
thereby betraying national interests (Corni 2018: 74–78). By employing
the argument of right-wing neofascist politics, the day for remembering the *foibe* and the exodus equates the *foibe* with genocide, that is,
ethnic cleansing of Italians, thereby equating Nazi violence with that
of the communists, and even describing it as the "Italian Shoah." The
commemoration of the *foibe* victims has set foundations for the creation of a new "appeased" common Italian public memory, which has
minimized or removed responsibility for the crimes perpetrated by the
fascist regime in Yugoslavia prior to the *foibe*. By abusing history for
political purposes like never before, Berlusconi's government set new coordinates for the national memory, the aim being to neutralize the previous discourse on anti-fascism as a factor for legitimizing/delegitimizing
political power and its replacement with anti-totalitarianisms that has
characterized European discourse especially after its eastward expansion.
A step further was taken by President Carlo Azeglio Ciampi between
1999 and 2006, with his attempt to construct common memory in order to unify all Italians and overcome the conflicts of different political
orientations and achieve reconcilement. To the mainstays of memory
that became the Risorgimento (the movement for Italian unification)
and the Italian resistance movement he added the Nazi-fascist killings,

which had hitherto been hidden in the so-called cabinet of shame, as well as the neofascist argument concerning the *foibe* victims. For many people, the search for common ground between the antifascist memory based on the resistance movement and the opposite memory of Mussolini's supporters was deemed unacceptable. In truth, this memory was equally controversial and selective as it only saw Italians as victims of either Tito's communists or the Nazi German SS divisions, while making no mention of the role played by Italians as occupiers and perpetrators vis-à-vis local populations, such as in the occupation of Libya, Ethiopia, or the Balkans. Thereby the myth of the "good Italians" and the "victimizing" paradigm are perpetuated, although some of Ciampi's acts also showed he was prepared to accept responsibility for the fascist past (Focardi 2020: 214–58).

Pamela Ballinger argues that all postimperial histories that coincide with the postwar period are uncomfortable for both scholars and society as they are in fact stories of defeat. That is why she uses the term "extruded histories" for these colonially displaced people (Ballinger 2012: 380). In the similar post-colonial context of the expulsion of the *pieds-noirs* from Algeria, Michéle Baussant (2002: 286) observes that they were "excluded from history" (Fr. *exclus de l'histoire*), "dismissed from history" (Fr. *licenciés de l'histoire*), or "forbidden from history" (Fr. *interdits d'histoire*). All these people "excluded" from history—from the *pieds-noirs* to the Palestinians, the Jews in Europe and in Egypt and more—are considered to be the bearers of negative heritages and imaginaries and are sometimes perceived to be toxic and old-fashioned, especially in the process of decolonization, where we are dealing with the memory of the losers who yearn for official recognition and the integration of their marginalized experiences in national history (Audenino 2015; Baussant 2019: 38, 155, 176).[9]

The Exodus in Slovenian Research

The impression of avoiding the "dark sides" of one's past may also be gained from border region historiography, which is obviously under the influence of political discourses and devotes itself primarily to themes that are crucial for Slovene identity: fascist violence and the antifascist movement as a response to it, the migrations of Slovenes, the Slovene minority in Italy, the national liberation struggle, borders, and more. Nevenka Troha (1997, 2000, 2002, 2006, 2010) is a historian who studied postwar migrations and the political questions of the time most systematically, but never published the results of her research in a monograph. Research into the exodus was carried out mostly by the Italian side, only some was Slovene or otherwise non-Italian: on quantitative demographic dimensions (e.g., Colella 1958; Colummi et al. 1980; Gombač 2005; Fornasin and Zacchigna 2007), on motives and political implications (e.g., Ballinger 2003; Pupo 2005), on the lives of "refugees" or *esuli* (e.g., Pupo 2005; Volk 2004), and on the lives of those who stayed in Yugoslavia as a national minority (e.g., Nemec 1998, 2012a). The exodus and the political circumstances at the time have recently been dealt with more extensively in doctoral dissertations by history students in Slovenia (Argenti Tremul 2016; Kosmač 2017).

A number of articles have been written, most by historians (see below), but in the field of Slovene ethnology or cultural anthropology no-one has studied postwar migrations and their consequences in Istria. There are also only a few individual studies on the consequences of the exodus in Istria, most of them recent (e.g., Titl 1961; Kalc 2019; Hrobat Virloget 2019; on architecture, Čebron Lipovec 2019). In addition to my postdoctoral project from 2012, a research project on the same subject has recently been confirmed entitled "Migrations and Social Changes in the Comparative Perspective: The Example of Western Slovenia after World War II." The project leader is Aleksej Kalc (both projects are financed by the Slovenian Research Agency).

Ten years ago, Franko Dota found that in Croatia relatively few studies were carried out on the subject of executions and the emigration of Italians. Nor had a comprehensive monograph been written. Any individual studies are Croatocentric as they polemicize and sometimes even compete with the Italian discourse. While the communist ideological charge has disappeared, the national motivation has been preserved (Dota 2010: 86), as is also sometimes the case on the Slovenian side.

Denying a difficult past and thereby ignoring the sensitive Slovenian-Italian relations in public discourse can be seen, for example, in the founding of the University of Primorska. When it was founded it was depicted as a "defender of Slovene identity" in the border area and initially refused to translate the name Primorska into the Italian *Littorale* because it is supposed to be a fascist term (Ivelja 2004). Oblivion enables the memory to free itself of the heaviest traces of one's past, so as to deny them and thence construct a positive self-image. In fact, oblivion is not a lack of memory, but a censure to create a positive self-image (Candau 2005: 94). Fabricated national memory is not falsified but selective as it preserves only a strategic selection of appropriate memories. By focusing the national memory on the guilt of "the other" and one's own victimization, we set up a protective shield that prevents us from hearing the memories of "the other," recognizing their equal status of victim and contemplating one's own responsibility and guilt (Assmann 2007: 16–17).

Furthermore, Italian and international historiography have dispelled the myth of the "good Italian" by uncovering colonial crimes and crimes perpetrated during World War II, Italian concentration camps, the failure to punish war criminals, and racist policies conducted against Slavs, Africans, and Jews. However, unlike academic research, the institutional memory is not yet prepared to accept responsibility for fascism and is still dominated by memories of Italian humanity as "saviors of the Jews," of violence experienced at the hands of the Yugoslavs or Nazis, but not the violence committed by the Italians themselves (D'Alessio 2012: 71–74; Focardi 2020: 37–58).

Despite the fact that self-critical research can be exploited by the political discourse of nationalist politics, this approach is essential. The most common Slovenian and Croatian discourse in international disputes over the exodus is as follows: we will admit our mistakes when the other side admits its mistakes (Dota 2010: 108–12). The main accusation leveled against the Italian side, which we will discuss below, is a lack of self-critical reflection about its role in the time of fascism (Corni 2018: 58). Moreover, at the time of writing this book, there are problematic processes of "heritagization" fascist architecture with positive connotations, and a rise in neo-fascism, which is why some people are labeling Italy "the sick man of Europe" (Arthurs 2010: 125).

Competing Discourses and Victimization in the Hands of Politics

Celebrations and History in the Hands of Conflicting National Memories

Despite the recent efforts made to achieve reconciliation, which will be described below, the memories of people living by the border who suffered due to these complex Slovenian-Croatian-Italian relations (that can still be conveniently exploited for political purposes), have unfortunately been silenced (Corni 2018: 79). After more than sixty years, the exodus continues to stir emotions and provoke disputes in international politics and public discourse (Dota 2010). One of the most high-profile examples of the abuse of painful memories by political authorities takes place every year on the Italian "Day of Remembrance" of the victims of the *foibe* and the exodus from Istria, Rijeka, and Dalmatia, which was instituted by the Italian right-wing government in 2004, the same year that the border between Italy and Slovenia became an internal EU border. It is set on the day on which the peace treaty in Paris was signed in 1947 (10 February), when Italy is supposed to have ceded parts of Istria and the Julian March to Yugoslavia (*Giorno del ricordo* 2021). The date is historically controversial as there is no cause-effect relationship between the signing of the treaty and the exodus, which was already underway. However, the aim is clear: to reiterate the injustice of the peace treaty. The first commemoration in 2005 was supported by the historically controversial film *Il cuore nel pozzo* (The heart in the well). The date of the memorial day is also controversial as it comes only a few days after International Holocaust Remembrance Day (27 January) (Corni 2018: 77–78). The implicit connection with Jewish suffering under Nazism is also evident in the political speeches of right-wing Italian politicians who equate the suffering of Italians from Istria with that of the Jews (e.g., Gianfranco Fini in 2003, see Ballinger 2015: 157). The controversial nature of the memorial day stems also from the generally accepted idea of the Italians being "victims" of World War II. By elevating the painful side of Italy's recent history to the institutional level of national memory and favoring the narratives of its victims, the *esuli*, the memorial day has distorted interpretations of history (M. Orlić 2015).

Every time the "Day of Remembrance" is celebrated in Italy, Slovenian and Croatian spectators are attentive to all the words and metaphors expressed. In 2019, the President of the European Parliament Antonio Tajani caused indignation in Slovenia and Croatia when at the commemoration held near the *foiba* in Basovizza/Bazovica, the Italian *lieu de mémoire,* he ended his speech by exclaiming "Long live Italian Istria, long live Italian Dalmatia and long live the *esuli*!" (Šuklje 2019). The event provoked heated debate and demands to apologize to Slovenians and Croats reverberated all the way to the European Parliament. The statement may be understood in the context that even nowadays Italy does not see the loss of territory on its eastern border as something due to it losing the war, but as an unjustified annexation and expulsion of the Italian population. Unlike Germany, which has accepted responsibility for the crimes it perpetrated during World War II, Italy lives under the illusion that it liberated itself from fascism on its own, thereby preventing it from facing up to its involvement on the side of Nazi Germany, e.g., in the Balkans, Libya, or Ethiopia. There has never been even a judicial investigation into Italian war crimes committed in the Balkans (Cogoy 2009: 19). At the commemorations held between 2007 and 2009, the left-wing politician and Italian President Giorgio Napolitano held a number of dramatic speeches about Slav expansionism and the barbarity and bloodthirsty rage of Tito's forces. He used this to legitimize the local history of the *esuli* and Trieste, which begins only in 1943 and ends with the exodus, and he completely omitted the twenty years of fascist violence against Slovenes and Croats beginning in 1919. This prepared the basis for the official Italian position that Italy was not a perpetrator but a victim in World War II (Fikfak 2009: 358–59; Altin and Badurina 2018: 189). In this discourse, historical events are interpreted only in the context of the conflict with the "slav enemy." Using the simplified term Slavs instead of specifically referring to Slovenes and Croats implies a broader category (the Slavic east), and this term acquired negative, pejorative (and clearly racist) meanings in the time of the fascist regime. In connection with "ethnic cleansing," the Slavs are stereotypically portrayed as being inclined to "bloodthirsty rage" (M. Orlić 2012: 16–17). The term "ethnic cleansing" comes from the war in Yugoslavia in the 1990s, and it replaced the term "denation-alization," which was previously used in discourse on the *foibe* and the exodus. The recent war in Yugoslavia was simply seen as a repetition of what the Yugoslavs are supposed to have done to the Italians a few de-cades ago (Ballinger 2004: 148). In this discourse, the *foibe* are also de-monized (by inflating the figures), mystified (by blurring the identities of victims and perpetrators) and removed from the historical context as something unique, thereby serving as defense against the collective guilt for fascism, whose aim was to erase ethnic diversity. When the *foibe* are interpreted as the consequence of ethnic cleansing, we actually reverse the roles of perpetrators and victims (Cogoy 2009: 18–19).

Since the fall of Mussolini, Italian governments have distanced them-selves from the fascist past with symbolic strategies of isolation from the regime by playing down its violent and criminal nature and claiming that the "people" did not support it. The mainstay of Italian collective memory of World War II was the stereotype of the "evil Nazi," like in other countries that were occupied by the Nazis, in conjunction with the stereotype of "good Italians," *Italiani brava gente.* In keeping with this myth, fascism is supposed to have deceived and lured ordinary be-nevolent people. The myth of the "good Italian," which was perpetuated by the film *Mediterraneo,* has a number of functions: shifting the blame for inactivity on someone else, giving excuses for military failures by say-ing that Italians are not cruel soldiers, and distancing the "people" from fascism (Del Boca 2005; Franzinetti 2006: 94; Dota 2010: 111; Purini and Ming 2014; Focardi 2020: 37–194).

Slovenia was quick to respond to the Italian "Day of Remembrance." Only one year later, in 2005, the Slovenian government instituted the national celebration of Primorska's reunification with the motherland. It is also connected with the Paris Peace Conference through the date on which it came into effect: 15 September 1947. In 2019, a political initiative wanted to replace the word "return" with "annexation," somewhat softening the discourse, but without success (Mekina 2021). If we realize that celebrations significantly help "imagined communities" (Anderson 1983) create interpretations of their past, help co-create a collective identity, mobilize patriotic emotions and acts, and give legitimacy to those in power, and if we see in them the buttresses of collective memory (Harvey 2001: 328: Jezernik 2013: 9, 12, 14), then the fact that the national commemoration was held in Koper, in the heart of the disputed territory in Slovenia, reveals the ignorant attitude of the dominant national memory to such a sensitive past. For the members of the Italian community, the celebration being held in Koper was like an implicit provocation, and they did not attend it, although judging by the Slovenian media, it appears that the Slovenian side did not understand their position. The hurt felt by the Italian minority because the celebration of Primorska's reunification with Slovenia was held in Koper, the town that had once been home to a majority Italian-speaking population, is clearly expressed by Michela:

> For example, if you want to celebrate Italy in Trieste, you won't go to Dolina, will you? [a village in which the majority of the population are members of the Slovenian minority in Italy] . . . And you see. Here they came to celebrate Slovenian Istria in Capodistria. They could have gone to Marezige, they could have gone to Šmarje [Slovene villages in the coastal hinterland]. You cannot celebrate this in Capodistria as every wall tells you it's Venetian, that it's Italian. . . .[10] Well, not even inappropriate, there's nothing left to provoke about, what's been broken has remained broken. Great harm has been done and Mussolini should be exhumed and cut up into little pieces, again, I know, because he was to blame for everything. (Hrobat Virloget 2014: 233)

As already reflected by the international disputes over terms such as exodus and "postwar migrations," each of the affected communities demands for itself the exclusive recognition of victim status, historical injustices, and the sole historical truth. The opposing national collective memory negates tragic events, reinterprets and censors them, and also refers to the concept of victim. Italian migrants explain their role of exclusive victim as the consequence of genocide perpetrated by the "barbaric" Slavs and the communist system against the Italians. Meanwhile, the other side, the Slovenes and the Croats emphasize their victim status at the hands of Italian imperialism and fascist violence (Ballinger 2003: 129–67, 207–44; 2015; Baskar 2010: 110–18; Dota 2010: 106–13).

In these discourses, competing for recognition of the genocide and suffering of one group, each side has its *lieux de mémoire*, places of memory: the Italian migrants and politics have the *foibe* (see Pirjevec 2009; Ballinger 2015), while Slovenian politics and the Slovenian minority in Italy have the Risiera—the Italian concentration camp for rebellious Yugoslavs (Ballinger 2003: 129–67)—and the monument to the heroes of Basovizza (Klabjan 2012: 678). Opposing views are evident also in the perception of the Risiera. In the Italian collective memory, it has primarily become a Jewish *lieu de mémoire*, but this is criticized because most of the victims were in fact anti-fascists (Ballinger 2004: 158). Commemoration of places of memory connected with World War II has multiplied the differences between Slovenians and Italians for more than half a century and consolidated ethnic identities along Italy's eastern border. In the same way the tragic memory of the *foibe* is used to strength the collective identity of the *esuli*, who make up a significant share of the Triestine population (Ballinger 2004: 145–46). However, the places of memory in the border area are not only places of mourning and foundations of collective memory but also have the function of marking national territories (Klabjan 2010: 403).

In keeping with the national versions of history, some reactions at the public presentations of my research included the question "what about fascism?" The discourse on voluntary legal "opting" is most widely accepted in Slovenia, especially among those who came to Istria from central Slovenia. Such is the case of Lieutenant Colonel Dragotin who was sent to Koper to command an army division in 1954 and who eventually bought a house from an Italian optant, the house in which he lived as a tenant when he arrived. It was unusual how he kept repeating every five minutes that the *esuli* were not refugees, as they call themselves, although my colleague and I asked him only once about this.

Maybe straight after the war the fascists and the like fled from the partisans, but otherwise they all went legally. Now and again someone says there was some pressure . . . There probably was, but I'm not allowed to say . . . [laughs] Otherwise, officially they left, they emigrated. In Italy they were promised housing, they got something, wages, and I don't know . . . Completely legally. . . . To tell you the truth there was no hostility. But that someone would think we kicked them out . . . It's possible there may have been some pressure here and there, I'm not saying there wasn't. But . . . It's not . . . It now says "refugees" . . . Not true. They're emigrants, they moved. There they had . . . They had a better standard of living there, they had connections and relatives and so on. They had to make an official request, which they had to put in six months prior to leaving, had to make an inventory of what they owned. That I would notice there was . . . There was this guy . . . I'm no nationalist . . . And we got on really well. He even authorized me to be a trustee, as did the neighbors. There were probably some disputes here and there as there are everywhere. So it's not . . . Like when you read, sometimes someone writes "refugees" in the newspaper. Not true. Emigrants . . . optants we called them optants.

According to Aleida Assmann these competing discourses about who is the greater victim are one of the tactics of remembering that European national memories have chosen after World War II. The tactic of righting injustices is actually a competition, where the only important memory is the guilt of the other, which blurs or minimizes one's own guilt. There is also in this case the tactic of competition between victims, where the struggle for one's own suffering being recognized comes to the fore. By placing one trauma in a privileged position, the other trauma is marginalized and becomes less important. The tactic of excluding other memories emphasizes the other's crime, thereby erasing one's own guilt (Assmann 2007: 20–21; 2010). It is the victim who gives meaning to remembrance. The memory of the tragedy is established at the same time as the group's affirmative memory, which is constructed and maintained through constant remembrance and recognition of suffering (Wieviorka 2004: 89 in Candau 2005: 82). Like identity, the collective memory (ethnic or religious) is constructed in opposition to other memories or by assimilating them. This is the case of Jewish memory, which has based itself above all on the Holocaust, thereby opposing Holocaust denial and anti-Semitism. In this way ethnic or religious memory focuses on suffering, which emphasizes the feeling of belonging (Candau 2005: 116). Following the disintegration of the postwar bipolar political context, after 1989 a general shift is perceived from a "history written by the victors to a history written by the victims" in Europe (Judt 2005: 829 in M. Orlić 2012: 14). Attention, almost obsessive at times, focuses on the victims, reflected on a universal level by the commemoration of the Shoah (Judt 2005: 829; M. Orlić 2012: 14). At this time, the shifting of attention to the victims, listening to them, became a moral obligation (Bazin and Perron 2018: 16).

Contested Heritage in the Hands of Political Conflicts

Population movements have long-term consequences that can reach beyond the generation that experienced the migration. They are often accompanied by impoverishment and the social degradation of the migrants, loss of property and therefore the possibility of a decent life, the impossibility of returning and the open wounds that are passed on to future generations. These include feelings of uprootedness, an individual's personal suffering, hatred, and the desire for revenge while perceptions oscillate between feelings of injustice to revisionist demands. The sense of belonging to a group depends also on common suffering, and this is why these feelings can so easily be exploited by politics. The past is frequently used as an argument that helps legitimize someone's point of view and their political demands. For example, the problem of the expulsion of the Sudeten Germans was politically exploited in discussions on EU enlargement (Bazin and Perron 2018: 19–20, 30).

Similarly, Italy as a senior EU member state set conditions for Slovenia's entry to the EU by demanding fair compensation for the confiscated or abandoned properties of *esuli* from Istria and Dalmatia (Šaunik 2001). On the basis of the treaties of Osimo and Rome (1983) all property and legal relations between the states were settled. As compensation for war damages, Italy was supposed to hand over the properties of the *esuli* to Yugoslavia, and in exchange for the properties located in Zone B, Yugoslavia would pay Italy US$110 million compensation in installments to be paid from 1990 onward. Prior to entering the EU, Slovenia had paid 70 percent of this amount by 2002, while Croatia did not pay the remaining 30 percent. For various reasons, Italy has not yet withdrawn this money from the bank. One of the reasons is Croatia's failure to pay the debt, another the demands by organizations representing the *esuli* to pay out the money, so the outstanding amount remains a useful excuse for international disputes and revisions. There is also ambiguity over the "law to correct injustices" suffered by victims of political persecution, adopted in 1997, which saw the *esuli* apply en masse with proof of communist violence against them. However, the state and some lawyers claim that the money intended for the *esuli* has been paid but that it unfortunately did not reach them (Šuligoj 2016; Šuklje 2019).

This problem is an example of a political power game, where a country with greater political power, that is, with full EU membership, uses its discourse to try to extort something from a country in a politically subordinate position. As far as I know, this is a rare case of compensation at an international level as none of the other countries connected with population movements, for example, the Czech Republic and Poland, and Germany on the other side, are opening up such sensitive matters that lead to serious diplomatic complications both because of the exiled population and compensation for war damages. History keeps repeating itself, again and again. In a similar way, Bulgaria is now trying to rewrite history by covering up the dark side of its past with a revised history. Being in a position of power as an EU member state, it is setting conditions for North Macedonia's EU entry by demanding it acknowledge that Macedonian is only a dialect of Bulgarian and that the words "Bulgarian fascist occupier" be removed from a World War II monument (!) (Milošević 2020: 13). All this has been seen before as each national memory draws attention to itself and its victimhood while erasing everything that is "unfitting" or unpleasant.

The population that was forced to leave feels it is its duty to remember that which enables it to preserve a collective identity. In some cases, rejecting oblivion is also a means of demanding "lost" territory or possessions or even the right to return (Bazin and Perron 2018: 30). The dispute over the restitution of Venetian artworks stolen from Istrian towns during World War II (paintings by Carpaccio and other artists and artworks from churches) fits this mindset. Even decades later this is still an open, unresolved matter between Italy and Slovenia. For the uprooted *esuli* these artworks are like relics confirming the existence of Italian (which they consider equivalent to Venetian) tradition on the territory of northern Istria. These artworks also provide a basis for their collective identity as exiles and are a political instrument of territorial demands. They are attached to them through the deep emotional hurt caused by their expatriation, and one might even sense some hope of returning. There are two possible interpretations: either the removed artworks are the property of the physical and geographical area from where they have come, or they belong to the historical and cultural context that produced them. In the latter case, explanations that are inclined to side with the *esuli* argue that the environment has already been "slavicized." We are dealing here with two processes of selective oblivion. On the one hand, the community of *esuli* is intentionally forgetting the presence of a Slav population in the hinterland of Istrian towns and their coexistence with these towns, while the Slovenian discourse is intentionally neglecting the Italian and Venetian contribution to the history of Istrian towns. As a result, the Slovenian general public is neglecting the urban Venetian heritage, which is why demands for the return of removed artworks are not more categorical (Babelič 2018: 68, 76–78).

From National to Regional Memory

The memory conflicts are reflected by commemorations such as the one held at the antifascist monument in Strunjan. The monument was one of the first to commemorate the early fascist violence in Istria. On 19 March 1921, fascists traveling on a train shot at children playing near the tracks of the Parenzana railway line. Two were killed and one was disabled for life (Brate 2007). In 1946, a simple vernacular monument was erected, commemorating the national liberation struggle. The monument was made by simple people, not artists, who wanted this obelisk to honor the local, innocent "martyrs," who became heroes and freedom fighters. With its two partisan caps, the monument's iconography reflects two ethnic identities in Istria fighting for freedom: one is the cap of the Slovene partisans, the *triglavka* or Triglav cap, while the other is the cap of the *garibaldini*, the members of the Italian resistance movement (Hrobat Virloget and Čebron Lipovec 2017: 51; Čebron Lipovec, Hrobat Virloget, and Preložnik 2017).

In Istria and all over Primorska, the monument assumed the symbolism of the *lieu de mémoire,* the basis of Slovene and especially regional Primorska identity, founded on victimization at the hands of fascist violence, heroic resistance against fascism and the national liberation struggle (Fikfak 2009: 359; Hrobat Virloget 2015a: 161). The monument's nationwide significance may also be deduced from the popular and prominent individuals who are chosen to speak at the annual commemorations. The speakers invited to address the people gathered at the celebration on 20 March 2015 were Milan Brglez, President of the National Assembly of Slovenia, and Peter Bossman, mayor of Piran. In their speeches, both politicians emphasized the above values as the foundations of Slovene and Primorska identity. The mayor (originally from Ghana) had a classic speech, typical of commemorations of the antifascist struggle during World War II:

> [On fascism as evil:] And we are proud that the Slovene people made an important contribution to the victory of the Allies in World War II. . . . We have shown that Slovenes will never be just helpless victims, but will always know how to hit back hard. . . . A nation that knows how to fight so bravely for its survival and its dignity can neither be stripped of its homeland, nor its future. Thank you.[11]

The speech by the mayor of Piran emphasizes the sacrifice and heroism of Slovenes in the context of typical nationalist discourse, where there is no room for the participation of "other" non-Slovenes in the antifascist struggle. As Stuart Hall (2008: 220–21) argues, nations create their collective identities by selectively choosing and binding together special events that must be remembered in a "national story" that is reflected in the national heritage. Those who do not see themselves in this story cannot truly "belong." In this case, it is the Italians who remained in Istria after the exodus who cannot identify themselves with these kinds of nationalistic discourses (Hrobat Virloget and Čebron Lipovec 2017: 52). Despite the links between the Slovene and Italian freedom fighters in the antifascist struggle, this element of brotherhood has very rarely outweighed the national agenda of the new Slovenian authorities in this area (see Rogoznica 2011: 298–304). Interviews with Italians from the region reflect their disappointment at being so frequently overlooked and even equated with fascists. According to Amalia, a former headmistress of an Italian school, the Italian minority was all too frequently overlooked and also hurt whenever she attended the commemorations with her pupils. It is clear from what she says that the different sides do not even agree on the ethnic identity of the murdered children, which is understandable for such a multicultural environment:

> But it was Italians who killed Italians. Those children killed in Strugnano were Italian. They were travelling on the Parenzana, they saw them and they began shooting. I mean, what do children have to do with this . . . But at these celebrations, sometimes the speakers, especially the older Slovenians . . . Something completely different comes out. They do not say anything against the Italians, against the fascists, but we are there, present, including the schools . . . And . . . It wasn't always pleasant. The school had to attend and so we went, but afterwards we said: "That's enough now, always listening to the same stories, always the same things, year after year, and we are always polite. But that's enough now!" (Hrobat Virloget and Čebron Lipovec 2017: 53)

Feelings of hurt caused by Italians from Istria being equated with fascists was a subject that most frequently cropped up in conversations with Italians. In the same interview, Amalia mentioned the burden of Italians being equated with fascists that she experiences in her everyday life.

> And also these fascists . . . The central theme of my whole life, ever since I was born, has always been: Italians—fascists. But enough of these stories! Sixty years have passed, enough . . . But no, every time someone wants to, how shall I put it, prod you, hurt you, they call you a fascist. This is really something I hate. When they want to hurt you [speaking in a low, contemptuous tone of voice], "you're a fascist!" (Hrobat Virloget 2015, 168).

Having experienced Yugoslav nationalism, imbued with the collective criminalization of Italians because of war crimes and fascist violence, most Italians with antifascist and socialist views living in socialist Yugoslavia experienced bitter disappointment after its promises of "Yugoslav-Italian brotherhood" (It. *fratellanza italo-slava*) and equality between all ethnic groups (Ballinger 2003: 129–67, 207–44; Nemec 2015; Hrobat Virloget 2015a).[12] As already mentioned, national memories focus on one's own victimhood, so as to overlook one's own co-responsibility and the "other's" victim status (Assmann 2007: 17). However, precisely this reflection on one's role in the victim–perpetrator duality could be identified in the speech by the experienced politician and left-leaning professor of international relations Milan Brglez. Although in his speech in Strunjan he also spoke about suffering under fascism, he nevertheless emphasized how victory could not be achieved without the mutual understanding and joint resistance to fascism by all Istrians, that is, Slovenes, Croats and Italians:

> This act [the shooting of children by the fascists] was yet another nail in the coffin of intercultural coexistence in this area. [Speaking about fascist violence and the repression of the Slovene language] Despite dark thunder clouds, the Slovene language and culture have survived. This is thanks above all to the Istrian Čedermaci, as the locals like to call them [nationally conscious priests], Alojz Kocijančič and others . . . . Without them Slovene would not now be spoken in these parts. Neither would this be possible without the brave men and women, whether of Slovene, Italian, or Croat origin, who liberated this territory from the fascist yoke. Without unity and coexistence, which were forged among the combatants in the forests, Strunjan and all of Slovenian Istria would now look different. But unfortunately, we must also admit that in this just struggle for liberation some things happened that, if we wish to be faithful to historical truth, we must admit and regret. One of these things was a drastic change in the population makeup of Slovenian Istria, which has significantly affected the following generations. Emptied villages and towns, empty streets, centuries-old names of streets, villages, and towns changed, all because of the postwar regime in this area.

Slovenian politicians very rarely speak this way, reflecting on the "dark" sides of postwar history including mass migrations and demographic and linguistic changes in Istrian society (Hrobat Virloget 2015a: 161–62). By focusing on intercultural coexistence and the joint multiethnic antifascist struggle, the speech is different from typical political discourses at regional and national levels. By acknowledging "our own" and "foreign" hurt, he indicates the road Aleida Assmann believes European politics should take in creating a common European memory. Such a memory will only come into existence when national memories succeed in establishing awareness of their role both as victims and perpetrators, which means they will have to face their own, sometimes overlooked memories, and listen to "the other" with empathy (Assmann 2007: 22–23).

Acts of Reconciliation

The Convergence of Political Discourses

A courageous step toward achieving international political reconciliation between Slovenian, Croatian, and Italian national memories was made in 2010, when the presidents of Slovenia, Croatia, and Italy—Danilo Türk, Ivo Josipović, and Giorgio Napolitano, respectively—symbolically acknowledged the "victimhood" of the "other" by jointly laying wreaths at key places of memory: before the *Narodni dom* (Slovene Cultural Centre) in Trieste, the burning down of which in 1920 is considered symbolic of the beginning of fascist violence against Slovenes and Croats, and before the memorial plaque dedicated to refugees from Istria, Rijeka, and Dalmatia located at the railway station in Trieste (Ivelja and Petkovič 2010; Horvat 2010; Hrobat Virloget 2015a: 160–61). In the inclined and less inclined reactions to the act of reconciliation, I found the direct connection made between fascism and the exodus by the Minister for Slovenians Abroad at the time, Boštjan Žekš, particularly interesting: "This is the beginning and end of an era. It began with the burning down of the *Narodni dom* and ended with the exodus" (Horvat 2010). As we saw in the section on competing discourses, the ceremony unfortunately had no major long-term impact on either side of the border.

At the time this book was being written, on 13 July 2020, a similar act of reconciliation was held at the presidential level to mark a hundred years since the burning down of the *Narodni dom* in Trieste. A contract transferring ownership of the building to the Slovene minority was signed. Prior to the ceremony in Trieste, the presidents of Slovenia and Italy, Borut Pahor and Sergio Mattarella, imitating the gesture previously made by the French and German presidents, laid wreaths and held hands before the memorial to the heroes of Basovizza and before the *foiba*. Again there was criticism that the *foiba* should first be investigated as false political myths were being created out of ignorance (A. Juri 2020). The Slovenian and Italian historians Jože Pirjevec and Raoul Pupo commented that political rhetoric wants neither the reality portrayed by historians nor the true numbers of victims (Širca 2020). The *foiba* in Basovizza has now been concreted over, and the Italians do not want to investigate it. In 1945, the British did not find a single Italian corpse, instead finding one hundred corpses of German soldiers and one civilian. The main reproach made by the Slovenians who protested on this occasion, and which is repeated by the Slovenian historian and author of a book on the *foibe* Jože Pirjevec, is that the *foiba* is being used for political manipulation and to distort history. This is also why

President Borut Pahor was criticized for visiting the *foiba* because he acknowledged the Italian "truth" (Lesjak 2020: 11), and why the Italians are constantly reproached for being incapable of acknowledging fascist atrocities without connecting them with what came before and after (Vojnović 2020). However, Jože Pirjevec believes that the Italian president paying tribute to the victims of Basovizza, the first people to fight against fascism in Europe and who are still considered terrorists by Italy, is nevertheless an important gesture as it is the first time Italy has made some sort of apology (Lesjak 2020: 10). The Italian media reported on the burning and return of the *Narodni dom*, but the main item of news was the visit to the *foiba* as Slovenian recognition of Italian suffering. Regardless of criticisms of Italian falsification of history, it is important to understand that the *foiba* in Basovizza is an Italian national place of remembrance so visiting such a place, together with the first victims of fascism, is nevertheless a significant diplomatic step. In the words of Sergio Mattarella, we cannot erase the difficult past but we can transform it either into mutual hatred or into common heritage from which cooperation and friendship will grow (Petrovec 2020).

As has always been the case, this attempt to bring the three national collective memories closer together again resulted in Slovenians and Croats criticizing the Italians for not having appropriately reported the findings of the Slovenian-Italian Cultural-Historical Commission from 2002 (Horvat 2010). When in 2000 the Slovenian and Italian governments appointed a joint commission of historians from both sides of the national border to study Slovenian-Italian relations from the period of 1880–1918 to 1945–1956, this was one of the most decisive steps in the attempt to bring together national conflicting memories (Kacin Wohinz and Troha 2001). A summary of the most crucial events on this territory is only eighteen pages long—this seems to be the greatest possible consensus historians on both sides of the national border could reach. While the Slovenian side has published its report on its government's official website, the Italian government website does not feature the report, however, it has appeared in a printed version and has also been published on the websites of some research institutes. According to Roberta Altin and Natka Badurina (2018: 188), the report did not generate any public interest.

Pacifying Memories in Literary Works and the Conflict between the Italian Urban and the Slav Rural Environments

Rather than in the dominant public discourse (with the exception of some of the examples above), pacifying memories may be found in alternative forms of collective memory such as literature, film, theater, and more. As already mentioned, Istrian writers were the first to mention the Istrian exodus after decades of silence (Dota 2010: 73–85). In the section on literature I do not intend to analyze the vast quantities of émigré literature on the subject of the exodus written by the *esuli* or their descendants. I am not an expert in literary studies who would be able to do this. As an ethnologist, the most I can do is list some literary works, theater performances, and public events on the subject of the disputed past that helped me get to grips with this complex topic or that I believe had a specific impact on Istria's current population. However, it is important to realize that these ways of interpreting the past are normally accessible only to a small circle of people, usually intellectuals and those who are particularly interested in the subject, and they unfortunately do not reach the general public as the normal media do. The general impression is that these cultural achievements do not reach most of the migrant workers from the southern republics of the former Yugoslavia who moved to Istria en masse in the 1960s and 1970s (Kalc 2019). These people are usually not seen in the audience at such cultural events.

Out of the writers who tackle the subject of people from the border area caught in the whirlwind of history, the first one we should mention is Fulvio Tomizza (1935–1999), who was born in the Croatian part of Istria, was also active in Koper, and then immigrated to Trieste. The works of the writer who "identified himself with the border" (Hladnik-Milharčič 2008) were translated into other languages, and he won various prizes in Slovenia and Croatia for his promotion of multiculturality, his efforts to overcome differences and antagonisms, and his avoidance of one-sided views.

In the words of Ciril Zlobec, he was recognized as a "symbol and positive literary reality of this trilingual, tricultural and triethnic space" (Hostnik 2002). As Franco Juri says, "he is a clear advocate of multiculturality. This is confirmed by the fact that he was not popular with any nationalists: not Slovene, not Croat, and certainly not Italian" (Hostnik 2002). It has already been mentioned how an Italian lady from Istria only discovered the exodus while studying Italian at university in Belgrade by reading Tomizza's novels. When reading Tomizza's books, I am always struck by the smallness of individuals who are sucked into these terrible whirlpools of political ideologies and violence. Despite their hybrid identities in the multicultural border environment, they are forced to choose just one identity. As Fulvio Tomizza writes in *La miglior vita* (The better life): "We were at war and we continued being at war simply because of the eternal question of whether we were Italians or Slavs, although in reality we were all of mixed origin" (Tomizza 1980: 303).

After the writer's death, the international Tomizza forum was founded in 2000, and it is held annually in Istria (in Trieste, Koper, and Umag/Umago) with the aim of connecting three bordering countries. The forums initially focused on the life and work of Fulvio Tomizza, but there are now also discussions about the border and its social, political, and cultural aspects ("Fulvio Tomizza." n.d.; "Forum Tomizza: Short Take." n.d.).

Out of the large amount of émigré literature on the exodus, my attention was caught by a graphic novel written by a woman from the third generation of emigrants, the daughter of an *esule* who left Istria as the child of a Croat-Italian family (Sansone and Tota 2012). Two stories intertwine in the book: one tells of a granddaughter whose search for her roots leads her in the opposite direction from the path taken by her parents and grandparents—all the way to Rijeka from where they originate, while the other story is of her émigré forebears in which we learn of their stereotyping as fascists and foreigners, and of journeys between refugee camps in Italy and the conditions in these camps. The title of the book, written in Italian, is *Palacinche* (pancakes). The word reminds the author of her childhood and this food, which has the same name in Italian, Croatian, and Slovene. This dish reflects Central European or Austro-Hungarian culinary heritage (Sansone and Tota 2012: 12), and it inspires much nostalgia for the old empire in Trieste at the turn of the twenty-first century (Ličen 2018: 44, 47). Traveling in search of one's family's roots is a common theme in literature, especially in connection with large migrations. In her analysis of German literature that deals with the search for family roots in the countries of Central and Eastern Europe, Catherine Perron (2017: 145) finds that émigré literature is a strong medium, which gives shape to and transmits cultural memory on representations of the past and reflections on it.

Few of the literary works on the Istrian exodus and its consequences have been translated into Slovene or Croatian. Most of the works are by Italian authors living in Istria, such as Nelida Milani Kruljac (2011, 2015) and Claudio Ugussi (2002) who live in Croatia. These books speak about the lives of the Italians who remained in Istria after the exodus, the deep uncertainties of fascism, World War II and the exodus, divided communities, scattered memories, hybrid identities, the loss of language, places of memory, identity, and more. ("Nelida Milani e la memoria tagliata" 2017; Mrđenović n.d.).

There is nothing going on here, absolutely nothing, there is nothing except the small town, and the dying Italian community . . . . This quarter means nothing to me, it is without meaning, without points of reference, this is a dull, static space, completely encoded in a different language . . . . The exodus, the eternal reference point that separates the before and the after, was followed by our being unprepared for the fate that befell us, then the death of things, life became a desert, just words in another language, words that take up all the social space. . . . Bilingualism? It wavers between chimeras. . . . (Milani Kruljac 2011: 64–66)

A comparable author from Slovenia is Franco Juri, former politician and activist and currently the director of Piran's Maritime Museum. He is particularly respected by one of my Italian interlocutors because "he has surpassed all these borders and is above all these small things," and he is one of the rare members of the Italian minority who has "stepped out of the minority and said, "enough of this minority, I am not a minority!" His novel, which has been translated from Italian into Slovene, tells his life story, of international proportions, and describes the difficulties faced by the Italians who remained after the exodus, including living with immigrants from all over Yugoslavia who frequently held the stereotypical view that Italians were fascists:

We played together in the different languages of this new Babylon: in Slovene, Italian, Venetian, Serbo-Croat, Macedonian, Albanian . . . Our nursery school was literally at the heart of the old town and a kind of summary of the new Yugoslavia, imbued with a loftier, indomitable honor.

Those of us who spoke Italian were often provoked by kids from other neighborhoods and when, after a long quarrel, we finally decided to play at "war," as if the war of our fathers was not enough, we had to assume the ungrateful role of villains—fascists. (F. Juri 2010: 164–65)

A view from the "slav perspective" is given by the Istrian writer and translator of Croat origin Milan Rakovac, one of the organizers of the Forum Tomizza. Similar to other Istrian authors, he does not describe the exodus as a clear-cut phenomenon but describes the combination of different complicated causes. The writer nevertheless presents a view of the exodus that goes against the dominant Yugoslav perspective, which held that the exodus was the emigration of fascists or people's voluntary decision to leave (Hrobat Virloget 2015a). His book bears the unusual title *"Riva i druži" ili, caco su nassa dizza* (1983), which is in the Istrian Croato-Venetian dialect and means "The comrades are coming or how are our children," and is practically inaccessible to anyone unfamiliar with this dialect, that is, for most Slovenians and Croats who are not from Istria and Primorska. The word *druži* was used by Italian Istrians to designate Slav immigrants, communists, so it is a new name for the "barbarian" or "ščavo" (Rakovac 1983: 29).[13] Milan Rakovac was born into an antifascist family whose name was Italianized under fascism, and his family fled fascist violence by moving to the Kingdom of Yugoslavia. In his own words: "In Istria, the Italians were struck by revenge and a terrible punishment. The punishment was merciless. That is why I wrote *Riva i druži*. Just like victory, punishment too has deep historical roots" (Hladnik-Milharčič 2008). Like most Slovenians and Croatians, he too accuses Italians of failing to recognize their own crimes (Baskar 2010: 110–18). "The only collective crime from World War II that was not punished is Italian fascism. . . . Germany carried out a thorough process of denazification and Japan underwent demilitarization. The Italians did not pay for their crimes. That is why amnesia has occurred" (Hladnik-Milharčič 2008). Rakovac says he wrote the book after translating *The Better Life* by Fulvio Tomizza, which talks about the Istrians caught up in the rapid succession of different states in the twentieth century. It made him want to "portray the South Slavs as being noble-hearted and broad-minded, and to show remorse, as Fulvio Tomizza did" (Hladnik-Milharčič 2008).

In addition to the question of fluidity of ethnic identities in Istria, Fulvio Tomizza, Franco Juri and Milan Rakovac all make the same observations about the impact of the exodus, which upended the centuries-old stereotyped contrast between Italian-civilized-urban and Slav-rural-barbarian (Baskar 2002; Dota 2010: 57–72). Through literature, the writer shows what Slovenian and Croatian public discourse are not prepared to recognize—that the exodus punished the Italians in Istria for never acknowledging fascist violence, and the deeply-rooted feeling of superiority of "civilized townspeople" over barbarian *sc'avi*:

> And yet, there was the impotent anger, the helpless contempt of the City that had to acknowledge the peasant's superiority. The Lord or the slave? The centuries-old relationship has fallen apart, the barbarian unworthy of even being looked at has taken his fate into his own hands. The wild, free and victorious peasant has stormed into the City, but the City could not accept this without suffering utter humiliation. This "Romance city of ours and its thousand years of culture" overwhelmed by the "barbaric Slav peasant" in a dance of victory, freedom and—revenge. Revenge for one thousand years of subordination, worthlessness, shame, anguish, famine and fear. Yes, the Istrian peasant delighted in taking revenge on the gentry and humiliated them mercilessly. The decisive blow did not come from some serious incidents, or tragedies, or pressure exerted by the victorious terror, but first and foremost from the most indescribable way in which the city's attributes, the core of its urban nature were desecrated. (Rakovac 1983: 32)

The postwar reversal of centuries-old relations of superiority, expressed in the opposition between urban and rural, is also reflected by Istrian writers of Italian origin such as Claudio Ugussi and Fulvio Tomizza.

> Nothing could have irritated these people [the citizens of Koper] more than that the idiom of the peasants was raised to the level of language and that it was expressed so freely that it must have been seen as a provocation. . . . And this animosity had always existed, even in times when the idea of a Yugoslav state had not even been born and the Slovene element consisted of timid peasants, standing at a distance from the area meant for carriages, who came to buy provisions for the whole month and who tried to speak Venetian, while their wives in brightly colored clothes with floral patterns walked around selling milk and they too were scoffed at because of the way they tried to speak the language. It is perhaps because I was the son of a woman who as a young girl carried milk cans through the streets of Piran that I could never entirely understand the feeling of superiority and at the same time insecurity that led them, long before the inevitable counter-attack, to take it out on this unarmed population, going to such lengths as to disturb their villages with punitive expeditions that were considered a legal and even holy duty under fascism. Now the tables have turned and every good citizen of Koper pondered the unpleasant consequences that awaited them. Besides being Slavs, the winners of the war declared themselves to be opposed to private property and religion. This meant everyone was affected: priests and devout people, merchants and aristocrats, workers and beggars, uninterrupted Italian tradition and mentality. (Tomizza 2015: 22)

> The language of the *sc'avi,* I thought to myself. . . . In Pula too, the Slavs from rural areas were called *sc'avi* and were mocked whenever they came to town with their oxcarts to sell wood and bundles of firewood. . . . And in Pula too, the fascists made sure the language of the *sc'avi* was not spoken. If anyone was caught speaking it, perhaps someone coming from elsewhere, the least they would have to endure would be a beating or having to drink castor oil. (Ugussi 1991: 41)

Most Istrian authors raise the subject of the superiority of the Italian population in Istria, which they equate with an urban, civilized identity in contrast to the rural and barbaric countryside, where the Slavs or *sc'avi* lived. Pamela Ballinger (2003: 168–206) observes that this derogatory term additionally emphasizes the ignorance of the Italians, and especially the *esuli,* in their evidently paternalistic discourse in which they still do not make the distinction between the Slovenes and Croats with whom they coexisted until not long ago. Faced with the stereotypical contrast of the homogeneous Slovene hinterland and the Italian town dwellers, the historian Marta Verginella (1996) emphasizes the need to bear in mind appurtenance to a particular social class. In a similar vein, the anthropologist Borut Brumen (2000: 129) interprets accounts of the haughty bourgeoisie in light of the conflictual nature of encounters between groups with different cultural and social values.

Unlike the above, typical interpretations simplify the conflict between Italian-civilized-urban and Slav-barbaric-rural to ethnic-national conflicts in Istria. This stereotype, on whose basis national borders and ethnic differentiation have been constructed in Istria since the mid-nineteenth century, has now been deconstructed with the argument that the situation in Istria was more complex. It is important to realize that in the censuses carried out in the nineteenth and early twentieth centuries it was not clear what "language spoken" meant when defining the national identity of bilingual Istrians: the language of interpersonal or working relations or language spoken in the family. In the nineteenth century, it was difficult to carry out censuses and determine Italian or Yugoslav ethnicity, and it is even harder to interpret them nowadays as people in this multicultural environment could easily switch from speaking Slovene or Croat to Italian. In the nineteenth century, there was evidence of increasing ethnic discord and stronger Italian, Slovene, or Croat ethnic identification, with Istrians in rural areas and in towns fighting for control of the public space and Istria's political future by founding different cultural or sports associations on the basis of ethnic affiliation. The borders between ethnicities also become more rigid as languages were standardized and the education system was further developed. The urban and rural areas that were mainly mixed or Slavic, and had been increasingly Italianized until the 1870s and 1880s, experienced a significant increase in Slovene or Croat identification. At the turn of the twentieth century, urban identity in Istria was still predominantly Italian, above all in the western part of Istria and in Labin/Albona (on the other side of Istria). However, Croat urban elements were increasingly visible in predominantly Italian-speaking towns and all the more evident in towns with a Croat majority in Istria's interior, the east, and on the islands. Regardless of this, many researchers uncritically equated towns, Italian identity, and civilization. This distinction between towns and villages was probably connected with an end to the growth of Slovene and Croat urban society following annexation to Italy, after their schools and associations were closed, and physical and psychological pressure was exerted on the elite to withdraw from the territory (in the direction of Yugoslavia). This turnaround fortified the superficial and static notion of national relations in Istria that was partly founded on facts, but also stemmed from the ignorance of Italian intellectuals concerning Slovenes and Croats and a lack of knowledge about changes that occurred from the mid-nineteenth to the twentieth centuries (D'Alessio 2006; 2008: 43–49).

The anthropologist Bojan Baskar draws attention to the frequent ideological distinctions between farmers and pastoralists, or urban and rural inhabitants, implying that the process of making ethnic opposites is connected with economic and geographic connotations. These opposites can be recognized in all nationalistic discourses, including in the recent siege of Sarajevo, which was described as a flare-up of an ancient conflict between rural and urban people.[14] The distinction between Trieste and Istria and the "barren" land above them on which Asiatic Slavs are supposed to have settled and dates back to the eighteenth century is of the same kind. It indicates the construction of a cultural boundary between the Triestine Mediterranean and the barbaric land above it or the essentialist drawing of ethnic boundaries between "Western" Europeans and Slavic peoples (Baskar 2002: 98–120).

Marta Verginella also appeals for the ethnocentric paradigm of the asymmetric multicultural environment, characteristic of the Balkan and Northern Adriatic region that was triggered by the process of nationalization and the politicization of the masses in the nineteenth century, to be problematized. An invention of Triestine historiography from before World War II and after it, Slovenian and international historiography continues to refer to it to this day, thereby prolonging the conviction that Italy's urban reality was the bearer of civilization whose opposite was the rural Slovene environment—entailing that the Slovene people are simple and uncivilized. As Larry Wolff argues, the invention of oppositions between urban and rural areas was functional for creating a frontier between the East and the West in the eighteenth century in the Adriatic region. Marta Verginella also emphasizes Braudel's appeal for the need for complex understanding of the changing relationship between urban and rural areas. Similar to Vanni D'Alessio, she also draws attention to the expulsion of the Slovene urban middle classes in the time of fascism (Wolff 2001; Verginella 2017). This old attitude of superiority is probably one of the main reasons why Slovenes and Croats cannot empathize with the suffering of the Italians, perceived as the former "perpetrators," when the age-old historical roles were turned upside down.

Views Expressed in Theater, Film, and Story-Telling Evenings

In the past decade, it was the theater play *Magazzino 18* written by Simone Cristicchi from Rome (first staged in 2013), that caused the greatest stir in connection with the unresolved frontier issues. The main professional criticism that can be leveled against this theater play, which deals with the *foibe* and the exodus, is a lack of deliberation on the responsibility of Italian politics (Hrobat Virloget 2017a: 42–43). Judging by the opinions of the Italians who remained in Istria, with their tears and enthusiastic ovations, the performance had a cathartic effect on them as it was the first time they experienced public recognition of their suffering and acknowledgment of the Italian "mother" nation's long silence on the subject. In the local Italian journal, the emotional feelings of Italian Istrians who remained are described in superlatives. It is emphasized that not many works can inspire emotions as strongly as *Magazzino 18*—named after a warehouse containing objects that belonged to the *esuli* in Trieste (Knez 2013a: 1). According to the local Italian historian Kristjan Knez, Cristicchi has told the tragic story of a completely uprooted Italian community and the centuries-old culture of this part of the Adriatic, "forgotten, covered by silence and oblivion although it was crying in pain" (Knez 2013a: 2). It actually paid for the sins of "Rome's unfortunate politics," fascism, violence, civil war after the downfall of the Kingdom of Italy, and other sins, and he emphasizes that the cause-and-effect relationship involving only the exodus and fascism is far too simple an interpretation (Knez 2013a: 1–2). Those who saw the play were moved by the fact that the silenced tragedy that befell Italians from Italy's eastern border was finally discussed in public after so many years of being confined to the privacy of personal memories. One woman said: "Usually, I don't even want to think about the painful past that struck us and our families as there was too much suffering" (Knez 2013b: 11). I also heard similar words from a member of the *esuli*, who did not want to go and see the play because bringing back memories of such a painful past would reopen a wound that simply hurt too much. In another comment, the exodus was linked to "the splitting up of families, including his own, contrary interpretations of facts by opposing political factions and opposing nationalisms that caused us who remained to suffer" (Knez 2013b: 13). Almost all who have seen the play agree it is the first portrayal of this very painful past, of the exodus, which has been carried out objectively and fairly as "every time the exodus was discussed someone was omitted. . . . You could feel that an effort has been made not to forget anyone" (Knez 2013b: 12). "Twenty years of fascism, the *foibe*, refugee camps, Goli Otok and much more besides. Not forgetting anyone, neither those who left, nor those who remained" (Knez 2013b: 12).

The overwhelming view that the play gives a fair representation of history stems from the fact that the period of Italian fascist violence is at least mentioned, while usually it is omitted from the dominant

Italian discourse on the eastern border, where history begins with the exodus (Fikfak 2009: 358–59). However, as the Italian historian Piero Purini wrote in a very well-founded review of the play,[15] only five minutes devoted to fascism out of one hour and forty-five minutes is like pulling wool over people's eyes. He accuses Cristicchi of forgetting the unpleasant parts in his desire to remember the forgotten tragedies of the *foibe* and the exodus on which Italian collective memory is based. Purini also accuses Cristicchi of completely failing to place the exodus in a historical context by omitting the terrible war crimes and fascist violence perpetrated against Slovenes and Croats including torture, concentration camps, murders, the burning down of Slovene and Croat villages, the killing of civilians for which no-one took responsibility, the closing down of Slovene and Croat schools, forbidding the use of language, brutal Italianization, the wiping out of the intellectual class, the flight of many to Yugoslavia to escape fascism, mass immigration of Italians to the newly conquered territories of Istria, and so on. In his opinion, equating Italians with fascists was not the invention of Slovenes and Croats but of fascist propaganda. Spreading the idea that it was no longer possible to "live as an Italian" in Yugoslavia, Italian identity being the only reason for which people were killed and thrown in the *foibe*, reflects great ignorance in simplifying complex ideological struggles and forgetting that Italians were granted national minority rights in Yugoslavia. When dealing with the exodus, he forgets the complex economic reasons, Italian propaganda, ideological and social contexts, the inversion of social roles, and more, in which the former master did not want to obey his former slave. In his opinion the play shows a complete ignorance of history and employs the usual stereotypes to simplify the extremely complex history of ethnic, linguistic, and national identities by again staging a "great amnesia" that complies with the myth of *Italiani, brava gente* (the Italians, good people). It "makes us blind to too many things, above all our racism" (Purini 2010; Purini and Wu Ming 2014).

Roberta Altin and Natka Badurina are similarly critical of the play and say that the content is historically inconsistent and biased because it presents the Istrian exodus as the destruction of Italian civilization in an exclusively Italian Adriatic environment. They too note that the short appearance by the Slovene girl, who testifies to fascist violence, appears intrusive and is a minimalistic attempt to achieve political correctness. As they have written, "what is on the stage is not the history of historians . . ., but history in a Freudian sense, a succession of fabricated events that are too unbearable to be memorable" (Altin and Badurina 2018: 195). Although the aim of the play was to "appease both sides," the anthropologists emphasize that the success of therapy following trauma depends on correctly understanding the local specifics of political violence. Without a correct understanding of history, collective therapy is doomed to failure (Altin and Badurina 2018: 193–96).

In the same way, the very complex border issue is simplified in two Italian films—in the already mentioned film that accompanied the introduction of the exodus and *foibe* remembrance day, *Il cuore nel pozzo,* and in the more recent film *Red Land—Rosso Istria* (2018) about wartime killings in Istria. From a Slovene perspective, the films perpetuate the one-sided Italian view of the border region's complex history, with the Italians portrayed as victims of the Yugoslavs and without any reflection on the preceding twenty years of fascist violence. Some historians, but also journalists, have in the case of the first film expressed agreement with the Slovenian public opinion: the aim of this politically guided propaganda is to erase the blame of one group (the fascists) and replace it with the responsibility of another (the communists); it distorts the roles of victim and executioners, occupiers and the occupied; it creates a new version of historical events, discredits the Yugoslav partisan movement, and shows the new neighbors—the Slovenes and the Croats—in a poor light (Verginella 2009: 44; Accati 2009: 192). The film is an attempt to radically change the coordinates of collective memory and to revise history by concealing events that would prevent an unambiguous memory based on the martyrdom of Italians in Istria and Dalmatia, and it is again only further proof that memory and oblivion are two sides of the same coin (Verginella 2009: 51–52). It is also necessary to be critical of Slovenian nationalistic discourse when talking about Istrian towns as being purely Slovene without any sensitivity for the Italian minority or about the unrecognized minority groups from the former Yugoslavia. Otherwise, the oldest Italian film to deal with the exodus is *La città dolente* (The city of pain) directed by Mario Bonnarda in 1949.

On the Slovenian side, Goran Vojnović tried to encourage reflection on postwar Istria with the film *Piran/Pirano* (2010). The story is a classic love triangle that brings together the life stories of two inhabitants of Piran: an Italian *esule* and a Bosnian partisan and liberator of Piran. The story of the immigrant, who has never swum in "his" sea of Piran, reflects the attitude of most of the working-class inhabitants of Istria's town centers to the local Mediterranean environment (see below under attitude toward the environment; Hrobat Virloget et al. 2016: 80; Hrobat Virloget 2017b: 22). Despite its good intentions, the film was sharply criticized for its unfortunate artistic realization and dramaturgy, and was also accused of "making history appear as simple as a cartoon" (Štefančič 2010). The film did not prompt any self-reflection on a national level about the drastic ethnic and social changes that befell mainly the Istrian urban population after the war nor on the complex intereth-nic relations.

A series of story-telling evenings were held at Koper Regional Mu-seum (2012, 2013) with the intention of assuaging feelings and hearing the "other's" story. They were organized by Neža Čebron Lipovec from the Faculty of Humanities of the University of Primorska, Maša Saccara from Koper Regional Museum, and Zdenko Bombek, a photographer from Koper (Čebron Lipovec 2015). As this was the first brave public head-to-head of the memories of Koper's inhabitants from different eth-nic backgrounds, the first evening resulted in an interethnic dispute.[16] However, it seems that the other evenings focusing on common urban points of memory succeeded in surpassing ethnic divisions and conflict-ing memories (Čebron Lipovec 2015). Also in the context of collecting memories of Istrians, there are a number of books that tell the life stories of people of different ethnic origin from Koper and Piran, who confront their views on the experience of "being" or becoming an Istrian (Pahor 2007, 2011, 2014; Menih 2011).

Through the Nationalistic Prism of the Northern Adriatic Museums

Museums dealing with population movements are undoubtedly ex-amples of the one-sided understanding of history. A case in point are the museums on the expulsion of Germans from Central and Eastern Europe after World War II (see Bazin and Perron 2018). A similar mind-set is evident in the Museum of the Civilization of Istria, Fiume and Dalmatia in Trieste (It. *Civico Museo della Civiltà Istriana, Fiumana e Dalmata*). The average Slovenian visitor will definitely be irked by the fact that there is no mention of the twenty years of fascist violence against Slovenes and Croats, and by the Italianization of Slovene and Croat toponyms, including places that never had an Italian population. Roberta Altin and Natka Badurina criticize the exhibition because it emphasizes solely the Italian historical perspective through Roman or Italian artifacts, and because its interpretation of the "catastrophe" that befell Italian culture in Istria, with a focus on the *foibe* and the exodus, ignores all the other components of what was a multicultural society. One may wonder why a museum should be founded in 2015, dedicated to a minority whose members were born after World War II and whose community was relocated seventy years ago. There is by all means an implicit aim to preserve a separate identity, the identity of Italians from Istria and Dalmatia, where the traumatic events of the "expulsion," the exodus, and the *foibe* are like the community's founding acts. Through an "imaginary" Istria, this museum reflects a community whose identity is based on homelessness and is constantly honored and found in "frozen" memories of trauma and absence. In an analysis of places of memory of the exodus in Trieste, the authors find that none of them has succeeded in surpassing the historical nationalistic trauma (Altin and Badurina 2018: 189–92).

Pamela Ballinger recognizes more implicit national discourses in her analysis of museums connected with maritime tradition in the Northern Adriatic. She believes they reveal indirect competition for symbolic control over the sea and coast and the mapping of ethnic-national identities on the territory. All three maritime museums in Piran, Trieste, and Santa Croce/Križ nad Trstom are supposed to reflect the local stereotypes of Italians with their high *civiltà* belonging to the coast and maritime culture, while Slavs belong to the rural culture in the hinterlands. In modern discourse this is supposed to be shown by a lack of seafood dishes and local fishing industries. For example, the focus of the maritime museum in Trieste is the once common coastal Northern Adriatic region. However, Ballinger is critical of the lack of discussion on national borders and ethnic identities. In her opinion, both Slovene museums, the Maritime Museum in Piran and the Fishing Museum of the Triestine coast in Santa Croce, Italy, are fighting against the stereotypical discourse by emphasizing Slav maritime culture: in Santa Croce by presenting the "centuries-old" Slovene fishing tradition with the *čupa* dugout canoe, and in Piran by reading maritime history through the "Slovene" prism, that is, by focusing on the history of Slovene seamanship. According to Ballinger, by drawing attention to Slovene sailors and their role in different navies, the museum unintentionally indicates that the coastal fishing tradition disappeared from the "slovene" coast after World War II with the exodus, although it denies the history of demographic changes. In contrast with the omission of Italian coastal traditions in the museum in Piran, these are emphasized in the Italian minority's museum in Rovinj/Rovigno, whose symbol is the local fishing boat known as the *batana*. Pamela Ballinger believes that unlike the others, this museum emphasizes the common coastal tradition shared by the inhabitants of Rovinj, regardless of whether they are Italians, Croats, Albanians, or Bosnian Muslims. By highlighting the success of the *batana*, helped by the socialist Tomos outboard engine from Koper, and the joint voyage of the *batana* and a traditional boat from the island of Vis to Venice, the museum goes beyond the discourse of ethnic boundaries by emphasizing the relations that run deep in this region (Ballinger 2006a).

In Croatia, the emigrants from Istria were the subject of an exhibition in the Ethnographic Museum of Istria in Pazin entitled "Suitcases and Destinies: Istria Out of Istria," for which a comprehensive catalog was also published (Nikočević 2011). If we look at the museums in Slovenia, however, we find that the subject of the exodus or drastic population changes in Istria are shrouded in silence. As will be shown below, even if the collection displays precious artifacts that remained after the exodus, such as porcelain in Koper Regional Museum's ethnological collection, there is no sign of self-reflection on the tragic fates of the people who gave these objects to the museum. However, there was recently a sign that things may be improving in the permanent exhibition on Koper's past in Koper Regional Museum, where one of the displays invited visitors to think about the painful upheavals caused by the different ideological and national systems in twentieth-century Istria. There was a drawer from which visitors could take both an archive source on someone's surname being changed into an Italian form under fascism and a request to move out after World War II.[17] Two painful truths from the time of fascism and the exodus, one alongside the other, the only such example in a museum exhibition in the Slovenian part of Istria that bravely considers different difficult pasts.

With the exception of some of the above attempts at appeasement, the different ethnic communities in the Northern Adriatic are all focusing on their own collective memory based on the black and white dichotomy of victim and perpetrator. So each ethnic community lives with its own painful truth that comes up against the "other's" painful truth. Roberta Altin and Natka Badurina also find that the accusations against the "other" in these nationalistic discourses are schizo-paranoid ways that lead to war and not peace, so it would be necessary to find a balance between awareness of one's own crime and the illusion of seeing oneself as "the good one." It would be necessary to undertake a precise historical analysis of each side's criminal acts and the complex psychological process of recognition (Altin and Badurina 2018: 189). Different truths continue to hit against each other—in their ignorance they can very easily be politically manipulated—and they draw their strength from deep-rooted stereotypes and untreated human pain.

Notes

1. Prior to emigration from Istria and before Germany attacked Yugoslavia in 1941, there had been organized emigration from Italian enclaves in Zadar and also Šibenik and Split (Volk 2003: 44).
2. The term "repatriation" ("return" to the motherland) is often used in these contexts, but it is problematic because it takes the motherland's point of view, while the "repa-

triated' immigrants consider the homeland to be the place they left (Čapo Žmegač 2002: 47–55; Tanc 2001).

3. More on the "counter-exodus," the Informbiro, and Goli Otok in the chapter on exodus in numbers.

4. An Adriatic island that was the site of a political prison after World War II in Yugoslavia.

5. Historical sources talk of between 25,000 and 30,000 migrants in only a few months of 1947, officially before the Paris Peace Treaty in 1947, which made it possible to opt for citizenship (Purini 2010: 250–51; Volk 2003: 45–46).

6. The author Lucia Castelli is the daughter of *esuli,* but the family never discussed its Istrian origins out of anger and sadness, but also because it was impossible to explain to people that did not understand them.

7. In Italian discourse, the *foibe* are deep natural sinkholes, commonplace on the Karst and in Istria, which are said to contain the victims of killings committed by Yugoslav partisans, civilians, and military personnel in 1943 and again in 1945 during the "forty-day occupation of Trieste." In the predominant Italian public discourse, they have acquired political and almost mythical connotations as in self-perception they are linked to ethnic cleansing because they are said to contain people who were killed simply "for being Italian" (Ballinger 2003: 129–67; Fikfak 2009: 358; Dota 2010; Radošević 2011: 243). On the other hand, Slovenian researchers claim that the *foibe* killings were motivated by ideology as many of the people killed were members of the Slovene anti-communist *domobranci* (home guard) and opponents of the new social system (Pirjevec 2009). Their interpretations in public and political discourses are based on old oppositions, from the *foibe* as an instrument of genocide to the *foibe* as the result of a spontaneous reaction by the Slavs to fascist brutality (Ballinger 2003: 145–56, 159; Verginella 2009: 53–67; Purini 2010: 189;). Numbers are also important. While studies of historical sources put the numbers of those killed and thrown in the *foibe* in Istria, Trieste, and the Julian March at somewhere between 1,500 and 2,000, the figures circulating in public of between 10,000 and 30,000 murdered individuals are excessive. This misleads the public into believing there was an attempt at mass extermination of the Italian population (Cogoy 2009: 16–17). Historians point out (Graziosi 2001; Orlić 2012: 19) that the *foibe* should be understood in a much broader context, from the perspective of the war and revolution, when a wave of violence was triggered in the final phase of the war throughout almost all of Europe. More specifically, they should be understood as a combination of the problems with violence and minorities, connected with the Axis powers, and events in Italy and a difficult end to the civil war.

8. More on this in the section Acts of Reconciliation.

9. However, with a change in the social context, the silenced memories of those "excluded" from history can become public, and they can even become bearers of national memory, as happened in the case of the Italian *esuli* when a national memorial day was introduced to commemorate them (see the section on competing discourses and victimisation).

10. As will be evident in the chapter on heritage, the Italians in Istria identify themselves with Venetian heritage—in line with the Italian identity construction.

11. I am grateful to my colleague Andrej Preložnik for providing audio-visual material from the event.

12. In addition to Slovenes from Primorska, the policy of "Slovene-Italian brotherhood" included primarily Italian communists and workers. It was formed by the leadership of the Slovene liberation movement and later the Yugoslav authorities with the aim

of jointly fighting for the annexation of the disputed territory around Trieste and Istria to Yugoslavia after World War II (Troha 1998: 188). Italian historians are critical of the selectivity of such policies, which only included a part of the Italian population (Pupo 2015: 31).

13. The word *druži* is used by Italian writers from Istria such as Nelida Milani Kruljac to denote Yugoslav immigrants. There is also the example of a derogatory exclamation by an Italian in a novel by Claudio Ugussi, "leave that dirty *drugarica*" (Ugussi 1991: 174)! (It. *Lasciala stare quella sporca drugarizza!*). The word comes from Croatian and Serbian and means "comrade"—a socialist way of expressing equality, i.e., that they were all on the same social level. However, in the Istrian Italian dialect the term acquired a negative, derogative connotation, similar to *titini*.

14. For more on the incursion of rural elements in the urban environment see the section on social boundaries with immigrants from the southern republics of the former Yugoslavia.

15. Purini also wrote a study on twentieth-century "ethnic metamorphoses" on Italy's eastern border (Purini 2010).

16. For more on this, see the section on interethnic relations.

17. The exhibition was prepared by the archaeologist and co-organizer of the story-telling evenings Maša Saccara, art historians Brigita Jenko and Tim Mavrič, and the designer Noel Mirković.

Chapter 2

The Exodus

Those Who Left, Those Who Stayed, and Those Who Came

The Exodus and Immigration in Numbers

Emigration from Istria ended the region's historical continuity and completely altered the ethnic, anthropological, and cultural aspects of Istrian everyday life. Immigration was not simply a replacement of the previous population and their jobs and homes, but the construction of a new social reality. Life continued in the existing urban centers in completely changed circumstances. The new inhabitants—who had come from near and far—gave the old built environment a new meaning, they built new suburbs, all within the new linguistic, ethnic, social, economic, and cultural-anthropological reality (Kalc 2019: 147).

Croatian researchers estimate that the territory joined to Croatia (Rijeka, Zadar, Cres, Lošinj, Lastovo) was abandoned by 180,000 people: 46,000 Italians who moved there after 1918, 117,000 autochthonous Italians, and 25,000 Croats. The total number of people thought to have left the territories joined to Yugoslavia is 237,000 (Žerjavić 1993; Volk 2003: 51). It is necessary to bear in mind that under fascism approximately 105,000 Slovenes and Croats emigrated from the Julian March (of which Istria was once part), and from 1918 to 1931 more than 130,000 Italians moved to this region (Kacin Wohinz and Troha 2001: 10; Kosmač 2017: 192). According to more recent Italian calculations, the figures for the provinces of Gorizia/Gorica, Trieste, Kvarner, and Zadar are as follows: Venetian Istrians—183,700; Italians who immigrated in the time of fascism—36,000; Italian administrative and military personnel from the frontier territory—24,500; Romanians, Hungarians, Albanians—4,400; Croats—12,300; Slovenes—5,300; anti-communist Slovenes from the hinterland of Gorizia—13,000 ±2,000). Slovene or Croat was the mother tongue of tens of thousands of these 300,000 emigrants (Pupo 2015: 26–28, figure 2). Out of the 10,156 optants from the district of Koper, analyzed by Jure Gombač (2005: 126), the proportions were as follows: the vast majority of emigrants were Italians—7,026, there were fewer Slovenes—2,992, and 1,056 of them also spoke Italian; out of the 138 Croats, 118 of them spoke Italian. As already mentioned, the numbers of emigrants quoted by Slovenian, Croat, and Italian interpretations differ—from 200,000 to 350,000— the latter considered by Pamela Ballinger (2003: 274) to be an excessive figure. Refugee associations speak of more than 300,000 or 350,000 people, although the foundation that helps refugees from the Julian March and Dalmatia quotes the figure 207,423 (the municipality of origin of 46,321 of these people being unknown). In 1958, 150,627 such persons were recorded in Italy (Kosmač 2017: 193).

Zone B of the Free Territory of Trieste—most of which is covered by this book—had 46,350 inhabitants in 1945, 18,500 of them in the towns of Izola, Koper, and Piran. After a slight increase in 1949, the population began falling and reached its lowest number in 1956 with 42,000 inhabitants. Then the population kept increasing until 1961, when it reached almost 50,000 people. These numbers clearly reflect the mass immigration to Zone A of the Free Territory of Trieste and to Italy, and emigration from Slovenia and other parts of Yugoslavia. In 1956, the exodus was more or less over, and the population reached its lowest number. From then on, the territory began to acquire a new identity. It is best reflected by the statistics of the numbers of Italians, which fell by 92 percent in comparison with 1945, and of their average age, which grew strongly (Titl 1961: 19; Kalc 2019: 149). The demographic changes in the concentration of Italians were most evident in the towns. While in 1945 they had made up over 91 percent of the urban population, by 1956 this had fallen to a little more than 10 percent. A similar fall is also evident in the rural areas where Italians had been present; in some villages they made up the majority of the population (Kalc 2019: 149).

Although the predominant term used in Italian and international literature is exodus—which suggests a uniform process, almost a unique event—the emigration took place in different forms and over a period of more than ten years. This is why Raoul Pupo (2015: 28) wonders if we may speak of one exodus or more than one, but he insists that the phenomenon should be treated as one because migratory waves were always caused by the same factors, albeit at different times and in different places.

Most researchers consider the end of World War II to mark the beginning of the exodus, but emigration accelerated in the early 1950s when it became clear that the Free Territory of Trieste's days were numbered. The possibility of opting out and thereby emigrating was enabled by the signing of the Paris Peace Treaty in 1947 and the London Memorandum in 1954. Similar to the London Memorandum, the text of the Paris Peace Treaty included an article that stipulated that adult Italian citizens (and their children) who on 10 June 1940 resided in territories that Italy ceded to other countries, would become citizens of this future state. By accepting the new nationality, they automatically lost their Italian citizenship. The treaty gave those people who met the conditions and whose "everyday" language was Italian the possibility of choosing (opting for) Italian citizenship. These people could make an application, which gave the authorities in their homeland a clear signal that they had chosen Italy. The successor state could demand that the optant moves to Italy within one year after receiving a positive response to their application. Both peace treaties gave people living on the territory that Italy ceded to other countries the right to choose between Italian and Yugoslav citizenship, thereby legalizing the emigration. This option ceased to be valid from October 1955 onwards, but it was prolonged for another year (Volk 2003: 47; Gombač 2005: 65). Choosing a nationality meant choosing the country of residence, so opting for Italian citizenship was followed by a move to Italy (Pupo 2015: 29). Meanwhile, members of the Slovene minority living on territory that was ceded to Italy, could opt for Yugoslav citizenship (Purini 2010: 249).[1]

According to Slovene figures, in the years 1945 to 1958, 49,132 people—including illegal migrants and people from the Karst, Notranjska, and Goriška—left the territory that was joined to Slovenia. Out of these, the number of true optants is thought to be 27,810 (Volk 2003: 51; Kosmač 2017: 193).[2] Most of them were Italians (70 percent), but there were also Slovenes and Croats (Volk 2003: 51; Cunja 2004: 89; Gombač 2005; Kalc 2019: 151). From the end of World War II until the adoption of the London Memorandum in October 1954, when the Free Territory of Trieste was abolished and the border between Italy and Yugoslavia was determined, around 14,000 people moved out. Immigration was at its height a year and a half after Zone B was annexed to Yugoslavia. In 1955, 8,000 optants moved out of the Slovene part of the coastal region and 2,200 had moved out by February 1957, when the deadlines for opting ran out (Lavrenčič 2012; Kalc 2019: 151). From the end of the war until the beginning of 1957, almost 24,400 people had moved out—almost 53 percent of the population recorded in 1945 (Titl 1961; Kalc 2019: 151). In a census carried out in 1960, after the final phase of the exodus, the proportion of autochthonous inhabitants in the Slovene part of Istria fell to 49 percent, with 65 percent in rural areas and 33 percent in towns. Researchers attribute these differences to the fact that the Italian population was concentrated in the towns while the population in the surrounding villages was predominantly Slovene (Titl 1961; Kalc 2019).

When discussing the exodus, the "counter-exodus" is often mentioned as an argument that migrations also took place in the opposite direction—from Italy to Yugoslavia. According to the Italian historian Raoul Pupo, this is only propaganda that aims to reduce the scale of the exodus as a kind of counterbalance, however, the numbers do not support this argument. The "counter-exodus" consisted of thousands of workers from Monfalcone and Friuli who settled in Yugoslavia with the aim of building a socialist state. Their number is most frequently put at around 2,000, or between 3,000 and 3,500, while some Slovenian sources talk of 10,000 people—including POWs. As Luciano, who was one of them says, the reason was ideological, but unemployment due to destroyed industry was another reason (Purini 2010: 263–72; Pupo 2015: 33–34):

> The first to leave were those from Monfalcone. Because they saw freedom, equality, brotherhood and other things. . . . There were 20,000 of them. From the whole territory. We were four families that went from Cormons to Pula. We were not alone. The others were from Pordenone, Gorizia, Cervignano . . . It could be said that in addition to the ideological factor, a very important reason was that the shipyard in Monfalcone had been heavily bombarded so it no longer offered work. As people were no longer farmers, whoever had become a blacksmith, laborer or mechanic was left unemployed. And people knew that there [in Yugoslavia] were many jobs.

Elda, whose husband later became a mayor in Istria and who came in the "counter-exodus," mentions that these immigrants were deliberately dispersed throughout Yugoslavia so they did not stay near the border:

> My husband . . . When they came from Italy—they had to decide where they were going—they decided to stay in Yugoslavia. . . . A truck came from Koper in 1945 with a trailer full of young men. There were thirty-five of them. And they did not even keep them here, you know, they sent them to Pula, Fiume, Bosnia; they separated them all because these people were not allowed to stay near the border.

Yugoslavia was in need of a workforce so it accepted the Italian workers with open arms as the exodus had left workplaces empty, especially in Rijeka and Pula. However, as my interlocutor experienced, the story did not end well as in the dispute with the Informbiro most Italian communists opposed Tito. The Yugoslav authorities were therefore suspicious of all Italian communists and some of them paid for this dearly with imprisonment on Goli Otok.[3] Some were persecuted in other ways by being laid off, forced to move, were beaten or taken to labor camps, so most of them returned to Italy (Purini 2010: 263–72; Nemec 2012b: 188; Pupo 2015: 33–34).

The Fluidity and Hybridity of Ethnic Identifications in Istria

When counting the numbers of ethnic Italians, Slovenes, and Croats who were caught up in the exodus, it is necessary to first ask to what extent counting such elusive ethnic identities is reliable in a multicultural environment where most of the population spoke at least two dialects, which was governed by five different nation-states in the twentieth century alone—Austria-Hungary, Italy, Yugoslavia, the Free Territory of Trieste, Slovenia/Croatia—and where the population had also experienced the violent fascist politics of denationalization or Italianization. As was already evident in the nineteenth-century censuses, it is not possible to gather reliable results on ethnic belonging in such a multicultural environment (D'Alessio 2008), and the same holds true for the twentieth century.

Through their "option," many Istrians chose or adapted their national identity to their desire to migrate. According to the Slovenian historian Sandi Volk (2004: 32–35), the exodus and the "opting" were decisive for the choice of national identity and a turning point for assimilation, when in the denationalizing process an unclear number of Croats and Slovenes chose an Italian identity. Choosing an Italian identity meant receiving help from the Italian state and associations of *esuli*. This is confirmed by some interlocutors.

> And what effect did it have that about ten, twelve people—my relatives—moved out, as well as another ten or twelve people—my ex-wife's relations. . . . Together with a friend we counted all the people who had moved out of our village—the northern part of Čežarji. About 15 percent of the people left, and they said this is our nationally and politically conscious village. In fact, 15 percent of them left, which we can consider

to be a statistically significant piece of information, that actually 27,000 or so people left, that probably a quarter of the Slovenes went across the border. . . . Everyone had to declare themselves to be Italian, otherwise they were not allowed to leave and this is why it was kept quiet.

An illustrative example is that of Slovene optants from Goriška who wanted to enroll their children in schools of the Slovene minority after moving to Italy, but the authorities did not allow them to do so. Many *esuli* mention in interviews that their parents or they themselves spoke the "Slav dialect." Due to difficulties with the Italian language, many children of *esuli* attended additional school courses. This could not have been solely the consequence of having attended Slovene or Croat schools for a few years. Sandi Volk (2004: 32–35) therefore assumes that these were Slovene or Croat children who had to be assimilated into the Italian culture.

According to the interpretations of the Italian historian Raoul Pupo and the Slovenian historian Aleksander Panjek, opting was like a safe-guard at a time when there was widespread disenchantment with the new regime in Yugoslavia, which led many people with undefined iden-tities to identify with Italian culture. "More or less voluntarily, more or less uncertainly, many (optants) chose their nationality, others changed it, and some declared it for the sake of convenience" (Pupo and Pan-jek 2004: 352). In an article entitled "Opting for Identity," Pamela Ballinger addresses the controversy surrounding the activities of the International Refugee Organization in the years 1948–1952 regarding the entitlement of the inhabitants of the Julian March to help, as they found that in defining who was entitled to help they could not rely on the indicators of national identity valid at the time: not place of birth, not mother tongue, not citizenship. As a result of the consequences of twenty years of violent, fascist Italianization, someone who spoke Ital-ian was not necessarily also of Italian origin. Therefore, the power of state-imposed categories to establish identities through external identity categories was problematic (Ballinger 2006b).

Pamela Ballinger (2006b: 129) noticed how identifications were changed to conform with people's wishes when she analyzed the *esuli* ar-chives. Those who wanted to migrate overseas did not define themselves as Italians in the hope that they would be helped by the International Refugee Organization, which only assisted refugees who had not come to their home country. That is why after analyzing applications and conversations with refugees, the organization commented that it was very difficult to categorize the identity of the inhabitants of the Julian March. In their opinion, it bordered on something negative, unstable, volatile, almost opportunism, even subject to change according to the interests of the refugees. Pamela Ballinger noticed a comparable problem of a "border peoples of 'indeterminate nationality,' whose customary language did not map onto ethnic self-consciousness," among the Masurians or "Polish-speaking Germans." In contrast with the Germans from the newly acquired territories, the Polish regime classified them as "autochtons" on the basis of the nationalist criterion of place of birth and demanded that they remain in their "native" land even against their will—with the exception of those deemed to have betrayed their Polish identity. This approach is reminiscent of the Yugoslav regime's frequent rejection of option applications (Ballinger 2006b: 124–25). In her analysis of the processes accompanying the formation of the Yugoslav state and nation in Istria from 1943 to 1952, the historian Mila Orlić also warns against classic historical studies, which place ordinary people in the role of "slaves" to the nation and address the Istrian context with the "paradigm of opposing nationalisms." Instead, she emphasizes people's indifference, neutrality, opportunism, and ambivalence concerning the question of national identity.[4] In Istria, whose future borders and national sovereignty remained uncertain for another ten years after the war, it is possible to observe the "national indifference" of ordinary people—mainly farmers—who rejected classification on a national basis even after the war. First the Italian and then the Yugoslav authorities used (and changed) surnames as proof of nationality and linguistic appurtenance to Istria. However, people did not necessarily consider a change in surname to be proof of their national belonging. The Yugoslav authorities were aware of the problem of the assimilation of the Slav element into Italian culture during the twenty years of fascist rule, so they tried to eradicate the feeling of "inferiority" and to "reawaken" the "Slav" multitudes. In order to prove Istria's "Slav character" a census was carried out in 1945, but Mila Orlić observes that a high percentage of people refused national identification—30 percent in the municipality of Buje/Buie, for example. It is evident that no connection can be made between declarations of belonging and the everyday use of language. In response to the Italian "nationalization" of history with an emphasis on the contrasts—urban/rural, Slavs/Italians—the Yugoslav politician Josip Smodlaka highlighted the diverse, fluid, undefined identifications in Istria, their hybridity and changeability, where the main question is not "am I a Slav or an Italian, but under whose rule will I be better off, under Italy or Yugoslavia?" In this way opting did not represent solely confirmation of one's political or ideological convictions, but also the search for social and economic strategies with the purpose of acquiring material advantages or job opportunities in the search of a better life. According to the author, the reasons for migration were not only connected with national belonging as from the 1950s onward they were more reminiscent of mass population movements in Mediterranean Europe from the countryside to urban areas, and from poor areas to industrialized ones (M. Orlić 2019: 565–69, 571–72, 575–83). Gianfranco, who comes from an ethnically mixed family, told me about these shifting identities in Istria that adapt to each new social authority in order to survive. When the Italian language was in favor, the people working in the salt-pans spoke Italian as Slovene was considered inferior. However, when the Slovene authorities took over, people adapted by speaking Slovene:

> And then they spoke Italian and no-one wanted people to know they were Slovene, but they were Slovene. Because it was *malvišto* [frowned upon, considered negative], as they say. They would be looked upon with disapproval. In order to save face, they spoke Italian; after all, there's no harm in speaking two languages. And that's how it was here too when we were working in the saltpans; we all spoke Italian. Then we began speaking Slovene when the bosses were Slovene.

And so he continues—from the former Italian schools he was sent to a Slovene school because it was necessary to learn the Slovene language. In this way, he adapted to the new national etiquette, Slovene this time:

> [Speaking about the fascists in Piran, whom the inhabitants of Piran did not like so they ran away] And then there was this hatred, then they began, because they were full of it . . . The ones who came from Ljubljana, because we had teachers from Ljubljana . . . When I was at school, they sent us to Slovene schools so we could learn our mother tongue. So we would say, "We are Slovenes and you must . . ." That is how they taught us that we were Slovenes. So that's it; we're Slovene. I don't mind what we are because we lived here in different countries. I didn't even know which one it was when I was younger; what did I know? And when I spoke, I spoke because my mum came from elsewhere. So my father had to speak Slovene.

The ethnologist Lidija Nikočević (2003: 104) noticed a similar fluidity of national identities on the Slovene-Croat frontier when the inhabitants of Pasjak above Rijeka spoke of their experiences in adapting to the prevalent political and social circumstances:

> Sometimes we had a Slovenian priest in the village, and sometimes a Croat. When the Slovenian priest was here, he would say: "You are, of course, Slovenian." We told him we were. But the Croat priest told us that we were Croats. We agreed with him also. The only thing we knew

Figure 2.1. Third Festival of Croatian Culture, Buje/Buie, 11 September 1949 (Department of History and Ethnography of the National Study Library of Trieste, collection Primorski dnevnik, author Mario Magajna).

was that we weren't Italians because, at the beginning, no-one under-stood Italian. (Nikočević 2003: 98)

Istrian authors often write about the fluidity or hybridity of Istrian identities. In his novel *The Better Life*, Fulvio Tomizza (1980) illustrates the shifting identifications of people that are sometimes voluntary and sometimes imposed. The lives of people living near the border are appro-priated by the changing state authorities to their advantage, and people have to choose just one aspect of themselves, despite having a broad pal-ette of identities and languages: "There were children or grandchildren of people who realized only when I was a child that they were Italians or Croats or Slovenes. But then they had to refute their original belief, which was formed through forced revelation and forced choice with an equal measure of prejudice and incitement" (Tomizza 1980: 316).

This undefined or fluid nature of identities was evident in most of the conversations. For example, when I asked Claudio, who comes from a Slovene anti-fascist family, if he was a native, he began explaining how Istrians have difficulties with national identifications:

Yes. Native . . . Ehh . . . Someone asks me, where are you from? Are you Slovene or Croat, what are you? I'm Istrian. Just like the people from the Karst say they are Kraševci [inhabitants of the Karst Plateau). . . . We're Istrians. We're a mixture . . . Every boot in history has trod on this land. And each one left something. Either a seed or culture or whatever. So sometimes it's hard to define what you are.

Figure 2.2. Second Festival of Italian Culture, Piran/Pirano, 1952 (Department of History and Ethnography of the National Study Library of Trieste, collection Primorski dnevnik, author Mario Magajna).

When under pressure by different states to choose an ethnic identity, Istrians always first refer to their regional, Istrian identity, which unlike the uniform, national identity is supposed to emphasize multiculturalism. However, in the case of symbolic borders this multicultural identity is also based on autochthonist ideas and, as will become evident later, it excludes all the "others from the Balkans," as well as all those who are not from this region (Ballinger 2003: 245–65; O. Orlić 2008).

By saying "we became Slovenes," Gianfranco, who comes from a Slovene family and who married an Italian native, clearly illustrated what anthropologists and historians say about the invention of national identity (Anderson 1983; Eriksen 1995; Hobsbawm 1996). In comparison with the construction of identity, which indicates the emergence of something completely new, the word invention suggests the creation of something that already existed in one form or another. There is also the concept of "awakening of national identity," but this is not very useful for humanities because it assumes an inherent theory of a "long dormant period" (Baskar 2002: 181).

You know how many Slovenes there were . . . We became Slovenes . . . In the past we did not say we were Slovene. If you're born in Italy, you're Italian. If you're born in Austria—before they were born in Austria—they were Austrians. But the Istrians here, we were Istrians—a people, like the Sytrians and the Dolenci, we are Istrians. People from Piran called those who were not from Piran *sc'avi*, they were a different people altogether, they were not "one of them." Because surnames such as Dessardo are Italian. One person lived in Piran, another in Vinjole or in Lucija, and when they came to Piran they were called *škarpa grossa* [peasant], they were treated like peasants. "You're all peasants." You who live outside Piran . . . They treated us like peasants.

While studying memories and identities in the village of Sveti Peter in Istria, Borut Brumen found that with the creation of the new state border in Istria in 1991 between Slovenia and Croatia—which was (and is still) politically and geographically undefined—the former common Istrian identity that shared the same cultural traditions has been divided into two separate ones—Croat Istrians and Slovene Istrians, or rather, Šavrini. On the one hand, this indicates the fluidity and adaptability of identification. However, the anthropologist observes that in contrast to anthropological theories of the fluidity of identity—according to which political borders should not overlap with cultural and social boundaries—with the "Slovenization" of Istria that followed the establishment of the new states of Slovenia and Croatia, this is exactly what has happened: new identities can clearly be made out on both sides of the new border in what was once one region (Brumen 2000: 398–405). Gianfranco's words also reflect the feeling of superiority of the townspeople over the people from the hinterland, who were pejoratively called *sc'avi* by the urban population. We have already discussed this in the section on stereotypical contrasts between urban, civilized and Italian, versus rural, Slav and barbaric. Claudio, an Istrian of Slovene origin, also mentions the feeling of superiority of the urban Italian population:

> C: We were . . . You know what, I'll also tell you this. There weren't big differences between the inhabitants of Piran or Izola. No-one took any notice if you were Slovene, or if you spoke Slovene . . . None of the ordinary people cared . . . But we had the feeling that we were second-class citizens. Wherever. Or in Koper! It was a bit worse in Koper because it was a bigger town.
> K: Why?
> C: Well, it was a bigger town, and people were harder on each other. . . . But in these places, Piran, Iz . . . Not to mention Lucija! Because we were already on the outskirts. We were . . . Simply different people . . . And we were considered to be worth a little less . . .

Although researchers emphasize that this is the ideological discourse of reducing ethnic oppositions to an economic and geographical level (Baskar 2002: 98–120), this conflict should also be considered outside the national context and in light of the conflictual nature of class encounters in the economic context, and the confrontation of groups with different cultural and social values (Brumen 2000: 129; Verginella 1996). The historian Sandi Volk believes that Italian identity was social rather than linguistic or cultural in nature. The inhabitants of towns and rural administrative centers—such as Grožnjan—considered themselves to be townspeople and looked down on the inhabitants of surrounding places. The pressure to assimilate was also greater in these towns, in which state authorities were present. It appears that Italian identity was inseparable from the superior social position (Volk 2003: 34).

The example of my own relatives would support this theory. They moved to Australia from Trieste in 1954. The mother had moved to Trieste from Istria and came from a Slovene family, while the father was an Italian from Trieste. They brought my aunt up as an Italian. She only began to wonder about her Slovene roots in Australia after marrying my Slovene-speaking uncle. She recalled her mother's unease in Trieste when they were contemptuously called *sc'avi*. By bringing her up as an Italian, her mother wanted to protect her daughter from being humiliated in this way by those who felt they were superior. The identification in my uncle's family is also interesting. My uncle was born in the Brkini hills, in Primorska, while his sister was born in Trieste because their family decided to seek a fortune elsewhere in the world, via Trieste. My uncle identified himself more as a Slovene while his sister identified herself more as an Italian (although they both had a primarily Australian identity), until she discovered her forgotten Slovene roots and relations—another illustrative example of how adaptable, temporary, and appropriated national identities can be in contrast to studies that speak of fixed national identifications and people as their captives.

In rare cases, feelings of superiority in the opposition between townspeople (Italians) and farmers (Slavs), existed in the other direction when Slovene farmers from the hinterlands looked down on the so-called Lahi—Italian townspeople who were considered to be much poorer because they did not have much land. This was the case with Bruno and Ivana from the village of Manžan:

> [When I first hear the term Lahi, I ask if he means Italians.] I: Yes, that's right, they were Lahi.
> B: We were on the outside, we were *sc'avi*, landowners. We who lived on the outskirts, we were *sc'avi* for them. And they were Lahi.
> K: So you did not like each other?
> B: . . . the Lahi and the *sc'avi* did not like each other, they were much worse off than we were.
> K: Why were they worse off?

B: They lived in poverty, we had coffee, oil, wine, pigs; they were poor.

K: I see, because you had larger farms?

B: Yes, we had everything. We weren't hungry.

I: And those from Koper, those Lahi had farms outside the town. They had a donkey and cart, and they transported manure. Actually, they kept these animals in Koper, under the stairs . . . In the morning they went from Koper to the fields; they took it out and that was it . . .

B: Yes, they were poor, they were worse off than we were.

The feeling of Slovene superiority evident in these words is probably due to the circumstances after World War II, when Yugoslavs assumed a superior attitude toward the Italians (see below). In the predominant identification of Italian identity with a superior position or higher culture, one may ask to what extent identity also changed in the other direction, that is, from Italian to Yugoslav. It was primarily people from families where they spoke Slovene at home that spoke to me about changeable identities and Istrian regional identities. However, the adaptability of identity to the new regime and economic circumstances is evident also on the Italian side. An example of this is Loredana's family—her Slovene mother came from northern Primorska and her Italian father was a local. Loredana and her brother both attended a Slovene school because after their parents decided to stay, and because they were employed in the public administration, they decided this would be better for them. The Italian father even learned so much Slovene that it became the main language of communication at home:[5]

Yes, well, at home they then decided—of course they enrolled us as Slovenes, my brother and myself—they recommended that we should be Slovenes, like our mother. [Asked about who recommended this.] No, no, probably my mum was advised at work because they were employed in the public security administration . . . I don't know, the UDBA [State Security Administration] existed back then. I don't know what it was, some kind of police; I don't know exactly. Well, and they recommended that if we are here . . . So my father too . . . He never regretted it. He always said: "Look, I decided to stay here, I chose Yugoslavia. I don't regret it. I also decided that you two should be Slovene, I accepted that you take your mother's nationality." But nowadays I meet people who ask me, when they see my surname [Italian], how is it that I'm Slovene.

Loredana remembers that her father suffered greatly because he felt pressure as a result of his identity, and because of the exodus of people who were close to him, including the only member of the family—his brother—so he left his job in the public administration to work on his own in fishing: "He decided he would rather work at sea because it was more peaceful there and less stressful, and there were no political arguments such as . . . Probably such as—who's Slovene, who's Italian, what are the advantages of one culture, what are the advantages of the other culture . . ."

In order to escape this pressure to choose an ethnicity, which is written about by Istrian writers, Loredana's father took refuge in regional identity: "I know they once came when there was a census, and they asked: 'What are you?' He answered: 'I don't know what I am. I'm an Istrian. I'm neither Italian nor Slovene; I feel neither Italian nor Slovene.'"

The pressure to assimilate is evident also in the youngest generation, which, judging by what was told, was mocked for being Italian on a daily basis. Ornella's son, who was educated in an Italian school, says that for the good of his children he will send them to a Slovene school:

> My son says: "Don't mention the exodus to me!" He does not want to hear about it. He was so, so very unhappy in the Italian school when he went out with his schoolmates, for example, on a boat. They always made fun of him. He said: "Mum, don't forget, if I will live here, my children will go to a Slovene school."

Vittoria tells a similar story: her son never wanted to hear about the exodus and he left his mother's side when she spoke the Istro-Venetian dialect on the bus. He moved far away because he felt constant pressure due to his mixed Slovene, Italian, and Serb identity. She was visibly tired because of this constant struggle for her Italian ethnic identity:

> I really hope the day will come when no-one will remind me I'm Italian. Someone said to me a few days ago: "What are you really, Vittoria? Are you Italian or Slovene?" I want to be Vittoria and nothing else. Enough! I am Vittoria. I'm fed up of having to define myself, I keep having to prove myself. . . . I have given up on bilingualism, on people speaking to me in Slovene or Italian. I no longer care, I speak Slovene anyway. I don't understand, OK, no problem, I'll speak. It's no longer a problem, I do more. Enough! Enough!

Her pupils at school told her they also felt ashamed about being Italian: "To become an equal among equals. And they spoke to us about the problems they had when they went out, to the disco and so on . . . God forbid they should speak Italian! They even spoke Slovene among themselves. Seventeen, eighteen, nineteen years old, they did not want to speak Slovene outside."

I don't know how strong the direct pressure on Italians in Istria, in terms of everyday denigration and mockery, is nowadays. It seems that in recent years the attitude has nevertheless improved as more and more parents send their children to Italian nurseries and then Slovene or Italian schools. The latter is especially the case with immigrants from the southern republics of the former Yugoslavia. One reason, according to what I have heard, is that Italian schools are cheaper. As Silvano Sau, a retired Italian politician from Izola warns, school is what determines an individual's national identity and young people nowadays no longer live under such ethnic pressure:

> [Concerning young people:] There is a difference between how they perceive Italian identity and how we, the middle generation—which was passionate—perceives it. That is how we had to be in order to remain Italian because those were different times. In the fourth year, I was dragged by force from an Italian to a Slovene school. Thanks to my father's intervention—he stood outside the school for a week out of fear that something like that could happen again—I remained Italian. If I had stayed in a Slovene school, I would now probably be Slovene. Young people now see Italians in a completely different cultural context: much more democratic and free. Their sense of belonging to the minority is no longer passionate, but perfectly natural. They are not plagued by the traumas we went through. Teenagers cannot imagine what Izola was like fifty years ago. It is perfectly normal for them to step into a shop and hear Slovene being spoken. (Kemperle 1997: 86)

Unlike older people, young members of the Italian minority are born into an already Slovenized environment. Rafael notices that Italians have assimilated to quite a large extent in this Slovene environment: "The old inhabitants of Koper have died. They've died. And now, any sons that remain have been Slovenized! They have become Slovene! You can't tell. They all speak perfect Slovene. You can't tell they're Italian. They still feel Italian; it's normal and only right, but you will find it hard to identify them."

However, we must not forget that identity depends on the social context; sometimes it is fluid while at other times it is solid and strong, as was the case when the Slovenia-Croatia border was established in Istria (Brumen 2001). It is known that an ethnic group is not formed in isolation but on social boundaries, where the members of different groups interact, and this is why identities are most distinct in border regions. Ethnic identity, which results from self-ascription and identification on the basis of inclusion/exclusion in relation to community members/non-members, becomes crucial when it is threatened (Barth 1969: 9–15; Eriksen 1995: 76).

For example, Jasna Fakin Bajec finds that on the Karst the fact that the Slovene national identifications were threatened under fascism had an important influence on the development and consolidation of Slovene national consciousness. The hostility between Italians and Slovenes strengthened both Slovene and Italian identity (Fakin Bajec 2011: 135). Piero Purini, who compared censuses carried out during fascist rule, noticed that fascist policies failed completely in their process of denationalizing Slovenes and Croats. Despite the violence, forced Italianization, prohibition of the use of Slovene and Croat in public, large-scale emigration to Yugoslavia and South America, and despite the immigration of a large number of Italians, the Slovene and Croat communities did not assimilate. On the contrary, censuses showed that the numbers of Slav inhabitants in the Julian March increased: while the number of Slovenes decreased by 8,000, the Croat population increased by 30,000 people. In all regional centers (except Gorizia), the number of non-Italian inhabitants increased, and in Istria, the minority communities also increased in size. The historian does not consider the reason for this to be immigration or a greater birth-rate, but the inaccuracy of the first census in 1921, in which many foreigners declared themselves to be Italian because of pressure from those who carried out the census and due to the change in regime. The 1936 census was intended more for verifying the success of denationalizing policies, so there were not as much manipulation and the results were therefore devastating for fascist politics (Purini 2010: 173–79). Pupo also observes that the linguistic minorities have only reduced by a small amount and unevenly—rather more in the urban contexts where the assimilatory pressures were stronger, and hardly at all in the rural areas. However, time is needed for denationalization to succeed without expulsions and killings—at least one generation (Pupo 2021: 72). Researchers from the Slovene minority in Italy are critical of such generalizations because for the Slovenes in the Italian environment, assimilation is not only a thing of the past but something they continue to experience today. So it is undoubtedly a long-lasting process that goes beyond just one generation.

Even nowadays there are many memories of the struggle for Slovene identity in the time of fascism. Under fascist rule, people who rejected "feeling Italian" and who did not join the Fascist Party found it very hard to find work (Purini 2010: 108). Claudio, a Slovene Istrian, remembers how his father could not find a stable job to support his family because he refused to join the Fascist Party. This was demanded of him if he wanted to keep his job in the national saltpans:

"Piero, go to Piran, get yourself a membership card." Because some were members of the Fascist Party. They weren't fascists. They joined in order to earn their daily bread! Istrians also joined just to keep their jobs. "Go there and join up." . . . And my father . . . He was neither anti this nor anti that . . . But . . . He was not, not for the Italians . . . He attended a Slovene school in Lucija. . . . "Father," they said to him, go to Piran, get yourself a membership card. Join the Fascist Party." . . . But he didn't go. The next day he was laid off.

Claudio's brother Rafael also experienced their father's unbending attitude toward the fascist regime when his father burned the only item of clothing he ever received in school, because it was fascist:

[Speaking about Befana:] Yes, she gives presents to children. He said [the teacher]: "What would you like? A *figlio della lupa* shirt [fascist organization for children]?" This was a costume for small boys. It consisted of knee-length shorts, trousers, a shirt, and a cap. And I had nothing, so I said, "Sir, I would like the *figlio della lupa*." Because I knew I would have something to put on. And I really got it. I brought it home. My father took it and threw it into the kitchen stove. He said: "You're not going to be a fascist!" I was a child! I wanted to be dressed! I did not understand yet because he was completely allergic to fascism . . . That's how it was . . .

Unlike Claudio's father, a minority of people joined the Fascist Party because they feared for their survival (Verginella 1995: 20–21; Brumen 2000: 143–44). However, there were also many Italians who were unemployed because of their anti-fascist stance, as was the case with Elisabetta's father: "We come from an Italian family, my father and my mother. My father never wanted to be a fascist. He was born an anti-fascist. . . . He didn't want to join and, of course, he didn't get a job, only part-time work because if you didn't have a [fascist] membership card you couldn't . . ."

Just as Slovene identity was consolidated during the violent fascist attempts at denationalization that lasted over twenty years, Italian identity was probably also fortified with the onset of the Yugoslav regime because the Italians felt threatened in the new linguistic and socio-cultural environment. The mutual hostility was very much affected by the twenty years of fascist violence. From the interviews with the Istrians who were among the first to immigrate, it is clear that there was much interethnic hatred. This will also be discussed below: "[On the inhabitants of Piran:] And I didn't have any problems with them, I didn't hate them. Italian or Slovene—we're all human. But there was a lot of hatred. 'That bloody Italian! Or the Italians: Look at that *sćavo*!'" (Pahor 2007: 121)

The Reasons for Emigration and the Regime's Attitude to Istrian Italians

Fascists, Re-Education in Schools, and "False" Italians

According to Mila Orlić, the emigration of Italians was not accompanied by an attitude as radical as when the Germans were expelled from Central and Eastern Europe after World War II. As we have already learned from the memories, Istrian Italians joined the partisan combatants so at least officially, the Italians were not considered a national enemy who must be expelled at the moment of liberation. This question arose later when a significant portion of the Italian population resisted the establishment of a new regime (M. Orlić 2012: 20).

Despite the absence of an official, negative policy against the Italians, it is clear from the memories that in everyday postwar life, much of the population was hostile toward the Italians. In the passionate reactions by Istrians to one of my first media interviews on the exodus, someone pointed out that the *esuli* were of mixed ethnic origin, and they do not identify themselves according to nationality but regional belonging. Nevertheless, despite this hybrid identity, a hostile attitude toward the Italians may be observed as they were collectively criminalized as fascists, so life was not supposed to have been easy for them:

> It was not only the Italians who opted, but also Croat Istrians and others, regardless of nationality. My family opted en masse. My family is of Croat origin but they considered themselves to be Istrian and they never concerned themselves with national appurtenance. . . . All who left were called fascists by the government. Fascists, my ass, everyone knows who the fascists were. Italians cannot identify with fascism. In the end, fascism in Italy capitulated without external intervention; it was toppled by the Italians themselves, their partisans. In Istria, where there were signs of the awakening of proletarian leftist ideas, they participated actively in the anti-fascist struggle, perhaps they even started it, Istrian Italians—well, Italian surnames. Anti-fascism is not purely the result of rebellion by Croats and Slovenes. The whole community resisted fascism, a logical resistance. So, there were fascists, but there were also these others, among the partisans. It would be fairer to call them anti-fascists, not communists. There were people who weren't communists; they were partisans, anti-fascists. But the government mixed up all these terms so it was a bit difficult being Italian in Istria. "They were constantly fucked around." (Branc 2015)[6]

Archival sources also show that those who left were collectively accused of being fascists, mostly the Italians. One source contains a list of 882

Figure 2.3. May Day parade in Koper/Capodistria, 1950 (Regional Archives Koper, collection SI PAK KP 344 – photo library, TE 5 and TE 8).

people[7] who left the district of Koper in the years 1945–1946 and "all left voluntarily, without the people's government exerting any pressure on them." The introduction to the list includes an explanation that this was "mostly the flight of war criminals and fascists, or the normal return of people who settled here during the war as refugees seeking refuge from air raids, either from Italy, Trieste, and who returned to their homes after 1 May 1945. Besides, the reasons for migration are the same as in normal times, for example, due to marriage, etc." Further down, a substantial number of people—whose names are given—are labeled fascists, war criminals, collaborators, blackshirts, Nazi-fascist collaborators, traitors, propagandists against the people's government, prison guards, *squadristi*,[8] and more. In most cases it is recorded that they escaped. For those who do not have these labels—the majority—it is written that they left for unknown reasons. In some places it is written that they returned to their homes for work. Only a few times health reasons or fear are mentioned.

The collective criminalization of Italians as fascists was experienced by most of my Italian interlocutors and is something that marked some of them for life. For example, let us remember the experience of Amalia, who refused to cooperate in commemorations at the Strunjan antifascist memorial because Italians were generally equated with fascists. A conversation with her friend Vittoria, the daughter of a communist who stayed because of his faith in socialism, reveals that they were both hurt by the way Italians were equated with the political system, which their families did not support.

> V: What was common to the Italians here and there [in Italy, the *esuli*] is that they were always considered to be fascists. Both here and there.

This is what we have in common and what hurt me most, us, our family members who decided to stay here.

A: It is unpleasant to be identified . . . Substituted for and identified with a regime.

V: With a regime with which we absolutely never agreed in any way at all, and under any circumstances.

A woman of Italian origin, who is publicly active in the cultural domain, once mentioned to me her family's pain because her father was considered a fascist even though he resisted the system. "My father [an Italian] was punished as a teacher by the fascists because he did not want to wear a fascist uniform. Then he was imprisoned in Yugoslavia for being an Italian" (note in field diary).

The Istrian Italians are even more hurt by being stereotyped as fascists as most of them were active anti-fascists, as Michela from the hinterland of Hrvatini/Crevatini emphasizes.

M: . . . After all, these villages here were all anti-fascist. They all participated in the people's liberation struggle. You see that house over there? I was born there in 1944 during the curfew. . . . I was born there and in the kitchen we had Germans and in the bedroom a partisan with a partisan doctor . . . This is why these people were not . . . Because those of us who stayed here—we were all fascists, you know, all of us. They called us fascists, and that was it.

K: They all did or only . . . What about the people who had already lived here before . . . Did they also call you fascists?

M: No, but the politics was like that. The politics was—everything that was Italian was fascist. For example, Rosa was teaching a Slovene the Italian language, and they came to the word "enemy," and she tried to explain what enemy means . . . "German," said the pupil. You understand? . . . And we, even on the bus, as children. Not all, not all, we must be fair.

K: How did they treat you?

M: Oh, of course, we were fascists, Italian—fascist . . . We were the ones who led the anti-fascist struggle, crazy . . .

Or as two residents of the old people's home in Koper put it—Tonin from Škofije (a Slovene Istrian) and Bepo from Roč (a Croat Istrian)—"after the war there was hatred and being Italian was the same as being fascist. It was hatred. If you spoke Italian you were a fascist" (note in field diary).

Each struggle to nationalize Istria involved changing surnames. From "restoring" surnames to their original "Italian" form during fascism (without foreign suffixes such as -ič and -ich), to the compulsory "restoration" of surnames (and toponyms) that were Italianized under fascism to their "Slav" form after 1943 or during the Yugoslav regime. Those who did not want this to happen had to make a written request for their Italian form to be preserved and were classified as "enemies of the people" in the eyes of the authorities (M. Orlić 2019: 570–72). The Italian Istrian Giulio describes how he resisted his surname being changed into a Slovene form: "Surname alterations. I was without my identity card for practically a whole year because I did not accept the identity card on which my name had been changed into a Slovene form." The same story is told by a man who speaks in an Istro-Venetian dialect when a journalist asks him about his surname Kavalič: "I was Cavalich, with a -c and a -ch, when we were under Austria. Because there had always been the question of surnames here . . . A mess . . . Because they even changed my name . . . That's disgusting . . . I became Ivan . . . My father Just, my mother Pavla" ("Nino e i suoi ricordi di Giusterna" 2009: 25). This is how my interlocutor Elisabetta commented on how the name of the Italian historical figure Pier Paolo Vergerio il Vecchio was changed into the Slovene form Peter Pavel Vergerij at a symposium in Koper a few years ago: "Did you not learn anything from history? If the Italians were wrong to Italianize all the names—we know the discourse—what are you doing now?" As will be evident in the section on heritage and Slovenization, all Istrian names were changed into the Slovene form, even those of non-Italian speakers.

In the Yugoslav perception, Italians with surnames of Slav origin (usually ending in -ič) belonged to "false" Italians, that is, Slavs who had been Italianized in the past and who in the eyes of the new regime had to be helped to regain their Slovene identity (Pupo 2015: 30). One of the ways to achieve this was through the education system as an element of the state apparatus, that is, by transferring pupils to the (newly founded) Slovene schools. Massimo remembers the almost completely emptied class in the Italian school on the island of Cres, after all the children with surnames of Slav origin were transferred to the newly founded Croat school. They found this very traumatic as they did not understand the Croat language. Studies of the Italian school system in Istria also mention this. People recall and internet sources speak about the Anton Peruško decree in Croatia in 1952, which declared that children with Slav surnames (ending in -ich and similar) had to be transferred to Croat and Slovene schools (Monica 1991: 43–44, 264–65; Miletto 2007: 113; "Dall'Istria alla Jugoslavia" n.d; "Il piacere di leggere" 2008; Gregorovich 2009; Castelli 2018: 81).

Figure 2.4. Italian school, first year pupils and teacher, Piran/Pirano, 1950s (Rovigno Historical Research Centre, Photo library, Unione Italiana – Pirano, nro. inv. 994-F-1).

Vittoria describes how this decree was very traumatic for Italian-speaking children who were suddenly lost in the middle of a foreign Slovene or Croat speaking environment:

The Peruško decree in Croatia. All children with "Croat" surnames or surnames that sounded Croat or Slovene—the same thing happened also in Slovenia—had to attend the schools of the majority population. . . . My school-mate's surname was Poretti. According to the Croat school authorities, her surname had been changed from Poropat to Poretti under fascism. [Speaking about the surname.] So they labeled her a Croat. She completed her first years of school in Italian, and she was then transferred to a Croat class for the remaining years. . . . She disappeared; we never saw her again. We saw her in the Croat class. She was always crying. After six months, she was sent back to the Italian class. But there were many children who couldn't return. It was enough if they had a surname ending in -ič, the parents could try anything they wanted but they could not be sent back to the Italian school. And look, I know many bright, intelligent children who could hardly wait to finish school. Although we wanted an education as this was truly an achievement of social justice. At last education was accessible to all. We could all complete grammar school, high school; almost all of us could go to university because there were many options to receive help and financing. Yet these children could hardly wait to finish. If they completed primary school, they found a job.

A large portion, at least 30 percent. And the exodus also had an effect . . .
If I think that in the school year 1954/1955 there were forty-three or
forty-four of us in the first year and . . . More than half of the children
disappeared in the course of that year.

As they did not know the language in the new school environment,
these children were condemned to failure in the long run, just like Slovene children had been in Italian schools under fascism. Vittoria also
remembered a conversation she had with a lady about how she and her
sister had been sent to different schools—one to an Italian school, the
other to a Croat school. Her sister suffered in the Croat school as she did
not speak a word of Croat.

> [About the sister] She should have begun year one, but despite her Italian
> surname they sent her to a Croat school. I don't know if this was her
> parents' decision or if it was compulsory, I understood it was something
> they had to do. . . . And she says: "My sister cried every day before going
> to school. And when she came home, we all tried to do her homework
> for her, but we didn't understand what we had to do. We didn't under-
> stand a single word. The first year was dramatic. But then she learned the
> language and she progressed, she did not change schools any more. So I
> completed an Italian school and my sister a Croat school."

We have already come across testimonies of children from ethnically mixed families being sent to Slovene schools because the parents
thought that would be better for the family. As Ornella from Koper
said: "People who are still alive can testify that if they did not send
their children to Slovene schools they could lose their jobs." Italians
felt the closure of Italian schools—especially in places where increasing
numbers were leaving for Italy—as one of many forms of pressure on
their national identity. In the following case, Giulia was sent to a Croat
school as a fourteen-year-old girl with the argument that she was not a
"proper" Italian. The Italian school was later closed down because there
were not enough pupils.

> G: They closed the school overnight. They made a list. There was a de-
> cree, and the decree determined who had to leave the school. And they
> said: "You're not a proper Italian. We're closing down the school, and
> you can do what you want. For you the Italian school no longer exists."
> K: Did they really close the school down?
> G: They left a few pupils from Albona, who then all went to Italy, so the
> school was empty. That is what they wanted to achieve, so for us Istrians
> the Italian school was no longer allowed to exist in Albona. And it re-
> mains closed to this day—there is no Italian school in Albona. It was a

tragedy for me. I came home, I can't describe, furious, in tears . . . I made a tragedy out of this event. I no longer wanted to go to school, I said I would not go to the Croat school as the headmistress had said . . . And she said: "Tomorrow you're going to the Croat school." As simply as if she had said hello, you understand? . . . I cried every day, my mother also cried with me. What were we to do . . . You have to go to school; you can't stay at home. I'm not going to the Croat school. [The solution they found was the Italian school in far-away Rovinj/Rovigno.]

People like Gianfranco, who come from mixed families in which both languages, Slovene and Italian, were spoken at home, also describe how Italian-speaking children were transferred to the newly founded Slovene schools after World War II. As already mentioned in connection with hybrid identities, they found it unusual that they were sent to Slovene schools with the explanation that the Slovene identity of the population had to be strengthened or restored.

> For example, from here to Sečovlje, where she was, but they . . . Because they considered that we Slovenes are oppressed, this and that, that now we want our mother tongue and they took her out of the Italian school . . . Because there was an Italian school here and they also built a Slovene one. . . . They removed those whose names had a č, or who were called Čendak, Abramič from the Italian school. Because they were Slovenes, and they had to go to a Slovene school. I'm talking about us . . . In Malija there was only a Slovene school because they considered there were Slovenes and only Slovenes up there. But in Malija there weren't just . . . There were many surnames from North Italy, Italian surnames. [Speaking about only four Italian families from Malija] They spoke both Slovene and Italian. For example, I spoke Slovene and Italian.

According to some testimonies, it can be concluded that transferring children to a Slovene or Croat school was not always done by force. As Giulio from Izola explains, his father rejected the move and also succeeded in having him sent back to the Italian school. It is particularly interesting, and can be sensed in literature and other commentaries such as the above, that this process of Slovenization or "return to Slav roots" unfolded primarily in the countryside. It was also an attempt to eradicate the "feeling of inferiority" that had been inculcated in the Slavs by twenty years of fascism (M. Orlić 2019: 569).

> Whoever lived in a village became a Slovene, which is normal, isn't it. But I found myself in a Slovene school. I came home, told my father—a farmer—about this new experience, I was happy . . . A new class, there's not many of us, and I said we speak Slovene . . . I didn't know anything

back then. The following morning, my father took me by the hand, took me to school [Italian] and waited until the end of the school day for a whole month so they wouldn't send me back to the other side [for this reason a Slovene anti-fascist warned him it would be dangerous for him to go outside in the evening].

There are different testimonies about transfers to Slovene schools. Valeria, who has an Italian surname, remembers how some children from the Italian school were transferred to a Slovene school, and as they did not understand anything, they sent them back to the Italian school after a year.

> A, B, C, D. There were four classes with thirty-five pupils in each class. When we entered the third year, all the classes slowly emptied because of the exodus. For example, before we had all these classes, but in the fourth year we had only one class. . . . We were all in one class. And in the third year—this is interesting—they came to school to tell us that those with Slovene surnames must go to Slovene school. . . . But these children who ended up in the Slovene school could not be assessed as there was no way it could be done. They had come from the Italian school, they didn't understand anything as they had only ever spoken Italian, and they were sent back at the end of the year with the same grades as at the beginning. . . .

Although these children were allowed to return to the school of their mother tongue, this was not always the case. The same woman describes how a friend abandoned school after being transferred to a Slovene school where he did not understand the language, and thereby destroyed his chances of getting suitable employment. Similar stories were also told by other Italians:

> And he was sent to a Slovene school, and one day, he said right here: "I went to Slovene school in the sixth year. They turned a blind eye. They let me progress. I had the grades to move into the next year. But then I no longer got good marks. I left school and went to learn a trade. So in this case, they destroyed me." I don't know, why were those children sent back?

Control over Emigration? The Contradictory Nature of Yugoslav Politics

Although the above testimonies clearly show that the Istrian Italians felt cornered by the new Slovene or Croat language, which they hardly knew, and by being stigmatized as "fascists," historians cannot find a single written source on a local, republican, or federal level indicating

Figure 2.5. Celebration marking the tenth anniversary of the Slovenian uprising, Koper/Capodistria, 22 July 1952 (Regional Archives Koper, collection SI PAK KP 344 – photo library, TE 5 and TE 8).

intentional "ethnic cleansing" of Italians in Istria. However, what is evident in written sources, is the aim of eliminating the "enemies of the people" throughout Yugoslavia, as well as throughout Central and Eastern Europe (M. Orlić 2012: 20–21; Corni 2018: 65). According to the Italian historian Raoul Pupo, the emigration of Italians appears to have been voluntary because the Yugoslav authorities had no official policy regarding this question. It is thought that the aim of the Yugoslav regime was to make life unbearable for the Italians, thereby encouraging them to leave (Pupo 2000: 188–89).

After the end of World War II, the Yugoslav federation formally adopted measures to protect Italians on its territory as their mass departure could cause disgrace and lead to sanctions by the international community. However, it was heard informally that the most senior officials encouraged the departure of Italians (Gombač 2005: 59–60). Despite the official protection, in line with the slogan of "Slovene-Italian brotherhood," it is possible to observe the contradictory behavior of the Yugoslav authorities. In some places like Pazin, where 90 percent of the population left, the Italian population was forced to rapidly leave en masse, while in other places the Yugoslav authorities tried to prevent mass migration by intimidating inciters (Corni 2018: 65, 68). Written sources show that local authorities were concerned that the local econ-

Figure 2.6. Ceremony to reward the most hard-working workers, Koper/Capodistria, 17 October 1948 (Department of History and Ethnography of the National Study Library of Trieste, collection Primorski dnevnik, author Mario Magajna).

omy would collapse because of the mass emigration of tradesmen who took with them all their tools and machinery. The secretariat in Koper decided that the communists would try to persuade the optants—especially the workers—to remain. However, this turned out to be futile. On the other hand, other people believed no-one should be pursued and that the optants should decide for themselves. Historical sources indicate that propaganda in favor of emigration and against it was present even among the Italians. This was the case in Koper. The extent of the chaos is shown by the fact that one week farmers in Izola encouraged people to emigrate, while arguing that it is better to stay the next. The memoirs of the politician Milovan Đilas show that he went to Istria with an eminent Yugoslav politician, Edvard Kardelj, to organize anti-Italian propaganda, to pressure the Italians into leaving (Gombač 2005: 59–60, 91–92).

The oral historian Gloria Nemec (2012b: 194) recorded a testimony in the Croat part of Istria about how people who had changed their minds, after submitting a request to leave, had to redeem themselves to the Yugoslav authorities by obstructing the people who were leaving, by attacking them both verbally and physically. Angela told a similar story—those who changed their minds about leaving had to redeem themselves by spreading propaganda against Italy.

Over there in Croatia, Pula and also here, I know one . . . They had to . . .
First they submitted a request to leave, and then, to save themselves as
they regretted it because they no longer wanted to leave . . . Then they
had to speak out against Italy . . . To sign that they really meant it, that
they were against; this was how they could save themselves.

The subject of Italians themselves helping to "purge" Istria of Italians
has already been discussed in the section on silence. A former politician,
who comes from an ethnically mixed family, describes how his father—a
communist and political refugee from Italy—had to prove his loyalty to
the Yugoslav authorities (F. Juri 2010: 86). Referring to the memories he
heard from his father and Tomizza, he describes the psychotic situation
after the war, when the regime changed and the roles of master and slave
were switched, and there were instances of personal revenge.

A psychosis ensued that was made worse by nationalistic intolerance
because as my father told me, so many people he didn't know weren't
members of the partisan movement [speaking about the white guard
and the Slovene home guard]. He said: "These are nationalists. They're
not communists; they're nationalists." And this nationalism, of course, it
made things worse . . . And also certain forms of primitive behavior . . .
Because it's a natural social phenomenon that the lower classes at last
rose up and could . . . And they weren't always very refined. When these
masses came in organized fashion to protest against something, they employed methods that literally terrorized the urban population. So this
sense of fear increased, and there were some events that made it even
worse—some murders or fights. They didn't allow the farmers to work . . .
For 1 May, for example. They beat them. They told me that . . . So the
people felt very insecure. Not because they were fascists, but because
they. . . . My father was a communist, he was very grateful to Yugoslavia,
so he wasn't anti-Yugoslav, but they expected him to help in the purge.
To go from house to house and advise Italians to leave. So the UDBA
[Yugoslav secret police] used Italians—those they kept a hold on who
had relatives in Italy—so they couldn't escape; they were frequently used
to exert pressure. So the authorities wouldn't get their hands dirty they
used these Italians to persuade the remaining Italians it would be better
to leave. These were very subtle methods. And my father did not want
to accept this because he knew; he got a list of people from Koper who
were supposed to leave. And then he said: "But they're not fascists, I
know them, they're ordinary, honest people." And then he too was given
an ultimatum to leave Zone B within forty-eight hours—to go either to
Yugoslavia or to Italy, but that he could no longer stay there. This was just
before the arrival of the allied commission, which tried to establish the
demographic and political situation. That was when strong pressure was
exerted to get as many people as possible to leave.

The Yugoslav authorities grew suspicious of the small number of "good and honest" Italians, anti-fascists and supporters of the socialist system, under the auspices of the politics of "Slovene (Slav)-Italian fraternity," after the Informbiro affair in 1948 (Pupo 2015), when large numbers of Italian communists opposed Tito's party (Kacin Wohinz and Troha 2001: 61–62). This is why the Italians who stayed in Istria had to prove their allegiance to Yugoslavia by participating in the political struggle for Istria to be annexed to Yugoslavia, in the political campaign against Italy, which was still considered to be imperialist and fascist, and in the fight against Italians who opposed Yugoslavia (Pupo 2015).

Memories also produce contradictory information about the promotion and prevention of emigration. In contrast to the above memory of being ordered by the Yugoslav authorities to persuade Italians to leave, Loredana—who comes from an Italian family—remembers how someone was sent from central Slovenia to Istria during the time of mass migrations[9] to persuade Italians to stay in Istria.

> He said he was sent from Ljubljana in those years, I don't know if it was 1954 or 1955, those years when so many Italians emigrated, he was sent to the Coast . . . I don't know from which institution he was sent—either a state institution or the police, I don't know . . . Basically to convince people not to emigrate. He simply told them that nothing would happen to them here. And he said he also visited my relatives and that he told them they would be OK; that they don't need to leave, and so on. So they didn't leave.

So there is no answer to the question of whether there was any control over emigration. Both historical data and oral testimonies are quite contradictory. We do not know whether this is due to the general state of confusion and different attitudes of the regional authorities or differences in attitude through time. As Sandi Volk (2003: 42) finds, the attitude of the Yugoslav authorities toward the Italians changed over time, however, the question has not yet been researched.

While mass emigration from the "Italianized" coastal urban centers was somehow considered acceptable, this was less the case in the countryside, which was considered "Slav." Many requests to "opt" were rejected. Reasons included Slav surnames, which were supposed to reflect Italianized Slavs, an upcoming military service, participation in labor brigades for postwar restoration, and so forth. Retaining repentant Italians in the spirit of "Slav-Italian fraternity," even after 1948, could have had a beneficent effect on repositioning Yugoslavia between the West and the communist East and was supposed to reflect the beneficent effect of Yugoslav socialism on people of fascist or pro-Soviet orientation

(Nemec 2012b: 184–87, 192, 198). For example, an analysis of the archives of the Ministry of Foreign Affairs in Zagreb showed that 26 percent of requests were rejected; out of 86,858 requests to "opt," 63,801 of them received a positive response (Žerjavić 1993; Nemec 2012b: 185). My interlocutors frequently recalled family members or acquaintances, whose requests were rejected, which led to unsuccessful escape attempts, like that of Amalia's father.

> How should I put it, there were options, they were free then, anyone who wanted to stay or to leave could vote. Many had their requests rejected. My father too wanted to leave. [About his Italian surname.] But they still rejected him and he wanted to escape on a boat, but they caught him and put him in prison. Because he considered himself to be Italian. [About how it is not known why they rejected his request—his surname was Italian.] But there were reasons because some weren't allowed to leave and some were. . . .

From May 1945 until Yugoslavia's expulsion from the Informbiro in 1948,[10] the historian Miha Kosmač showed that the Yugoslav authorities were aware of the inappropriate attitude to the Istrian population, especially the Italians, and they tried to deal with the problem (Kosmač 2015).[11] In 1943, the Anti-Fascist Council for the National Liberation of Yugoslavia (AVNOJ) planned for the Yugoslav authorities to include representatives of the Italian minority. Even before the end of World War II, the Slovene political elite strove to find individuals who would represent this area's Italian population in the political structure. The bodies of the popular government encouraged brotherhood and unity, which had already taken shape during the national liberation struggle (Argenti Tremul 2016; Kosmač 2017: 104). Yugoslavia already ensured the protection of the Italian national community with the Paris Peace Treaty in 1947, while the system of protection of autochthonous national communities was completed by the mid-1980s (Kavrečič 2008; Sanzin 2015: 15–20). However, despite the postwar desire of the Yugoslav authorities for brotherhood, unity, and legal protection, the Italian population was unequally represented in government committees in comparison with the Slovenes and the Croats, and there were also various other irregularities: limitations on the use of Italian in public offices, the removal of Italian signs, and delays in the reopening of schools, encroachment on the safety of individuals and property, instances of inequality before the law, false accusations, arrests, punishment without trial or long-lasting procedures for arrested persons, and so on. According to Miha Kosmač, these irregularities were caused by various problems with the functioning of lower levels of government—in districts and towns—from an inability to execute orders, different interpretations of orders, a lack of experienced and disciplined staff, an overly bureaucratic state apparatus, and even cases of personal revenge and shifts in positions of power from the hitherto "leading" (Romance/Italian) to the "subordinate" (Slav/Slovene, Croat) ethnic communities. Until 1948, the Yugoslav authorities emphasized the need to respect the right of Italians to their own education and culture. There was a fear that an inappropriate attitude towards the Italians could threaten the existence of the whole of Istria, knowing that the actions (and mistakes) of the local authorities, whose sole aim was to achieve social transformation, were experienced by the Italian population mainly as an attack on their national identity. Until 1948, the Yugoslav authorities tried to stop the Italian population from leaving with counter-propaganda, by exerting stricter control over laissez-passers, and by taking more time to approve requests to move (Kosmač 2015: 116–17; 2017: 106–7, 137). Toward the end of 1947, the first requests to return were made by optants—especially by those from around Pula, where the largest migrations had taken place due to fear and panic. However, the senior authorities rejected almost all applications, only making rare exceptions for people who had learned trades that were given special consideration (Kosmač 2017: 189–90).

All historians agree that the Informbiro dispute in 1948 played an important role in emigration, when Italian communists from Zone B of the Free Territory of Trieste opted en masse against Tito's party (Kacin Wohinz and Troha 2001: 61–62). After the dispute, even the small group of "good and honest Italians," anti-fascists and supporters of the socialist system—who embodied the policy of "Italian-Slav brotherhood and unity"—became even more suspicious than before (Pupo 2015; Kosmač 2015). While the Yugoslav authorities initially tried to prevent the Italian population from leaving, after 1948 the governments on either side of the border made efforts to promote emigration. On the Yugoslav side, they canceled the policy of "Slav-Italian brotherhood" and looked with favor on the emigration of Italians. New outbreaks of violence accompanied the elections in 1950 and the Trieste Crisis in 1953, from the elimination of undesired individuals to the closure of the border between the zones. The Yugoslav authorities obstructed the passage of people into Zone A, which was a problem for those who went to work in Trieste, and they made changing currencies more difficult, evicted families whose members were employed in Zone A, and so forth. At the same time, the Italian authorities launched an extensive propaganda campaign encouraging the population to leave, warning against the violence of the neighboring country's totalitarian regime, and promising jobs and flats in Italy (Troha 1997: 58–59; Kacin Wo-hinz and Troha 2001). Following the signing of the Udine Agreement on local border traffic between Italy and Yugoslavia on 23 May 1955, the Yugoslav authorities finally gave up, and despite the concern that now "everyone would have the right to go and it was hard to reject an application" (Gombač 2005: 94), all who applied were allowed to go as there were no longer any administrative hurdles. They also decided to give faster positive responses to applications without any procrastination (Gombač 2005: 94–95).

Two interlocutors gave evidence on the change in attitude of the Yu-goslav authorities. The first was Emir, whose story of his father—an early immigrant of Turkish origin from Macedonia (1952), who found his cake shop's previous Italian owner in tears—has already been told. According to the testimonies of his father and other Italians in Izola—especially fishermen—emigration was voluntary at first, followed by gentle pressure and later strong pressure to leave.

> This is basically what he said: first of all, when they left here—this exo-dus, when they were leaving—it was like this: they could sell what they had, voluntarily. He sold up and went. Later, he said, this is what they told these locals: "Now take as much as you can carry and go!" . . . That was the second round and the third round simply had to go. Not, "What will you take with you?" but, "Go!" . . . The third round had to go. You simply had no choice.

The memories of Karlo, an intellectual from Koper with Slovene roots—who gives much "credit" for the mass emigration of Italians to the later politics of the politician Kajtimir—are in line with this story of voluntary emigration that turns into violence. In 1954, Kajtimir was replaced by Jurij Beltram—one of the first Yugoslav political officials in Zone B who led an open policy of "Italian-Slav brotherhood." A change can therefore be detected when Istria was joined to Yugoslavia.

> Janko Beltram worked hard for this *fratellanza*, then came a new line that moved him to Ljubljana, . . . Kajtimir came . . . Beltram was removed and sent to Ljubljana [1955] then Kajtimir was in charge here, and he carried out the purge. . . . They had this uncompromising policy, to re-solve this territorial problem, to get rid of as many Italians as possible. I think they encouraged people to leave as much as they could. . . . Politics changed. In the past, there had been a policy of rapprochement, but now there was a policy to fix the national structure. To get rid of the Italians. A sort of expedition came . . . to resolve this, that was Kajtimir, a politician, and a foreigner here.

Here is a brief summary of the reasons studies give for migration, and which I will later compare with the memories: a negative perception of Italians, a worsening of living conditions, job losses, rejection of drastic changes to the economy, the change in language, threats (of revenge), arrests, "epuration committees"[12] and trials against supporters of the fascist regime, deportations and liquidations (in the beginning), fear, Italian propaganda about a better life in Italy that had an effect on frightened people, obstructed movement or closed borders between Zones B and A when Trieste was Istria's economic center (from October 1953 to August 1955), fear of being stranded on the wrong side of the "iron curtain," socialist coercive measures against wealthy inhabitants that affected primarily the Italian bourgeoisie and rich farmers (confiscation of private property and land from the rich with the agrarian reform, and distribution among poorer people—the destruction of the system of *coloni*, a hostile attitude toward tradesmen and higher taxes for them, worker cooperatives, the removal of religious practices from the public domain, and more), Yugoslav policies against "enemies of the people" and "class enemies," the closure of some Italian schools, the loss of a social network, rejection of the change in social power (after fascism and Nazism inspired a superior attitude in the Italians toward the Slavs, whom they considered to be "subhuman"), pressure exerted by the authorities whose totalitarian nature prevented the expression of national identity, the ideological struggle that was sometimes intentionally or unintentionally linked to ethnicity, and other such things (Kacin Wohinz and Troha 2001; Pletikosić 2002; Ballinger 2003: 207–44; Volk 2003: 35–42; Fakin and Jerman 2004: 119–22; Bonin 2004; Gombač 2005: 84–85; Kralj and Rener 2010; Rogoznica 2011; Hrobat Virloget 2015a, 2015b; Argenti Tremul 2016; Kosmač 2017: 133–37; Kalc 2019: 150).

The Italian inhabitants realized that in the new circumstances they would not be able to preserve their national identity "as a set of life habits and emotions that go far beyond the bare political-ideological dimension, so for them emigration meant choosing freedom" (Kacin Wohinz and Troha 2001). Some Slovenian researchers emphasize that Slovene Istrians also suffered as a result of most of the above communist measures connected with the establishment of the communist system (Rožac Darovec 2012: 694–700). However, it is important to understand that the population movements may also have been caused by indirect pressure when people felt threatened in an ethnic sense and no longer saw a future for themselves in their home town or village (Ther 2001). Most migrants also believed, or hoped, that the migration would be temporary, and this is also evident in the oral testimonies. However, it turned out to be permanent. The requests to opt show that people who wanted to leave Zone B were motivated by various factors: unemployment, low wages, lack of prospects, or tensions in the family due to their estates being too small. They were attracted to the other side of the border by work, health, money, pensions, and education. None of the reasons listed in the written applications are connected with nationality. With the exception of criticisms about land being seized for the construction of the airport, there is no sign of other criticisms of the system as the applicants probably feared their request being turned down (Gombač 2005: 115–16, 118).

Indirect Pressure: Intimidation, Negative Attitude toward Italians

How are the above complex and very diverse reasons for the exodus evident in the memories of people from Istria? The intimidation of Italians, especially by banging on windows in the night and breaking into houses, has already been mentioned in the section on silenced memories. Elisabetta remembers the intimidation of an Italian teacher from Koper:

> They wanted her to speak, to describe the situation, to practically be a spy. To tell who is still working . . . To spy on colleagues, as she did—we're talking about the years 1949, 1950—also in prison, etc. And she really had to leave because her father died that year, in 1949. He was a lawyer [name]. The police came in, they threw everything out, the whole office, the books; it was really hard in those times.

Elda also remembers cases of violence against lawyers and teachers in Koper:

> E: When I came, everyone had left Piran. But in Capodistria, when I was still there . . . The most fanatic party members threw even the mattresses and furniture of people who were leaving through the windows. . . .
> L: Of the people who had left?
> E: No, those who were leaving. To get them to leave.

Although in principle the authorities supported the ethnic rights of Italians in Istria, sources indicate that they had difficulties with Italian teachers who were not deemed "reliable" enough as they doubted their support for the Yugoslav movement and the annexation of Istria to Yugoslavia (Kosmač 2017: 108). As is written in an archival document from Koper in 1947: "Regarding Italian teachers and professors, they are all negative elements, each and every one of them, and in the schools they follow the old education system. . . . These people were ordered to stay here by the CLN[13] in order to preserve Italian culture and this is what they aim to do in schools."[14]

The memories of Italians, especially those who left, are pervaded by fear. If we compare the published memories of those who left and those who stayed (Castelli 2018), we notice that a large number of migrants were full of fear of violence by the new Yugoslav regime. In contrast, only some of those who stayed mention the general atmosphere of fear. They also mention the Italian propaganda, but their desire to adapt to the new circumstances is more evident, especially their pride when as children or teenagers they succeeded in learning Slovene or Croat, which became the new majority languages, especially in schools. There is a clear difference between the Italians who stayed and continued to live in Istria, who gradually adapted to the new environment—the situation probably also calmed down gradually—and those who left, whose memories remained frozen in time, probably in the time immediately after the war, in the time of greatest social upheaval.

Fear can be sensed among most of those who left. As one woman said, "after the war we lived in fear" (Castelli 2018: 58). There was fear of violence by the so-called *titini*,[15] the sudden disappearance of people and physical violence, sudden imprisonments and confiscations, threats, persecution of priests, and hostility toward Italians. People were constantly afraid of having their houses broken into, having their doors beaten down, being mocked in an incomprehensible language, having their property seized by force, and so forth (Castelli 2018: 39, 41, 53–63). Here are some testimonies on this subject: "And some people came from the OZNA [the Department for People's Protection was Communist Yugoslavia's security agency]; they smashed all the drawers of the cupboard and the chest of drawers, and took all the money we had—there was a considerable amount" [according to memory there was enough to buy two flats] (Castelli 2018: 61). "After the war the atmosphere was very tense; if you went to church, they called you a fascist, and also if you didn't speak Slovene . . . like a form of psychological terrorism" (Castelli 2018: 63). People were threatened with having their private property confiscated: "We left in February 1956, because they took all we had, we were a large family, the *titini* confiscated our grocery store" (Castelli 2018: 69). "We were afraid. Then my daughter died in Capodistria, we didn't speak the language and they called us 'bloody Italians.' We fled. . . ." (Castelli 2018: 70). A better life, pressure because of religious practice, and problems due to not understanding the new language are mentioned only occasionally (Castelli 2018: 38, 64, 66, 72).

Violence and fear are two reasons for the departure of many humiliated Italians. A descendant of *esuli* from Koper shared with Neža Čebron Lipovec a terrible testimony about her grandfather's departure due to shaming and maltreatment.

> My mother was born in 1947 . . ., my father was a fisherman and mandolin-player. They did not plan to leave. But the Yugoslav soldiers hounded my father and shamed him: they stripped him of his clothes and he had to walk around the town naked (!), down to the small harbor and back . . . They couldn't take it any longer, and in 1952, they moved away and lived for years in shacks meant for refugees [speaking about the terrible conditions and abuse].

The testimonies by Italians on violence in Istria are shocking—for example, those mentioned in *History in Exile* by Pamela Ballinger (2003). Miha Kosmač also writes about violence in Istria during the war and immediately after it (until 1948), which was accompanied by the powerful propaganda effect exerted by fear of the Istrian *foibe*. These killings occurred in the period when no-one was in power—after the capitulation of Italy on 8 September 1943 and the German occupation of Istria in the beginning of October 1943. The realistic number of people that died then is considered to be between 350 and 500. In Istria, there were reprisals due to fascism; people took revenge both as a social group and personally. Violence was aimed primarily against presumed fascists, collaborators, representatives of the fascist apparatus and some civilians. This was typical of most European countries after the war. The OZNA had the task of "sweeping up" the newly liberated territories, not on a national basis but on a "fascist basis," that is, by acting against the "enemies of the people." These were tried in special "people's tribunals to protect the nation's honor." Inhabitants, including Italians who did not accept Yugoslav nationality, were court-martialed. You could be considered an "enemy of the people" simply for not participating in demonstrations and political and propaganda campaigns in support of Istria's annexation to Yugoslavia. The persecution and repression of the population coincided with revolutionary processes, as the settling of accounts with the so-called class enemies partly coincided with the settling of scores with collaborators. In addition to the OZNA, military units of the Yugoslav Army and the people's militia also helped carry out the repression. In 1944, the Yugoslav authorities were informed of the arbitrary nature of their decision-making and the inappropriate treatment of the population, and they tried to prepare countermeasures as they were aware of the propaganda effect of "terror" on the anti-Yugoslav forces (Kosmač 2017: 96–102).

The psychological and physical violence had a negative effect above all on the Italian population, regardless of whether it was in the form of unfair trials or day-to-day intimidation. Giulio, a politician with Italian roots, gives the example of a public trial against a suspected terrorist from Izola that is thought to have had a crucial impact on events that led to mass emigration.

> He was arrested in Isola. The trial was one of the most frightful imaginable . . . The trials were held out of ideological and political reasons, with young men accused of terrorism, even if they were only between twenty and twenty-five years old. He was put in prison, his family was sent away, and then he was pardoned after eleven years in jail, in Maribor and Strugnano, I think. [He was a member of the first Health Committee, which consisted of people of all political orientations, and he operated in secret under the Germans, and is thought to have helped liberate Isola in 1945.] In 1945, after two or three days, they were removed and sent back underground—they moved to Trieste as members of CLN Istria. And this was like the beginning of the traumas that followed from 1945 to 1954, 1955, 1956. The beginning of the process that developed particularly in 1953, and which caused 90 percent of the population to flee across the border. [Speaking about how the Italians hoped until the end that Zone B would stay in Italy. For the other parts of Istria it was already known what would happen with them.] And it was not allowed to speak about them. For forty or fifty years, it was forbidden here to speak about Luigi Andrioli and the band of terrorists. The trial took place in 1948, in the year of the Informbiro, with great fanfare, with megaphones in the town square transmitting the trial live.

Many interlocutors, especially Italians but also others, spoke about intimidations that took place in the town streets. The intimidations were mentioned both by those who were intimidated and those who carried out the intimidations. Ornella, who experienced the exodus in Koper as a child, tells the frequently heard story of intimidations or pressure to leave that took place on the doors of houses belonging to Italians. We do not know if this is an original memory or not, as we are aware that we remember together with the society in which we live, and we also remember with memories that do not belong to ourselves but to the society we are part of (Halbwachs 2001).

> O: But they fled like crazy because they came to the doors of houses: "If you don't go this evening, we will kill you tomorrow." And you know what happened?
> K: But is this about the doors true?
> O: Of course, I remember it myself. Except I was small and I experienced these things as though it was theater. They beat on the doors . . . But I . . . But they were terrorizing people, who disappeared from one day to the

next; you couldn't understand how. It was incredible. And then this emptied little town, empty, so few of us remained.

Some people, like Lucija, remember the testimonies of those who exerted this indirect pressure on the Italians:

> L: I was told by a professor [name], who is now already dead, in Maribor. He said they went on holiday for two months to Portorož in 1945, and their task was to annoy a little Italian (at least one every two days) to such an extent that he would begin ranting and raving at them so the police could then arrest him for a few days.
> K: "To annoy"?
> L: Like children do: "Get lost you Italian!!!" [in a contemptuous tone of voice] Or they would pick a fight, or anything. So there were these *skojevci* [members of the League of Communist Youth of Yugoslavia], these youngsters; I won't say everyone did it, but this regime also did some things in a—we could say illegal, hidden way—to get them to . . .

Anton, who moved here from central Croatia and is married to a Croat Istrian, says that pressure was exerted on the Istrian Italians by people who moved here from elsewhere—Slovenes from the interior:

> A: Most of those who left already had someone there. And the ones who were really staunch Italians were afraid! Some were afraid. I can give you an example. My neighbor, she was Italian! They beat on her windows every night. [Tense feeling, silence.]
> K: Really?
> A: Do you know who beat on the windows? The locals, the locals . . . Actually Slovenes, who had moved here!
> K: But was she politically compromised, so to speak, or was she just Italian?
> A: [Shakes his head in silence.] There was that! There was! There was that! That I must say. I know of cases. [Does not want to say any more about this.]

Anton's ensuing silence reflects the unpleasant feelings which accompany claims that do not conform to the national collective memory. This was expressed by the Yugoslav politician Julij Beltram (1986: 191) in his memoirs as follows: "In Istria there was neither terrorization, nor intimidation, and there were no anti-Italian incidents." Such memories about the indirect intimidation of Italians on the streets were not rare. Vittoria heard them told by other people:

> V: Đilas said in 1991 that he remembered how he and Kardelj received an order when they arrived in Istria . . . Make sure that as many Italians

as possible are removed from Istria, that they are driven away in any way possible. All means were allowed, all of them. I've told you how the students at the Maritime Institute organized themselves and were armed with small guns . . .

K: No, you didn't tell me.

V: No? When whole classes were taken out of the Maritime Institute, they sent them onto the streets of Piran at night with small guns, and they shot with them—pim, pim, pim—making a noise on doors and shouting: "Italians, we're going to kill you all. Italians go!" People who had been terrorized by the nationalizations, by all this, what could they do? Some of them didn't even close their doors, they simply left.

We have already quoted the memoirs of the politician Milovan Đilas, who together with another politician, Edvard Kardelj, organized anti-Italian propaganda in Istria and persuaded the Italians to leave (Gombač 2005: 59–60). The intention to intimidate may even be sensed firsthand by those who were involved in exerting indirect pressure—probably immediately after the end of the war. After my public lecture on the exodus, a Slovene from Istria reacted furiously to my public testimonies of pressure on the Italians with a testimony of his own participation in such activities:

> We have no illusions because what followed 1945 was truly brutal. It's true that the Italian professors avoided teaching Slovene for those two, three, four hours, so it was somehow logical. And it's right that they drove them out [the Italian teachers who refused to teach Slovene], that they sent us into the streets to beat on the doors, to get them to leave if they didn't want to learn a little Slovene.

The negative perception of Italians can be attributed to the Slovene population's anger and desire for retaliation after all the fascist violence. Historians too notice how some activists took it out on the local Italian population. It was both for this reason and because of the dispute with the Informbiro, when most Italian communists in Zone B declared themselves to be against Tito's party, that the Italian-speaking inhabitants were afraid of retaliatory Yugoslav measures (fear of killings) (Kacin Wohinz and Troha 2001: 62). However, there was not only talk of threats in the streets; my interlocutors also spoke about violent expulsions. This is commonly cited as a reason in the memories of migrants (see Ballinger 2003; Castelli 2018). Massimo tells the story of his grandfather, a big landowner from Umag, whose son was killed in unclear circumstances, and whose family was threatened and forced to leave overnight. In the refugee center he died because of the feeling of disappointment that he had been ruined by his own neighbors:

M: The same thing happened to my grandfather [he had to sell all his property in exchange for a few oxen]. He lived near Umag. They came in the evening and said: "If we find you here tomorrow morning, we will shoot the whole family." . . . So that night he loaded everything onto his oxen and left. And he left everything . . . But this is again because my grandfather owned a lot, he had vineyards, he had a house, he had everything. So they seized all this. He had to go away.

K: Why did he have to go?

M: Well, they killed his son and they came . . .

K: Why, how?

M: They shot him, near down there, near Umag. He went into a field, and they said it was the Germans, etc. . . . And he was an Austro-Hungarian soldier, and he had an Austro-Hungarian pension; it was unheard of at the time that someone should receive a pension from Austria. And they even took his book, his bank book with his money, but this again is what I told you earlier; it was the ones who were not on top. And they did this to gain something for themselves, nothing else. Then my grandfather complained to someone higher up, and they gave him his book back. And so on. [Speaking about the departure] I was still small, I was born in 1952, so it must have been in 1955, thereabouts. Then the state paid my mother something like €1,000, something like an inheritance for what they took from them. [Speaking about the refugee camp] He was sad all the time, and he had never smoked or drunk before. And before he died, he asked them to bring him a liter of brandy and cigars. He was sad because it was actually his fellow villagers who did this to him.

As has been mentioned in the discussion on silence, pressure should not be understood solely as tension due to differences in nationality or ideological opinion, but it was also the consequence of interpersonal relations and the struggle for power in the local community. With the collapse of the old social order and the transformation of the social hierarchy, resistance movements frequently conceal social conflicts, power struggles and civil wars (Pavone 1992; Portelli 1997; Van Boeschoten 2005: 39; Rožac Darovec 2012).

The fact that former neighbors became enemies left deep wounds. Throughout the interview my interlocutor emphasized that it was those "who were not on top," who caused problems for the Italians, and this corresponds with the observations made by Miha Kosmač (2015; 2017) on the incorrect functioning of the low-level Yugoslav authorities and not that of the central regime. If we leave aside the ethnic belonging of the expelled landowner and remember how disappointed he was with his neighbors—his poorer neighbors—we cannot ignore contemporary moral-ethical questions of coexistence and betrayal that emerged during the COVID-19 crisis when this book was being written. It was the mass denunciation of those who did not abide by the government's anti-COVID-19 measures that revealed all the depravity of human society, or as Miha Mazzini (2020) wrote, the envy of the self-righteous toward those who dare and are happy has been revealed. As the psychiatrist Željko Ćurić warned during the COVID-19 crisis, "very often people's fates in wars and even the worst massacres were determined by the closest neighbors, regardless of whether it was a question of racism, nationalism or religious superiority" (Lorenci 2020). The historian Jan Gross (2012) showed in his book *Neighbors* that during World War II in the Polish town of Jedwabne, the Poles murdered their own neighbors, the Jews, without being forced to do so by the Nazis. This is why he poses the rhetorical question: can a community be both a victim and a perpetrator (Gross 2012: 144)?

The unexplained disappearances of family members cut deep wounds into both the *esuli* and those who remained. An Italian lady, who lost her brother in unclear circumstances as late as the early 1960s, has similar memories. Even nowadays she senses fear when she thinks of the evil acts perpetrated by the communists, and above all the local authorities—evil acts that know no chronological boundaries. This general atmosphere of fear was heightened during the war by rumors of the *foibe*. As Greta illustrates: "All of them. They all went. One went, and a second, and a third . . . That this, that, and the other would happen, that they would kill them, this and that, that they would be thrown in the *foibe*, and they fled."

Psychological violence against the Italians in Istria is therefore quite strongly present in memories. However, it is unclear who was behind this violence—the central or regional government, or was it simply revenge carried out by individuals? Neither is it clear how many people exerted psychological violence against the Italian-speaking population, and how many were in favor of a policy of "Italian-Slav brotherhood." As already mentioned, those who stayed here are more at peace with their memories and do not exude as much fear as the *esuli*. Mario described the negative attitude toward the Italians, who were even beaten, and then made the following comment: "I stayed at home, nobody bothered me . . ."

A similar calmness in the new system can be sensed in the following account of a life story:

> Everything changed after the war. It was no longer the same. The people left. Many sailors left. . . . My father did not want to leave. He said: "I was a prisoner for four years in Russia, and I know what a refugee camp looks like. I'm not going anywhere. I'm staying at home. We're not going

to die of hunger or from being treated badly." And it's true that they always respected us. No-one ever said anything to us. (Pahor 2011: 59)

Although for some Italians memories of intimidation are still traumatic, others have no such memories—they stayed and adapted to life in the new social reality. Some only experienced gentle forms of pressure, but even in this regard many were of the opinion that it depended to what extent you resisted the system, that is, regarding children being sent to Slovene schools, the Slovenization of Italian names, hateful comments, and so forth.

Judging by the interviews, most Istrians believe the reasons for departure were very complex. A typical example of someone who lists diverse reasons is Štelio, a Slovene Istrian from the hinterland of Istria, whose mother—of Slovene origin—also wanted to go to Italy. He says people left for economic reasons, to avoid military service, out of fear of Yugoslavia, and also because Italians were generally unwelcome. Like some others, they emphasized the contempt for the Istrians—both for those who spoke Slovene and those who spoke Italian. As will become clear later, the predominant discourse in these opinions was that pressure was exerted against people to leave and make room for people coming from Slovenia's interior.

> Some went to work in Trieste. They weren't allowed to go dancing. The others who went were those who were later forced to leave because they were Italians. And the third group left for economic reasons. And then those who chased after the Italians also went away. The locals. Those that had to do military service. So as not to have to do it . . . They were better than us. In Trieste, in Italy, they earned more. They had better wages. . . . They were afraid of Yugoslavia . . . Here where we are . . . There was . . . Tito. . . . I'm very skeptical because that was ethnic cleansing. The aim was to get rid of the Italians. I don't know who was the commander. The aim was to get the Italians out so others could move in. Because Izola, Koper, Piran had Italian-speaking inhabitants.

The memories of Italian-speaking Istrians clearly show their unease in the face of the hostile attitude of those newly arrived from Slovenia's interior and other Yugoslav republics. These people were not aware of the local reality and adopted the generally widespread stigmatization of Italians.

> The people who came from elsewhere were hostile to Italians, to Italian culture, and the Italians no longer felt at home. . . . I remember a man [name] who used to come sometimes, he's already dead now—and he

used to shout in the street under the windows: "Bloody Italians, get lost!" I remember this and will probably remember it for the rest of my life. I didn't understand why they persecuted us. My mother was at home; she never went to work. She cooked, cleaned, and looked after the house. My father did nothing bad to anyone, neither during the war nor before the war. But we suffered under this scourge; in reality, we were rejected because we were Italians. (Pahor 2007: 55–56)

There was a similar testimony in the chapter on the stigmatization of Italians as fascists, where the locals blame politics "from outside" for the exodus. Many interlocutors, including Gianfranco who comes from a Slovene-Italian family, claim that the pressure on the Italians was exerted predominantly by new arrivals:

For example, in Sečovlje . . . The locals left because those who came from elsewhere also intimidated them; they came because a mine was opened, and they didn't have enough workers. And these young people came from Velenje and Trbovlje, and they slept in the old barracks. That's where they made their home. These young people shouted all over Sečovlje: "These are Italians!" . . . That Italians are bad and this and that [speaking about conflicts with the locals].

In a study on the so-called exchange of populations between Greece and Turkey in 1923, after the Balkan Wars, in which Turkey accepted 380,000 Muslims from Greece, and Greece took 1.1 million Christians from Turkey, Barbaros Tanc (2001) showed that immigrants from both sides remembered a harmonic coexistence with the "others" prior to the conflicts, which were said to have been incited by external actors. Angela and Guido also talk about the complex reasons for departure, giving a series of reasons, from fear of the new system, uncertainty due to propaganda from Slovenia's interior, and so on.

A: They were afraid . . . After the war . . .
K: That the borders would be closed?
A: Not just the borders, also the . . . Regime, how . . .
K: The communist regime?
A: They were terrified, as my husband said . . . One spoke . . .
G: One persuaded another . . .
A: I'm sure some would have preferred to stay . . . But they didn't know how the story would end. There was that too . . . Many left.
G: Then there was propaganda, there was so and so who came from Slovenia, he spoke Italian, for example . . . "Sell up because tomorrow you'll lose everything, sell your house, you can't do anything." . . .

A: Yes, they were afraid and then Tito . . . Then this regime, how would
it treat those who stay . . . That was . . .
K: Did they frighten them?
A: There were also provocations . . .

It was not just the Slovenes. I also heard the Italians speaking about a
harmonic coexistence until the war and the state border cut in, followed
by the great fear of the unknown Yugoslav Army and system. Michela
tells the story from her own point of view and the view of a friend, an
esule.

[The narrative of the *esule* friend.] In this village, we lived together like
one big family. Some would say *buon giorno* [hello], others *dober dan*
[hello]. No-one minded. But then came the border and Yugoslavia, and
various grudges and animosities began surfacing, but where did they
come from? From the war. Because it was all a mess. "And we," she said,
"lived so nicely." So you can understand the sadness . . . How many
people we knew died of heart attacks. On the day the Yugoslav troops arrived, I was in that house [as a child]. When they were coming up the hill
with a cart and mules, on that day I had a fever of 40 degrees. The first
to come into our house was a doctor from Capodistria. It was a shock for
everyone, but I never regretted it because I am strongly attached to my
house, my local environment; I would die if I had to go far from here.

From the testimonies we have already seen in the chapter on the
stigmatization of Italians as fascists, it seems that after the war, people
were quite hostile toward Italians. As we have seen many times in history—from the burning down of the Narodni dom in Trieste (Slovene
Cultural Center) to the postwar situation in Yugoslavia, and as we saw
in the COVID-19 epidemic, when there were so many reports of neighbors "behaving unacceptably," not by the authorities but by the "people
underneath"—"enemies" quickly emerge in times of fear, panic, and uncertainty. This is also shown by a couple from Istria—Stanka of Slovene
origin and Mario with Italian roots—who mention a general negative
attitude toward the Italians and even beatings:

M: Because of the coming of Yugoslavia. They didn't want to live under
Yugoslavia. Because this came under Italy . . .
S: At one point, there was terrible hostility toward the Italians. . . .
K: What was this hostility toward the Italians that you mentioned?
S: Well, it was they that came, the Slovenes, one and the other, especially
the communists, the communists were against them.
M: Communism was against them, they even beat them . . .
S: And here, where there were Italians who left, we came to live there.

M: Yes, but some of them didn't give in . . . They created such propaganda . . . Such *dimostrazion* [intimidation, demonstration]. No war brings anything good. . . .

S: I was there in the street when a woman from Nova vas came here. And Italians lived here, an elderly couple. She told a neighbor to remove the greenery growing on the wall so they could repair the window. I was there, together with another woman, and she said: "Bloody Italian, go to Italy!" "Ey!" I said, "She's on her own property. What and you, where are you? She'll go away and you'll go and live on her property," I said. "But I wasn't talking about you . . ." I'm not Italian, my husband's Italian and I'm not, but you should not say such things! . . . I was married [to an Italian], and why did I give my children Italian names [they reproached her for this]. . . . And why did I send them to Italian schools. "These are our things," I said, "and I want to learn Italian myself, even though I'm not Italian." "No, as you're not Italian, you shouldn't have sent them to the Italian school." Some people gave in, but not everyone gave in . . .

Even if the above examples of pressure were more indirect in nature, we can still empathize with the people who no longer felt safe, or a part of the newly established society when faced with such hostile attitudes on a daily basis.

The Uncertain Economic Situation, Socialist Economic Measures, and the New State Borders

The economic situation in Istria was very bad in the interwar period, and this is why it was considered to be less developed than other Italian provinces. Most of the population lived in difficult economic circumstances, and with the new postwar regime the situation deteriorated even further. The land, especially the best land, was in the hands of a small number of large landowners, while most people could barely make a living. The Italian bourgeoisie and the landowners were the main targets of the new regime, as socialist measures envisaged their expropriation, a ban on itinerant trade, restrictions on private property, a ban on the *colonus* system and the distribution of expropriated land to the laborers, *coloni,* and poor farmers, and so on (Volk 2003: 35–39; Gombač 2005: 85; Purini 2010: 244–45). As Gianfranco and many others described, land was taken from the rich and distributed to the laborers, poor people, and the colonate:

They took it from these rich people, the ones who were a bit better off, they took the larger plots of land from them and gave them . . . In Jernej, they formed an assembly. They did not call it an assembly back then. And they took the land from these landowners. The landowners left. They left for Trieste already in 1950. [Speaking about the agrarian reform.] Before he was a farmer who worked up there for the padres, up there at Krog there was a large . . . They were priests, and they had half the valley and half the entire hill. And these farmers worked for them, half-time or three-quarters. Then in 1945, they took this land that belonged to the padres and gave it to anyone who had a small house. They gave them this land so they could cultivate it themselves. . . . Here, some were in favor of Yugoslavia because before it was bad. Before they were all *coloni*, they all had to work; everyone had to work on half the land, one-third. That's why they preferred Yugoslavia—now we are masters, landowners, they gave houses for free, they got it back. The ones who went got houses, where they lived, they immediately got land and houses. Up at the priests it was the same situation: they gave them land; what they used to do for the priests, it's all for you now. It was ideal. . . . And then they began taking this land, created these cooperatives and then it all went into ruin.

An elderly Italian local describes the violent expropriation in the post-war state of lawlessness. As he says, people "from elsewhere" broke into houses and drove out the Italian *coloni* to their relatives in the towns:

> People came from outside. And they would go into the house, and throw out the old *coloni* who had lived there for centuries [surname]. Then there's another family further on [two surnames] . . . Some went up the stairs, the others down. And they grabbed the oil and wine, whatever they had became theirs. [Speaking about the fact that these were the *coloni* of Count Totto.] There were no laws back then, and even if there were, they weren't respected. Like bilingualism nowadays. ("Nino e i suoi ricordi di Giusterna" 2009: 27–28)

Some reasons for the departure of many Italians were the already-mentioned socialist measures of confiscating private property. This can be gathered indirectly from the memories of immigrants who lived as tenants in villas that once belonged to the Italian bourgeoisie. However, as Danilo—one of the first immigrants who lived with his mother as a tenant in a villa that belonged to two Italian ladies in Portorož/Portorose—says, this was not pressure exerted on an ethnic basis but a socialist measure, although for many it was the final straw:

> K: Did you live in the house, which they [the two elderly Italian ladies] sold? That means it was probably seized from them. Did you pay them rent?
> D: No, they had to have us there by decree. That was the order; I don't know who paid the rent to whom. It was a villa after all, 100 square meters on each floor. . . .

K: Yes, but this is already a form of pressure, which you cannot see.
R: Of course, but it was not connected with nationality as it also happened in Ljubljana, Maribor, everywhere. People who had too much had their possessions confiscated or taken away, to be given to those who had nothing.

And as he later describes in reference to Portorož: "But all around, what I remember of these villas is that there were these new settlers everywhere." Vittoria also describes how her uncle was a hated "capitalist" whose fishing boat was nationalized—confiscated—and he was thereby forced to leave:

> He had disputes with the party. He was in conflict. He was the director of a fishery cooperative. I don't know precisely what the problems were, but it was mainly to do with defending the Italian fishermen. There was nationalization, they took their boats, they had to give their boats . . . That's the case of my uncle, the husband of my father's sister, who left with his family, his three children and wife, in 1952. They went, *esuli* . . . They took his boat because he's a capitalist. It was a motorboat for fishing that he bought on credit, and worked eighteen hours a day to pay it off. He transported sand, transported stones, from Quarnaro to this other side of Istria and took great risks. . . . He was therefore considered to be a capitalist.

Raoul Pupo observed that everyone who did not make enough effort to purge the fascists, or did not show enough "fervor" for the new system, was considered to be an "enemy of the people." The bourgeoisie belonged to this category, whereby the term referred to large and medium-sized landowners, businessmen, professionals, intellectuals, and the upper and lower middle classes in towns, and they were predominantly Italians. They were often the target of repressive tactics including intimidation, injustices, violence, arrests, and disappearances. The general feeling of uncertainty was also heightened by the confiscation of companies, shops, work equipment, boats, and goods (Pupo 2015: 31). The hostile attitude toward fishermen can be explained by Yugoslavia's very negative view of self-employed tradesmen. In the desire for a more "honest" economy—for which the communist leadership in Koper was striving in 1954—they were considered to be the main obstacle to the implementation of this "new economic policy" because they were said to be constantly "speculating" and opposing the authorities. Besides, they did not want to join state "cooperatives" for workers because they wanted to remain independent (Gombač 2015: 122).

Some Italians, such as Vittoria, saw the socialist economic changes as deliberate pressure on the Italian community. As we have been taught

Figure 2.7. Inside the factory, Izola/Isola, 1948 (Department of History and Ethnography of the National Study Library of Trieste, collection Primorski dnevnik, author Mario Magajna).

by history, toppling a nation's financial and cultural elite is an efficient way of silencing and even eliminating a national minority—this is what happened to the Slovene minority in Austria (Pečenko 2020). It is impossible to know to what extent this was deliberate as Yugoslav politics surprisingly had contradictory attitudes toward the Italian population in Istria. Vittoria draws attention to the forgotten aspect of the economic impoverishment of Italians:

> The economic dimension is lacking in all this discourse that takes into account the social and psychological aspects of migration. It is right to say that the Italians felt betrayed on an ideological and political level—with all the consequences—but they were also robbed. We were robbed as our banks were closed down, our factories were nationalized, and the machines taken away so the workers were forced to leave [Isola], the boats and motorboats were nationalized and taken to Dalmatia, the shipyards, ships for transporting people and goods, etc. People were left without work. The laboratories were removed from the technical schools in Capodistria . . . And of course, the schools were closed down, etc. This crucial dimension is completely missing. The motivation for the exodus was primarily economic, and then political and linguistic . . . We often forget this, including myself. In exchange, the state gave us "subventions" so we cannot die. We are on a reanimation bed with a drip in the vein, incapable of reacting, grateful to still be alive . . . What an irony!

Figure 2.8. Arrigoni factory, Izola/Isola, 1948 (Department of History and Ethnography of the National Study Library of Trieste, collection Primorski dnevnik, author Mario Magajna).

The fact that the new authorities were not exactly soft on the Italian population in Istria is shown also by the report prepared by the joint Italian-Slovene historical commission, which mentions not only the cutting of economic ties with Trieste, but also many other reasons for emigration. During their temporary administration of Zone B, the Yugoslav authorities tried to annex it to Yugoslavia by force. While the Slovenes were granted the ethnic rights to which they were not entitled under fascism, there were attempts—including by intimidation—to force the Italians to agree to the annexation of Zone B to Yugoslavia. The severance of economic ties with Trieste undermined the economic basis of the Italians' leading social role, and this was accompanied by the disintegration of the leading Italian classes. At the same time, the government also tried to destroy the Italian community's cultural strongholds by gradually removing Italian teachers and Italian schools, and by defaming them. As will be evident in the memories below, the Italians even felt the persecution of the faith to be pressure exerted on their nationality. There were also activists whose anger against fascism spread to Italians in general, and they did not even conceal their intention to get rid of those Italians who stood up to the authorities. However, this commission also finds that there are no indications of the intentional persecution of Italians (Kacin Wohinz and Troha 2001).

The uncertainty in postwar Istria was heightened by the difficult economic situation, which persuaded many Istrians to leave. It is vividly described by Luciano, an Italian who moved to Pula (outside Zone B) from Friuli because of his father's desire to "build the socialist state" in the already-mentioned "counter-exodus." As a result of the difficult economic situation and other "annoyances," he moved back to Italy after ten years.

> Someone has a house . . . and then they come and say, "This is not your house any more, how many of you are there?" "Three." "This flat with two rooms is enough if there are just three of you, you can live here, the rest will be for social housing." . . . So whoever had a house was affected. And whoever had some business, especially a trade, that was it. . . . The only ones who could keep their trade were a barber and an ice-cream seller. He was Hungarian. All the other shops closed down. They weren't allowed . . . Only cooperatives. Whoever was a farmer, didn't live in a town, and had land was sent to the *kolkhoz*. [Speaking about the unfair equality based on assets.] In the shipyard, there was no work because of the bombing. Then—as happened to us—if you had a nice flat, someone "with connections" turned up. You were sent away, to a small flat, and the nice flat was given to those "with connections." [Speaking about his house for which they had to pay rent.] Opposite us lived an OZNA lieutenant, a navy commander, and an air force lieutenant. [Speaking about the departure of people from Pula who even took coffins with them and destroyed everything they left behind.] The problem was that there was nothing to eat and nothing to put on. [Speaking about different kinds of food vouchers, the poor quality, milk, meat, gas; being categorized according to social class—his father who was a shop owner had the least rights; the endless queues for all sorts of goods]. If you put all these things together, you can understand why people became *esuli*. We got along somehow because they closed down our shop, no business was allowed.

Gianfranco tells a similar story; with the closure of the border, it was almost impossible to obtain life's necessities. "It was bad, you know, it was really bad, it was bad because we had hardly anything in the shop. And we went to Trieste for goods, but when they closed the border crossings, we too were . . ."

Rationing was in place in Istria until 1952 (Gombač 2005: 85). Like elsewhere, the problem of hunger and supplies was chronic in the postwar years. However, unlike elsewhere, the Istrians could opt for a better life. In addition to the already-mentioned socialist measures against the wealthier inhabitants, who were mostly Italians, the socialist reforms (the agrarian reform, the establishment of agricultural cooperatives, a surplus of farm products that had to be sold at agreed prices, new taxes on production) also deterred the rural inhabitants—Italian, Croat (and Slovene). A negative role was played by the ruptured relations with Trieste, which is where the farmers usually sold their products. Speaking about the area around Buje—from where approximately half of the population (both Croat and Italian) moved out—those who stayed said it was the chaotic politics in rural areas that caused people to leave (M. Orlić 2019: 581). I often noticed that the Istrian farmers had a cynical attitude toward those who moved here from elsewhere and the agrarian reforms, which were unsuited to farming work, as Gianfranco and many others described (see below under symbolic borders):

> A man came down with two horses and a cart and this was all the co-operative had. This cart and the two horses. And they went to work on the land at eight in the morning, and at four in the afternoon they went home. But they went with a flag and accordion; our farmers didn't want to go just like that. They said: "This can't last." But the others were all happy . . . This lasted a few years, but not many years, they soon saw that it didn't work.

The population's difficulties began to increase with the introduction of borders. The border between the zones made even the simplest day-to-day tasks difficult—for example, going to work in Zone A, selling farm products and seafood at the market in Trieste.[16] Besides, the Allied Military Government sometimes closed the border. Until October 1953—when Zone A was administered by the Allied Military Government and the fate of Zone B remained open—the delimitation did not limit daily migrations too badly. The most decisive factor for emigration was the closure of the border between Zones A and B between October 1953 and August 1955 as ties between the district of Koper and Trieste were cut for almost two years. Fear and a sense of uncertainty were increased also by the hardening of relations between Yugoslavia and Italy in October 1953 when diplomatic relations were tense, and there was a danger of conflict. All this caused people to fear for their social security as they were afraid of losing their pensions, length of time in service, employment, and more. The economy in Zone B in the 1950s was not sufficiently developed to employ the entire workforce that had until then been centered on Trieste. The situation in the Slovene coastal region did not normalize until Italy and Yugoslavia signed the Udine Agreement on 20 August 1955 (Kostov 2005: 73; Argenti Tremul 2016). As Michela from Hrvatini says, everyone, including some of her family, went to Trieste because of employment:

> Here in this village, only we stayed—one, two, three and four, five families. The others all left as they had jobs in Trieste. Our people didn't leave

because of politics, otherwise they would have stayed here. Our people went where the jobs were. Because, for example, those who stayed, I stayed with my mother and father, I was ten years old. My sister and brother had work in Trieste, and where did they go? Where the work was. They didn't go for political reasons. After all, these villages are anti-fascist.

When talking about Piran, all the interlocutors emphasized that it emptied almost completely, and as Guido says: "Because they were sailors, most of them were sailors and they went there because of work . . ." Trieste was the center of overseas ocean shipping. Claudio—who comes from a patriotic Slovene family from near Piran—similarly emphasizes the mass departure of sailors from Piran due to work in Trieste, and their strong sense of being foreigners in the new Yugoslav environment.

> K: But why do you think fewer left Izola and more left Piran?
> C: Because they were more attached to these places . . . They did not feel simply superfluous. . . . Because they had . . . The factory in Izola continued to work at full steam even after the end of the war! The Yugoslav Army ate fish spreads—where did they come from? From Izola, the factory (*laughs*). Like in Maribor, where they made trucks, for who? For the army, the Yugoslav Army. As soon as we went apart, one factory went under, and that factory, how many factories closed down? Because before we had worked for a bigger country, more consumers. Suddenly we were left without them and the factories went.
> K: So in Piran, for example, they didn't really turn to this, they rather . . .
> C: Piran . . . First of all, the sailors were tied to Trieste. Because Trieste was . . . Lloyd . . . A shipping center. And many of them were employed on large ships and all the ships belonged to Lloyd Triestino. And they had work there, their contributions were paid . . .

From the archival sources, it is possible to gather the Communist Party's concern over the mass departure of people from Piran. However, written sources do not mention the sailors, but sixty shipyard workers and thirty workers from the Salvetti factory. They also mention the departure of workers from the De Langlade factory in Koper (Gombač 2005: 92–93).

Gianfranco and Maria describe the fear of the border with Trieste—the city with which Istrians had not only economic but also close family ties—being closed:

> G: But then they closed the border crossing. It was impossible to travel in either direction. This frightened people. That's what many of the people from Piran who left now say . . . One woman in Piran . . . For years and years, he was at sea, and he used to send home money via the bank—she

lived here. When they closed the border crossings, they closed the banks, you couldn't have any more contact with Trieste. She said she had to go up, to apply. Because they blocked everything, they gave those who wanted to go to Italy another two years to decide. And that was a big mistake. They said "whoever wants to go," they intimated them; ours said: "Go, go!" They [?] pushed them to go.

K: Our side encouraged them?

G: Yes. "If you go to Trieste often, then go, go!" There were people like that among us.

As I have also heard elsewhere, Gianfranco blames the departure of 90 percent of Piran's Italians—especially sailors employed in Trieste—on fear of the border closing, along with the undesired socialist measures: "Everyone left Piran, as they keep saying, but 90 percent of the people definitely left Piran. Because they sailed and then they closed the border crossings, and these women then left because they didn't have any money. That was then."

As he describes, they felt cornered with the closing of the border, both on the Italian and the Croat side:

The biggest mistake was that people left when they closed the border crossings. That was that. And then you didn't know what to do—you were shut in. There was the border. We were there, like in a box. You couldn't do anything. You couldn't go to Trieste, to go up you had to have documents, a passport, to go to Istria, down across the Mirna, you had to have documents. We were wedged in.

According to Valeria, panic in the face of the complete closure of the new state border was the main reason why her extended family left:

And when this story of the exodus arrived . . . My cousin helped our uncle with work in the salt pans. When he left, my uncle who didn't have children, wondered: "What shall I do now? Who will help me in the salt pans? Why are all these people I know leaving?" So they left too. Two uncles from Piran were working on a boat, and the boats were sailing for Trieste . . . They were transporting sand, all sorts, but the boats went to Trieste and returned to Pirano. . . . They suddenly found themselves in Trieste with the thought that they would no longer be able to go there and back. And families didn't want to stay here, so they left. This whole family . . . When [one uncle] arrived in Argentina, someone . . . There were boats coming, and they said to him: "They're shutting down the border!" [people didn't want to go back for fear that the border would be closed.] My aunt from Capodistria . . . left with her two small children because they were closing these borders.

The introduction of the state border, fear of not being able to cross it, and feeling like a foreigner in one's own home are the reasons for departure that are cited repeatedly. As Ornella summarizes:

> It's clear that people left as they saw that this was no longer their home. Of course, their language was no longer in use, there were no more books, they worked in Trieste. There were obstacles, they were inside, the customs officers would keep them waiting outside for a whole day . . . They made life difficult for them, of course. And they couldn't take it anymore . . . My sister also left . . .

In connection with the decision to leave for Zone A, there is the tragic story of a Slovene family from Škofije/Scofie—close to the newly created border—which lost two houses, one after the other, due to the shifting of the border. The father—who commuted to work from Zone B to Zone A—tried to avoid the forced labor he was subjected to because he refused to pay the taxes on his work that would take away 75 percent of his earnings, so he moved with his family to Zone A. Similarly, 108 workers from Škofije who worked in Zone A decided to leave with their families, prior to 1950, because of all the obstacles the Yugoslav authorities put in the way for those who wanted to cross the border between the zones. One personal life story also reflects the differences in wages between Zones A and B, which was undoubtedly also a reason to leave (Pecchiari Pečarič 2020; Cunja 2020: 175–77).

The consequences of the severed ties with Trieste—Istria's economic center—were evident also in trade, especially for fishermen, as Tonin, a Slovene Istrian from Škofije, explains. "Koper emptied. A fisherman had nowhere to sell his fish. The farmers in Koper were strong. When they went to Trieste [emigrated], they couldn't even take everything with them. They left behind many tools, enormous presses, barrels, they left everything behind and it all decayed" (note in field diary).

The Yugoslav regime tried to separate its economy from Zone A and connect it more closely with Slovenia and Croatia. Due to mass emigration and the continuing emigration from Zone B, the disintegration was so much greater following annexation to Yugoslavia, which also cut social ties (Panjek 2011: 50–51; Rogoznica 2011: 253–310). The new state borders cut social ties, including the closest family ties, which was the reason why many people moved and, as we will see later, this was the greatest source of pain for those who stayed. Maria from the hinterland of Portorož, who is of Italian origin, mentions emigration that took place to avoid family ties being severed, as well as the fear of Slovenes moving in:

Figure 2.9. Border crossing at Škofije/Scofie, 25 October 1948 (Department of History and Ethnography of the National Study Library of Trieste, collection Primorski dnevnik, author Mario Magajna).

When they enabled those who wanted to leave, to leave, that's when it emptied. The odd person here and there left, those merchants and teachers, they left. Others no. Workers, ordinary people who were poor, they all stayed. Then the young began, who didn't have . . . They were always in these fields, and they saw the opportunity to go up to Trieste. Some of our people here worked up in Trieste. . . . These young people escaped, they went away, they stayed up there. There was a family up here in Parezago [name]. He came one day and told us his daughter wanted to leave because she was training to be a seamstress, she would get a job up there, they wanted to go because they don't have jobs here . . . "And they want me to leave," he said, "but I'm not letting them go. Otherwise they'll run away. I have to go too." . . . He was crying because he didn't want to leave. There were also other examples, such as Jernej: "Yes, if you're going, then I'm going too. What will I do here on my own. Then the Slavs will come, these Slovenes will come . . ."

The Italians as Foreigners at Home: The Breaking of Social Ties, Change of Language, Reversal of Social Power and Propaganda

Below we will discuss indirect social pressure exerted on the Italians, who felt the changed social environment put them under pressure not to express their national identity. The Italians quickly obtained their national rights, the right to bilingualism, their own media, newspapers, radio, and television, and more. For example, Radio Koper / Capodistria was founded in 1949 as the Radio of the Yugoslav zone of Trieste—Radio Trieste zona Jugoslava—and it broadcast in Italian (50 percent), Slovene (35 percent), and Croat (15 percent). After 1954, it broadcast mainly in Italian, but in 1979, it separated into Slovene and Italian programs. It is interesting because it played an important role during the Cold War. The fact that it was a frontier region and minority radio meant that for many years it was one of the most listened to radio stations in all of Italy (Vidmar 2009; "Radio Koper praznuje 70 let" 2019;), and it played a key role in spreading pop culture across borders. However, regardless of all the constitutional rights, the conversations show that the Italians felt like foreigners in the new country. Due to the changed social and political circumstances, the change in language and the disrupted social networks, the Italians felt like "foreigners in their own homes" (Ballinger 2003: 220–44; Hrobat Virloget 2015a: 164–67). As we have seen indirectly in the memories we have heard so far, knowledge of the new language—Slovene—was necessary to survive on a daily basis and for employment. The new language, which most of the Italian speakers did not know, became dominant in their local social environment. As some of the interlocutors explained, the Italians in rural areas already had some knowledge of Slovene or Croat, while in the towns they were linguistically distanced from the rural, more Slovene environment. One should also not forget the twenty years of fascist rule, during which Italian dominated in the public sphere and the use of Slovene was forbidden. Ornella says they found themselves in an empty town in which they no longer felt at home. Before it emptied, it provided them with an extensive social network, while after the exodus they found themselves cornered in a foreign environment:

> Capodistria was like an extended family. Why? I could walk to my auntie's house, then I went to see my grandma, then there was my father's sister . . . There were all these extended families. . . . Capodistria was a center and there were all these families because in Capodistria people lived outside; people lived out in the street. The children . . . No-one locked the door; children played in the squares. And as you walked down the street: "Hello Sorenina, good day to you. How is your father? Well, thank you, and you? Hello . . ." Because everyone was out in the street, when it was warm they sat outside on little footstools . . . like one family. That's how it was, you never closed the door. And then we, who were at home, I suddenly felt like a guest in a world that was no longer mine, where other people gave me orders and I had to ask for permission. It's like being part of a family in a house, then everyone leaves, other people come, and you who were in your own family and gave all the orders, you

suddenly find yourself cornered and even have to ask permission to wash your hands. In fact, you no longer know where you are, who you are, and what you're doing. It was very hard. That's how it was.

Both those who stayed and those who left feel nostalgic about the lost "Italian" world of which only traces are left in Istria. Although they did not leave physically, those who stayed experienced a kind of displacement inside themselves as they found themselves to be living at home in a completely foreign environment (Ballinger 2003: 220). The memories of Istrian Italians are focused on an idyllic picture of a past that was destroyed by a wave of foreigners with incomprehensible languages and cultures, and the exodus that cut all social ties in the urban environment (Hrobat Virloget 2020: 26–27). Amalia, who we have already met in the section on unhealed wounds due to families being separated by the exodus, describes the feeling of complete alienation in the middle of a new, incomprehensible language environment in their home town of Rovinj, in the Croat part of Istria:

We went to the shops and couldn't understand what they were asking us. No, we spoke Italian, they didn't understand us. They didn't understand us, and we didn't understand them so we were a little, how should I put it . . . My grandma wondered "How is it that no-one understands me here at home?" speaking in her dialect. There were people who understood us, but other people moved to where we lived on the hill of San Martin because all the houses were empty and we found ourselves . . . [Speaking about her grandma who did not understand the language of her neighbor, a Muslim]. Then I went to school and found that a different language existed that I did not understand. We didn't begin to learn Croat at the beginning, as is the case now, but in the fifth year. Then I began to understand slowly and I used to speak to my grandma. Poor grandma knew only three words, "thank you," "hello," and "good evening," she used to say. Three words, and a fourth one, "goodbye," that was all. My grandma was too old, but I learned it. [Speaking about the shameful occasion, when as a diligent schoolgirl she had to hand Tito a bouquet of flowers, but forgot the Croat words of welcome as she did not understand them.] Rights existed, there was everything, but my town changed, it was no longer as nice as it had once been. All the signs were in Croat, logically, nothing in Italian . . . I don't know if I felt like a foreigner in my homeland back then, but later I did.

While Slovene and Croat toponyms were strictly forbidden during the years of fascist repression before World War II, after Istria's annexation to Yugoslavia the previous Italian toponyms were replaced with Slovene and Croat names. The Slovenization of street names did not happen in one go but was a long process that began after 1945 and was most radical after 1958 (Cernaz 2008; Čebron Lipovec 2018: 107–8). As Vincent Veschambre (2008: 10) finds, it is through interventions in space through heritage and the destruction thereof, and new architectural constructions, and so forth, that colonizers change the toponymy to symbolically mark the new political power and their appropriation of the territory.

It is possible to gather from memories that many Italian speakers did not understand the new Slovene language, and they were therefore a target of psychological violence: "I still keep the letter written by my poor, desperate mother who was hospitalized in Piran in 1970. She wrote how terrible it was because she couldn't understand anyone—neither the doctor not the nurses. And even worse: they insulted her and shouted at her for not understanding Slovene" (Menih 2011: 89).

Vittoria remembers her mother on the Croat side of Istria who simply could not learn Croat after the war, even though she made an effort. Moreover, due to her Yugoslav surname, she was stereotyped as a false Italian, a converted Yugoslav:

[My mother] never learned Croat; my father did. However, my mother really tried. She attended courses but never learned it. . . . Besides, she had a Croat surname [ending in -ić] so they never answered her in Italian, only in Croat. . . . In our long conversations, she would always describe how in certain shops, at the post office, at the water pump, people were rude to you, refused to serve you, or left you out; you were invisible, they didn't see you, they left you out.

She had problems herself when she moved to Piran from the Croat part of Istria in the early 1970s. She was afraid of external social contact as it made her feel like a foreign element, driven to the edge of society.

Social relations were hard, life outside, in communication, going to the shops . . . I didn't speak Slovene yet; I spoke Italian. It was extremely difficult. I had to know in which shops the people would answer me in Italian. Also, because when I spoke Serbian, which I knew well [from her husband], Serbo-Croat, they were very rude to me. . . . Neither Italian, nor Serbo-Croat was OK. Neither of them. So this feeling grew . . . Of being pushed to the edge of society. Really pushed away, rejected, always considered a foreign element, of being problematic.

Ornella also describes the language barriers in the new Slovene society in Koper:

> Those who didn't have work . . . Began coming. And then we looked at each other . . . "Who are these people here?" It was crazy, they didn't understand us and we couldn't understand them. And then my mother spoke like a pidgin language, "I, Albina," "I, Tončka" . . . Crazy. But these Slovenes who arrived first, respected us, treated us as equals, never said anything rude to us.

Knowing that memory is a trace of the past in the present and that the past has no chronological framework, the sense of foreignness is logically stretched into an undefined period—a period "after," when the social picture in Istria changed completely as a result of the exodus. There are many similar testimonies, such as the occasion in Izola when they refused to serve her father Massimo because he spoke Italian. "There was an old tavern there before, an old one. She just said 'We speak Slovene here' and refused to serve him."

Jure Gombač (2005) also notices in archive sources that language was one of the main reasons for disputes between the Italian Istrians and the first new arrivals, as the latter did not want to conform to the (former) majority language in the towns and demanded communication in the language of the "victors."

As Elda and Antonella from Piran commented: "Everyone spoke Italian back then." "But who spoke Slovene here? No-one spoke Slovene here!"

There is an eloquent example from 1949 of a complaint by the authorities regarding the Italian language still being predominant in towns, especially in Koper: "As a rule, the political situation is very bad in towns such as Koper, Izola, and Piran, where the Italian element is very predominant."[17] A document from 1949[18] also mentions the predominance of the Italian language, or "Italian element," stating that 60 percent of the press is in Italian, 34 percent in Croat, and only 6 percent in Slovene. "The current policy demands there should be a strong emphasis on Slovene culture in the district of Koper as until now the Italian side has been emphasized too strongly. This side continues to dominate to this day, especially in Koper. It is found that bilingualism is not being respected, to the detriment of Slovenes. Slovene signs are of an improvised nature, and for the most part there are no Slovene signs at all, only Italian ones." One of the sources mentions that bilingualism will also be introduced with the removal of those people from public administration who cannot speak Slovene:[19] "Those 10 percent of protectors, who cannot speak Slovene or Croat, will be removed from posts where they come in contact with people."

As one man who stayed in Istria, although his application to opt was approved, said: "The atmosphere was difficult for us as we didn't know the language [Slovene]. When I was looking for my first job, I was handed a form to fill in, but I left it empty as I didn't understand the language" (Castelli 2018: 85). Other interlocutors, such as Angela, also mention how not knowing Slovene was a big hurdle when looking for work: "Also in offices. It was compulsory there. Because I didn't know Slovene back then, I learned it gradually while working. But if I had spoken Slovene as well as I do now, I would perhaps have been employed in public administration."

It is clear from the archival sources that in introducing bilingualism in Istria, they laid off or relocated officials who did not know Slovene. In their place they employed people who were loyal to the new authorities and who were capable of operating in both languages (Gombač 2005: 84). An important reason for leaving was the feeling of foreignness in the new linguistic and social-cultural environment, which demanded knowledge of Slovene for careers.

> Elda: [Speaking about the emptying of Piran.] It emptied completely because they were all Italians, and also because many of them worked as sailors on ships. That's why they left because they already had jobs.
> Antonella: It was because of jobs, wasn't it.
> Elda: The last to leave were those who didn't have work, who didn't have anything. And you know what else . . .
> Antonella: What our grandma, who left, said: "But who will I talk to . . ."
> Elda: For the schools, for everything . . . That was the beginning . . .
> Antonella: And if you didn't speak Slovene . . .
> Elda: My brother . . . Mine didn't know any Slovene . . .
> Antonella: They didn't get work . . .
> Katja: There was no more work, was that the main reason?
> Elda: Yes, of course, like everywhere else.
> Antonella: There was a shortage of all the job profiles of those who left— at least that's what I was told—engineers, doctors, school teachers.

After World War II, the situation was turned upside down. Free at last from the yoke of violent fascism, the "victors" demanded their national rights in the newly liberated territory and despised everything that reminded them of the previous occupier's system, although evidently the "teething troubles" of establishing the new official language were quite serious. However, these complaints clearly show that the authorities did not introduce the new language in a violent way. As Mila Orlić (2019: 569–90) observes, in the Croat part of Istria it was the Croat press that was the key element of the "Slav reawakening," along with the changing of toponyms and surnames. However, the people only knew the Istrian dialect (and not the official Croat language) and were educated only in Italian schools.

As a result of indirect pressure and negative perceptions, it was evidently better for Italians to adapt to the new system and language as best they could, as has already been shown by the decisions to send children to Slovene schools. The following extract from a biography describes the process of adapting to the new system and forgetting Italianness:

> You know, I spoke the language [Italian] well, but after the war we weren't allowed, we had to speak only Slovene. . . . The teachers indoctrinated us. When I was eighteen, I fell out with all my relatives. . . . I told them they were fascists; and that they went to Italy because they were fascists while we stayed here. . . . Around 1975, I slowly began to realize I was Italian, that I had Italian culture. My mother was really Italian, although she didn't bring me up in this spirit. We lived here, and you simply accept what's closest. My name probably appears on some list, although I was a member of the Communist Party. . . . As a professor—I taught at the Italian school until 1985? . . . I felt a certain distrust in our society. . . . They still see you as a foreigner. You're a foreigner at home, where you were born, where your family built a house, worked, paid taxes. (Pahor 2007: 55–56, 59–60)

After the war, the social situation was turned on its head. If before the war communication in Slovene was considered shameful, after the war it was the opposite. That is why people adapted to the new social norms, which meant Italian speakers learned Slovene through contact with the new arrivals.

> [Speaking about how they didn't understand Slovene in her family.] When it was still Italy and someone—like a tourist—came past and spoke with my grandma, who didn't understand, she would say: "Wait, I'll fetch Mrs. Ana who may be able to help you." And she would say: "No, absolutely not. How can you allow yourself to ask something like that!" But when Yugoslavia came, she spoke Slovene very well. In short, they went to mass, and I heard the daughter speaking. . . Next to me, I thought it was in Italian, but they spoke during the mass in Slovene, so they knew it but didn't want others to know that . . . In short, it was in a way, how can I put it, "I don't want you to understand who I am." This was the only family that could, how can I say—that spoke it, perhaps a little, but they spoke it. While all the others who came, they all spoke Slovene, these neighbors of ours . . . But we always had good relations, even if we didn't understand each other [speaking about learning her first words of Slovene through contact with children].

Although in the narratives heard so far, most of the feelings of foreignness have stemmed from not knowing the new language, foreignness is not connected only with the linguistic environment or a different place of origin. The environment may also determine you as a foreigner for other reasons, and proceed to exclude you from its community. This is described by an *esule* from Izola who lost his job and could not even make a living selling vegetables in the market because he was considered a fascist.

> It wasn't even a case of them being expelled, they simply had to go if they wanted to survive . . . They were in effect economically incapacitated; they lost their jobs [officials], then they tried selling the vegetables from their garden but no-one wanted to buy them. In short, they became poor; they were literally hungry, so they packed their bags and went to Trieste. One of this lady's brothers never returned to Izola because of his feeling of sadness, although he lives in Mestre [approx. 200 km away].[20]

As Simona Cerutti finds, becoming a foreigner does not depend only on geographical or territorial origin, but also stems from the incapacity to appropriate a sense of local belonging; in a particular moment of their life, an individual is seen as a foreigner, so their full access to local resources is hindered (Cerutti 2012; Baussant and Foscarini 2017). As we will see below in connection with social boundaries, the concept of foreignness—like identity—is not fixed, but changes depending on changes in socio-political reality.

The report by the mixed Slovene-Italian commission found that one of the reasons for the unease of Istrian Italians at the change in regime was the new regime's persecution of religion in the case of the Italian clergy. This inadvertently became a denationalizing element (Kacin Wohinz and Troha 2001: 17). Historians mention the fact that the Yugoslav authorities exerted pressure on the Italian-speaking clergy, culminating in the attack on the archbishop of Trieste and Koper Antonio Santin during a visit to his diocese in June 1947 (Corni 2018: 61). Bishop Santin supported Italian national politics, and this caused a rift with the Slovene clergy, which strove for Slovene national emancipation (Blasina 1993). In the eyes of the Yugoslav authorities, priests were seen as agents spreading propaganda in favor of emigration by organizing religious processions, which were supposed to be attended only by Italians. This was thought to prevent their development in the "socialist reality." Priests were also believed to be promoting opting by persuading people that the faith could be freely expressed outside Yugoslavia—in Italy or Australia (Gombač 2005: 85, 94; 2015: 123). Amalia, an Istrian of

Italian origin, felt that the ban on religious ceremonies—in addition to the new language—was another form of pressure exerted by the new authorities to prevent the expression of one's identity. Although, unlike her grandma who practiced her religion, she does not practice religion; she says it was more a problem of limiting the freedom to express oneself and one's tradition and heritage:

> And we found ourselves together because the new arrivals, how should I say, also had different traditions. One of our traditions was the Christian religion. [Speaking about her grandma's religiosity and that of her family.] She went to church, but not everyone could as the Church was not respected. And then there were our feasts—Christmas, Easter, and so on . . . Our traditions meant a lot to us, and we did things like in the past. But these things that were connected with Church traditions were not seen in a good light. And that's not all. People were afraid of going to church. I'm telling the truth. [Speaking about decorating a Christmas tree in secret and traditional Easter dishes.] Yes, my grandma always went to church. But she was already older, she didn't work . . . But for people who had jobs, it was hard. I still have this, this fear of expressing how I feel. And I'm not religious, even if my grandma was, but it's a question of being free to do something or not. . . . More than many other problems, many feelings, not being free, not physical freedom, but freedom of expression, to do things as you did them before. [Speaking about multiculturalism, in which freedom of expression is essential.]

Or as Michela commented sarcastically, "In Yugoslavia, in Croatia all the saints died," which of course is not valid only for Istria. From an ethnological point of view, tradition is used to create groups, and at the same time it is an instrument of identity politics, but it can also be the medium that indicates a group's disintegration. Tradition creates and confirms a sense of identity. Cooperating and sharing common traditions in a particular group enables group members to feel they are part of it, regardless if this is on a national, regional, or family level. As tradition gives us a feeling of belonging, we become attached to it. It can connect us with past generations, through ethnic or religious identity or with certain people. The more we are attached to an identity, the harder we will try not to lose this tradition (Mugnaini 2004; Lenclud 2004; Habinc 2009; Poljak Istenič 2012: 88). Feasts (and tradition) are not just symbolic acts, which unite members of a homogeneous community and speak about its values, but according to agency theory, power relations may be recognized through them (Habinc 2009: 32). By suppressing a group's tradition, we indirectly suppress the group's identity. In socialist Yugoslavia, religious groups had to withdraw from public life and go into hiding, as power and with it the right to public expression were taken over by other groups and celebrations connected with the new state (Habinc 2009). The Italians felt this extra pressure as just another in a series that made them feel insecure and afraid to express their Italian identity (Hrobat Virloget 2014: 231–32).

The feeling of being confined by not being free to express their faith was just another aspect of the foreignness experienced by the Italians in Istria. They were also increasingly pushed to the edge of society in their working lives—something that was increasingly reflected in the reversal of social roles. Massimo, an Istrian Italian from Izola, uses the example of his father's professional demotion to explain that all the important jobs were increasingly being held by people from Slovenia's interior, while the Italians were losing their previous (leading) positions and also leaving because of this:

> Italian was spoken everywhere here after the war, in the town halls, everywhere, and it was in those years that large numbers of people came from Štajerska, because they wanted to Slovenize, or how should I say, fill this territory with people who weren't here before. And that's why enormous numbers of Italians, natives I'd say, who were born here generations ago, were forced to move away. We almost left ourselves. . . . Because my father was a secretary at the town hall, and then it happened . . . So, he didn't agree with this immigration, with the things that were happening because . . . What happened . . . They appointed mostly people from Štajerska, and they put them in leading positions. So now . . . But they never felt like locals. They cared for Štajerska. . . . That's that side of the story and then it so happened that my father became a driver. . . . I don't know, I think he was laid off . . . I was only small then, I was eight or nine. But, I would say, he suddenly became a warehouse employee, driver, or something like that. In those times, some people moved out or fled to Italy because of this.

Mario, an Istrian of Italian origin also speaks about the new leadership that ousted the Italian one: "They came from Croatia, from Slavonia, from Bosnia, even Serbia. The offices were full of them. They were in charge; they were leading. Like that, overnight . . . They pushed our ones away. You were *costretto de andar*! [forced to leave] You were forced."

The new postwar regime in Istria caused a reversal in social positions at all levels, beginning with the professional level, and this is certainly one of the complex reasons for Italian emigration. The new Yugoslav social system turned on its head a decades-old social system of "superior Italian civilization and Slav barbarism" under fascism. The Italians had for a long time looked upon Slovenes and Croats as though they were subhuman—*sc'avi*—while fascism and Nazism inculcated in them a feeling of superiority and the conviction that Istria belongs to Italy (Ballinger 2003; Pirjevec 2012: 151; Verginella 2015; Kosmač 2017: 134). Lucija, who moved from the Vipava Valley to Dekani and then to Koper in 1948, says one of the reasons for the departure of Italians was their feeling of cultural superiority:

> L: The first reason is that they were afraid of the new government because, the bourgeoisie in particular, were not pro-fascists, but they weren't anti-fascists either. They weren't anti-fascists, not the majority. Koper . . . had the worst fascists, the *squadristi* . . . [Talking about surnames.] Well, some of them were definitely politically engaged as fascists. But most of them were neutral, yet tacitly in favor. I'm not talking now about the militant fascists, but people explained to me how they helped fascism, therefore Mussolini's social project, to succeed. They grew maize on their window sills; a very large number of them did that. . . . Of course, these people here, faced with the possibility that the partisans, the *Slavi*, the *družeti* were coming, said.
> K: Yes, *družeti*. Do you yourself remember that they said *družeti*?
> J: Yes . . . *La xe del druxe* [She's the *druže*'s daughter], that was me. . . .
> K: But because they called you that, did they also treat you differently?
> L: . . . Absolutely not. The first reason was this inclination. I won't say for fascist terrorism, but for example, this Italianness, culture and also in literature—which you can read—they considered us to be illiterate. I held a literary evening with Tomšič in Trieste, in the Istrian club . . . and those who are leftists . . . And then a man from Pula, a writer, stood up and said: "Excuse me madam, but we didn't understand. Only now do we understand that our Slavs are not illiterate. And that they have culture, and what culture, but we didn't understand any of this before." . . . So, those people left who couldn't accept that this culture that had previously been scorned was now equal to them or even in power. Then there were those who remained . . ., a lady from Piran, a native, told me so many times. Some of the natives: "But the Slavs are also good people," that's why they gave her strange looks.

The educated Italian speakers, officials, and school staff moved out because they did not want to relinquish their senior positions and conform to the new situation in which the people they considered inferior became their equals or superiors (Volk 2003: 39). Claudio, a Slovene Istrian who held various senior positions (director of different companies), says the reasons for the emigration of Italians included a feeling of superiority, not belonging to the new state, rejection of changes connected with the reversal of social roles when the *sc'avi* became equals of

the Italians (see also Nemec 2012b: 202), and the fact that they failed to
see a future in the new system.

> C: Well, and when this happened in 1954, the Italian population saw
> there was no more room for them here. Grandpas and old people who
> had nowhere to go, or people who were particularly attached to their
> house and so on, stayed. But few, very few remained. The others . . . In
> droves! . . . Because here [in Piran] they felt . . . superfluous! Before we
> were unwanted, and suddenly they became unwanted, so that's how they
> felt and that's why 90 percent of them left! Because they saw no future
> here. Some of them stayed, but most left. Fewer of them left Izola. . . .
> Well, and I tell you that politics did its own share. Why? The Italian
> right—what remained of fascism—said: "Go, go away from there! The
> *Žlavi* [Slavs] live there. They will do this and that to you. They will take
> revenge! Go away from there!" Well, and that was the propaganda. One
> side. Our side had a different policy: "Let them go!" They didn't lift a
> finger to stop them! "Thank God, let them go!" Well, that's how it was.
> And we the locals, who were attached like those who left to our home
> towns and villages, to watch people leaving for no particular reason . . .
> "But this is your home, you were born here, your great, great [grandfa-
> ther] is from here, but now . . ." "Yes, but what will I do here, yes, but
> what about the schools here, they will be Slovene now, and . . ." Basi-
> cally, it was . . . Terrible! Terrible! For those who left and for those of us
> who stayed! Some of us, who knew they didn't like us—they never liked
> us who were second-class citizens—we said: "Thank God! Go!" But we
> didn't actually escort anyone or say: "Go!" Because some say—the politi-
> cians, right-wingers on the other side, that we booted them out. But it's
> not true! We didn't force anyone to leave! On the contrary! We tried to
> persuade them to stay! But they didn't see any future! Not in culture, not
> in the education system, not even in employment, nothing! . . . But . . .
> A house is a house. There were farmers who had land down in Istria. They
> left everything and they went. They went over there, and only when they
> got there did they see what was waiting for them.
> K: And why? Did everything go to ruin here or why was . . . I mean, if . . .
> Did their businesses collapse in this time or . . . Why didn't they see a
> future?
> C: First, they felt alienated. Like this was no longer their homeland.
> They were Italians, Italy was on the other side. This was Yugoslavia. They
> weren't Yugoslavs. Just like we were second-class citizens under Italy—
> we the Slavs—while they weren't, they expected to become what we
> had been, second-class citizens. The others there invited them to come.
> "Come, come, come, here you will have this and that . . ." There was
> also propaganda, politics, because this was their way of proving, politics,
> "Look what they're doing, they're kicking our people out!" No, we didn't
> force anyone to go. That's just how it happened. [Speaking about refugee

centers.] Because there weren't any houses and flats and jobs waiting for them. Oh no! They lived there [in refugee centers] for years!

Rafael, Claudio's brother, a teacher and recognized sportsman, also highlights the Italian incitement against the so-called *titini*, Italian propaganda and Yugoslavia's neutral attitude to emigration. He differentiates between Istrian Italians who were haughty, those who were hostile, and those who were "our equals":

> To begin with, I'll be like a left-wing politician, but I'll tell the truth. The Church played an important role. The Church. "The *titini* are here," I don't know if you've heard this nickname *titini*. "They're dangerous; they're this and that. Go to Italy, you'll get everything. You don't belong here; go where you belong." And this was such strong propaganda that some naively left and then really regretted it! That they had gone. But they went! And left everything behind! . . . To live in shacks!!! [Speaking about the terrible conditions in the refugee centers.] Some left out of principle because of their conviction, out of hatred for us and so on. But the vast majority left through naivety. I must add that our propaganda was also bad. Poor propaganda. Like, "They want to go, let them go! Let them go! Let them go!" Why? Because people from all over Slovenia could hardly wait to move here. And in a couple of years this fluctuation was so great that . . .

As has already been mentioned, both conversations again show the unclear position of the Yugoslav authorities regarding emigration. On the one hand, some were prevented from leaving, while others were allowed or encouraged to go. It has already been shown that there were different attitudes at different times and in different places—as though there was no common strategy—and it was not until after the Udine Agreement in 1955 that the Yugoslav authorities stopped hindering emigration (Gombač 2005: 94; Corni 2018). Both brothers confirm that there was strong Italian propaganda, including incitement of fear of the socialist system. Gianfranco, who comes from an ethnically mixed family, also testifies to the strong Italian propaganda and particularly emphasizes the influence of the CLN:

> G: "If you sign up to go to Trieste, we will write . . ." They wanted as many people as possible, to sign up, to go up, who will quickly come back under Italy.
> K: The logic was that they would come back?
> G: Back, yes. They put them all . . . Here it was so, they always thought . . . The more of us go up, to show the Americans that Istria, that we are in favor of Italy, not Yugoslavia. This was the work of the CLN.

The Yugoslav newspapers back then blamed the exodus on the CLN, and they also considered it to be the source of "Italian chauvinism and irredentism," that fanned the flames of hatred between Italians and Slovenes (Gombač 2015: 122). As Piero Purini (2010) writes, pro-Italian organizations began openly pressuring the Italian population to emigrate, giving reasons similar to those for the mass exodus from Rijeka—"to show the compactness of the Italianness of the territory and the injustice of its annexation to Yugoslavia" (Purini 2010: 248). Similarly, Sandi Volk (2003: 40) believes that mass departures were seen as "plebiscites for the Italianness" of Istria's population, and that they were intended (unsuccessfully) to be a form of pressure in international negotiations concerning Istria's belonging. Gloria Nemec believes this is an argument of the old Yugoslav historiography, as in her opinion testimonies do not confirm this theory. She also believes that the Italian government tried to prevent mass migrations, at least until a diplomatic solution was reached. Keeping as many Italians as possible in the disputed territory was thought to give more weight to diplomatic demands for territory (Nemec 2012b: 204–5). The memories of both Italians and Slovenes that I recorded showed otherwise. Most of them, especially the Slovenes, emphasized that the Italian propaganda was a strong factor in the exodus. The Italian Radio Venezia-Giulia was a powerful pro-Italian propaganda machine, whose target audience were the Italians in Istria and the Julian March from the end of World War II until the London Memorandum. The radio tried to influence the Italian population in both regions by opposing and criticizing the Yugoslav authorities. There was a constant struggle for control, or at least mutual obstruction, between Zones A and B, and Radio Trieste (which later became Radio Koper under the control of the Yugoslav authorities) was also involved in this struggle. Even Tito tried proving to foreign diplomats that Radio Venezia-Giulia clearly expressed territorial aspirations not only for Zone B, but also for the rest of Istria and Dalmatia (Spazzali 2013; Han 2014). Neither should we forget the role played by Radio Koper / Capodistria, which was founded in 1949.

In any case, a domino effect was triggered. Thousands of people left Istria (Purini 2010: 248–94) for very different reasons (political, economic, psychological), and this will be discussed below.

The Dilemma of Whether to Stay or Go

Many interlocutors speak of mass emigration as the consequence of a chain reaction that only rare individuals resisted. This was the experience of Luisa, who moved from Trieste to the surroundings of Izola in

1932. Her parents were originally from Istria and the Triestine Karst. She is also an example of hybrid borderland identities. While living in Trieste, they spoke both Slovene and Italian at home, but in Istria, her language of communication became Italian:

> They were afraid there would be this or that. And they left everything and went away. I also told my mother when we remained on our own. "Mother," I said, "let's go from where you came from." But she said she wouldn't go [to the refugee centers, she'd rather die at home]. Me, what did I do? What should I do? I don't know. Leave her alone? She was already old. I didn't even feel like getting married. To leave my mother alone, hmmm . . . The border crossings were closing. It would not be possible to come down in future. What would we do then? Mother could die! No-one knows what may happen. So I stayed here with my mother. There you are.

The predominant Slovene discourse states that the mass exodus was the result of herd mentality. Those who remained often consider the emigration to have been caused by herd mentality, and they consider the *esuli* to have been weak opportunists, attracted by the promise of a better standard of life in Italy (Nemec 2012b: 203). Almost all of my interlocutors of Italian origin were on the point of opting, but the decision to stay was made at the last minute. This is what happened with Valeria's family, in which the decision to "opt" was rejected by her grandma because she was afraid of having to live as a refugee:

> [They had agreed that a family that had already emigrated to Trieste would take in their grandma while they would go to a refugee center.] I remember, it was 5 January 1955, my birthday; I was 14. [A neighbor came to tell grandma that she would not opt.] On that day she sat on a chair by the window with her arms folded in her lap, and I had these applications [for opting] in my hand. My mother was at the door wearing a headscarf. And there was I with these applications in my hand . . . Still filling out the application. . . . And my grandma said: "I'm not going!" "What do you mean you're not going? But we've agreed to go; we've written the applications, including for you?" "No, I'm not going. I've a roof over my head here; I own this house, I can do my own things . . ." That's how it was. She was seventy-eight at the time. "To go out into the world now, no, I'm not going!" I could have handed in our application, but as I watched my mother standing in the doorway, with red eyes and in tears, I tore the application into a thousand pieces. I don't believe I ever regretted it.

People decided to stay at the last minute—to stay with elderly members of the family or out of fear of the unknown, being refugees, wandering around the world, and living a miserable existence in refugee centers in Italy.[21] In her study of the memories of the Italian minority in Croatia, the historian Gloria Nemec (2012b: 181–82) noticed that a small number of Istrian Italians abandoned their plans to emigrate or gave up this possibility because of their involvement with the new authorities, a poor level of professionalization, skepticism regarding what Italy was offering, and responsibility for older people and young people. There were even some who left but then returned because they felt so attached to their home town or village.

Faced with a future living in refugee centers in Italy, many people, including Giulia's family, decided to stay home, where they at least had a "roof over their heads":

> We should have gone too. We had practically filled everything out. My father was a farmer, he had no connections with the authorities, neither before nor after. . . . He worked in fields that didn't belong to him. . . . He was a proletarian through and through. But a proletarian without any ideological connections with anyone. . . . And of course, he filled out all the applications to leave. Then we went one Sunday . . . It was in 1954; I was twelve. We went to Trieste and Padriciano, where we had relatives. We visited our cousin. . . . And when he saw the conditions in which people lived, he said: "I'm not coming to live here." He said: "I have my own house, the worst they can do is kill me . . . But to live the life of a prisoner, no . . ." That's why we stayed.

Although her father tried to escape because his application to "opt" was rejected, Amalia's grandfathers decided to stay because they had already experienced what life was like as a refugee or migrant:

> When families were deciding whether to stay or go, there were people who didn't want to leave. My grandma said: "During World War I, I was in Wagna . . .," that she was in Hungary and then in Wagna, "come what may, I'm not leaving home again!" And my grandpa, logically, agreed with her—also because he had socialist tendencies. [Speaking about the family splitting up.]

While towns and villages were emptying, the opposite phenomenon was happening simultaneously—people were changing their minds about their applications to "opt." The first reason was that the Istrians were informed about the difficult living conditions in the refugee centers. These did not conform to the idea of a "free and flourishing world" that had been proclaimed during the previous years. The other reason was that Yugoslav politics gradually changed, especially after the Informbiro dispute when the Soviet development model was abandoned (M. Orlić 2019: 582–83). The stories of *esuli* who returned were particularly highlighted by Istrian media. They said the refugee centers were like "concentration camps" or "death camps." They described how they were attacked by irredentists and how they waited in vain to register, and of centers that organized further overseas voyages. The disappointment of those who had suffered only hunger, hospitalization, and humiliation in the capitalist "paradise" were supposed to serve as an example to all who yearned to leave (Nemec 2012b: 194–95). As has already been shown in the section on control, those who changed their minds after having handed in their application to "opt" had to prove their allegiance to the Yugoslav authorities by inciting people against Italy and against the optants. Even nowadays, a fair number of people who live in Istria commented that many *esuli* regretted leaving. For example, Mario quotes an *esule* who believes that "those who stayed here live like lords" and that "some came back, still think of coming back, but the houses in which they lived before are now inhabited by other people."

Maria's family also decided not to leave because they had been frightened by what they saw. She says she burst into tears when she arrived in the refugee center in Padriciano/Padriče. It was clear from the conversation that the decision to stay was almost harder than the decision to leave, as most of my interlocutors were left without their families, both immediate and extended. As Maria's husband explained, his father stayed because he wanted to have a roof over his head; only richer people departed: "[The father:] 'That they would send me up into some village and give us a house there . . . My house is here, I have my own land, where should I go? I'm not going.' . . . And we didn't go, none of us. Only one family went up . . ., he left. He was a richer farmer."

Many interlocutors spoke of richer farmers who left everything or were dispossessed. The story of the president of a French association of *esuli* in Paris is heart-breaking, but not unique. Alberto left Istria as a young man. He was the only person from his family to leave—in search of a better life and to study in Trieste. He cried as he told the tragic story of his trustee—a rich farmer who experienced desperate disappointment after the exodus robbed him of his rich world in Istria and made him a "nobody" in the "promised" land, marginalized, on the edge of society like a pauper, a foreigner and an unwanted *esule*, which is why he committed suicide:

> I was happy then . . . After all, I was going to study. . . . Now, when I think back, I can see the faces of all the people who returned to Verteneglio . . . Yes, because here . . . My trustee committed suicide after one year . . .

> Because he went from his own world into a world where nothing was left of him, he was nothing . . . He had a shop. . . . There was no more trading, no shop . . . He went from a life in which he had fields, land . . . He produced wine, oil . . . To come to Trieste . . . Where he was nothing. His old friend employed him. . . . It didn't last long, then he committed suicide . . . To come to nothing . . . He didn't find anything . . . of what he had dreamed of . . . He hoped . . .

Throughout Italy, the *esuli* were labeled fascists by the local population. They were welcomed reluctantly, with hatred, and sometimes ghettoized and isolated, even after they had moved out of the refugee centers (Fakin and Jerman 2004; M. Orlić 2015: 479–80; Castelli 2018: 42–43). This meant they were ascribed the ungrateful role of fascists on the Yugoslav side, and communists or fascists on the Italian side as Štelio, an Istrian of Slovene origin, comments. "The worst thing that these *esuli*—of whom I know many—experienced is . . . That they were considered fascists here . . . Up there as communists . . . Neither black nor white . . ." Or as one of them who was never a fascist said, "we were fascists here and fascists there!" (Nemec 2012b: 194). Vittoria says the same: "They too were fascists. But they weren't. And we were also fascists. Although born later in Yugoslavia . . . And always fascists."

In these dilemmas of whether to stay or follow the masses, both studies and memories indicate that emigration was greatest from the coastal towns. In the discussion that accompanied the presentation of the book by Lucia Castelli (2018) on the memories of those who left and those who stayed, one of the latter said that more people left the towns because they were not attached to the land like farmers. Besides, they confiscated their shops, among other things. It was his farm and his land that made his father decide not to leave. The Italian native commented that more people left the towns than the villages because in the villages there was less fear caused by the media, and less fear of coexistence with the Slovenes: "In the countryside, people didn't have radios; there were no newspapers; and they had relationships with their Slovene neighbors . . . They knew each other, got on well, so there wasn't that much fear. Unlike in Capodistria, Isola, Pirano . . ." ("Nino e i suoi ricordi di Giusterna" 2009: 29).

Interestingly, an analysis of permits for Italy from the district of Koper shows a different picture. Out of 4,160 permit holders—and a further 5,996 family members connected with them—the largest proportion were farmers (1,197), who found it hard to leave their land. They were followed by 722 housewives, 549 workers, 447 pensioners, and 129 fishermen (Gombač 2005: 120). It is important not to forget that many of Koper's citizens were farmers who had land outside the town, as is confirmed by most of the interlocutors. The above memories are confirmed by most historical studies as most of the Italian population were urban dwellers, as writes Aleksej Kalc (2019: 146, 149), so the consequences of the exodus were most evident in the towns, where their share of the population fell from 91 percent to only 10 percent between the years 1945 and 1956.

Who Stayed?

As is widely believed in both Slovenia and Italy, quite a number of Italians in Istria stayed because of their ideological convictions, that is, their belief in communism and socialism. In a number of interviews, Vittoria remembers her father who stayed despite his wife's objections, due to his deep faith in socialism, which he was convinced would conquer nationalism. He was also a partisan, the son of a socialist who died in prison convicted by the fascist court in the province of Reggio Emilia:

> My mother wanted to leave, after 1951 she applied to opt, she wanted to go but there was no way my father was going, despite having some problems with the party. He always believed these were only mistakes on the road to socialism and communism becoming established and that sooner or later things would sort themselves out; that nationalism cannot win. [He left the party out of disillusionment in 1970.] He was in favor of Yugoslavia. He wanted a more just, social state. It was not important to him if that was Italy or Yugoslavia—at that time Yugoslavia was promising this. He wanted to live in a socialist, communist state and nowhere else. But he never thought he would feel threatened because of his linguistic and cultural identity. Never. And that's where the betrayal began, and they felt abandoned by everyone because for as long as he lived in Rovigno—where most of the population was still Italian—things were OK. But even there, a rift occurred between those in favor of Tito and those who favored Stalin.

The dilemma between ideology and ethnic identity faced by Italian socialists is also highlighted by historian Alessandra Argenti Tremul, who notices that the memories of Italian partisans in the Yugoslav national liberation army reflect discord with members of the nations of the Socialist Federal Republic of Yugoslavia. The latter were not only fighting for their freedom but also for their country, while the former were only fighting for the idea of international socialism/communism. When Trieste was liberated, the laboring masses in Trieste who supported the establishment of a socialist state were surprised that the partisans raised Slovene and Yugoslav flags and not the red flag (Argenti Tremul 2016). If we remember all the Triestine workers who came to Yugoslavia to "build socialism" and were forced to leave after the Informbiro dispute, and if we compare this with the declarations made by Italian socialists like the above, then we may confirm the previous findings that Italian families with anti-fascist and socialist views were bitterly disappointed by socialist Yugoslavia and its promises of brotherhood and unity of all nations when they experienced Yugoslav nationalism and collective criminalization (Ballinger 2003: 129–67, 207–44; Nemec 2015). Disappointment with the criminalization of Italian anti-fascists, who were frequently equated in the Yugoslav perception with the stereotype of Italian—fascist—is also evident in the comment made in passing by a cultural figure of Italian origin from the Slovenian part of Istria. "My father was a teacher, and he was punished by the fascists for refusing to wear the fascist uniform, then he was imprisoned in Yugoslavia for being Italian" (note in field diary).

There are also written archive sources that show that people stayed for ideological reasons. Alongside the fear of Koper losing good workers, the district committee also believed the capitalists were leaving, while for those who stayed, "political belonging was more important than the nation" (Gombač 2005: 93). This was the situation of a family from Piran that chose to stay despite having to tolerate various forms of "mischief" and hear people in the streets shouting that the Italians should go away: "My father was the eldest brother in his family. . . . He was never actively involved in politics, but he had a socialist way of thinking. If he could, he always helped those in need, and he was in favor of just relations in society. That's also why he stayed here. Although he was provoked [speaking about the persecution of Italians in the streets]." (Pahor 2007: 55).

Some believe that the wealthier people and the intellectual elite left in greater numbers, as they were most affected in the new system by the socialist measures against the richer classes. Meanwhile fewer people from the lower classes are supposed to have left due to their faith in a better life and equality under socialism. It is, however, evident that these people also left, enticed by promises of "a better life" in Italy. A lady from Piran, of Italian origin, remarks that most of the wealthier people and the elite left, and only the poor stayed. "They all left . . ., the engineers, doctors, teachers. . . . Only those who couldn't afford to leave and who weren't educated stayed." Although she spoke earlier about pressure exerted on the Italians and said that it is not good to speak publicly about this, she added: "You didn't actually need much courage to stay. If I don't provoke you, you won't provoke me either." However, in contrast to this statement that emphasizes courage, I think that in light of the mass emigration, more courage was needed to stay than to leave. The Italian Ornella describes—with a fair dose of irony—the example of her father who, like most of the poorer population, stayed because he believed in socialism and that the rich and the poor would become equals:

> Who stayed? Those with hungry mouths like my father who said: "Dead here or there, what should I take?" What's more, my father believed in communism because communists, what were they? Poor people who hoped that with communism they would have something like the rich do. "We too will become high society [It. *siori*], we will also eat bread like the rich people." They always made these comparisons with high society. My mother also worked "for high society." And so this communism, which promised that "we will all be equal, everything will be wonderful, all brothers . . ." Of course, my father who was poor dreamed of this communism . . . So why should he go to Italy if he had communism here. And then there were many of these Slovenes coming from Italy, these Italians coming from Italy, who were politically persecuted, they came here [names]. They all came from Italy because they had problems with the authorities there.

As will be evident in the section on immigration, the Slovenes, who moved back to Istria from Trieste where they had sought refuge from fascist violence, were joined also by the already-mentioned Italian working class, which came out of ideological reasons in the so-called "counter-exodus." These ideological immigrants from Monfalcone and Friuli are mentioned by Elda, whose husband—who was also a mayor in Istria—was part of this wave: "From Friuli, from Italy. They were from Ronchi, where the airport is, all the way to Udine, all those villages there. . . . Yes, they stayed in Yugoslavia, in Slovenia. Because they had Tito, they stayed because of Tito."

The decision to stay or to go depended largely on the extent to which an individual could adapt to the new political system and the socio-linguistic environment. Maria, of Italian origin, who is married to someone from a Slovene Istrian family, remembers how she adapted quickly and learned the new language because of work:

> [In the refugee center in Italy.] "And you who are so young stayed?" "No," I said, "firstly because I loved my parents and I am Italian . . ." When I had to learn the language, I also learned Slovene because I had to learn my trade [as a seamstress]. [At school in Vipava.] My teacher said, "Don't be afraid!" He was a little older. "If you can't speak Slovene, just speak Italian." . . . And I said: "Those who went to Trieste and America had to learn a language." So I took this attitude.

Or as Giulio quoted his father, a farmer, who decided to stay after seeing the miserable life in the refugee centers: "I survived fascism, I'll survive communism. I'm not going away from here!"

It would be wrong to think that only those who believed in socialist ideas stayed in Istria. It would also be wrong to believe that only those with hybrid identities decided to stay, especially those from ethnically mixed families, as we have seen the difficulties they had learning the new languages—Slovene or Croat. However, it seems that this idea prevails in the broader Italian discourse, and even in the more open left-wing discourse. I began to wonder about this after a discussion on those who stayed—based on the title of my lecture—together with the famous Italian ethnologist Fabio Mugnaini from the University of Siena who organized a sort of counterbalance to the historical revisionism of Italian historical discourse prior to the day of remembrance in 2021, in cooperation with the Italian partisan association (ANPI).[22] When I proposed to call my lecture "The Forgotten Ones: The Italians who Remained in Yugoslav Istria," he said he doubted if these ethnically mixed identities in Istria can be called Italian, but his doubt was dispelled after he heard my argumentation. Basically, those who stayed were not only those with mixed identities, and they did not stay exclusively because of socialism. The people who stayed were ordinary people who did not want to have anything to do with any political side. I was struck by the comment that it was primarily the townspeople who left because they were influenced by media propaganda and fear. Meanwhile, the rural people did not have access to the media and, unlike the urban dwellers, lived in a more multicultural environment where they coexisted with the Slovenians and Croatians and were therefore not as afraid of the Yugoslav *titini*. It is in this light that we may understand the comments made by Elda from Piran who said that the elite left and "everyone was missing: engineers, even doctors and teachers," and only the elderly and the poor remained.

> Only a few of them stayed then, these natives like in Capodistria, Isola . . . Only the oldest people remained, or those who . . . But the others left. How could I put it . . . They put pressure on them, they told them this and that . . . [Quite a lot of interview content in between.] The people back then, only those remained who couldn't go away, who were uneducated, something like that.

It is interesting that Elda's husband was a mayor in an Istrian town, so he probably did not come from a lower social class. However, it is true that most memories and also Italian historiography tell the same story (e.g., Pupo, Nemec). Mass emigration took place primarily from Italian urban environments and most of those who left belonged to the upper classes, the ones hardest hit by the socialist economic measures and who probably felt that the expression of their national identity was under greater pressure. Those who stayed were people in the countryside, farmers attached to their land, older people, poorer people, and those more accustomed to interethnic coexistence who were not connected to any political or ideological system. We have heard a number of old people relate how young people did not leave for the "promised land" because their parents or grandparents decided not to go. Of course, this is not a rule; we also know that some villages emptied completely—as Tomizza writes in the case of his Materada—which only proves that the situation was very complex, and general conclusions are difficult to make.

Voluntary Migrations?

Testimonies about deciding whether to move out or remain therefore go against some highly simplified explanations—especially on the Italian side—which only highlight ethnic reasons. These are present in the fear that in the new Yugoslav state, Italians would no longer be able to express their ethnic identity—something that seemed increasingly realistic with the arrival of growing numbers of Slovene speakers. On top of that, their identity was undesired and despised in the dominant discourse due to collective criminalization. On the other hand, we have seen that politics failed to guarantee all the national rights of Italians despite the principle of "Yugoslav-Italian brotherhood."

However, these are only some of the many different fears that existed in this complex decision-making process. Emigration was caused by diverse reasons connected with the new delimitation of territory and the new political and ideological state system—from the uncertain economic circumstances and socialist economic measures that affected above all the wealthier, Italian population, to the establishment of the state border and the cutting of economic and social ties, feelings of being a foreigner at home, negative perceptions of Italians as fascists, pressure felt due to not knowing the new dominant language (Slovene), direct and indirect intimidation, as well as strong pro-Italian propaganda, promises of a better life, an attempt to prevent the severing of family ties with the departure of the majority, and so on.

Most Slovenian and Croat historians insist that the migrations were voluntary, and from the point of view of the legal possibility of opting, this is true. As Giulio, an Italian politician commented, for Slovenians, the *esuli* are optants, but were they really free to decide?

The president . . . does not speak about the exodus. He talks about optants. Slovenian politics talks about optants. To be an optant means you have the freedom to choose. But it was not a free choice. For none of the 5,000, or even 7,000 individuals who left [Izola]. It was not a free choice. . . . There was a moment when 7,000 people decided to leave because they were given this possibility. But there was no attempt to stop them. "My dear people, you're leaving everything, your home, your cemeteries, your culture, everything. Why?" No-one ever asked them what they were afraid of, not even Italy.

This was a comment made by many interlocutors, Istrians, both Slovene and Italian—no-one ever lifted a finger to stop them. We should nevertheless delve deeper into the circumstances that led to these "voluntary" decisions. The historians Philipp Ther and Krystyna Kersten differentiate between direct and indirect forms of pressure. When force was used in connection with population movements in Eastern and Central Europe, people were actually not free to choose whether to leave their homes or not. However, if they chose to emigrate as a result of indirect forms of pressure, this was because they felt threatened or failed to see a future in their old home environment (Ther 2001: 54; Kersten 2001).

A similar case is the exodus of Croats from Srijem in Serbia, which took place in the 1990s during the war in Yugoslavia. Unlike in Istria, there was no international treaty to regulate the migrations as the Croats exchanged homes with Serbs living in Croatia on an individual basis. Researchers speak of forced population transfers, although in Srijem there was no direct military pressure, but there was no alternative for the migrants. The reasons given by migrants for their departure include the threat of having to serve in the Yugoslav Army (against their own nation in the time of war); they were the targets of verbal threats, insults, armed attacks on their houses; there were many murders and disappearances—threats came from not only everyday sources but also the political leadership (Čapo Žmegač 2007: 15–16). If we make a comparison, all these circumstances were also noted in the exodus from Istria: people—mainly those who migrated—talked about the fear, intimidation, and negative perception of the Italians. Many feared not only for their Italian identity, but were also afraid of the new socialist system and the Slavs (as the Italians would call them), coupled with the changes in the economic system and the uncertain economic circumstances, feelings of being superfluous and foreigners in the new environment, and so on. It is possible to imagine their predicament. We should not forget the powerful Italian propaganda, which further increased fear of the so-called *titini* and promised a better life. It really was a combination of the most diverse and complex reasons that forced people to make difficult life-changing decisions. Although they appeared to have been made voluntarily, it is nevertheless clear it was the difficult circumstances that forced the population to make "voluntary" decisions. This is why from an anthropological point of view I find it hard to talk about voluntariness.

On the other hand, in Istria unlike in many other cases of population movement in Central and Eastern Europe, there were people who decided to stay despite the very difficult social circumstances. They are the ones who prove that the decision to stay or to leave was nevertheless voluntary. They were a minority as we know that only about 10 percent remained. Considering the huge numbers of people moving away, it seems likely that more courage was required to stay in the completely changed social circumstances than to leave. For those who remained, it would appear that a key role in the dilemma of whether to stay or go was played by faith in socialism, in international ideas of a socially just life that surpassed national limitations, as well as strong ties to the land and home, and the sight of the misery in the refugee centers, which shattered illusions of a "better life." Above all, those who stayed had to have the strength to adapt to the completely new socio-political situation. So, voluntariness yes, but when 90 percent of the population decides to leave, this voluntariness becomes questionable. That is why I find it difficult to agree with historians who talk about it so lightly; even if in a legal and political sense leaving was voluntary. If from an anthropological perspective we put ourselves in people's shoes, imagine their dilemmas and experiences, then reality is revealed in a different, more human way, in which it is no longer necessary to argue who was right and who was not, or which national standpoint is right and which one is not . . . I am afraid that on both sides the cruel fate suffered by people is only being used for political purposes, often supported by scientific studies that are uncritical of their own national discourse.

We should also not forget that in the case of the Istrian exodus, the official position of the Yugoslav authorities on the Italian emigration was never recorded. Attitudes changed through time, and the decisive shift came with the Informbiro dispute and the final annexation of Istria to Yugoslavia. At the same time, different trends may be observed—from emigration being encouraged in some places, while elsewhere, or even in the same place, efforts were made to prevent emigration only a little later.

Neither should we forget the problem of fluidity or hybridity of ethnic identities in Istria. As has been shown, people in this multicultural environment—where national authorities changed hands on many occasions—were forced to adapt to each new demand to define their national appurtenance. It is important to realize that choosing to leave was at the same time a choice of national identity. Whoever left this multi-cultural environment—in which some, particularly the urban dwellers, found it harder and others easier to switch from one identity and spoken language to another—made a final decision to choose the Italian iden-tity, in many cases for personal benefit. Just as Slav identification could be transformed into Italian under fascism—although many resisted this staunchly and further strengthened their Slovene identity—the same thing happened on the other side, when it was no longer Italian but Yugoslav identity that brought benefits. In the new Yugoslav system, some people remained firmly rooted in their Italianness, others were open enough to learn the new language in order to survive and coexist in harmony, and a third group sent its children to Slovene schools so they would adapt better to the new system. For the latter, Slovene identity became the number one priority. Of course, we know that identities are changeable and depend on the prevailing social circumstances within the multiplicity of collective identifications and, as Maurice Halbwachs (2001) would say, the multiplicity of collective memories.

The diversity of memories on both sides is also interesting from an anthropological point of view. Those who left could only define their community through their rootlessness, with memories "frozen in time" and from which fear emanates. These are memories that reflect the "freezing in time" of the moment in which their life's continuity in their home environment was terminated. On the other hand, there are mem-ories of those who stayed, but who do not show any signs of fear. Even if this was, for them too, a time of uncertainty and great dilemmas, they nevertheless adapted to the new circumstances and some of them par-ticipated actively in building the new socialist society. So for them life did not end or "freeze."

Relations between Those Who Stayed and Those Who Left

The exodus radically divided the Italian community in Istria in two, so I will only mention the question of relations between those who stayed and those who left, although I usually did not ask my interlocutors about this directly. We have already seen that the departure of most of the Italians had a strong impact on those who stayed as both family ties and social bonds were severed. In the course of the study, people who stayed often told me about the pain of the *esuli* who came to see their abandoned houses after years of life as migrants.

This was also one of the main themes in the film *Piran/Pirano* (2010), in which an *esule* visits his former girlfriend (who turns out to be deceased) and the abandoned house in Piran that is now inhabited by an immigrant from Bosnia. The director Goran Vojnović probably got the idea from his mother who is originally from Pula. Ornella describes, in tears, the suffering of the *esuli* in an environment that was hostile to them in Italy, and their emotional visits to their former homes:

> Certainly. We suffered, but all suffered . . . All the people who left. Look, when I see someone touching a wall, I go up to them and say: "Where did you live?" "Oh, I lived here." Because they come and touch . . . That's . . . When you leave the place where your family grew up, you have all your emotions from childhood and the teenage years, your loves; you can never forget, never. If you don't go back to those places, they've cut your roots, they've cut off a part of your life. . . . You must come back. They were afraid to return, they didn't come for fifty years. And how they suffered! I have friends, for example, they threw themselves out of the house, they couldn't live. When they left, they were put in a hotel. He went up to the top floor and threw himself down. There are tragic stories, tragic. And these people . . . We suffered, but they suffered just as much because they were despised, they were treated badly, people didn't want them—just like migrants—they didn't want to see them. Some went to America, some to Australia, they went all over . . . When I visited Abitanti [in Istria] and saw this emptied village, with chairs, tables, a cupboard inside, it broke my heart. I felt so bad because my children refused to speak Italian.

More memories describing how the *esuli* were afraid of returning because of the violence they had experienced can be found in the book by Pamela Ballinger (2003). For example, there is the sad story of how an *esule*, a former farmer who now lived in Trieste, observed his abandoned home every day through binoculars (Ballinger 2003: 168–206). Tonin from Škofije remembers this despair, especially that of farmers on their way to Italy: "In Škofije, there was a tavern next to the walnut tree. The poor people just stood and stood there! Poor farmers!!! Used to working!!! They were in groups of four, propping their heads up! They had never been in a tavern before and they waited . . ." (note from field diary).

When comparing the collective memories of *esuli* communities and those who stayed, Pamela Ballinger notices that "they do not speak" the same language. In the eyes of the *esuli*, those who stayed are not "true" Italians, so they ignore them and only see themselves as true, autochthonous, and authentic Istrians. They create a discourse about themselves, which sees them as the only victims of the *foibe*. They see their "purity" in two senses—as innocent victims and as authentic Italians, persecuted by Yugoslavs who carried out ethnic cleansing. Meanwhile, those who stayed refer to the language of authentic hybridity, referring to the regional Istrian identity and not nationality. While the *esuli* demand the return of Istria and see themselves as martyrs, those who remained—having participated in the anti-fascist struggle and been let down by Yugoslav nationalism—see themselves as martyrs for a just Istrian society (Ballinger 2003: 168–244). It should, however, be taken into account that Ballinger studied *esuli* communities that unite people with more distinct political convictions, so she probably failed to capture all the nuanced opinions of people who do not belong to certain communities, especially those who maintained regular (family) ties with those who stayed. My studies confirm that the Istrians refer to Istrian hybridity, yet, in contrast to the dominant Italian view, they also refer to their Italianness—especially those who do not come from ethnically mixed families. In the section on memory, it was shown that the *esuli* discourse—in which history begins in 1943 with the beginning of the exodus, completely omitting the twenty years of violent fascism and Italian war crimes—has since the 1990s been accepted on a national level as the Italian collective memory, reflected annually by the commemorations held on the "Day of Remembrance." In this memory, Italy is presented as a victim, forgetting its previous role of perpetrator in the time of fascism and the occupation during World War II. In the section on pacifying memories, we have already seen that those who stayed felt forgotten by their mother country. Seeing Cristicchi's theater play was actually the first time they felt they had been heard. Not only were those who stayed marginalized and unheard in the context of the Slovene or former Yugoslav collective memory—their truth as a national minority did not coincide with the collective memory of the "victors of the war." They were also forgotten by their mother country. Giulio, an Italian politician and member of the national minority, mentions in passing that Italy forgot about them:

> [The first Italian consul] came in 1956 or 1955 as a result of the London Memorandum; before that there was nothing. It was interesting to hear his observations when he explained that when he tried to get help from the Italian government he didn't get any. So the Italian government, the Italian side that stayed here, that did not leave, was erased; they are *titini*, they no longer exist and the first meeting—I was president of the Italian union at the time, Istria and Rijeka—our first meeting with the Italian government as a minority was in the 1980s, in 1983/1984, I think, when I was director of RTV Capodistria.

As a politician, he also drew attention to the Italian minority in Yugoslavia by speaking in Italian in the Yugoslav parliament in Belgrade in the 1980s.

> There happened to be a discussion about symbols, national symbols. . . . I had the support of some wise politicians here in Slovenia. . . . I said, I'm going to speak in Italian . . . I began; first I spoke in Italian for over a minute, a minute and a half. They all put their headphones on because they all had headphones . . . [He continued speaking in Serbo-Croat and Slovene.]

As already mentioned, Yugoslavia ensured protection of the Italian national minority with the Paris Peace Treaty in 1947, but the system of protecting autochthonous national communities was not completed until the mid-1980s. There was a parallel process to protect the Slovene national community in Italy. By signing the treaty of Osimo (1975), Yugoslavia was obliged to protect the Italian minority (Kavrečič 2008; Sanzin 2015: 15–20).

While Yugoslavia rapidly introduced measures to protect the Italian national community—at least in a legal and formal respect—those who stayed were ignored both by Italy and the *esuli*. Vittoria commented that very few members of the minority succeeded in establishing good relations with them. One of the rare individuals who succeeded was the Italian politician mentioned above. Otherwise, relations are mostly poor, even hostile in some cases. He mentioned the occasion when a monument was erected in memory of the *foibe* victims and the *esuli* thanked neither the mayor nor those who stayed. Such conversations show the contempt of the *esuli* have for the present-day Istrians—regardless of their ethnicity. Pamela Ballinger (2003) also provided evidence of this. The *esuli* were mentioned by the interlocutors more in the context of family ties. In Vittoria's opinion, the main accusation leveled by the *esuli* against those who stayed was the fact that they stayed: "And those who left never admitted that we suffered because we stayed. [Speaking about the difficult lives of the *esuli*, who were seen as fascists.] You understand? And they blamed us for not leaving together with them."

Meanwhile, Vittoria explains how those who stayed reproach the *esuli* for leaving and say that everything would have been different had they not left. When the *esuli* reply that that was not possible, those who stayed emphasize that they were left alone and survived despite all the pressures.

There is also a difference between the two communities in terms of memory—the *esuli* memory is frozen in time, while the other one has adapted to the Yugoslav social reality. According to those who remained, part of the pain felt by the *esuli* also lies in the realization that their expectations that life would be miserable in Yugoslavia did not materialize. As Vittoria says, unlike the *esuli*, they were able to study in Yugoslavia. Valeria also mentions the envy felt by the *esuli* because of the good economic standing of the families that stayed in Yugoslavia, while they left out of fear of Yugoslavia.

> In short, those who left and now live in Trieste, and come and visit, they have always been, how can I put it, angry when they see we are making progress and are OK. What they want is, how should I put it: "We left because things could have been bad for us, so we don't want to see you're OK." [Speaking about her husband's good wage.] Basically, we could afford things, we bought a gramophone, television, many things we couldn't afford before. And we had a fridge that used a lot of electricity and our aunt came from Trieste. . . . And my husband said: "You know what, we're probably going to buy a new fridge." And she replied: "What use will it be to you here?" You know, they were rather narrow-minded; more than we were. I don't know how to explain . . . "What use will it be to you?" [Speaking about buying a color television.] [In Trieste:] "You know, uncle, father bought a color television." "What? Color television? Not even my son has one!" You could sometimes hear, "But how could you get one if I haven't got one" [they did not come on the day of the *šagre* (the annual village celebration) but one day before or after, as though they did not want to celebrate together].

From this and other conversations, it is clear that both groups developed into separate, and sometimes even hostile communities, with each group blaming the other for the postwar situation in Istria. People emphasize that the conflicts are mainly on a political level while intimate relations between families are preserved, however, some unease is nonetheless evident in their relations . . . Those who stayed adapted to the new socio-political reality and, as we have already seen, most of them do not regret their decision. On the other hand, there are the *esuli* with their memories frozen in time, many of them with a feeling of superiority, and uprootedness, and often with unresolved hatred and grudges. We must nevertheless avoid seeing the two communities as distinct from each other because everyday conversations show family ties and diversity that surpasses the apparently dominant political persuasions. There are also different examples of art that bear witness to the establishment of ties between those who left and those who stayed—for example, the book written jointly by two authors, one from an *esuli* family and the other from a family that remained (Mori and Milani Kruljac 2012), or the recent photobook by Lucia Castelli (2018), which tells stories from both communities.

Notes

1. While only a small Italian ethnic minority remained in Yugoslavia because many decided to leave, a larger Slovene ethnic minority remained in Italy as most did not opt for Yugoslav nationality (Širca 2020).
2. For memories of the different phases of emigration and immigration, see the chapter "After the Exodus: The Renovation of Istrian Society, Social Relations, and Heritage."
3. Approximately 150 from Rijeka and Istria, which is a large number considering the size of the Italian community (Purini 2010: 271).
4. An increasing number of historical studies have been carried out on the subject of national indifference, e.g., King (2002), Judson (2006), Bjork (2008), Zahra (2008, 2010), Bjork et al. (2016), Van Ginderachter and Fox (2019), as Mila Orlić kindly pointed out to me.
5. The father's adaptability in terms of identity may also be due to the fact that he lost his Italian-speaking parents while still a child and was brought up in Slovene families. However, her parents initially wanted to send their daughter to an Italian school, but they changed their mind at the last minute and said they did not like the school.
6. Commentary from someone with the pseudonym "Franci for president," translated from Croatian.
7. Arhiv republike Slovenije. SI AS 1589/III: Arhiv Republike Slovenije, Centralni komite zveze komunistov Slovenije, Fond tržaškega okrožnega komiteja KP JK; leto 1945–46, škatla 48, mapa 1515, Seznam oseb, ki so pobegnile oz. so se izselile iz Kopra v Italijo ob koncu vojne (Archives of the Republic of Slovenia. si as 1589/iii: Archives of the Republic of Slovenia, Central Committee of the League of Communists of Slovenia, Depot of the Trieste District Committee kp jk; 1945–46, box 48, file 1515. List of people who escaped or moved out of Koper to Italy at the end of the war).
8. Blackshirts and *squadristi* were the terms used for Italian fascist soldiers who fought against communism and socialism using violent methods.
9. As will be shown below, this took place in the last phase of the exodus between 1954 and 1957 (Kalc 2019: 151).
10. On 28 June 1948, Yugoslavia was excluded from the Informbiro with a decree because of its departure from Marxist and Leninist ideologies, and its hostile attitude toward the Soviet Union. It was issued in September 1947 with the aim of coordinating the activity of Soviet, Polish, Hungarian, Czech, Romanian, Bulgarian, Yugoslav, Italian, and French communist representatives under Soviet leadership (Purini 2010: 268).
11. The author places the term "Italian population" in inverted commas because of the problematic nature of border identities. However, the same should be done with Slovene and Croat population for the same reasons.
12. The purge of fascists and their collaborators began in the area under "Tito's" authority immediately after the end of World War II in 1945. The new regime set up people's courts for judging fascist crimes and designated members of the purge commissions (Pletikosić 2002: 465–69).
13. Comitato di Liberazione Nazionale dell'Istria (National Liberation Committee of Istria, CLN), which was supported by the Italian state. It supported the spreading of pro-Italian propaganda in Zone B. It provided financial support to those categories of the population—for example, teachers—who were important for the preservation of the Italians in Istria (Pupo 2015: 34).

14. Arhiv republike Slovenije. SI AS 1589/III: Arhiv Republike Slovenije, Centralni komite zveze komunistov Slovenije, Fond tržaškega okrožnega komiteja KP JK, leto 1949, okrajni komite KPS Koper, d. Poročila ekip; Poročilo o kadrovskem stanju v posameznih panogah gospodarstva v Istrskem okrožju, Koper, 14. 8. 1949 (Archives of the Republic of Slovenia. SI AS 1589/iii: Archives of the Republic of Slovenia, Central Committee of the League of Communists of Slovenia, Depot of the Trieste District Committee kp jk, 1949, District Committee of kps Koper, d. Team reports; Report on the staffing situation in different business fields in the Istrian District, Koper, 14 August 1949).

15. In Italian, the term *titini* is connected with the postwar period and refers to followers of Marshall Tito (Širok 2007: 377).

16. See also the section on uncertain economic situation and new state borders.

17. SI AS 1589/III, Centralni komite zveze komunistov Slovenije, Fond tržaškega okrožnega komiteja KP JK; škatla 48, mapa 1515, Istrsko okrožje, 7. IX. 1949 (SI AS 1589/III, Central Committee of the League of Communists of Slovenia, Depot of the Trieste District Committee kp jk; box 48, file 1515, Istrian district, 7. ix. 1949).

18. SI AS 1589/III, Centralni komite zveze komunistov Slovenije, Fond tržaškega okrožnega komiteja KP JK; škatla 48, mapa 1515, O agitacijskem in propagandnem delu v Kopru, 1949 (SI AS 1589/III, Central Committee of the League of Communists of Slovenia, Depot of the Trieste District Committee kp jk; box 48, file 1515, Agitation and propaganda work in Koper, 1949).

19. SI AS 1589/III, Centralni komite zveze komunistov Slovenije, Fond tržaškega okrožnega komiteja KP JK; škatla 48, mapa 1515, Poročilo o naturalizaciji poitalijančenih priimkov, o izdaji osebnih izkaznic v coni B STO-ja, o kaznovanju za kršitve ponovne odredbe o dvojezičnosti. 24. 8. 49; ae:III/ dokument III/50-713/16 (SI AS 1589/III, Central Committee of the League of Communists of Slovenia, Depot of the Trieste District Committee kp jk; box 48, file 1515, Report on the naturalization of Italianized surnames, the issuing of identity cards in Zone B of the Free Territory of Trieste, punishing of violations of the renewed order governing bilingualism. 24 August 49; ae:III DOCUMENT III/50-713/16).

20. I was told this story by Martina Vovk, who heard it from her aunt who spoke with this man.

21. The inhabitants of territories lost by Italy (their former provinces in the Balkans and former colonies in Africa) gained rights in Italy as national refugees, which meant the Italian state took responsibility for them and tried to integrate them in Italian society on the peninsula (even after years living in refugee centers). In contrast to the displaced persons who identified themselves as Italians, foreign migrants were cared for by the United Nations Relief and Rehabilitation Administration and its successor, the International Refugee Organisation (Ballinger 2006b, 2015: 77–78).

22. The title of the short conference that took place online on 9 February 2021, was "Le radici dell'odio. La dominazione italiana nella regione giuliano-dalmata. Per una conoscenza storica e antropologica della violenza innescata dal dominio coloniale fascista" (The roots of hatred. Italian domination in the Julian-Dalmatian region. For historical and anthropological understanding of the violence triggered by fascist colonial rule).

Chapter 3

After the Exodus

The Renovation of Istrian Society, Social Relations, and Heritage

Memories of the Emigration and Immigration Processes

The process of immigration to Istria depended directly on emigration. That is why memories of the two processes are dealt with in the same chapter. While all existing literature focuses on the process of mass emigration, the process of immigration and setting up a new social reality in Istria has been almost completely overlooked by all studies that have been carried out so far (Kalc 2019: 147–48).

Similar to the statistics on emigration and immigration,[1] memories also show large fluctuations in the process of emigration. From memories of sporadic, sudden disappearances of Italian neighbors typical of the early phase, when the 1947 Paris Peace Treaty introduced the possibility of opting, to memories of the mass exodus that happened in the final phase of emigration, when Zone B was annexed to Yugoslavia with the London Memorandum in 1954. The highest rate of emigration is recorded a year and a half after the annexation. Memories are dominated by a feeling that the first people to come to Istria arrived in what was still a completely Italian urban environment. Lucija's parents—a teacher and a partisan who later had a business—moved to Dekani in 1946 and later moved to Koper. She remembers a completely Italian environment in Koper with only a few Slovenes, and she only spoke Slovene with her parents. She spoke of the language barriers in the Italian environment that she experienced as a child, and of the sudden disappearance of her childhood friend, an Italian, when she discovered the splintered door of his home.

> [Speaking about there being only two Slovene families in the block of flats:] Slovenes, the others were all Italians. [Speaking about difficulties communicating in the shops:] Of course, it was an elderly lady and two adult women who didn't understand what I was saying. And I said, "three fresh eggs," and they said to each other: "Ma cosa vol 'sta *fia* qua, ma cosa la vol." [What does this little girl want]. . . . Mum taught me not to say "three fresh eggs," but "tre uova fresche" . . . And I would repeat "tre uova fresche, tre uova fresche" all the way down from the third floor and around the corner . . ." and in the end I said: "tre fresche" [three fresh] [*laughs*]. And as she didn't understand me, I told her, in Slovene of course, that I wanted three fresh eggs, and when I repeated this in Slovene they were even more surprised, they understood me even less. And then I repeated in both languages and the shop assistant said to me, "ah, tre pesce!" [*pesca* means peach in Italian], and offered me three peaches. . . . Later I spoke only Italian. I only spoke Slovene with my parents. [Speaking about telling children stories from Slovene books in Italian; about the Italian newspaper that published her photograph with the caption: *I ragazzi slo-veni sono uguali ai ragazzi italiani*. "Slovene children are just like Italian children."] [How she went to fetch a toy she had forgotten at the house of an Italian friend:] I went up to their door and it was in splinters. Then two planks were nailed diagonally across the splintered door, and I never saw Valter or his grandma again. . . . That was in 1952 or thereabouts.

When Colonel Dragotin arrived in Koper in 1954, everything was still completely Italian. However, he says that in the end only five Italian families remained:

> They're all from Trieste, ninety-nine . . . Allegedly about five Italian families remained in Koper. One of them was here in our garden, and even they then moved into their own flat somewhere up in Istria. So it's not . . . There were only Italians here . . . ninety, if not more. . . . All Italian and we, my father; it was bilingualism at the town hall . . . Even the mayor was Italian when I came down here.

Memories of "disappearances" of Italian neighbors from the Italian-speaking environment have their opposite in later testimonies of the mass departure of Italians who left the Istrian towns in droves. This was the final phase of the exodus that followed the annexation of Zone B to Yugoslavia, as described by Claudio, a Slovene Istrian:

> C: In Piran . . . Piran emptied. It was practically emptied! I'll say . . . If there were 90, let's say, but maybe even more than 90 percent Italians.

Proper Italians! Slovenes in Piran . . . Even if there were any, they were hidden! They didn't admit to being Slovene, no.

K: And when you came, when you came here as a commander, when was that roughly?

C: Ah . . . That was in . . . Hold on, I finished in Piran in 1950 . . . About 1946.

K: I see. And what was your experience? When you came here most of the people were Italian or had some already left?

C: They were all here! There were already some new arrivals. But all the inhabitants of Piran were still here. It wasn't until 1954 that it began emptying rapidly. When it was decided. When it was decided there would be no Free Territory of Trieste. Because that's what all of them were waiting for. That it would materialize. [Speaking about the Free Territory of Trieste that did not come alive.] And goodbye . . . It was the end of the Free Territory of Trieste.

K: And then what, the people . . .

C: Well, and when this happened, in 1954, the Italian population saw there was no more room for them here. Grandpas and old people who had nowhere to go, or people who were particularly attached to their house, etc., stayed. But few, very few remained. The others . . . In droves! . . . And Piran was left empty . . .. There were trucks loading up the bedding . . . They loaded what they could on trucks and . . . It was all clear to see. There was a queue at the border! Every day! Not only here, from all of Istria, from Pula . . . In droves! In droves! In droves! . . . They went to refugee camps. Just a little further on from Škofije. There was a refugee camp there. There were shacks. There was a tent city. . . . It was terrible to watch! I felt like crying! When I saw it. I saw them, I knew many of them, many people, poor people . . . Who left in tears! And even for us who stayed it was hard! Watching this.

In another interview, Rafael, a teacher and the brother of the interlocutor mentioned above illustrates the complete emptying of Piran after Zone B was annexed to Yugoslavia. He remembers how the full classes in the Italian school, where he taught physical education, were almost empty a year later, and he was left on his own playing basketball with only three children:

Yes, clear. Because as you went in through the doors, "si parla italiano" [we speak Italian here], without any exceptions. And there were three classes in every year! Three classes at the Italian school. Upper and lower. The next year! The next year I had three pupils in one class, and I was the fourth, and we played basketball two on two because there wasn't anyone else. . . . This happened in one year . . . 1953, 1954. What a difference! Such a change! The streets! My brother can tell you this too. Empty streets! There was no-one! There were trucks! All day and all night, everyone was in a rush. And I had another year. The next year in summer I saw there was a job going at the primary school in Piran, and I went to the Slovene primary school in Piran because I was afraid I would be out of a job. There were so few Italian pupils, there was a danger it would all be abandoned. . . . It wasn't just the children, the teachers also left! All of them! Everything Italian left. Teerribble! A terrible change! Well, and then things slowly settled down as the years went by, so this grammar school existed more as a name, and the primary school, as it is now. It was terrible!!! When I came to Piran there was no handball. I played football. There were only Italians, one Dalmatian, and myself! There was no-one!

The complete emptying and veritable mass exodus is described by Giulio in Izola, where he says parents waited until the end of the school year before leaving en masse following Zone B's annexation to Yugoslavia:

I finished the seventh year of primary school here in Isola, in the old Italian school and there were . . . 7c, there were thirty-five of us in the class, I think. In September, the beginning of the new school year, we found ourselves in that courtyard, a few groups of three or four people; year eight began the school year with five of us. During the summer it all went empty. . . . That was in 1955 . . . People actually waited for the end of the school year. They didn't want to interrupt the school year. They emptied everything in three years. The streets were filled with trucks. . . . This lasted throughout 1954, 1955, and partly 1956.

The emigration therefore went from being sporadic to very visible at the height of the exodus. We also hear about this from the other side—the new arrivals, such as Kristina, the daughter of a partisan who came from Primorska, but waited for accommodation in Istria after its liberation in a house that had belonged to Gottschee Germans.[2] Kristina came to Izola in 1955:

There were still many Italians. But almost every day there was news that someone was no longer there, that they had left. I remember wondering at the time: "Why doesn't anyone inform us of this in advance?" No-one gave any prior explanation. They simply disappeared the following day. I must say that it wasn't just the Italians who left, also immigrants from Slovenia's interior. The destinations were the same: the refugee camp in Trieste. . . . It went *liscio* [smoothly]. There was no debate about it. And there were no political tensions or persecutions.

Marko's family was also considered a "returnee" family as they had to flee the area around Trieste and move to Yugoslavia because of their

Figure 3.1. Portorož/Portorose, 28 April 1948 (Department of History and Ethnography of the National Study Library of Trieste, collection Primorski dnevnik, author Mario Magajna).

antifascist activity. They waited there for the opportunity to "return," and he has childhood memories of how people simply disappeared overnight: "I remember that many people disappeared all at once, we had no idea how. Children, friends with whom you used to play, were no longer there the next day."

Memories of completely emptied towns reflect how the population of Istrian towns changed completely. This happened in the final phase of the exodus following the annexation of Zone B to Yugoslavia, as Ante remembers from his arrival in 1957: "When I came here in 1957, well, not here [Koper] but Piran! Every door was empty [?], it was terrible in Piran! It was 1957, we slept there, and we went down the streets, looking around a little. For sale, fully furnished. For sale, fully furnished. All of them, 90 percent of the houses! You could buy a house with one wage!"

Memories of a "Bunch of Keys"

The state of degradation and neglect of the towns at that time is best reflected by the urban story of a "bunch of keys," which the new arrivals received when they arrived in one of the three Istrian towns and with which they looked for a roof over their heads among the neglected, degraded flats. The story turned out to be true as many interlocutors had a similar experience—both those who received keys to flats and those

Figure 3.2. Piran/Pirano, 1948 (Department of History and Ethnography of the National Study Library of Trieste, collection Primorski dnevnik, author Mario Magajna).

who distributed keys with the aim of attracting immigrants, as we will see below. In her memoirs, a nurse describes how she was appalled by the degraded state of the abandoned flats in Piran that were unfit for habitation. She walked from flat to flat with a "bunch of keys" in her hand, looking for a flat for herself:

> [Describing how she first found a room.] Then we began looking for a flat. There were many flats in Piran, but they were unfit for habitation. I don't know how these people used to live. Perhaps they destroyed everything before leaving, but I don't believe that. All the stairwells and flats were in a state of neglect. Maybe it doesn't sound nice, but it was impossible. That was in 1955, when the largest number of people were moving out. Perhaps it was because of that. Or perhaps because I came from elsewhere and I saw everything in an even more negative light. What's clear is that it's incomparable with what it's like today. Unfortunately, it wasn't even clean. When we began looking for flats, I actually received a bunch of keys at the town hall and walked through almost all of Piran. Someone walked with me, I was not alone. But I didn't find anything; there wasn't a single flat you could move into. I took all the keys back and said I didn't like old flats like that [After a few days she and her work colleague found a flat that had been inhabited by a family that was just moving out, and which even had a toilet—unlike all the other flats]. (Pahor 2007: 205).

Figure 3.3. Nova vas, 1948 (Department of History and Ethnography of the National Study Library of Trieste, collection Primorski dnevnik, author Mario Magajna).

Emir's father, who moved to Piran from Macedonia in 1952, told his son how in 1954, when he moved to Izola and received the abandoned cake shop from the municipality, he was also given a "bunch of keys" to the abandoned flats:

> [Asked if there were any Italians in the town upon his arrival.] Yes. At number 1 Koprska ulica [Koper Street 1]. There was only our family, at number 2 there were some other Macedonians—two families, on the other side of the road there was a family [name], and another two families, so there were no Italians. At number 4 there was [name], then in the next house there were Italians, who still live there now. Mainly Slovenians. When I arrived, about 20 percent of the families in our street were Italian. I'll tell you another interesting thing: after my father got the shop, he went to ask at the town hall if he could get a flat. They said to him, "Here are the keys for Koprska ulica," a bunch of keys, "go and choose one." So they were empty.

This urban story of the "bunch of keys," which I found incredible when I came across it at the beginning of my research and which ten years ago other people would not have believed either, shows to what extent the population in Istrian towns changed. Practically all the inhabitants were replaced, bringing drastic changes in terms of ethnicity, eco-

nomic structure, culture and the way of life. The stories of immigration
and the differences between the first to arrive in the still Italian urban
environment and those who came later to an already Slovenized environment, will also be seen below, in connection with the occupational
structure and origin of the immigrants. On the other hand, it is necessary to highlight that my lecture in Koper entitled "A Bunch of Keys"
annoyed many people who did not have the privilege of being allocated
a flat. Allocating flats to some and not to others not only caused tensions
but also begs the question: who were the "chosen ones" who were given
a "bunch of keys," and to what extent did these privileges depend on the
time of arrival? We may assume that privileges were used to attract the
early immigrants when the need for social and economic reconstruction
was greatest in the wake of the exodus. A Slovene Istrian who came to my
lecture commented that this may have been true in the early years, the
1950s, but later, probably after 1957, these flats were no longer available:

> Bunches of keys, you can see him to this day, you can meet him in town,
> a man, an electrician who came to Koper around 1950, and I listened to
> him here with a colleague about twenty years ago. He says, I had them
> here, they gave me a whole bunch of keys and I walked around the town
> looking for a flat for myself. And you looked for a flat, they said. Well,
> it's true that he chose the worst he could, that's his problem. A few years
> later, 1956, 1957, my wife and I, both employed, she had been working
> a few more years and we had a baby, but there were no flats here in Ko-
> per. The bank did not want to give us one where I was working . . . The
> cooperative bank did not want to give it because my wife was employed,
> so I went to inquire at the town hall. And what did they say? They didn't
> say anything. The man in the office just looked at me as though I had
> fallen from the moon and that I'm completely mad. And basically I can't
> find a flat.

The daughter of early immigrants from Gorizia and Trieste reacted
in similarly reluctant fashion to the statement that flats were "given for
free." It is interesting to see that they did not see themselves as immigrants but as natives because they were Primorci (from the Littoral
Region; see below). Again, we can see that the earliest immigrants came
from the frontier region and spoke Italian. However, evidently not all
received flats, as they did not receive one. So although the urban story
of the "bunch of keys" turned out to be true, it appears not everyone
had this possibility:

> I would also like to say why I came today. I felt challenged by the title
> "A Bunch of Keys." I was born before 1950 in Koper. We weren't new-

comers, I mean, my mother came from Gorizia, my father from Trieste, but we never felt like new arrivals. I don't know what this bunch of keys was; I agree with the gentleman. I will tell you what my parents experienced. My father had—I think—quite an important function in Koper. That's why he came. You didn't come to Koper just like that in 1948. My mother was pregnant, close to giving birth, and she came on foot every day from Izola, where they were renting a flat, to look for a flat in Koper as there was no transport. What's more . . . She always told us how she went from house to house asking if they had even just one room. There was no chance. And then we got two rooms in Kreljeva ulica [Krelj Street], where my poor mother also died, but you know, our Slovenes had one, they also got two rooms. One on one side of the hallway and one on the other. We were in the palace and we had a toilet and water in the garden. Some didn't even have this. And for years my father . . . So, my mother always said they were afraid of me because my father had a senior position, that's why they gave me that room. It was real misery and in 1954 my father, who had been a partisan from 1942—he joined the partisans when he was sixteen . . .—he decided to move away from us. He didn't get a bunch of keys either. Despite his job and the fact he had been a partisan, he still had to live in a room with a water leak. He never got any other flat. I don't want anyone to leave this lecture thinking that those who came to Koper simply received this bunch of keys, walked around Koper, looked around and chose what they wanted. I can't understand, I understood in 1948, but I couldn't understand that my parents in 1954 or 1956, or I don't know when there was this bunch of keys . . . They couldn't get a flat. Not just mine, also all my neighbors, we're all old neighbors. No-one could move away.

So we could say that during the time in which the Istrian towns were emptiest, the authorities used the "bunch of keys" to try to attract people to come. This will be evident in the next chapter, in the memory of someone who invited people to come. It is, however, obvious that not everyone had this privilege. Although it seems this privilege could be linked with the time of arrival, this theory also proved questionable.

Who Came and from Where?
The New Demographic Structure in Istria

The process of immigration corresponded to the processes of emigration. Only 2,600 cases of permanent internal migration to the Slovenia's coastal region had been registered by 1954. However, there was considerable migration within Istria as people from the hinterlands moved to the Obala (The Coast) and close to the coastal towns, leading to the emptying of Istria's villages (Kalc 2019: 151–52). Antonio and Pina testify to the movement of Istria's rural inhabitants to nearby coastal towns. They remember how Manžan and other Istrian villages emptied completely after farmers moved to abandoned Italian houses:

> A: Yes, my uncle up there went to Izola, another one went to Koper. They dispersed. . . .
> P: You know what they got—those Italians from Koper and Izola went to Trieste, didn't they—and they got big old houses; but they got farms in Koper; they left Marezige, Manžan, all these villages, they got new houses, and they went, including my cousin who left Marezige, he got a nice house, but some didn't get anything, they were paupers even in Koper. . . .
> A: Yes, then those left. The order came to clear these people out. They weren't allowed to be here, and the people moved away.
> K: I see, and then the village emptied, Manžan.
> P: Some went to Trieste, some to Koper, some to Izola . . .
> K: And then, who came here?
> A: From the south [meaning the southern republics of former Yugoslavia].
> K: They even came to the villages?
> P: The village is full of them. There are still forty-one families. The village was full of people, there was a school up there, an Italian school, there was a pub, there was something, but then it was . . . It was cleaned out and came to nothing.

Some rare studies of the population structure show that in the time of the Free Territory of Trieste most new arrivals came from the interior of Slovenia's coastal region, together with immigrants from Zone A. In the early years, immigration was primarily connected with employment in military and civil administration and in the newly founded social and economic structures. There were many political migrants from Trieste and its surroundings who had fled fascist violence in Yugoslavia in the years 1920–1930 (Kalc 2019: 155). There was Marko, who we have already mentioned, whose family had to move from Trieste to Kranj because of its antifascist activities. The family returned to Trieste following the liberation, and moved to Koper in 1948.

> They had to flee . . . My uncle was in the same group of people who were shot in Bazovica [because of antifascist activities in the time of fascism]. But they warned him so the whole family fled to Kranj [in the Kingdom of Yugoslavia] from Trieste [in Italy]. So they lived in Trieste from 1930 until the war, and then after the war, they immediately returned to Trieste, then they all came to Koper. . . . The whole family had to flee. They packed their bags overnight and had to move to Kranj where they weren't

really welcome, as is always the case with refugees. You're always seen as someone who is taking jobs away from the locals so they're not really pleased to see you. Of course, then after the war they immediately came back down. But then they were in Trieste for a very short period of time as it was still ours, and then they simply moved to Koper.

The archive sources also clearly show that the first immigrants came from Primorska (the Littoral Region), from Zone A and Yugoslavia. An important magnet was the restoration of the school system. Slovenian schools had been abolished under fascist rule so this area had no trained teaching staff. As a result, schools and departments were united and combined, and teaching was entrusted to teachers who had not completed their training (Kalc 2019: 152). The memories of the first arrivals confirm that the first to arrive in the Istrian towns were those who were already adapted to the majority Italian environment, i.e., people from the surroundings of Trieste or from Primorska, where they were familiar with the Italian language because of contact with the region's economic center Trieste and the two decades of fascism (when Italian was the only language allowed).

Many of these people were patriotic Slovenes who fled fascist violence and sought refuge in Yugoslavia, waiting there for an opportunity to return to Istria, although it was on the other side of the border. Many of them were intellectuals and teachers. The authorities needed bilingual teachers in the still predominantly Italian environment. Three of my interlocutors came from such families. Both parents of the above "returnee" family that fled fascist violence were teachers—the mother taught in a Slovene-Italian combined school.

> We first lived in Bošadraga [a part of Koper], then when I was one year old we moved up to live above the primary school in Markovec [a district of Koper], and that was a primary school that was half Slovene, half Italian. Actually, my mother taught the Slovene classes from years one to four, there was no . . . Then one of her colleagues taught the Italian children, also years one to four.

Immigration from Zone A of the Free Territory of Trieste soon came to an end and staff began arriving from other parts of Slovenia and Croatia, particularly from the Istrian hinterlands. The immigrants came predominantly from the municipalities of Hrpelje, Sežana, Ilirska Bistrica, Postojna, and the region of Gorizia, which was cut off from its urban center Gorizia that remained in Italy after the demarcation in 1947. Both regions shared a common history with Istria as they were part of the joint administrative region under Austria-Hungary and the Julian March under fascist Italy. Lucija's parents, both teachers who we have already mentioned, arrived from the Vipava Valley early on, in 1946. When they moved to Koper in the same year, they were one of the few Slovenian families there. Their mother left for Ljubljana to finish her education and when she returned in 1955, the town's ethnic makeup had changed completely:

> My parents came here as envoys from the Vipava Valley. In fact, they were teachers in the Goriška Brda at the time, despite not having undergone formal training for this profession. But then they had, they probably had some experience. . . . They came to Dekani in 1946. [The father soon left the education system.] But mother stayed in the school system. [When they moved to Koper,] I think it was just our neighbors and us who lived on the third floor . . . Slovenes, the others were all Italians.

Her husband Danilo has a similar story. He also came from Zone A as a child early on in 1952, together with his mother who was a bilingual teacher and came from a family of partisan national heroes. Unlike Koper, Portorož consisted predominantly of immigrants so Italian was not the main language, although it seems a little early for the dominance of other languages:

> I came with my mother who was sent to the Obala [the Coast] as a teacher. She was the first Slovene nursery school teacher on the Obala; there had not been any before. She completed a one-year course for nursery school teachers in Ljubljana, and she came down together with me, a two-year-old; I think it was at the beginning of 1952 or something like that. . . . But in Portorož, like Lucija said, most of the children were new arrivals, at least as far as I can remember. And they came from all over, soldiers called Mikolič, Kocetič, these were all my schoolmates . . . [Asked if they were from Yugoslavia:] Yes, also. They were all sons of soldiers who stayed on, officers who . . . There was a hospital there so. There was quite a mixed bunch of children and Italian was by no means the main language.

As can be gathered from the testimonies, many of the immigrants from other parts of Primorska were former partisans. The story of a well-known political figure, Kristina, the daughter of a partisan from Primorska, is particularly interesting. After the war, her family moved temporarily from the Brkini hills to Kočevje, to live in a house that had belonged to the Gottschee Germans, where they waited together with other families for the possibility to return to Primorska, after it was "liberated."

> We knew we weren't going to stay there permanently [in Kočevje], and we waited all the while for the border between Italy and Yugoslavia to be determined. We wanted to know if Trieste would be ours, what would be

Figure 3.4. Portorož/Portorose, 1948 (Department of History and Ethnography of the National Study Library of Trieste, collection Primorski dnevnik, author Mario Magajna).

ours, and this separation was finally carried out in 1945, wasn't it. And we immediately began preparing to return. After that we . . . I think all the families returned. . . . It's not true that all the Italians went to Trieste. They left behind empty homes; they weren't houses . . . So it was possible for us to return. The men were the first to go again. My father and most of the men then began working in construction because something new was being built, and these families settled on this territory again, some of them in Bertoki, and in Hrvatini; probably the ones who missed having a farm, we were never proper farmers. . . . So we moved to the town. My mother said "we're moving to a town." And that town was Izola.

The early immigration was connected with setting up the new socialist government and administrative structures as well as employing the already mentioned cultural sector and military staff (Kalc 2019: 152). Colonel Dragotin, who came to Koper in 1954, describes this need for administrative staff. Interestingly, there is no longer any sign of a need for bilingualism; this man did not speak Italian, although he notes that upon his arrival most of the population was still Italian. As he recounts, the need for administrative staff was great, so most people were accepted:

[Speaking about his arrival:] In 1954, immediately on 15 October, to be the commander of the military unit here. And then we took over; until then soldiers had not done military service, then we began summoning them . . . The inhabitants here. [Answering the question from where he had come:] From Ljubljana, most of the employees, I won't say all of them . . . To put it bluntly, anyone who knew how to write came here because the district council, the new authority was being set up, new staff were needed in the bank, etc. When I came there were still Italians here. Let's not forget that at least 90 percent of the inhabitants of Koper were Italian.

Immigration increased greatly after the London Memorandum, which was accompanied by the introduction of a planned economy and the integration of Zone B in the Republic of Slovenia. Although the Free Territory of Trieste did not allow any Yugoslav interference, the Communist Party introduced a socialist economy and the social concept to Zone B, and tried to reduce the dependence of Istria's economy on Trieste (Rogoznica 2011: 290; Kalc 2019: 156). Projects of national importance were undertaken such as the construction of the Port of Koper, industrial plants such as Tomos, Delamaris, Splošna plovba, and others. Much effort was invested in the development of agriculture, fishing, and salt production. Construction and merchant companies were founded. All this called for a new workforce with different qualifications (Rogoznica 2011; Kalc 2019: 156). Claudio, the former director of a utilities and construction company who drew various craftsmen to come from the Karst region to Piran with the help of a "bunch of keys," describes how great the need for a new workforce in the emptied Istrian towns was:

C: [Speaking about the establishment and the construction company's operation] How the people came. The craftsmen left. Only a few remained, some old ones, there were no joiners, no builders, no this, no that, there were no electricians . . . And we went around the interior inviting people to come and work here.
K: I see. The interior . . . Where? In Istria?
C: Why am I telling you about this Konstruktor now? I didn't have any builders here. So where did I go? I went to the Karst region. I know the Karst. I was a partisan up there. I know there are builders in Renče, I know there are joiners in Dutovlje . . . And I came up here, we had a meeting, and I said "Listen. We need builders down there. Are you prepared to come? You'll get a house, a flat." That's what you asked me earlier. I went to Dutovlje. "I need carpenters and joiners if you can come." You understand, a joiner's a joiner. And I got builders from one place and joiners from another. . . . And I went to the housing office, to the town hall. "I need a few flats for the people I'm going to bring here." And the boss gave me a cardboard shoebox full of keys! There was a sticker on it

with the street name and house number. "Here you are," he said, "choose what you want!" [*laughs*] And with those keys . . . I'm not exaggerating but there were a hundred inside! I went to our company, gave them to the head of human resources, and said: "Here are the keys, whoever applies can take their pick! They can go and take a look . . ." And that's how it was. And they went down the street . . . "Yes, not that one, yes, not that, I prefer that one, that one's better, what will you have . . ." Etc. It was a joke. People could choose what they wanted.

K: And then they paid a rent here or how did it work?

C: That was the housing authority. Because that was one authority, it wasn't just like that, partisan style, no. It was one authority, one owner, everything belonged to the state! Everything they left behind—those who left—became the municipality's property!

K: I see, and then you were the one who invited . . .

C: Yes, and also the teachers and the school staff? Exactly the same! They could . . . There weren't any teachers here! Few! There was a college for teachers in Portorož. But the staff was still undergoing training, they weren't ready yet. Basically, there was a shortage of staff. You asked me what happened with the houses. Some of them filled up with the arrival of new people, new workers, new, etc. And then many of them were offered to companies as holiday homes, holiday homes were in fashion at the time! From the square, Zelenjavni trg, down to the Punta, all holiday homes!

In addition to confirming the story of the "bunch of keys" for empty flats for new settlers, two other comments by Claudio are also interesting. The first mentions the handing over of abandoned houses to immigrants from Slovenia's interior, and will be discussed in the section on symbolic frontiers. The second refers to the already mentioned lack of teachers needed to set up the Slovenian education system that had been abolished twenty years before (due to fascism). It appears that this staff was also invited in a special way by being given somewhere to live. Martin, a local antique collector who moved here in the 1970s, says these flats were intended for those who were ordered to come. A negative attitude can be sensed toward the "privileged" immigrants of higher social status from the southern republics of the former Yugoslavia. We will also deal with this later.

Those who came helped themselves; they took large flats, the best flats. The keys you mention, they were given to verified people . . . A few keys, and this flat, and that one, and that one, and choose which one you like. It wasn't a bunch of keys, but these flats had already been taken; it was professors and teachers who received orders to come to the Obala [the Coast]. They're the ones who came. . . . Yes, for example if someone from

Figure 3.5. Sv. Marija na Krasu, 1948 (Department of History and Ethnography of the National Study Library of Trieste, collection Primorski dnevnik, author Mario Magajna).

> Kranj was ordered to come. They taught in Kranj, schools, professors . . .
> Books were written . . . That they're going to the Obala. They were guar-
> anteed flats here. They also said to him "here, do you want this, do you
> want that." And so he got this bunch of keys. Look, he didn't get a bunch
> of keys to go from door to door looking, that key's for that street, well,
> here's two, three keys, you decide . . . That was . . . [A large part of the
> interview.] Many people with surnames ending in "ić" came on the list;
> they brought them here from all over. They crammed the flats with them
> and they got flats . . . [A large part of the interview.] So here, they got
> privileged flats, good flats, they did and the dentists and all those needed
> by the system were given good flats. And they were nice flats.

We have already seen that bilingual teachers were the first to be sent
here. However, this changed when the towns became more Slovene.
Miroslav from Kranj told an interesting personal story. He was forced
to serve in the German Army, defected to the British in Normandy, was
captured and returned via the overseas brigades as a young teacher. In
1946, he volunteered to be sent to Zone B of the Free Territory of Trieste to help set up the Slovenian school system. My attention was drawn
by his comment that teaching positions in Istrian towns were reserved
only for privileged individuals, that is, Slovenes from Trieste or teachers
with experience:

M: After I had finished my military service, I applied to this teacher training course in Kranj, and then around twenty-five of us [out of sixty] decided to go to Primorska. Most of them were activists in the "national liberation struggle" and former partisans. . . . So I completed this course then went down to Primorska; we volunteered to go.

K: I see, you volunteered, but why Primorska? Had you heard or what? [About the liberation of Istria.]

M: We were young and, I don't know, full of those ideas, and we went down to help renew this education system.

K: OK, I see, it was known that people were needed in Istria.

M: Yes, there were no educated people down there, you can say. If there was one or two, it was a lot, most of the people were farmers, and those employed in the factories in Izola, there were these fish factories [speaking about the predominance of farmers and laborers]. So I applied to go to Primorska. And then they sent us out to the villages. I don't know anyone that was sent to the towns; those positions were reserved for the chosen ones.

K: And who were these chosen people?

M: Well, some former Primorci [people from the Primorska region] who were employed in schools in Slovenia or whatever, and who then returned to Primorska. . . . It was already Zone B, and we came later. We were sent down in the direction of Croat Istria.

K: So Slovenian teachers were transferred down to the Croat side?

M: Yes, it's Croatia now. . . . But it wasn't back then, it belonged to Koper. I came to Sveti Anton. . . . Yes, I went there, some went to Dekani, one went to Valdoltra, to the school of the children's hospital, then some went to Marezige and the villages back there, Pomjan, Babiči, and to Šmarje [speaking about other villages in Istria's interior]. Yes, only to the villages; you couldn't get to the towns. In the towns there were other older staff or teachers, or Slovenes from Trieste, for example, that's who went to the towns.

K: Mm, perhaps because they also spoke Italian; Italian was still spoken in the towns at the time.

M: That's true, most were Italians, the towns were Italian while the countryside was Slovene or Slovene-Croat; that's also a mixture.

Judging by the testimony, the teachers who were sent to the towns were people who returned to Primorska, while other Slovenes were sent to the rural Istrian hinterland. As Kristina noted above, the "returnees" were also sent to villages if they preferred, but her family wanted to be in a town. There is even a saying in the Brkini hills that states that Izola is the largest town of the Brkini.

According to archive sources, in this time the immigrants were coming from all over the Republic of Slovenia (19.5 percent). The largest waves of immigrants came from Ljubljana, Celje, Novo mesto, and

Murska Sobota (Kalc 2019: 155). Kristina remembers how upon her arrival in Izola in 1955 the environment was still predominantly Italian. However, with the new arrivals it very rapidly became Slovene:

> Also, many of the people employed in the public services spoke very poor Slovene . . . That was in 1955. My sister, who was in the second year of school, forgot how to multiply and how to write while we were moving house. So, for her too it was a culture shock. Italian was very much present at the time. These things changed incredibly rapidly. I'm talking about Izola. Perhaps it was different in Koper. The empty homes filled up very quickly and new blocks of flats were built . . . They were filled up with people who came from Štajerska; many people came from Maribor and also from Gorenjska, Jesenice. It's no coincidence. Maribor had many people who were trained in industry. And Jesenice also had its steelworks . . . These people, this staff was very welcome because in Koper, and later in Izola, mechanization began because of Tomos. It filled up very quickly. In the second half of the eight-year primary school . . . We already had schoolmates who had come from all over Slovenia. So when I arrived, I was alone. Then young families came streaming in from everywhere. So, I began speaking Italian in passing. For the people who came and who had contact with other people, like shop assistants and doctors, they organized an Italian language course as they had to speak it because it was widely spoken . . . I learned very good Italian in one of these evening classes. This made it easier for me to play cops and robbers—that's what we used to play then—but as I said, this area filled up with Slovenes very, very fast. Those who came a little later didn't have the contact with Italian culture that I did. The strongest contact with Italian culture was in the music school on Gregorčičeva ulica, where the headquarters of the Circolo Italiano di Cultura [Italian Cultural Association] used to be. Shortly after my arrival we had a television; we used to watch Sanremo [an Italian festival].

People who came later, after 1955, came into an already Slovenized environment, and they had no contact with Italian culture because the Italians were already a minority. This will be discussed in the section on symbolic borders in the newly founded Istrian society, when it will become clear that immigrants in this time felt no need to speak Italian. The former Zone B of the Free Territory of Trieste within Yugoslavia was not only attractive to Slovenians, but also to immigrants from the rural hinterland of north Istrian towns in the region of the Republic of Croatia. In 1945, fewer than a hundred inhabitants of Croat ethnicity were registered, while in 1956, 2,800 inhabitants came from Croatia, and in 1960 this figure had risen to over 5,000, representing 11.7 percent of the population. Many of them came from around Buzet, elsewhere in Istria and the Croat coastal belt. They mainly replaced the occupational structure of the emigrants, primarily in fishing and food production, some of them in shipping, while others settled in the countryside (Kalc 2019: 156). Ante's story belongs to this context. His wife's father was summoned from Buzet to come to this part of Istria because he was a baker. Interestingly, he mentions in passing that Slovenians did not want to go to Istria:

> Because the Italians were leaving! That's what I wanted to say. And there were no bakeries or bakers! From Slovenia, those Slovenians didn't go to the Obala [the Coast]! And they called the old man from Buzet to come and work, that he had a job! Someone asked him to come [in 1953 . . . Long interview in between]. That was in 1953, 1954, 1955 and so on. In the beginning, they didn't look so much, but to . . . Because the Italians were leaving, the fishermen, all the trades and so on, and they needed. That's why I'm telling you, those up there didn't have the "affinity" to come, and the government and the inertia . . . Like happened to me . . . I didn't, it never occurred to me that I would come and live here [they invited him to come as a teacher although he didn't speak a word of Slovene].

A lack of interest in moving here can also be gathered from the archive sources. The reasons given include modest possibilities for accommodation and a low standard of life, which is mentioned by the above interlocutor and will be discussed below. For these reasons, doctors came only on a temporary basis, various companies active in trade and commerce could not find managerial staff, and many immigrants soon left (Kalc 2019: 157). The interlocutors describe their profound disappointment with the situation in the Istrian towns. For example, one lady was disappointed to land in Piran simply because she could not return after giving up her job in Maribor (Pahor 2007: 204). Interestingly, later on in the interview Ante emphasizes that the authorities later preferred Slovenes, a tendency that was abandoned with the arrival of workforce from other former Yugoslav republics in the 1960s and 1970s. It is not entirely clear from his words, but it appears that during a certain period—the year 1957 is mentioned—new arrivals from other Yugoslav republics were required to have proof of accommodation and employment, although this was not mentioned by anyone else.

> A: Yes, that's how it was. Conditions were deliberately set by, what was his name . . . [discusses names] There was the registry office, and you had to register. You could only apply if you had, if you could say "I have a flat." Then he would first check who you were living with and so on. . . By which criteria. I was living with my wife . . . So if you had that, the next question was: "Do you have a job?" If you didn't, you couldn't get

residence. And that's how it was until the port began functioning. And they wouldn't give you it. They had criteria—only Slovenians. [Speaking about the immigration of Croats.]

K: Yes, but if you say they primarily wanted Slovenians . . .

A: To begin with they didn't check . . . Not when there was the military administration, the important thing was that they came, just as long as they're ours . . . We'll make sure in the census there are so many, you understand? They didn't check. But then when I came they were already checking. That was in 1957. They checked yes, to keep the number of "brothers from the south" [an ironic way of referring to people from the southern republics of former Yugoslavia] to a minimum, that's what they said. But then when the port came alive, and then Tomos . . . Suddenly there weren't any natives . . . Why should someone from Maribor, from Metalna or whatever it was called . . . From there . . . Come down here . . . There weren't even any toilets. Low standards, the standards of sanitation were extremely low.

He was not the only immigrant who felt this superior nationalistic attitude toward "southerners" from the Balkans, as this could also be felt in the words of other immigrants and locals. We will discuss this further below. Colonel Dragotin also spoke in a nationalistic tone when describing immigration from the former southern republics of Yugoslavia to some rural parts of Istria: "All these employees—I would say a couple of hundred of us—came down because there were no officials here. They got those flats immediately. And they came slowly, one after another. In Hrvatini, where many left and they brought these "southerners," we called it the "southern border." And even now, up there, just look, there are many . . ."

If we stick to this subject of immigrants from the Croat part of Istria, we must not forget there were also Italian speakers among them, such as Livio's father who came to replace the fishing workforce:

My father from Vrsar in Istria, my mother from Vižinjan in Istria. Both of them Italian speakers. My mother wanted to flee, a house near Gorizia was on both sides of the border and you paid to go through it into Italy—they caught her. My father got work as a fisherman in Izola; many Istrians—also fishermen as the old fishermen left Izola—made one of the largest fishing centers in the Adriatic. My father did not try to flee, he had not been in any army. . . . Initially only the chosen ones—the ones desired by the authorities—could come to the coastal towns. Istrians from Croatia could come, otherwise only the chosen ones could come [officers and people favorably disposed towards the socialist authorities]. Workers began coming only after factories like Tomos had been built.

Only the select few also had other privileges, not just flats but also child allowances, etc. (note in my field diary)

It is therefore possible to make out from oral testimonies that the first settlers in Istria, especially in the towns, were people ordered to come, chosen ones who were employed in the civil and military administration. Completely new staff was required to set up the Slovenian school system. It seems there were a large number of partisans among the new arrivals who were rewarded for their wartime activities by being provided with accommodation and jobs. These people were also desperately needed to set up the new sociopolitical system. However, the advantages with which they tried to draw trained employees and others to the "wild west" inspired unease and jealousy in the locals who did not enjoy these favors. This will be further discussed under symbolic borders but first let us take a look at the living conditions upon arrival in Istria.

Living Conditions in Istrian Towns upon Arrival

As has already been shown, both archive sources and memories indicate that the emptied Istrian towns did not represent the "promised land" for all the new arrivals, with the exception of the Primorci (people from the Primorska region). Many people, much workforce and managerial staff had to be enticed with privileges to come to this "ransacked" "wild west." Colonel Dragotin describes how the present-day Slovenian part of Istria was considered no-one's territory and above all an unknown land. He says the Slovenian collective memory spoke only about the conquest of Trieste.

> You must understand that when I was in primary and secondary school before the war, Koper was never ever mentioned. You know what I mean? All we said was, "Well, we still have the sea . . ." That's all, and nothing about where it was. And also in the partisans, when I got the order to go to the Slovenian Istria, they didn't say Koper, but Trieste. Only after the war, then, but before the war . . . Not Koper. Everything was focused on Trieste. At least that's what the mindset was here.

As has already been said, the main problems in annexed Istria were the poor accommodation and low living standards as there were no toilets or sewage systems (Kalc 2019: 157). Ante described the low living standards, without bathrooms, toilets, or running water:

[Speaking about empty Piran upon his arrival] The houses were one story higher than in Koper because the space was limited, they built them up. In Koper, there was enough room so they were low. That whole part of the town called Bošadraga, it's terrible! Even nowadays you wonder how anyone can live there. Think what it was like fifty, sixty years ago. The lowest standards of hygiene! In former Yugoslavia, not in Slovenia! In former Yugoslavia, these three towns—Koper, Izola and Piran. . . .—in terms of hygiene. I mean, they didn't have toilets; they didn't have water, a sewage system. They didn't have anything. . . . Even towns in Kosovo and Macedonia had this in place. And this . . . Why? The government changed. Higher standards were introduced, bathrooms, toilets, etc.; they used to have toilets in the garden! My neighbor. Five hundred years ago the house had been divided into two. And when I moved in, my house had a toilet in the garden!

In contrast to the Istrian conviction that the immigrants from the southern republics of the former Yugoslavia were coming to a highly civilized urban environment—as will be evident below—these words show that the new arrivals had the exact opposite view (Hrobat Virloget 2020). In 1957, the state of the sewage system in the district of Koper was still very problematic. Only 40.3 percent of flats had toilets (in Ljubljana the percentage was 43.6 percent), and the remainder had "primitive 'dry' toilets," some of them outdoors. The percentage of flats with no toilet amounted to 20.6 percent, unlike in the countryside where only 1 percent of houses had no toilet. In 1950, in the coastal belt, only 1.3 percent of flats had a bathroom, which combined with the 7.6 percent share in the hinterland was actually a lower percentage than elsewhere in Yugoslavia. In the towns within the district of Koper, only 27.1 percent of flats had water, 19.4 percent had water in the house, and 3.1 percent had water in the courtyard; 50.4 percent of the flats were without water altogether (Čebron Lipovec 2018: 111–12). This is how Colonel Dragotin describes the poor living conditions in Koper:

D: No sewage system, you know that. This flat already had a toilet and also, we had a bathroom . . . But we just left it, but it already had a flush. Our neighbor downstairs had a wooden toilet down in the corner and it's now been built over. It was a wooden toilet in the courtyard. And don't forget, only the *"casa nova"* [a multi-apartment building from 1910] had bathrooms. . . . Yes, normal ones . . . I don't know if any other house had a bathroom. But toilets, 50 percent of them weren't even in the houses. When we went looking for a flat we came in the morning, and everywhere there were chamber pots in the bathrooms. [Speaking about the conditions in 1956.] Because there were neither toilets nor water. Water was in the wells. This house already had water and electricity. Some had electricity that came via overhead cables . . . Then they made—we said it was for the Montenegrins so they wouldn't have to work hard, they would simply push with their shoulder. Because before we had to wind it up. [Speaking about Koper and the different town planning.]

K: And you, when you arrived here, did they let you see a number of different flats or did they simply give you this room?

D: No . . . I still have the list somewhere, 150 flats. And I spent fourteen days choosing, but there was no toilet anywhere, just this room already had a flush toilet and I chose this, where I am today.

In addition to the non-existent sewage system, some people like Marko mentions the absence of a water supply, the stench and the rats.

What was a bigger problem, life was hard back then; Koper was dirty, the Italians really did nothing for the town. . . . It was so dirty, everything smelled of rats. There was an open sewer, a ditch had been dug in the middle of the street with boards placed over it and the sewage flowed down it into the sea. And the rats . . . I practically lived with them . . . They broke into the flat. . . . You know, we got a flat that was poor, dirty, without running water, with a lodger, you understand. . . . My father got a flat down in the Triglav block of flats, you know the one opposite the market? That was the first thing they built, and we already had keys to the flat. We moved down there, and then they found there was an engineer from Tomos . . . It would be better if he [name] got it, and they showed him [my father] a wreck of a house, and easily satisfied and modest as he was . . . There in Bošadraga. My mother cried for a month after we moved in. . . . A black kitchen and hearth . . . My father had to renovate everything; the rats . . . We took baths in a tub, mother poured warm water over us . . . In the town center. She came down from the Karst, from a village, but she said the way Istria was down here . . . She first taught in Boršt, up there, and she said it was a culture shock. They didn't even have toilets here in Istria, in the villages. Simply, wherever it came, not even water. They just went to a nearby pool, and if there wasn't one, they went to the nearest pond.

Archive sources also mention the dilapidated state and poor accessibility of flats in Istria. Most of the buildings (84.5 percent) were older than fifty years, that is, they had been built before 1900. In the town this percentage was 74 percent and in the hinterland 54 percent. In the towns, less than half of the flats were well maintained, 14.7 percent requiring major repairs. The portion of flats unfit for living was 0.5 percent but the portion of buildings with unsuitable installations was even greater (Čebron Lipovec 2018: 112). This is why the administration made efforts already in the early years to gain the population's support by "raising the standard of living and culture" through the construction of schools, halls of residence for school pupils, cultural centers, hospitals, by carrying out maintenance on the water supply, purchasing chlorination appliances, renovating the sewage system, opening public bathrooms, electrification, and so on (Rogoznica 2011: 207, 287–88; Čebron Lipovec 2018: 72). The dismal state of the building stock and the rapid population growth dictated the new urban development plans and the intensive construction of flats, mostly in the hands of architect Edo Mihevc (see Čebron Lipovec 2018, 2019). However, such a low standard of living represented a "better life" for only a handful of immigrants who had come from even worse conditions. This was the case with Emir's family of Turkish origin, which came from Macedonia. Despite the catastrophic state of the flat they chose in Izola, they nevertheless came "somewhere better":

> Mother, when she came, she said we lived with rats. She had to clean and scrub for a few months. She was used to working—it wasn't hard—but to get it in a roughly normal state because there was no money to buy furniture. There was a small stove, I'm not sure now if there was, or if father bought it later. There was water only downstairs in the entrance hall, and nowhere else in the house. There was a tap, wooden stairs, but in a very bad state, half rotten away you could say. They slowly . . . When I was around six, seven years old, they began renovating the building with the help of the housing fund. In 1964, 1965 they also installed water and wastewater pipes in the flat. There was a tap downstairs, it was right next to the entrance. . . . That was all . . . Considering that in Macedonia it was even worse this was an improvement [*laughter*]. At least we didn't have to draw water from a well. They were still better off, although by a minimal margin.

Despite being disappointed with the low living standards, Ante mentions that for some people life was nevertheless better because of the "zone allowance":

> In all of Istria, the part here that was under Italy, they had white bread, white flour; they had a higher standard than in the rest of Yugoslavia. When the peace treaty was signed, pluf! They fled. But in this part, in Zone B, they didn't so much because they stopped them; the standard was higher here. And they had, let me tell you, 5,000 dinars of zone allowance. But the wage was already good if it amounted to six, seven thousand.

The "zone allowance," which was supposed to prevent excessive differences in wages in comparison with those over the border in Italy, is not mentioned only by Slovene and Croat immigrants (see also Pahor 2007 on higher wages in Istria), but also Luciano from Italy who came to Istria out of ideological reasons in the "counter-exodus" from Italy. He noticed that the living standards were better in Zone B, not only because the wages were higher than in Yugoslavia, but also because the border with Italy could more easily be crossed and because of smuggling:

> There was a big difference. In the former Zone B from Buie onward and on this side from Risana, people were able to go to Italy four times a month. And they could even take certain things with them. Various little things were smuggled. The other interesting fact is that the wages were 20 percent higher than in Yugoslavia. That's in Zone B. If not, the difference with Italy, i.e., with Trieste, would have been too great. At least as far as Slovenia was concerned. There were people who took meat to Trieste and returned with new shoes, or took cigarettes and came back with a golden chain, which they then sold on. Then there was the period when the car market was liberalized; I think it was in 1958. Where the harbormaster's office used to be in Capodistria, there were many old cars because new ones cost too much. Everything that could be taken to Trieste came back here. There was no lack of anything.

Archive sources also show that until the end of the 1940s, that is, until the period that corresponded to the outbreak of the Informbiro dispute, the authorities in Zone B tried to "artificially maintain" a somewhat higher standard of living in comparison with Yugoslavia, so as not to lag too far behind the Zone A standard. They mention the supply system, lower taxes for the farming population, higher salaries for the working class and full employment. Similarly, until the beginning of the 1950s, political and tactical reasons were behind the large investments made to improve the population's social standard with the aim of consolidating new social and national relations in Zone B of the Free Territory of Trieste (Rogoznica 2011: 287).

Going back to the problem with accommodation, we can say that due to the low standards, Istrian town centers were purely transitional in nature for many immigrants who later settled elsewhere in the surroundings. Many flats were not on hand to the local authorities as the departing *esuli* gave their houses to relatives or other administrators to look after (Kalc 2019: 157). This was the case with Colonel Dragotin, who was given a flat to look after by the previous Italian owner from whom he had rented a room. He later bought the flat from the municipality:

Him? Yes, I paid him; he was a very friendly Italian. I only knew a few
Italian things. . . . Well, and then he applied to leave, he authorized me
in court to be custodian until 1962, when it was nationalized. It wasn't
until 1962 that the municipality. . . . Then I lived in here, first paying a
small rent to the municipality before later buying it. As did the others
for the most part. Meanwhile, the others bought according to Jazbinšek's
law, when it was cheap . . . [Speaking about the former owner and two
children who came to visit] And they came to visit me here every year;
they brought me coffee . . . We went out into the garden and even in the
garden he would sit and cry . . . You know, it's there's after all . . . I can't
say anything against them. They even wrote to me sometimes, well, now
the son too has died; he's gone.

Neighbors, Istrians, could also be authorized to look after a house, so
such dwellings were not available to immigrants.

[From Škofije on the border:] An *esule* gave me his farm to look after. I
was entrusted with two houses and a farm to look after. The farmer asked
me before he left. He had to get someone to hand them over the farm. He
sorted out the papers—I was the caretaker. I was the master. He left with
the papers. When they sorted out the borders he could have returned to
live here. We would have welcomed him back with pleasure if only his
papers were in order. (note in field diary)

There is an interesting comment on the nationalization of abandoned
flats that was made in a tense part of the interview with Ante, who
bought the house of a departing Italian on the outskirts of Koper:

No, no. In the towns they . . . they had—I happen to know this because
I knew people who worked for the police and that—they knew so and
so . . . They had informers among the local population. Anything they
said: "This neighbor from . . . such and such a street is leaving for good
tonight." Then they seized these houses; they simply took them and nationalized them.

From 1947 to 1950, personal property was handed over to the
Commission for the Temporary Management of Property Belonging
to Absent Persons, which rented it out to various applicants, individuals, organizations, and offices on the basis of instructions. Property in
danger of falling into ruin was also sold. Property that was fictitiously
sold to individuals was managed by a special commission. Following
the signing of the London Memorandum in 1954, the sale of real estate
was stopped. Until 1955, real estate was managed by special representatives. From 1956 to 1958, it was taken over by competent popular

committees. After that, most of it became the general property of the people and was given to the relevant municipalities to run (Rogoznica 2011: 45–57). We must not forget that "rich people" had their property confiscated, including parts of houses that were given to immigrants to live in. We have seen this in the testimonies of both the colonel and Luciano, who mention that the Italians felt cornered when they were forced to have tenants from elsewhere living in their town houses. Danilo, who moved here from the Triestine Karst also remembers this. He commented in passing that he and his mother felt better in the villa when they lived together with the Italian owners, who were in a subordinate position because they were forced to accept new occupants, than when they later lived with the Slovenian owner who bought the villa in Portorož from the two *esuli* ladies:

> [The house] that belonged to the goldsmith remained until—I don't know now whose it is—they might still be its owners. What I want to say is that relations with this immigrant from Ljubljana were considerably more difficult than with those two [Italian] ladies. They must certainly have felt they were in a subordinate position because we had come to live in their house by force. Later, we felt we were in a subordinate position against someone who had a lot of money and the power to throw us out. So, in fact, the tables were turned.

He remembers that in the early period of immigration there were no new constructions so the new arrivals were put up anywhere there was room:

> Those were villas. After all, Portorož was a cosmopolitan . . . It had hotels and already back then there were hotels that were in operation. Hotel Central, Hotel Riviera, and so on. All these people were put up in some of these large buildings. Some of them were in houses that had already been abandoned by Italians, and there were quite a number of them. And some of them were in these big houses; nothing new was built.

The fact that "nothing new was built" when the first people arrived in Istria reflects the situation in Zone B of the Free Territory of Trieste, where despite some urban development plans prior to 1950, no major architectural plans for new constructions were made due to the territory's unclear fate. This is why extensive urban planning began only after the London Memorandum, when the fate of this part of Istria was finally decided. On both sides of the border, architecture became a tool for national and ideological marking of space (Čebron Lipovec 2019: 201–2, 220).

Symbolic Borders in Istrian Society

Social Borders between People with the Same Ethnic Belonging

Giving flats to immigrants to use was a strong factor that created or deepened the symbolic borders between the new arrivals and those who stayed in Istria. As related studies into "population exchanges" of Croat, Serb, Greek, and Turkish refugees have shown, people may all belong to the same nation but the new arrivals and natives set up symbolic borders with each other (Hirschon 1989: 30–35; Čapo Žmegač 2010: 189–92; Čapo 2015a).

Renée Hirschon, who studied the "exchange" of populations between Greece and Turkey after the Balkan wars, was the first anthropologist to draw attention to the fact that if the migrants and the host population were of the same ethnicity, this did not make integration any easier. Other elements of social life were more important. So despite sharing the same ethnic identity, the immigrants continue to be the "others" (Hirschon 1989; Čapo 2015a). We have already mentioned a similar aversion to immigrants of the same ethnicity in the relations of Italian natives with the *esuli* (Fakin and Jerman 2004). The same phenomenon can be sensed in Marko's commentary on how Slovene political refugees from Italy, in the time of fascism, were welcomed in Yugoslavia. The comments by interlocutors also clearly show that the benefits accorded to the new arrivals, with which the authorities lured them to come to the Istrian "wild west," were very unpopular with the locals. This is what an Istrian native with Slovene roots had to say: "The new arrivals were given free flats, even whole farms! They made them into landowners! They created cooperatives. The worthless ones were sent to collective farms. They went to the fields with an accordion and carrying flags!!!" (note from field diary).

Not only did Istrian farmers ridicule such behavior, which had nothing to do with the established agricultural standards, they could also not believe how poorly adapted the immigrants were to the new circumstances. They were not acquainted with the local farming conditions, as Bruno from the hinterland of Koper explained:

> [Speaking about the immigrants "from the south" in his village:] They didn't know much . . ., and they had no clue you can plant them here, in this soil. They were accustomed to soil in which nothing at all grew, not even to feed goats. Because they didn't know how. They didn't know how. We knew where to put things [where to plant them].

In the words of Štelio, a Slovene Istrian from the hinterland, one can sense the contempt the Slovene and Italian Istrians felt in the eyes of the new sociopolitical system, combined with their perception of the immigrants as privileged people:

> Most people from Štajerska were in Piran . . . Because a bus from Maribor went to Piran. The Bosnians came to Koper because the train went to Koper. A man said to me: "I stopped in Koper because the train didn't go any further." They came from all over. The aim was to change the environment here. There were many people from the Brkini hills. People who were up for it . . . They gave them everything . . . If you said you were from Malija, you weren't worth anything. I got into many arguments. I'm not a chauvinist, you can't call me that. They were very rude to us. They said to us, "you're from Malija?" . . . It was also like that for the Italians at the time.

In the same interview, he also ridicules the agrarian reforms of the new communist authorities when he explains how they cut down old olive trees: "Because our . . . communists said . . . They came from Russia, that we will plant pine trees, build a factory."

The distanced attitude of the locals toward the privileged immigrants is also reflected in Claudio's memory of how his Italian landlord offered to sell him his house in Piran for a favorable price, but he had to reject the offer because he was a member of the Communist Party, and it was against the rules. The way he says that all the property in the Istrian towns was bought up by immigrants who made good money from it suggests a feeling of injustice:

> Well, and when the owner left, he said I was a tenant in the house. "Listen," he said. I was standing up there on the Punta. "Listen, I'm leaving," he said, "but not because of politics, you know, this is my land, I was born here, I would rather stay here, but what can I do? I spent a lifetime there as a sailor for Lloyd [maritime company in Trieste]. I've every right there. I'll get a pension there. What would I do here?" And he left. And he left me his house! . . . And he left me his house. Left his house . . . "I'm going," he said, "you stay here, buy this house of mine." I said, "But I'm a civil servant, what will I buy it with . . . I have a small wage." "Don't worry about that," he said, "when I come down I'll need money for . . . A party, you'll quickly . . ." I worked for the municipality and was friends with the mayor who lived in this house here. He lived up there; he was Italian, a Friulian. I said: "Listen, the owner of my house is leaving, he said . . . he invited me to come to the court to transfer ownership of the house, I'll pay it off slowly." "What!!!??" he said, "don't you see," he said, "we're not allowed to buy from Italians who are leaving, we communists are not allowed!" I was a member of the party. "We communists must not buy from them! Because they'll say we sent them away or that we're taking their houses! We

mustn't! You'll get a flat when you want . . ." . . . Basically, he persuaded me not to touch it. Well, and I, of course, because I was a member of the party, I obeyed . . . But then they came down from the interior and bought everything up! Including that house of mine. They bought it, then sold it and made a profit. Basically, we stuck to the rules . . .

Such symbolic borders between people of the same nationality can also be detected in other conversations with Slovene Istrians. Tonin, a Slovene Istrian from Škofije who resides in the old people's home in Koper, laughed as he commented on the numerous social borders in this renovated Istrian society: "Two women from Štajerska were having a conversation on Čevljarska ulica in Koper, and they heard two old ladies talking in Italian. And the two ladies from Štajerska said: 'We've still got foreigners here.' They had come from Maribor—therefore foreigners—thought they were one of us!!!!" (note from field diary).

No fewer than three symbolic borders can be made out in this comment: Slovene Istrians did not consider Slovene immigrants to be "one of them," just as Slovene immigrants did not accept Italian Istrians as "one of them," while Slovene and Italian Istrians felt they were together on the "other" side of the border as "us." In conversations with Slovene Istrians, one frequently gets the impression that they consider immigrants to be privileged, as was expressed in a conversation at the old people's home in Koper: "The newcomers moved into these houses for free or for next to nothing" (note from field diary).

All these testimonies reflect a social border between natives and immigrants of the same nationality, which can be compared with a study by Jasna Čapo Žmegač (2007, 2010) on the Croats who migrated from Serbia to Croatia after the last Balkan wars. Although all these "population exchanges" involve migrations of people who speak the same language or belong to the same ethnicity across national borders, the situation is comparable with Istria, as people of the same ethnicity and nationality—Slovene or Yugoslav—moved into the emptied territory, although in Istria, it was a case of mass migration within state borders (Yugoslavia). Jasna Čapo Žmegač problematized the term "co-ethnic migration" as it envisages a "return" to the homeland and the problem-free integration of migrants in society on the basis of an apparently natural connection between a person and the ethnic group, the homeland. However, such views of ethno-nationalistically oriented politicians do not coincide with the reality of migrants, despite the fact that they are ethnically privileged migrants who acquire all rights in the new homeland (citizenship, political rights, they do not have refugee status; unlike other refugees they have no desire to return). It is only in the beginning that the loss of home is alleviated by the idea of belonging to the same ethnic group as the local population, which however shows no interest in the new arrivals and gives them a "cold" welcome. The ethnic privilege therefore lasts only for the time of migration as it determines the goal, eases the acquisition of citizenship and alleviates the feeling of being obliged to leave. But gradually ethnicity ceases to be a privilege. The natives reject the new arrivals and the idea of the problem-free integration of co-ethnic migrations turns out to be delusive as the migrants continue to be rooted elsewhere—in their lost home. It becomes clear that migrants cannot be labeled according to their external criteria, but must instead be considered on the basis of their everyday experience and practice (Čapo Žmegač 2010).

In the same way, Algerian migrants of French nationality who fled en masse to France, their "motherland," following the Algerian-French wars, were stigmatized and continue to be stigmatized. The state authorities call this "repatriation." In the eyes of the natives, the so-called *pieds-noirs* continue to be seen in a negative light. They are considered to be exploiters, violent, loud, vulgar, racist, and responsible for their sad fate. They are therefore blamed not only for their own fate, but for the whole weight of colonization, with all the shame and guilt placed on their shoulders. All this stigmatization means that for immigrants with the same nationality there is a large difference between integration and the existential feeling of foreignness. The *pieds-noirs* are therefore caught between two worlds—Algeria, which was their homeland, persecuted them, and France their "motherland" rejected them (Baussant 2002: 249–56).

There are various kinds of symbolic borders. In Istria, especially in rural areas, a clear distinction continues to be made between Istrians and the so-called *forešti*, or foreigners, as has already been written about by Borut Brumen (2000). He observes that the word *forešt* has a flexible definition that depends on the context. In the village of Sv. Peter it may refer to villagers who have moved there from surrounding villages, people who come there because of marriage, people doing errands in the village, or visitors from coastal towns. But it may also refer to people who come to the village in an official manner, as tourists or on business. When there is talk of the latter—who are often also seen as representatives of the authorities—the former group known as the šuperski *forešti* (*forešti* of Sv. Peter) become natives. It is expected of them that they will behave in accordance with the unwritten moral code called *krjanca* (a word use throughout the region of Primorska). The community will watch closely that it is respected and any inappropriate behavior will be sanctioned with gossip. It is expected that they take interest in and participate in village activities (Brumen 2000: 379–84).

How strong the symbolic borders with the natives continue to be even decades after moving there is testified by immigrants who even after having spent more than seventy years living in Istria still do not dare identify themselves as Istrians. This rift between "autochthonous" Istrians and those who have "moved there" could be detected at the roundtable events at which the speakers always specified to which group they belonged. This uncertain identification of immigrants as Istrians was clearly displayed at a roundtable held on 27 November 2019, when a man who had moved to Koper seventy-five years ago said it was not until recently that he first "referred to himself as Istrian":

> I'm an Istrian. Two months ago, I was asked where I came from, who I was, and for the first time I said the word "Istrian" because, when I was still a child, my uncle said to me: "Hell, you're as thick as an Istrian!" You know, and Istria got a . . . This shy opinion that they're worth something less—if there are any Istrians here, please let me know if you agree—because there was the feeling that they are something less and . . . And also, we who came before—I've lived in Koper for seventy-five years—it was the first time, as I'm telling you, that I said I was Istrian.

Social Borders between People of Different Ethnic Identities: Slovenes against Italians

What has been described above begs the question: who in Istria feels they are "on their own land," and who is excluded from this community? From the above humorous account, we can conclude that the immigrants nevertheless felt they were "on their own land." This was probably emphasized by the dominant Yugoslav memory, according to which the Italians they came across on Slovene territory (fewer and fewer of them over the years) were foreigners. This is evident from the comment made in passing by Roza, a teacher of Slovene who came to live here from Ljubljana. She said the Italians, whom she refers to as natives, moved "back" to Italy. "There were still some natives here but many of them moved back to Italy from here." This statement clearly shows that the new arrivals considered them to be only temporarily present—the predominant view was that they came here in the time of fascism.

The perception of Italians as foreigners on Slovene territory suits nationalist ideology, according to which cultural borders should correspond with political borders, that is, the state should only contain people of the "same type" (Gellner 1983). Interethnic hatred from the time of violent fascism and the war left profound consequences on interpersonal relations in Istria. This is evident in the relatively strong social border between Italians and the newly settled Slovenes. Even nowadays, the two communities do not engage with each other as each has its own repressed memories. A conflict occurs when these meet, as happened at a public event for telling memories about Koper entitled "Telling the Town's Story: Urban Legends and Anecdotes." It was organized in autumn 2012 by Neža Čebron Lipovec, Maša Saccara, and Zdenko Bombek.[3] A stir was caused by memories publicly expressed—one after the other—of mutual contempt and humiliation. One spoke of a Slovene woman, who had just arrived, being humiliated in the street by Italians in Koper, and the other of an Italian woman being humiliated by Slovenes.

> And I was going past [the Loggia in Koper], probably on the way to work, when someone hissed behind me. When I heard her, I hit her so hard that I frightened myself and began shaking.
> They said to me, "Maledetta Italiana!" [Bloody Italian!], and I pushed them up against the wall. [The moderator Neža Čebron Lipovec tried to calm things down—the Slovenian and Italian residents of Koper sat in separate groups.]

An Italian native from Koper reacted to these memories by highlighting the injustices Yugoslav socialism caused for Istrian Italians, from the confiscation of private property and the transferal of Italian children to Slovenian schools, to being labeled fascists and the privileges enjoyed by the new arrivals:

> But, for example, Tomos [a factory] was built on land that was stolen from my grandfather and no-one ever gave it back to him. He was neither a fascist nor a communist; he was just a farmer who worked honestly. And it must be said that some who came to Capodistria were lucky. They had work and a home, but some people who had nothing to do with any wrongdoing had to suffer many injustices. In the 1950s, there was talk of education but the system was not idyllic. Italian children were forced to attend Slovenian schools. . . . This meant there were many children in Slovenian schools who did not understand Slovene as they had never spoken it at home. It is important to say that with the desire to repair certain injustices, other injustices were caused. [Speaking about the headquarters of Radio Koper, which used to be the headquarters of the Italian communists; and about the mayor of Capodistria—a communist—who was elected in 1922.] The people of Capodistria never voted for the fascists. It is important to remember this as lies are often told on this subject. Isola was run by Christian Democrats while in Pirano it was the Communist Party. Very often they were defined as fascists, simply because they were Italian, even if they were communists or had some other political persuasion [speaking about the closing down of schools]. (Hrobat Virloget 2015b: 546)

It was in the tense atmosphere of this public event that a decades-old northern Adriatic conflict about the superiority of one ethnic group over another came to the surface. During fascist rule, the Italians as representatives of the *civiltà*, felt superior and more "civilized" than the *sc'avi*—which was and continues to be a derogative Italian term for the Slav population. The attitude of contempt and ignorance is reflected in the failure to differentiate between Slav ethnic and national groups, such as the Slovenes and the Croats. Instead, they bundle them all together into one Slav group. This opposition between the Italians and the Slavs is equated with the urban-rural social conflict (Baskar 2002; Ballinger 2003; D'Alessio 2008; Verginella 2015; Wolff 2021). In the new postwar social reality, this relationship was turned upside down, especially from the Yugoslav perspective in which the Italians were collectively seen as fascists and occupiers (Hrobat Virloget 2015a). Each side concentrates only on the concept of its own victimhood while denying it to the "other" side. Neither side sees itself as a perpetrator (Assmann 2007; Hrobat Virloget and Čebron Lipovec 2017).

In all the conversations with immigrants, one of my standard questions was whether they had learned Italian in the new environment. It is a telling fact that hardly anyone learned the language, with the exception of those who had already spoken Italian before, including a gentleman from Montenegro. As we have already seen in Kristina's story, after this environment was Slovenized, there was no need to speak Italian. This attitude also shows that later arrivals did not feel the need to understand the complex and delicate history of their new living environment. Jelka's story confirms this. She came to the Obala (the Coast), as she calls this area, in 1962:

> [Asked if she had any contact with the local Italians:] No way! I didn't speak Italian! And I can't speak it now either! [Despite learning the language, she cannot speak it. But she can understand them and has relatives in Italy. Speaking about her daughters:] She has no trouble with Italian. They did well at school. They accepted the bilingual area, but I didn't. I didn't . . . It's only now in my old age that I've come into contact with Italians. I went to Trieste, but they spoke Slovene with me. Otherwise I didn't feel the need. But now I do, I see them often.

This helps us understand the large difference between the Italian minority's official right to use its own language in public and reality. As Ornella from Koper said: "Because if I speak Italian, they answer 'yes,' they speak to me in English." I once witnessed a conversation in English between an Italian guest and a waitress in Koper. Most Slovenians would say that Italians should speak Slovene! When Vittoria asked in Italian for *radicchio* (Italian chicory) in the market in Koper someone said to her "If you want to buy *radicchio* in Italian then go to Trieste!" Ornella, an Italian from Koper put it nicely "there is a thin line of antipathy. To speak Italian in these parts is like picking at something, it's better if you don't do it."

This indicates a rift between immigrants from Slovenia's interior and the Italian natives, while there is no sign of a similar conflict between Slovene and Italian natives, as we shall see below. Some Slovene Istrians even say that the conflict between Italians and Slovenes was brought "from outside," as Tonin and Bepo from Škofije and Roć, suggest.

> They fled. But 90 percent of them didn't know why! The politics was tough. Politics was to blame that you had to leave all your belongings! Politics applied pressure! We were fifteen, sixteen years old at the time; we didn't understand. But now we can see; we understand. There was hatred. Whoever spoke Italian was a fascist. Ljubljana and Zagreb are to blame!!!! For the emigration! Politicians are to blame. To have new people move in. The Istrians they didn't [respect]. Before that, it was similar under Italy. (note from field diary) (Hrobat Virloget 2015b).

A related study by Jasna Čapo Žmegač (2002: 117–30) on the migration of Syrmian Croats from Serbia to Croatia after the war in Yugoslavia in the 1990s—a case of co-ethnic migration like in Istria—finds that the refugees from Serbia blame the Serbs who recently fled from Croatia (i.e., immigrants) for the ethnic conflicts. In his study of the population "exchange" between Greece and Turkey in 1923 after the Balkan wars, Barbaros Tanc (2001) shows that immigrants on both sides remember harmonic coexistence with the ethnic "other," prior to the conflicts that were supposed to have been triggered by external actors, in this case also immigrants.

The Social Border with Immigrants from the Southern Republics of the Former Yugoslavia

On the one hand we can make out the conflict between the Italian natives and the new arrivals in Istria. It appears that the latter are predominantly Slovenians who came "to their own land" under the influence of the dominant collective memory of Italians as the enemies of the people. On the other hand, it is evident that a border is established that separates the "natives" and the early immigrants from those who arrived later. For example, Marko, who came to Koper as a "returnee" with his antifascist family that fled fascism in Trieste and sought refuge in Yugoslavia, highlights the similarity between Italians and Slovenes in Primorska, as they had already coexisted in the past. This suggests a superior attitude toward the immigrants from the southern parts of former Yugoslavia:

> [Speaking about the arrival of workers from the southern republics of the former Yugoslavia in Koper for the needs of the port, Tomos, and other industries:] Another culture breaks in, which actually . . . There was less difference, much less, between us and the Italians, as we actually lived on the same territory, one side happened to be Slovene . . . This has been the case for millennia. My father was born in Trieste . . . But this is when a completely different culture breaks in. They took people down there, from the villages, you understand, they were shepherds . . . They carried bags here and so on. That was more difficult. On some cultural level.

Marko continues using this orientalistic discourse when he describes the farmers from "the Balkans," who settled in the highly urbanized Istrian towns. Again we come across the stereotypical discourse about the low rural and high urban culture, this time in a different social context:

> This is why conflicts occurred because they actually brought people—let's put it bluntly—shepherds. You put them in a highly developed urban environment, and they couldn't cope, of course, they were afraid here and reacted in self-defense. . . . The problem was the language. These were people who had been brought from the hills who weren't used to this. They spoke their own language and that was that. It's all very well telling them to "learn Slovene!" But they didn't even know their own language. I don't know if they knew how to read.

In contrast to the above, a study carried out in the 1980s on immigrants from the southern republics of Yugoslavia refuted the widespread stereotype that most of these people were uneducated as it showed only small differences in the levels of education of Slovenians and non-Slovenians. The educational structure of Slovenians was also "low," although in terms of employment and career progress this was less evident than the low education level of immigrants (Mežnarič 1986: 73–74). A similar, superior attitude toward immigrants from the southern republics of the former Yugoslavia may be sensed in the perception that they have come to a highly urbanized culture. This is evident when Italian Istrians like Ornella speak of the relationship immigrants have with heritage and the local environment:

> This first Slovene part [the first Slovene immigrants] is the one that respects us the most. . . . When they came, they couldn't say "you weren't there," as they bumped into us. Any they're the ones who came from

elsewhere as we were already here. . . . Then a different group of people arrived, all these people from Bosnia, from that war. With all respect to them too, but they've occupied this land . . . Occupied and . . . they've brought along, of course they've brought their traditions. They've brought their own world. They've brought little respect for these places where they've come, not much (Hrobat Virloget 2019: 172).

The "otherness" of the immigrants from the southern republics of the former Yugoslavia is reflected in the eyes of Koper's Slovene inhabitants by their different mentality and their violent behavior that does not comply with "local" standards, as described by a lady from Istria whose family owned a restaurant:

> [Speaking about the large influx of people "from the south" when the factories opened in the 1970s:] These people brought with them their own culture, which was unknown to us here. They drank a lot, smashed things, got in fights and literally brought so much unrest and discontent to the pubs that the locals preferred to withdraw because of them. So they literally overran the town. Especially on payday. The entrance to the port was just near here and it was clear when it was payday from the amount of drinking, and for us who worked in pubs and restaurants work became very hard . . . There was money. But it was very hard to work because these people were . . . There was a lot of alcohol, violence, fights, police . . . It wasn't very pleasant in the period I'm describing, from around 1978 until 1985. [Speaking about their departure:] The largest number left around 1991, when there was war where they're from. Quite a lot of them left then. But others came up. Some of them also assimilated, calmed down a bit, but it was bad in those years.[4]

The study entitled *The Established and the Outsiders* can partly help us understand why violence is ascribed to the "other." Norbert Elias and John L. Scotson (1994) analyzed why young people from immigrant "outsider" families are considered to be delinquents. Despite the fact that only a small percentage of them do not conform to the behavioral standards of the original population, their delinquent acts are convenient for denigrating and confirming the "inferior" status of immigrants in general. Unlike children who grow up under the collective supervision of settled, established populations, children in immigrant families that are not connected within a community, are left to be brought up only by an individual family and are therefore without broader societal supervision. The children of immigrants identified themselves with the negative stigmatization of their parents from a young age. In the past, family instability and a deviation from social norms were mostly ascribed to poverty, rootlessness in the search for employment, and the volatility of working-class employment. However, this was not the case with the analyzed community of workers, where the main reasons were connected with personalities. People came to this city from all over, with different standards and patterns of social behavior that collided with the "civilized" behavior of the already established community.

This "different" behavior may therefore be ascribed to the incompetence or aversion of certain families to the standards of behavior established by the community consisting of the oldest inhabitants. The young generation has preserved the social borders employed by their parents and has made them even more rigid. On one side, we have the pride of young people who come from the first "established" families and their contempt for the immigrants, and on the other side, the roughness and "inappropriate" behavior of young people "with a lower status." The latter have been provoked and rejected from their childhood onward, so they have reacted by harassing those who rejected and despised them, which led to the latter feeling even more threatened (Elias and Scotson 1994: 117–45). Although in our case there is no mention of a second immigrant generation, which would mean we could easily apply this explanation to them, we may ask to what extent the "deviation" in the behavior of a minority of immigrants from the southern republics of the former Yugoslavia was caused by revolt and identification with the stigma of the "lower class" and the negative meaning of the name *Balkanci* [people from the Balkans] they were given upon their arrival.

Discourses about the Balkan "other" may be heard both among Slovenians and Italians in Istria. It is clear from daily practice in Istria and throughout Slovenia that immigrants from the southern republics of the former Yugoslavia are the "ultimate other." As Ana Kralj (2008) says, immigrants in Slovene society are generally uninvited, although it has been shown that in Istria they were "invited" to help build the new social and economic order (Hrobat Virloget 2019). Anthropologist Irena Weber finds in her contemporary study, as part of the "Piran: My Town" project, that ethnic intolerance is still strong in Piran. It is expressed through pejorative names like *Šiptar* (derogative term for Albanians), *Italijanar* (derogative term for Italians), *južnjak* (somebody from the "south"), and more. Through seemingly tolerant statements that actually reflect intolerance like: "I've got nothing against them, but . . ." She finds that cultural differences are smallest between ethnic Slovenes and Croats—those from Istria and Dalmatia—and the greatest between ethnic Albanians and other groups (Weber 2006: 3).

In Istrian society, researchers have already noticed strong regionalism and the attachment of Slovenes and Italians to the common, hybrid, Istrian identity. Unlike the Italian *esuli*—the Italian postwar migrants from Istria who in the language of superior purity and autochthonous homogeneity perceive themselves as the sole Istrian Italians, as there were supposedly no true Istrians left in Istria following the exodus—the *rimasti,* Italian-speaking inhabitants who did not leave, and the other Slovene (and Croat) Istrians proudly refer to the language of authentic hybridity. We are therefore not Croats, not Slovenes, and not Italians, but Istrians, yet different from the non-Istrians, especially those of the Balkan kind. The discourse revolves around the rhetoric of "historical rights" to the area, and emphasizes the autochthony and cultural superiority of Istria in comparison with the Balkans. These stereotypes are reflected in spatial terms—the Balkan immigrants are seen as inhabitants of the abandoned Istrian town centers who live in the flats abandoned by the Italians. They are accused of not taking up the Istrian dialect, are seen as a mafia (the Albanians), are accused of making the town centers appear neglected with their "uncivilized" traditions—an example of the old discourse of farmers occupying the center and degrading it. Although it appears more multicultural at first, this Istrian hybridity (Italian, Croat, and Slovene) is also exclusivist in its orientalizing discourse (Ballinger 2003: 245–73). A recent study by the Croat anthropologist Olga Orlić of the frequently acclaimed Istrian multiculturalism has shown that it actually conceals an exclusivist discourse, not unlike the discourse on European multiculturalism, which excludes people from non-Western Europe and non-autochthonous inhabitants. The coexistence (It. *convivenza*), so greatly extolled in Istria,[5] actually refers to coexistence with the Italians as an autochthonous group, while the relatively new minorities such as the Serbs, Bosnians, Albanians, and Chinese are excluded. Members of these minorities and the Croat immigrants who came from beyond Mt. Učka (the equivalent in the Slovenian part of Istria would be immigrants from above Črni Kal) see themselves as "others," who are expected to adopt the Istrian identity, dialect, way of life, and mentality. Istrian multiculturalism is therefore present nowadays only on a declarative level in its attitude toward the autochthonous, native Italians. However, in relation to the new arrivals it only expresses a need for assimilation, which goes against the idea of multiculturalism (O. Orlić 2008).

In the contemporary context of postwar Sarajevo, Alenka Bartulović (2013: 277–308) notices the persistent perception—imbued with orientalism—that the "rural" or "uncultured," "backward" and "Balkan" has intruded into the "urban" or "cultured" and "European." She also quotes other studies that found similar perceptions throughout Yugoslav history. In the eyes of the people of Sarajevo, after the war the city's "urban character" was killed by the "invasion of nationalistically oriented peasants." The concept of the "ruralization of cities" is not just a Yugoslav phenomenon as the conflict between "urban" and "rural" is also deeply rooted elsewhere, especially in the Mediterranean. The category of "urban provincial" prevailed in the explanation of Yugoslav history after 1944 when rapid industrialization drew masses from the countryside to the cities. After moving, they were said to remain in an awkward liminal position. The problem with the perception of the "urban provincial" also lies in the ascribed homogeneity that is imposed upon the immigrant population, and in the neglect of the historical context. The establishment of socialism was connected with rapid urbanization and the construction of an industrialized society. This involved intentionally stimulating people to move from the countryside to towns and cities in line with socialist aspirations to depart from the stigmatized backward "peasant society." For example, it is said that the "rural newcomers" never felt Belgrade was there true home. Instead, it was a place of discomfort, which they tried to make more home-like by behaving like peasants. This liminality or "double life" lived by the immigrants is also supposed to have hindered urbanization and "progressive thinking" due to a lack of education and the absence of motivation for cultural life (Simić 1973: 13; Blok and Driessen 1984; Miličić 1985: 100, 106; Allcock 2000: 164; Brown 2001: 419). These urban stereotypes of "maladjusted," "rural" practices in the "urban" environment have been around in Koper for decades, and include the widespread stories of immigrants "from the Balkans" growing potatoes or keeping pigs in urban Venetian palaces in the old town center. Unlike studies of rural immigrants in Yugoslavia, who mostly share the same ethnic identity, the "rural others" in Istrian urban environments are not of the same nationality, or rather, even if people of the same (Slovene) ethnicity came from the countryside, this urban folklore does not refer to them but exclusively to the "Balkan others." The latter admittedly belonged to the joint but fragile Yugoslav identity. This fragility was clear to see when Yugoslavia broke up and the very distinct ethnic identities emerged, leading to the "erased"[6] (Zorn and Lipovec Čebron 2008).

Regardless of the fantastic basis of symbolic borders, these were internalized by immigrants from the southern republics of the former Yugoslavia. Their everyday experience of these borders was very real. The son of Macedonian parents who came to live in Koper describes the alienation caused by the negative stigmatization of immigrants from the Balkans:

> I didn't associate with the locals but with immigrants from other Yugoslav nations. It was still Yugoslavia at the time. . . . I always wonder what

I did wrong to not be accepted as I would want to be. Why do the locals first look at my name and surname and then decide not to enter my cake shop? Foreigners don't care, and they come and buy what they want. However, the foreigners come once and then go away, but the locals live here (Menih 2011: 67–68).

In Piran, Irena Weber observes the constant separation of "true" and "false" inhabitants of Piran. This includes the question of who has the right to call themselves a *Pirančan* (native of Piran). Although this right is granted, in a specific context, to those who were born in Piran, this is not the case with all ethnic groups. "I was born in Piran, but I have been called a *Šiptar* (derogatory term for Albanians) all my life," said my interlocutor. Who exactly qualifies as a *Pirančan* depends on the context of the conversation as identity is not fixed but movable (Weber 2006: 68).

The experiences of immigrants from the southern republics of the former Yugoslavia, who felt their "otherness" and "foreignness" as unwanted citizens in the new Slovenian environment, did not correspond to the official discourse, which promoted the "brotherhood and unity" of all Yugoslav nations. In principle, they belonged to the same Yugoslav nationality, and yet they were "others" as the republican identity was obviously stronger. Andrea Smith calls this contrast between public discourse on the one hand and personal experience as a migrant on the other, conversational or cognitive dissonance, and also observed it in Maltese immigrants in France and Algeria. For example, she quotes a Maltese immigrant who openly confronts the official discourse with the "melting pot" of migrants and her own experience of "otherness" (A. Smith 2006: 134–40). It is very reminiscent of the memories of alienation, being accepted and also unaccepted, described by Adela, an Albanian immigrant from Kosovo. She kept emphasizing how her family was welcomed by the Istrians, but also highlighted that her family kept making efforts not to appear different from the natives—for example, by keeping their traditions in the privacy of their home:

That the locals failed to welcome us here . . . it would be very dishonest, as they actually stood by our side. If anyone made life hard for us it was the Udba [State Security Administration] back then. . . . And as we had a business—because in those times you were a capitalist if you had a business in that system. [Speaking about the regime's resistance to Catholic practices.] That you were . . . I can't say you were an opposing element, but you were by no means in their . . . I mean, we suffered this pressure that the Udba exerted on us. Otherwise no, you know, the people we lived with, no. They accepted us. . . . OK, I was lucky to grow up in such a family. It was made clear to us that we had come here, to an area, and that our first duty was to accept the people, to be exactly like them. All the rest you have in the family. So, our church services, we simply had them at home [other Slovenians also performed their Catholic practices at home in secret]. . . . No, it would be unfair to say they didn't accept us. It would be very unfair. . . . If you come here and are not aware of why you came, and you have no respect for the natives who are here, anything else can happen then. Because I say that if you come to a new place, it's right that you assimilate and adapt, and not the other way round. Which means, first the language, and all the rest. . . . You have all the rest at home. OK, I know I've often heard this other story, that I'm Albanian and that I'm Muslim. And before it was explained that it's not true . . . that I'm Catholic, it was hard. OK, they gave you some strange looks, yes. But did they chase me away to keep me out of their society? No, that didn't happen. You know, in the end, it's clear you're not one of them. But not to the extent that they would hate you or anything. Not like that. . . . For example, there was no emphasis on this at home. We made more efforts in the other direction. We were actually more neat and tidy when we stepped out than all the others. Just so they wouldn't hold this against us. . . . They were sad because you have to be aware that many people who go somewhere, you're a foreigner and they probably treat you like a foreigner. . . . I never understood my father and I said, . . . "Why didn't you go to Italy if you'd already traveled a thousand kilometers? [The father:] "But do you think it would be any easier for you?" I said: "For me, yes, because I'd be a foreigner abroad while here I feel like a foreigner at home." I explained this to him as I was growing up when I didn't understand—I simply didn't want to accept the communist system. . . . I experienced it that way, not because I was Albanian or anything. Not in the smallest way from the locals. I experienced it more from those higher up. . . . You have to realize you've come somewhere, and respect these people who've given you the opportunity to be here. I mean, the first thing you should do is learn their language.

This passage reflects what Andrea L. Smith notices in connection with the question of assimilation, which is often a conscious process for people with migrant roots. When they notice in their external environment, in the street, or in school that their origins are seen as inferior and that they can distance themselves from their native environment, this leads to denial of their identity background (A. Smith 2006: 138). As Adela emphasizes "any way you take it, it's clear you're not one of them," and the cognitive dissonance with the official discourse is very clear from her statement that "you're a foreigner at home." This will be discussed further below. Adela constantly refers to not being accepted by the communist authorities, which were in fact a part of the everyday reality throughout Yugoslavia, including in her native Macedonia. Cognitive dissonance is evident throughout the interview as a permanent, recurring conviction that they were accepted by the locals although they made special efforts not to be "different" from them. This feeling of exclusion that is experienced by immigrants from the southern republics of Yugoslavia is condemned by the Italian Istrian Vittoria:

> I wonder how many years they must live here for them to become equal citizens. I keep asking myself this. Why do we always say "us" and "them." Why? How many years have to pass? Why am I . . . "Have you come from southern Istria?" OK, I'm working. I'm paying taxes. I'm a citizen like everyone else. They work. they work hard. Why? Here, with the Albanians who're selling vegetables. . . . And they tell me, I understand, judging by what they tell me, that they live apart, a foreign element in Slovenia. Their community, closed, difficult . . . And I told this man who sells, I ask myself, why do they live apart like that? Why don't we know anything about you, your wives and children. And yet I buy vegetables. I come here. I speak with you. Terrible if you're not here. I ask you about your family down there. I don't want you to leave and go down to Kosovo. "Bring your family," I said many times. "You're a citizen here like everyone else."

Research into immigration to the northern Istrian towns is still in its early stages, however, the interviews that have been held so far with immigrants from the southern republics of the former Yugoslavia show both a feeling of separation and of being accepted by society, as has been emphasized above. For example, a lady from Bosnia who moved here in 1955 stressed that the Italian locals blamed the Bosnians for the lack of jobs: "and when there was no work, they said the Bosnians should go away, that the Bosnians were to blame, and that this is their home and that they need work, not us."[7] As comparative Mediterranean studies have observed, the complex social and ethnic circumstances may be stable as long as the economic situation is stable. However, when the latter is shaken, social and ethnic tensions are also activated (Weber 2006: 6).

On the other hand, when asked if Slovenians have accepted her and her Dalmatian husband, both of them repeatedly affirm that they have. "We never had any problems with Slovenians, I was respectful and fair so they were like that to me too." The lady from Bosnia says the reason they were accepted by Slovenian society was that they were hardworking—a quality that is probably particularly prized by Slovenians. "We never had any problems because we were hardworking and paid everything like they did. That's why they accepted us like we were one of them. Your grandma always said to me we were like them, not like the other lazy Bosnians."

In some of the other interviews the question of integration in the new social environment did not reveal a strong symbolic border either. Many of them referred to equality among workers, for example, the above interlocutor from Bosnia:

> No, no, it wasn't like that. I personally had no problems with Slovenians, nor with them [the Italians] because I knew how to stand up to them. Look, I came here and got a job. . . . We both worked, had a family, and paid the full taxes. We weren't a social problem. But those who were a social problem, they insulted them and made life difficult for them. They told them they had come from Bosnia and that all they do is eat bread and that they have to work for them. Us two—who were on a par with them, got the same and paid everything just like they did—never had any problems. He [her husband] asked to get a flat and whenever he asked, he got what he wanted, so these Slovenians, the director and the others were always fair to him.

A study carried out in the 1980s on Bosnians in Slovenia bore the telling title "Bosnians: but Where Do Slovenians Go on Sundays," which reflects the clash of lifestyles between "us" and "those who are different." It nevertheless shows it is necessary to differentiate between immigrants with and without families, when dealing with processes of social integration. Living in a family circle brings with it a much more complex everyday life. A young "Bosnian" immigrant family adapted more quickly to Slovenian society and way of life, and also considered this to be "modernization." The author observes that in the time of Yugoslavia, the immigrants emphasized not so much the distinction between Bosnians and Slovenians, but "we, below" and "them up there"—referring to the administrative class. This classification according to class did not include the national or ethnic element, but indicated the unequal access to basic resources and control in society, that is, power relations in the everyday life of a laborer (Mežnarič 1986: 202–7). We must take into account that most immigrants from the 1950s had families or at least created them here, and most of them were working class. They were different from the immigrants in the 1960s and later, for whom the Tomos homes for working men were built, for example.

It therefore appears that ethnic borders were not experienced the same way by all. It must be emphasized that views such as the ones expressed above, which highlight the equality among workers that was supposed to surpass ethnic borders, come from the perspective of immigrants from the southern republics of the former Yugoslavia. In the eyes of the Slovenian locals, they are still the "ethnic others."

The Social Border between the Natives
and the Oldest Immigrants, and the Later Immigrants

Was the ethnic element always equally potent in creating social borders? As will be shown below, it appears to have had a stronger role in the time preceding the exodus, when society was divided into Slav-rural and Italian-urban inhabitants. We could also assume that it was more distinct in the time following the breakup of Yugoslavia in the 1990s, and became particularly clear with the phenomenon of the "erased" (Zorn and Lipovec Čebron 2008). The above memories and testimonies about the feeling of home (in the next section) indicate that the new group "we" consists of Italian Istrians and the first group of immigrants, most of whom came from Primorska. They had already "coexisted" with the Italians in the interwar years and arrived in the first phase of the exodus, when emigration and immigration was only sporadic (Hrobat Virloget 2019). This group evidently set itself up in opposition to the latter, larger group of immigrants who came as a reaction to the mass emigration that followed Istria's annexation to Yugoslavia. It is not possible to say that we are dealing only with orientalizing discourse in the ethnic sense toward the immigrants from the southern republics of the former Yugoslavia—especially toward those who came in the 1960s and 1970s because there was a need for workers in the Port of Koper, Tomos, and other industrial plants. This is evidently a social border with all immigrants who came in the wave of mass migrations. It appears that the role of ethnic differentiation has eased off somewhat, and has been replaced by "sociological" age, that is, length of residence, which was noted by the sociologists Norbert Elias and John L. Scotson (1994). For example, Kristina who comes from a family from the Brkini hills in Primorska, and who waited for the liberation of Istria in a house that had belonged to the Gottscheer Germans, remembers that upon her arrival in Izola in 1955, the environment was still predominantly Italian. However, it was Slovenized very quickly with the new, mass migrations so the later arrivals came to an already Slovenized environment.

> So when I came, I was alone. Then young families came streaming in from everywhere. . . . But as has already been said, this area filled up very, very quickly with Slovenes. Those who came a little later didn't have this contact with Italian culture that I did. . . . We got to know it at least a little. [Speaking about the need to learn Italian, which was greater at the beginning than in the time of mass immigration:] Yes, precisely, neither was there any need for my schoolmates who came later; there wasn't the concern I had when I arrived. I felt I was completely lost, lonely and that

> I must master it somehow [the Italian language], but I ascribe this to the fact that we were Primorci. I didn't come to this environment as a complete foreigner. After all, we came from Primorska, not from way over there . . . And, of course, with parents who spoke Italian, so I understand.

We can sense from these words that there is a separation of "we"—those who came to the Italian environment first and who speak Italian—and "they," "from way over there," not from Primorska. We have also seen from the memories told so far that those who spoke Italian were also the first to move here. This differentiation between "us" Primorci (people from the Primorska region), that is, those who speak Italian, and "them" from elsewhere, will be evident in the next section when we ask who feels at home and who feels like a foreigner in the new Istrian environment. As will be shown, not only the Istrians but all Primorci—from as far as Gorica—said they felt at home.

When studying migrant societies, Norbert Elias and John L. Scotson (1994) noticed that although immigrants were all of the same nationality and belonged to the same working class, the "old families," that were the first to arrive, consider themselves better, superior, and reject contact with the immigrants they consider to be "outsiders." Their research has shown that there are no objective differences within the immigrant groups, no differences in ethnicity, nationality, race, color, occupational structure, income, and education. They all belong to the working class and the only difference between them is their "age" in terms of period of residence. The old inhabitants consider themselves superior and see the immigrants as a threat to their established way of life. This relationship between the "established" and the "outsiders" is entirely of social origin, a collective fantasy. At best it is a question of control over the principal resources of power, which the "older" inhabitants control better because of their greater group cohesion, solidarity, uniformity and self-discipline. They have established all this as a group in the course of their longer period of coexistence. At the same time, they exclude the immigrants from these resources. For the "established" inhabitants, it is their common past, common memories, belonging, emotional ties, group cohesion and subjection to group norms that are important. All this involves the opposition between "us" and "them." This superior attitude toward "outsiders" is a result of the stigma that is often reified by the immigrants. Immigrants, who always have to establish a relationship with those who are already established, actually internalize the ascribed feeling of inferiority. This is augmented by the fact that they live "by themselves" and have no leadership or any form of group cohesion. Besides, the "outsiders" do not follow group norms and do not even have any collective memories, which is why the "older" residents reject, stigmatize, and humiliate them even more. By distancing themselves from the immigrants, rejecting them and giving them a lower status, the older residents retain their ("higher") status and position of power (Elias and Scotson 1994; Čapo Žmegač 2007: 153). Irena Weber (2006: 67) makes similar findings in a contemporary study of Piran. She notes that it was mass migrations that influenced the formation of a fragmented urban community, which has not succeeded in forming a sense of belonging because of discontinuity.

Social Borders between "Native" and Immigrant Italians

Another group of people who moved into the north Istrian towns were the Italian Istrians from Croatia, who also came in search of employment. It seems that the locals categorized the Italian immigrants from the Croat part of Istria purely as immigrants, despite the fact that they are of the same ethnic identity. Vittoria, an Italian from the Croat part of Istria says that for the people of Piran—referring to the old Italian citizens—they are all "newcomers." In her words, Italians like herself who came from elsewhere are second-class citizens, Slovenians third-class, and all other newcomers fourth-class. These different categories of social ranking of "Italian natives" were also felt by immigrants from the southern republics of the former Yugoslavia. This is evident in the interview featured below that was carried out with immigrants from Dalmatia and Bosnia who arrived in Istria in 1955.[8] Throughout the interview the interlocutors emphasize the social border and the feeling of superiority the Istrian Italians have toward immigrants. The relationship is similar to that of the Slavs (*sc'avi*) and the Italians (*civiltà*) before the exodus.

> N: They had to move out. Those who stayed here . . . When we began moving in, they behaved as though they were higher.
> K: The Italian natives?
> N: Yes, as though they were cleverer than us.
> K: They thought they were superior?
> N: Yes, and if you spoke Croat or Serb, they took you for a Bosnian. Regardless of whether you were from Bosnia, Serbia, or Croatia. And when they came to the town hall, they spoke Italian so as to have an advantage, to get work. To have an advantage, they wanted to be something more. Or if we were at work. Those of us from down below did not speak Italian so when they wanted to criticize us they criticized us. . . . They said mean things about us, behaved as though they were more developed than us, and that this is their place, and that they have more rights to find work than us, and to earn higher wages, even if we do the same work. But there were no differences in Yugoslavia, as we all got the same. And when there was no work they said the Bosnians should leave, that the Bosnians were

to blame and that this is their home and that they need work, not us. These were the differences; that's how it was.

... N2 (husband): No, the Italians kept in small groups and only socialized with each other and stayed together. They didn't mix much with the other nations.

How should we understand the comments that the Italians kept themselves to themselves? On the one hand, we can understand this as they did not understand the new majority language, but on the other hand, we have already spoken about the self-attributed superiority of some Italians and their deliberate maintenance of the social border. Some Italians from Istria remain critical of this superior attitude to this day. As a politician and member of the Italian minority said, "It even occurs that some Italians don't want their book to be published in Slovene. It seems to me that we all stick to the 'this is ours, this is yours' mindset too much, instead of building a common, open, truly bilingual culture" (Ivelja 2004).

The other aspect is language. Not understanding the language was a major obstacle for the Italians who moved here from the Croat part of Istria, and as Vittoria says, as an immigrant from the Croat part of Istria, she will always be an immigrant in the eyes of Italian Istrians in the Slovenian part of Istria. This makes integrating into the new environment so much more difficult. Upon her arrival in Piran, she had problems because she did not understand Slovene, and also because she felt uneasy speaking her second mother tongue, Serbo-Croat, which she had learned in her place of origin:

In school I felt OK, it was an Italian environment. But social relations were difficult, life outside, shopping . . . I didn't speak Slovene yet, I spoke Italian; it was very hard. I had to know exactly in which shops I would receive an answer in Italian. Also, because when I spoke Serbian, which I spoke perfectly, Serbo-Croat, which I spoke perfectly as a second language, they answered in an unfriendly tone.

Amalia, an Italian from the Croat part of Istria, also says that when she moved to Piran she felt like a foreigner again, surrounded by people who spoke a language she did not understand a word of. She first felt like a foreigner after the exodus when large numbers of immigrants arrived in the town in Croat Istria, as has been mentioned in the section on the foreignness of Italians. This happened to her again when she moved to the Slovenian part of Istria in 1966:

After university. And again, I didn't know the language. A complete foreigner yet again. And then Slovene and Croat; even nowadays I sometimes mix things up because some things are so similar, but the grammar is completely different. . . . And then I slowly began meeting people who spoke both languages. And so it was that in their company I somehow began speaking and then I began to understand because, with the exception of pronunciation, these two languages are similar. But I always mixed things up with Croat. Then slowly, slowly, somehow—I never studied Slovene—I attended Slovene language courses, but I never studied it. So I don't speak excellently.

It was interesting to hear the story about how these ethnic Italians from Croatia were also on the verge of being "erased." An example is Vittoria who is married to someone from a southern republic of the former Yugoslavia. Contrary to widespread belief, they didn't have Italian but Yugoslav citizenship, like most members of the national minority:

> We could have been among the "erased" if in December 1991 the family had not decided to apply for citizenship, after twenty years living in Slovenia. We all applied for citizenship; we could have been "erased." . . . We never defined my son's nationality or citizenship. [Speaking about her husband:] Because he was . . . [from one of the Yugoslav republics. They said he could obtain Croat or Serb citizenship due to the place of birth of one of his parents, or] he can be Slovenian because he's born in Slovenia. And my husband said: "Can he be Yugoslav?" "No." He tore up the piece of paper and went away. He got angry and left. We never defined his citizenship but he had a red Yugoslav passport, everything. In 1991, . . . we had to decide. . . . We said, we have a house. We have work. Our son goes to school What will happen to us if we will no longer be nationals? . . . And then we said, my husband and I: "Enough, we're here. We're staying here. Tomorrow we'll fill out the forms and apply also for our son's citizenship." [Asked if she does not have Italian citizenship:] No, I don't. I never had it, never applied for it. I was born in Yugoslavia and moved around within Yugoslavia perfectly normally. That was my homeland, although everywhere was my homeland. It was my homeland both emotionally and ideologically. Now Slovenia's my homeland.

There was only a thin line that kept one from being "erased" as before Slovenia's independence everyone, including ethnic Italians, had Yugoslav citizenship.

Concluding Thoughts on Symbolic Borders in Istrian Society

It could be said that the symbolic borders in Istrian society are multiphase, but most depend on the duration of residence in a certain place and are connected with the fantastic social ranking system. Although the ethnic element, from the phase preceding the exodus, was abandoned during the process of establishing groups that followed the exodus, in favor of the new element of duration of residence, it cannot be said that ethnicity has completely gone out of the picture. This important "definer" of groups has remained present within orientalizing discourse toward the Balkan "other." It appears that the border is movable—each group that precedes another feels superior to the one that comes after it. First come the Slovene and Italian Istrians who consider all immigrants as lower categories and refer to their own autochthony, or more precisely their regional autochthony. The next "we" group appears to be the Italian Istrian urban residents and the first immigrants who came from the immediate hinterland of Istria and wider Primorska, Trieste and Gorizia. These create a feeling of "us" that is in contrast with those "from over there"—immigrants from other Slovenian regions who came later and in greater numbers. They no longer came to an Italian environment as it had meanwhile been Slovenized. Further social borders emerged within the Italian ethnic category in which people again separated themselves into "autochthonous" and "newly arrived." The most excluded from this Istrian society, the "ultimate others," would appear to be the third group—the immigrants who were the last to arrive from the southern republics of the former Yugoslavia, who came as a workforce and are most lacking in internal cohesion in comparison with those who became established as a society before them. In contrast to the so greatly extolled Istrian multiculturalism that present-day Istrians are so proud of, we can say that it actually conceals the exclusion of all "Balkan others."

All these different collective memories and social borders indicate that people are "strangers either way" in Istrian society, as Jasna Čapo Žmegač (2007) describes relations between co-ethnic natives and immigrants in Croat society. Similarly, Istrian society after the exodus is described by the title of our collective monograph: *At Home but Foreigners* (Hrobat Virloget, Gousseff, and Corni 2015). However, these relations are more distinct in the urban environment, while in rural areas, the borders of belonging are more permeable and the linguistic environment is more mixed and adaptable.

The Sense of Belonging and the Attitude toward the Environment and Heritage

Immigrants from Primorska: Between "Like at Home," "Severed Ties," and Broken Porcelain

The symbolic borders in the migrant society of north Istrian towns become even more apparent when home is perceived as a social and physical space in which someone recognizes others as "their own," and feels they are a member of the community (Hage 1997: 103; Bartulović

2013: 278). Unlike most similar studies of "population exchanges" (Hirschon 1989; Čapo Žmegač 2007), the situation in Istria appears to be more complex as there is not only the relationship between "natives" and immigrants, but there are several phases of emigration and immigration in which a strong role is played by regional belonging and ethnicity. The latter changed to nationality after the breakup of Yugoslavia. So we could say that after the exodus in Istria we have different groups with symbolic borders and conflicting memories: Italians who stayed, Italians who either moved here from the Croat part of Istria or who moved here from Italy, Italians from ethnically mixed families, Croat immigrants from Istria, Slovene immigrants from the broader Primorska region, including the "returnees" who sought refuge from fascism in Yugoslavia and "returned" to the Slovenian part of Istria. The latter groups were accustomed to co-existing with Italians. In addition to these groups, there are also the Slovenian immigrants from continental Slovenia and the immigrants from the southern republics of the former Yugoslavia. Here again there is a difference between those who came sooner and those who came later. Due to this complex social situation, also affected by the breakup of Yugoslavia in the 1990s, I will point out some preliminary findings about the sense of belonging and feeling at home, although it is clear that further studies should be carried out. As I mentioned in the beginning, the focus of my study was primarily on Italian and Slovenian immigrants and there were fewer interlocutors from the southern republics of the former Yugoslavia. Hardly any of the latter were from the last wave of immigration in the 1960s and 1970s. The question of the establishment of a new society in Istria after the exodus harbors great potential for further research. A comparison with Nova Gorica will be interesting as, unlike the Istrian towns, it was deliberately created from scratch as a counterbalance to the loss of Gorizia as regional center due to the new state border (Jerman 2008; Ramšak 2015).[9]

It has been shown thus far that the Italians who remained felt "at home but like foreigners" because of the exodus, the new social reality, the new dominant language, the different political system and the broken social networks (Ballinger 2003; Hrobat Virloget 2015a). They went from being the majority in Istrian towns to a national minority, albeit with acknowledged national rights. In the previous section, we saw that the initial opposition between urban-Italian and rural-Slav was transformed into those who were old(er) residents, in contrast with those who came "later," based on the duration of residence. The ethnic element was abandoned in this form of differentiation. It can be gathered from the interviews that the Istrian Italians and the first immigrants—mainly Istrians from the hinterland and other people from further afield in Primorska—joined together as a group of "us" versus "the others." Both sides—the Italians and the immigrants from Primorska—emphasize the coexistence of both ethnicities. For them the "others" are all the many immigrants who came later, and the "ultimate others" are the immigrants from the southern republics of the former Yugoslavia. Marko, who comes from a family of Triestine "returnees" who were among the first to arrive, bilingual and employed as teachers, emphasizes that coexistence with the Italians was completely harmonious:

> For example, my mother . . . The šjore [*signore,* in dialect *siore,* meaning ladies in Italian] taught her how to drink coffee. There was none of this, what you're describing, that there were some . . . There were no conflicts between people. Even here, where we've been living for a long time because we moved . . . the Italian neighbors always used to chat with my mother. Although she was a passionate communist, but this did not . . . I never experienced a conflict on such a basis that Italians . . . For us it's perfectly normal that, for example, Juri [Italian] was the town mayor. The people here, I don't know . . . Simply Italian, Italian, what the hell . . . You wouldn't see something like that in Trieste—a Slovene mayor. [Speaking about children's games] The games were mostly Italian. . . . *Toka–važo* (cops and robbers). There were also counting-out games . . . Most of the streets kept the old names: Calegaria . . . Although there weren't many Italians left, not many at all.

Kristina, the daughter of parents from the Brkini hills in Primorska, emphasizes that after spending her childhood in the vast forests of Kočevje and its villages, she felt a culture shock in Izola with its "compact mass of houses." However, her parents felt at home because in the past they had had regular contact with Trieste and Italians. "Yes, very mixed. Mother was at home, my father was at work, and she felt very much at home because one of our neighbors was Italian . . . There were still many Italians." A remark made in passing by a woman who came to my lecture and who did not agree that the immigrants given the "bunch of keys" were privileged, indicates that immigrants from the wider region, even as far as Gorizia, felt at home in the new environment. "I was born before 1950 in Koper. We're not newcomers, I mean, my mother came from Gorizia, my father from Trieste, but we never felt like newcomers."

Other conversations with people from Primorska—the first immigrants—also show that they did not feel like foreigners in the predominantly Italian environment but that it was in fact because of the Italian environment that they felt "like [they were] at home." Otherwise, the early immigrants from Primorska also admit to it being hard for them to identify as Istrians, as was described above. Marko emphasizes the "severed tie" as a reason that the immigrants, even if they have come from the broader region of Primorska, are not bound to the urban environment by "deep roots" or intergenerational memories.

> No, no, they were all Slovenes. Here, the Istrians, that's a strange mixture. I somehow don't really feel like an Istrian. Your parents give you a lot; for example, my mother talked a lot about the Karst, and these stories actually make you feel more attached to those places. We miss that here where we've been . . . Connections, those stories, for example, what happened in a certain house, who was . . . This bond was severed when the majority left back then. That's why we don't feel a connection to certain buildings, for example. It's different in the case of your ancestors. . . . A cut has definitely been made here . . . And it would be really good to revive these stories about the town . . . [Hinting at the storytelling evenings.] So you know. Here, every stone that's been worn smooth is interesting, but you don't know why it's been worn smooth. Over there in Pliskovica, I know the well from which I used to draw water. I know all about every stone because I went there on holiday. But here we children used to explore on our own, that's why we used to go up in the attics and on the roofs. As a child you explore, but you don't know the old stories. Next to our flat the name "Paolo Carbonaio" was written on the wall and obviously someone in there was selling coal and had an awful lot of spades in there. We found them and scattered them around. Or in the neighboring house, which really was empty, we went up into the attic and found ceramic dishes up there, amazing ones . . . Soup. There was a lot of this if I think now, but the problem was that we children played with it and smashed it all. But I remember mother watching us smashing it, but back then plastic plates were in fashion and no-one valued this. That was this severed tie.

In this well-illustrated feeling of a lack of inner ties with one's hometown, it is worth highlighting the interlocutor's thoughts about severed ties due to the almost complete replacement of the town's population. These immigrants feel they lack bonds with the place, even though they have come to feel at home in the town and although their Primorska identity makes them feel at home. We will come back to exploring the traces of an unknown past, but before that we should look at a similar testimony by a younger immigrant to Koper who did not experience this population "exchange." It is, however, significant that he too emphasizes that this emptied and repopulated town "lacks a soul." In his opinion, this is also the reason for the weak local identity.

> So, who is a *Koprčan* [a native of Koper]? Now . . . Until 1954, completely different people lived in this town. They left in this exodus; 99

percent of the Italians left. The ones that stayed . . . You can count them
on the fingers of one hand. And people from Slovenia's interior came, and
also from here, well, from Koper's hinterland, and as some factories were
built—from all over former Yugoslavia . . . I feel this city [Koper] lacks
a soul. I don't feel now that it has centuries of tradition, although things
have remained here; those who left didn't take everything with them.
Although they did carry away precious paintings from the churches. But
we—other people—have inherited the rich heritage here. So it is being
recreated, and the identity has not yet been formed completely.[10]

As we could see above, in the towns, the immigrants—regardless of
where they came from and especially their children—uncovered new
pieces of buried, unknown, we could say hidden, silenced, or even neglected past. In the eyes of the adults, it was the past of the "others" and
they were not interested in it. The dominant perception was that it was
the past of the fascists. A similar experience of uncovering the traces of
the former inhabitants of the towns is described by Lucija, the daughter
of early immigrants from Primorska. She moved with her family from
Koper to a flat in a villa in Izola in 1955:

They were Italians. . . . But I know that as children we used to play in the
garden in Izola, and in many places where we dug, we brought up beautiful pieces of porcelain, colored glass. They said that the natives used to
live in the flat we were living in; except there were two Slovenian families
there before us [names], then we came. So the previous owners escaped,
and as they could not take everything with them, they smashed the dishes
and crystal and buried it deep down. And if the garden was ever dug up
properly, who knows what else would be found. . . . And we played then,
and I know that I wasn't allowed to play with it because it was smashed,
and I could cut myself. And there was, for example, a quarter of a plate,
but it was proper porcelain. That's where I got the blue-white ones, etc.
That's it. But there were even finer examples with golden rims, and one
little bowl was almost intact. But what I can remember best is some very,
very thin porcelain that had a creamy color, and you could see through
it, and on top it had a thin golden layer and a thick line. And I argued
that that was mine.

Heaps of objects made of expensive porcelain—like the mute remains
of the silent past of those who left—are kept in the depots of Koper Regional Museum, as we were told by the ethnologist Tina Novak Pucer.
When I learned of this, I wondered if the museum staff saw the artifacts
purely as objects requiring classification, or did they see in them traces
of the people who left and therefore felt empathy for them. These people
were able to take with them a large fortune (Gombač 2005: 106–10),

however, perhaps due to the fragility of the objects, or because they had to leave fast, they could not take all their luxury objects with them.

The image of uncovering a silenced or neglected past—even if only by children—through the material remains of the former town dwellers, is reminiscent of the studies carried out by Olga Sezneva in the city of Kaliningrad—the former Königsberg. After the mass expulsion of the German inhabitants, the new Russian population faced the city's ideological hegemonic discourse on the one hand—its (socialist) history only began in 1945 after it was conquered—and the material remains of the "erased" inhabitants and the Prussian past in their everyday lives on the other. After the city was conquered and the German population expelled, its identity was transformed (similarly to Istria) into a Soviet one with streets renamed, the Prussian past erased, German architecture devalued and demolished, and replaced with modern architecture, etc. With the complete expulsion of the previous population (unlike in Istria), the erasure of the memory of the city's prewar past was guaranteed. However, on the basis of the material traces present in the city, the new inhabitants created another, alternative history, as a form of resistance to the official Soviet representation (Sezneva 2003). In most cities in the former communist countries of Eastern and Central Europe, the new urban population was under the influence of the hegemonic discourse of the new nation-states, which changed the urban histories ideologically to align them with the state's uniform vision of the past. The state ideologies tried to "reinvent" history, as Yugoslavia and Russia did with the history of the national liberation struggle. They tried to recreate the "place" from scratch, but in their everyday lives the new majority population—the immigrants—still encountered physical reminders of the former townspeople (Ruble 2003; Sezneva 2003).

The Sea as a Metaphor for Feelings of Homeliness and Foreignness

A powerful metaphor that reflects the feeling of foreignness in the new land is the sea. Goran Vojnović's film *Piran/Pirano* features an immigrant Bosnian for whom the sea was something so alien that he never swam in it. This is how an immigrant from Bosnia describes the alienness and fear of the sea he felt upon his arrival in Koper (Baltić and Harčević Ćatić 2015: 12.48 min):

> When I came here I was so frightened by the sea! It was the first time I saw such a large amount! This grandeur of the sea! I had never seen so much water before! There was the old bus station [in Koper], and when I stepped out of the bus here, I was rooted to the spot and could not move

forward. This relative of mine pulled me and shouted "Come on, what's wrong with you, what are you waiting for . . ." I couldn't even breathe; it was as if I was drowning on dry land!!! That's how frightened I was by this great mass of water! Endless! There's no shore on the other side . . . That was an experience for me, I'll never forget it. I didn't even know how to swim! And then little by little I got used to the sea [he worked in the port and had a view of the sea].

Dijana Harčević Ćatić, a co-author of the documentary film from which the above testimony is taken, made the interesting comment that some immigrants, the Bosnian Muslims in particular, only lived *by* the sea while others learned to live with it.[11] Judging by the stories, the sea was what surprised the immigrants the most as they were not used to this great expanse. Some even described how people—in their ignorance—tried drinking seawater. This is what Emir, whose parents came from Kosovo in the early years, had to say:

> I'm talking about 1953, when the Slovenians were arriving. They came to fill up this place because it was empty; people were needed so they came. People who came from Slovenia's interior didn't even know what the sea was. They didn't know it existed and my father told me some of them went to drink the water. "Mum, Mum, this water's salty." "Bloody Italians, they've poisoned the water." And that's true, you know; if something's new to you . . .

Ante, an immigrant from the Croat part of Istria whose wife was a rower and demanded they live in a flat by the sea, also describes how unacquainted the Slovenian newcomers were with life by the sea: "Well, they were invited to come . . . The Slovenians weren't particularly fond of the sea. . . . They didn't have a feeling for the sea. Let me just tell you this. Near the harbor office [in Koper] they fenced off the sea so no-one would fall in. I'm not lying. They put up posts and those chains . . ." (*laughs*).

On the other hand, it was because of the sea that some immigrants fell in love with this Mediterranean urban environment, as Rozalija who moved to Piran from Dolenjska explains. She chose to stay here because of the sea, which she considered a substitute for the large cultivated fields of Dolenjska:

> [Asked how she grew accustomed to life in Piran:] Yes, very quickly. Because when I saw the sea, I said to my mother who came to visit, I can see our wheat field. And Mum said: "Yes, my child, are you OK?" The sea meant everything to me. This open expanse, the sea . . . It replaced everything for me, the forest and the vineyard. I didn't miss any anything, I fell in love with the stone, the narrow streets, I don't know. And I said: "I'm not going anywhere!"

Figure 3.6. A rower from Koper/Capodistria training near Koper's main pier in 1956 (Privat archive Zdenko Bombek).

The relationship with the sea in this Adriatic environment is very significative, especially when we consider how well the natives know the sea. It has already been mentioned that Italian dialectal terms are used in fishing, as they had the most knowledge of the sea and fishing in these parts. Tonin, a Slovene Istrian from Škofije, describes how he shared a hospital room with an Italian from Piran. A particular dialect was spoken in Piran, which he imitated with a singing voice, and the sea was used to predict the weather, something that most other Istrians were not familiar with. "And the man from Piran said: *Il mare a le strade, sara piovi* [The sea has "stripes," rain is coming]. When the sea's nice and blue, it'll be sunny, when it's pale or has clouds [a sandy color], there'll be rain."

The sea as a strong element of the new Mediterranean environment proved to be a metaphor for the unease felt by immigrants in the face of such a wide expanse, and on the other hand, the familiarity of those who are used to living near it.

Immigrants from the Interiors of Slovenia and Yugoslavia: Between Two Homelands and "Foreigners on Their Own Turf"

While the people from Primorska came to the Istrian towns with at least some knowledge of the complex and sensitive Italian-Slovene and Croat past, it appears that the people who came from continental Slovenia and the southern republics of the former Yugoslavia knew nothing. This is not only true of the immigrants from the southern republics of the former Yugoslavia, but also those who came from Slovenia's interior. Some of them took to the Mediterranean environment because they fell in love with the sea, but I more frequently heard expressions of nostalgia and stories of returning "home" like the following:

> I always wanted to go back to Štajerska, as did my husband. I once managed to get a job in Ptuj but didn't find somewhere to live. So we stayed here. . . . In Piran, I missed the snow most of all. I really did. In winter the cold northeasterly wind blew here, but I missed the snow. So I liked going back up, home. Sometimes in winter but definitely in summer; I went up at least twice a year. Or rather, we went. (Pahor 2007: 206)

I felt the immigrants from the southern republics of the former Yugoslavia were strongly divided between their current home and their original home. This was clearly expressed in an interview with an immigrant from Serbia who used to work in the Tomos factory as he explained how his life revolved around Tomos, the blocks of flats outside Koper's center, and the football pitch.[12] When he described the workers' strikes in the center of Koper, it was obvious that he did not know the name of the most visible element of Venetian architecture, the Loggia. When asked if after so many years living here he felt like a true *Koprčan* (native of Koper), his answer shows the typical sense of division felt by immigrants between their original and present homeland: "Yes, of course. After all these years I feel like a true *Koprčan*. My wife, daughter and son-in-law are here, my family's here. But my Vojvodina (in Serbia) is still in my heart, and I like going there for holidays."

Jasna Čapo Žmegač similarly observes that for Croat immigrants from Serbia who settled in Croatia, after twenty years the feeling of "home" is tied above all to the family they have created. This is particularly true for women. The feeling of "home" is also rooted in a sense of security that contrasts with the violence and war in their original homeland. They feel at home in the construction of a house with which they can identify or a farm and the activities connected with it. However, the feeling of a new "home" relates only to their dwelling place and not the whole settlement or region. Unlike "home" in their place of birth, which included the area surrounding their place of dwelling, migrants do not feel that the new physical and social environment is their "own." They say their new "home" is soulless. Their attitude toward it is therefore purely functional, and they have only established an emotional relationship with the unit of dwelling, house, and/or property. It is a practical relationship with "home" in which the true symbolic ties are not inscribed in the whole place of residence. This is particularly the case with elderly people who have not been shaped by the experience of living in a new place and who do not have long-standing social relations there (Čapo Žmegač 2010: 185–87). However, this is not so often the case in Istria, where, judging by the interviews, people mainly came while still young.

Similar to the Croats who migrated from Serbia to Croatia, who have a weak social network and no long-standing relationships in their new place of residence and who maintain their native social and mental landscape by socializing with other immigrants (Čapo Žmegač 2010: 187), it appears that immigrants from the southern republics of the former Yugoslavia also predominantly socialize with other immigrants. Like the above interlocutor who has "his Vojvodina in his heart," the immigrants feel appurtenance to where they have come from (Čapo Žmegač 2010: 188–89). This was already visible in the section on symbolic borders and everyday practices, for example, when an immigrant admitted to socializing only "with immigrants from other Yugoslav nations" (Menih 2011: 67–68), and the comment made in passing by the above immigrant from Serbia who said that after work at the Tomos factory in Koper the "natives" went to work in their allotments while the "other" immigrants socialized and played football. The latest study by Jasna Čapo on the subject of *Gastarbeiters*[13] in Germany entitled *Dva doma* (Two homes, 2019), clearly shows that after some time, the migrant generation creates a home for itself in the country of residence. At the same time, they preserve emotional ties with different places, including their parents' place of origin (or where they spend their summer holidays), as well as where they live. This dual or parallel set of life references in relation to where they live abroad and their place of origin means they have developed the feeling that they have two homes in two lands. This view contrasts with the view that the feeling of home is singular and is tied only to the land of origin. The researcher has thereby refuted the hypothesis that the dominant feeling experienced by migrants is dual exclusion, that is, from the place/country of origin as well as the place/country of reception, and that they are therefore long-term "double" foreigners. In contrast to the hypotheses concerning the lack of emotional identification with the host country, Jasna Čapo (2019: 346, 360–62) observes that migrants create emotional ties with where they live. This is nicely shown by one of her interlocutors, who said she does not feel like a foreigner in Germany, as she does in her native Croatia, despite the fact that she is perceived as a foreigner by the Germans (Čapo 2019: 337).

A similar aversion to being labeled foreigners by the natives is also sensed among the immigrants from the former southern Yugoslav republics, who feel "at home" in Koper despite their immigrant past. We have already heard the immigrant woman from Albania who said that "you're a foreigner at home." Just as significant is the title of the film *Tujec na svojem* (A Foreigner on One's Own Turf), about immigrants from Bosnia and Herzegovina in Koper that was produced by the Behar Association (Baltić and Harčević Ćatić 2015). In the interview, workers say they do not feel like foreigners in Koper. It is a known fact that a large part of present-day Koper features postwar architecture (Čebron Lipovec 2018; 2019). This is why we can understand the statement made by an immigrant worker from Bosnia who said that they, the workers, built "present-day" Koper, so he does not feel like a foreigner here as "we're walking on home turf": "We built the flats, the port; we the workers, employees, we built all this. So we don't feel like foreigners here today; we built this, we're walking on home turf! This is my second homeland and I'm connected with it. But there's always a big desire to return to your hometown, that's normal" (Baltić and Harčević Ćatić 2015: 15.33 min).

Before making the above statement, the interlocutor repeated that his roots are here as this is where he invested himself! Speaking about the construction of the Port of Koper: "We cooperated, we invested ourselves, a lot . . . Our roots are here as far as we're concerned!" (Baltić and Harčević Ćatić 2015: 14.00 min). As has been shown in the case of the Italians who moved here from Istria, they too had a hard job coping with all the new languages, especially Italian (Baltić and Harčević Ćatić 2015: 8.18 min):

A: The strangest thing when I came was this mixture of languages . . . I found it hard to cope.
B: More Italian was spoken than Croat . . .

Another immigrant from Bosnia and Herzegovina says Koper felt more like home for him than his previous, temporary home in the Netherlands, and he believes a person puts down roots wherever they live (Baltić and Harčević Ćatić 2015: 16.04 min): "I have the feeling that a person gradually puts down roots here, where they live, where they work . . . I lived in the Netherlands for twelve years but never felt my—how can I put it—presence there like I can feel it here, properly, in Koper and Slovenia."

Although the study should be broadened to include later immigration, this small sample confirms the hypotheses concerning the transnational nature of migrants. However, it does not reveal their dual foreignness but a dual sense of feeling at home (Čapo 2019). This is clearly described by an immigrant from Bosnia who describes the duality of the lives of Bosnians in Slovenia. They have to renovate the flats they live in while at the same time building a house back home where they come from. They feel they owe this to what they have inherited and to their grandchildren who, however, do not intend to move to Bosnia. Probably unaware of the title of the book by Jasna Čapo (2019), who describes the *Gastarbeiters*, his grand-daughter Taira says: "We have two homes" (Baltić and Harčević Ćatić 2015: 20.23 min). This feeling of home, of being "a foreigner on one's own turf," is probably emphasized so much more because of constant opposition from the local population, who persistently establish symbolic borders with the "others," who actually don't feel as "other" as is generally purported.

Heritage and Tradition in Istria as a Reflection of Social Changes

Degraded, Neglected Heritage in the Old Town Centers

Although the immigrants created a new home for themselves, we have seen that it is mainly connected with the immediate place of residence, the house and its surroundings. It is not known to what extent they identify with the heritage of the environment in which they live, as we know that heritage is directly connected with collective identity. If people identify with heritage they perceive it as their own, they have to believe in it, they have to be caught up and motivated in it and for it (van de Port and Meyer 2018: 20). What does the heritage of the Istrian towns mean to the different groups that inhabit them? If we begin with what has been written above, then we can say that people in Istrian towns feel a lack of multigenerational connections with the environment. The immigrants from Serbia displayed a of lack of knowledge of Venetian urban heritage, and we saw that the immigrants uncovered pieces of the unknown past through the material remains of their new home, thereby discovering an alternative silenced past like elsewhere in Eastern Europe (Sezneva 2003). Similar examples of the silenced past and heritage being uncovered may be detected in parts of Slovenia that had a German population prior to World War II. They were expelled after the war, together with millions of other Germans from Central and Eastern Europe (Hrobat Virloget et al. 2016).

Tourists voted Piran one of the fifty most romantic towns in Europe, however, they get to see only the idyllic side of the town in the summer bustle—an "authentic illusion"—to use Ahmed Scounti's (2009) words. Those of us who have experienced Piran in other seasons know that the town is completely lifeless in winter, full of marginalized inhabitants, drug and alcohol addicts who do not live with the sea the whole year round. The Venetian urban architecture is dilapidated, neglected, inappropriately renovated, and the flats are empty—most of them only used as holiday apartments.

It is said that Piran emptied later, in the 1970s, when everyone who could afford it moved to the new flats in Lucija/Lucia. Only those who could not afford it stayed in the old town. This was the case with most old town centers in socialist Slovenia. Evgenija, an immigrant from Slovenia's interior, remembers the cramped conditions and dilapidated state of buildings in Piran, which is why everyone wanted to move to the newly built flats in Lucija:

> I spent one year living in Piran—from 1973 to 1974—in that old house. Then I lived for ten years in Lucija. Back then, to be in Lucija, in the flat, not here [in Piran] in the old, smelly flat. . . . That's how it was, back then; forty years ago Piran was not what it is now. And I saw flats—the light on all day, you look through the window, you see into another kitchen, another room. And there were loads of flat like that between the streets. Everyone could hardly wait. Whoever could went there. [In Lucija:] Many buildings were constructed back then, all those blocks of flats, the school. . . . And you went from a bad flat to a better, nicer one. [When they had a child:] We were looking for somewhere else to live. Piran? Over my dead body.

Similar stories were heard in the case of Koper, only those who could not afford something else stayed in the old flats in the town center. Nowadays, the old, rather neglected Istrian town centers, especially of Piran and Koper, are mainly inhabited by immigrants from the southern republics of the former Yugoslavia, mainly working-class people. The fact that some north Istrian towns are mainly populated by an immigrant population from "the Balkans" is also evident from graffiti in Piran: "Piran = Mala Bosna" (Piran = Little Bosnia).[14] As we have already shown, the term "Bosanci" (Bosnians) is a pejorative label for all immigrants from the southern republics of the former Yugoslavia. The marginalization of urban heritage can be linked with the population living around this heritage being marginalized—in this case, mainly immigrants from the southern republics of the former Yugoslavia. Their marginalization increased with Slovenia's independence in 1991, when they experienced deep social marginalization and became second-class citizens, many of them "erased" from the register of Slovenian inhabitants (Zorn and Lipovec Čebron 2008). Unlike Brežice in eastern Slovenia, where immigrants from the southern republics of the former Yugoslavia represented the elite, military class—privileged people with a significant influence on decision-making in the town, the immigrants in Istria mainly belong to the working class (Hrobat Virloget et al. 2016: 80, 85). Although the immigrants from the former Yugoslav republics are actively present among "us," they are a distinctly invisible group as they are not protected by legal means such as laws governing national minorities (Kržišnik-Bukić 2014; Buić 2017), and therefore remain hidden minorities (Promitzer, Klaus-Jürgen, and Staudinger 2009). In any case, the process of heritage being marginalized is related to what the geographer Stanko Pelc (2018: 35) calls marginalization of nature, or pushing human elements to the edge—in our case urban priorities. Degradation begins with a fall in the quality of life due to the incapacity of inhabitants to properly maintain their habitat. Reasons are usually economic and frequently connected with the existing policies. The reason why Istrian urban heritage is neglected is probably not only due to the immigrants not identifying sufficiently with their "new" urban environment, but also stems from economic issues as most of the town center inhabitants are descendants of economically weak working-class immigrants (Hrobat Virloget et al. 2016).

Material Heritage as an Anchorage for
Italian Identity and an Object of Nostalgia

We have seen that people in Istria have now established complex relations with each other and the environment in which they live, as "foreigners to each other" (Čapo Žmegač 2007), some of them "at home, yet foreigners" (Hrobat Virloget et al. 2015) and others "foreigners, yet on their own turf" (Baltić and Harčević Ćatić 2015). At the same time, everyone is at least some of all of the above. While the immigrants had to establish new connections with the new environment and put down roots, the Italians who remained were strongly rooted in the physical reality of the Istrian urban environment. It was like a refuge for them— the only remaining connection with familiarity in the completely different social situation. Their memories are anchored in the material, urban environment, which is their only source of emotional support and an anchorage for their identity (Halbwachs 1971: 130; 2001: 151–52, 175–76; Čebron Lipovec 2015: 190–96; Hrobat Virloget 2020: 26).

In Piran, this continuity with emplaced tradition, as a support for the identity of the "old" inhabitants of Piran, may be seen in their attachment to Trg 1. maja (1 May Square). Its traditional layout is like a form of opposition to the changeability of times and society. On the other hand, they reject the modern architectural intervention in the main square—Tartinijev trg (Tartini square)—saying that the aesthetics does not belong to "our" space, and that the architect comes from a different cultural environment—a "continental." Those who frequent this newly transformed square, which the "true" *Pirančani* (natives of Piran) say has been destroyed because of the modernity of the intervention, are uniformly referred to as Bosnians, that is, immigrants and "false" *Pirančani* (Weber 2006: 48).

The new postwar architecture in north Istrian towns demanded the mass demolition of historical buildings. This was especially the case in Koper and is the most obvious reflection of tectonic changes in the population. We may understand the demolition of the historical center as the manifestation of a modernistic, "progressive" approach, but it may also be understood in the perspective of forced oblivion and the practice of erasing anchors of memory in order to establish a new social and ideological system—the symbolic marking of territory by the new Yugoslav authorities. Moreover, this modernist architecture—which has in the meantime become heritage and an anchor for the identity of Koper's new inhabitants, the immigrants—was also being demolished until recently (Čebron Lipovec 2015: 193–94; 2018; 2019). We may therefore talk of the creation of *lieux d'oubli* (sites of oblivion) (Candau 2005: 162), as an antithesis to *lieux de mémoire* (sites of memory) (Nora 1984, 1986, 1993). Nowadays, the Venetian heritage of Istrian towns is promoted as a tourist attraction, however, in tourist and other dominant discourses its connection with the Italian population that once prevailed in the Istrian towns and their exodus is silenced. This silence is painful for Istria's Italian speakers, who identify with the Venetian heritage in accordance with Italian national discourse. After mentioning the Italian minority's hurt because the celebration of Primorska's reunification with Slovenia was held in Koper, the town that had once been home to a majority Italian-speaking population, Michela clearly indicates the Italian perception of Venetian heritage as the basis of their national identity: "You can't celebrate in Koper as every wall tells you it's Venetian, that it's Italian."

The emplaced memories of the Italian Istrians have been and continue to be hurt by each new urban intervention in the historic urban environment, and by the sight of old buildings decaying. I could sense Elisabetta's emotional distress seeing the urban Venetian heritage being left to decay, as well as opposition to the introduction of foreign practices by immigrants into this Adriatic region, reflecting a strong symbolic border between them.

> Kreljeva ulica [Krelj street], where the palace they're renovating stands, but with European funds, for . . . ages . . . But it's always closed. It's very

run-down; they don't look after it. People go in. . . . So many things in
Capodistria; they should have more respect for the environment. From
the trees that are simply chopped down, but the trees, I don't have anything against palms, but look, they're wonderful trees. And if you went
around Capodistria, if you knew palms used to grow in Capodistria. . . .
In the gardens, but they were born here and were strong. And also the gardens, for example Capodistria was full of gardens, open spaces, but now
these spaces are all built over. I can understand that you build these . . .
But all the same, space is important, space is open. And then, even when
they leave it open, they close it all. And I'll give you an example, for
example Triglav [now Hotel Koper]. There was a space at the front and
it was all covered in greenery. There were even grapevines, it was wonderful. Because in summer it gives shade, then it falls and we have some
sun, excellent. And what did they do? They cut it all down and put some
artificial, plastic things, all. It means they don't feel . . . They say we're in
the Mediterranean . . . We? Look, we're living here, who used to be . . . I
never felt I was someone from the Mediterranean, for me the Mediterranean, we know where the Mediterranean is, but this is the Adriatic. We're
people who were born by the sea. We love light; that's normal. Those
who came, OK, accept this light. No, let's cover everything, heavy roofs,
everything covered. Do that in another climate but not here. It means
they don't feel, or bring something from somewhere else . . . But this is
the case with the environment also when it comes to culture, climate, in
all these respects.

We have already shown how the degraded state of the built environment in the old urban centers can be connected on the one hand with
an inappropriate attitude toward heritage, and on the other with the
inferior situation of the majority population—the working class from
the southern republics of the former Yugoslavia. It is, however, possible
to recognize complex power relations behind the "(non)heritagization"
processes (Harvey 2001). Demolition or devaluation means denying
the memory of the people who identify with these spaces. It may also
be interpreted as symbolic violence, expropriation, the denial of identification marks to part of the population and an expression of power
(Veschambre 2008: 7–15, 115–17). As has already been said, heritage
provides cultural foundations for the creation of national identity and
memory, and those who cannot identify with these stories stay outside,
they do not belong to the nation. Those who have colonized the past
have an impact on heritage. However, a turnabout in history suffices to
make heritage the subject of revision and conflicts (Hall 2008). Those
who have "stayed outside" when it comes to Slovenian national heritage certainly include the national minorities, both the unacknowledged
ones such as the immigrants from the southern republics of the former

Yugoslavia and the recognized ones such as the Italian national community. For them in particular, heritage can be one way to acquire visibility and legitimacy on the contested territory. In this context, we may understand the recent attempts by the Italian communities in Istria to declare the old town cemeteries in Piran and Izola cultural heritage. The gravestones of the old Italian urban families are the best possible *lieux de mémoire*—symbols, indicators of the age and primacy of residence of the Italian community.

As Ornella, an Italian from Koper points out "they're the ones who came 'from outside' because we were already here." Pamela Ballinger finds that both the *esuli* and those who stayed rely on the material traces of the autochthony and purity of Italians in Istria, such as architectural monuments, cemeteries, and houses, with which they legitimize their historical demands. Memory and space are therefore directly connected (Ballinger 2003: 168–206). Heritage is what proves the so highly esteemed autochthony—the element that nowadays justifies a community's rightful claim to a territory. We Slovenians are similarly proud that Slovene place names in Carinthia (Austria's southernmost state) are featured on the Austrian national list of intangible heritage (Piko-Rustja 2012; Židov 2019: 16), as this means the "other" is recognized through recognition of their heritage within a homogeneous national heritage discourse (L. Smith 2006; Jezernik 2005: 11–24; Harrison et al. 2008: 7). Heritage is not heritage just by itself, but only becomes heritage after (new) symbolic meanings are attached to it—to the material or immaterial remains of the past—in the process of heritagization. This symbolic power of remnants of the past has been employed throughout history by various groups, religions, and ideologies that anchored themselves to them, thereby gaining their authority (Harvey 2001; Halbwachs 1971). As Vincent Veschambre (2008) argues, groups demand legitimacy, which stems from their "age in a place," so heritage is the best medium for the appropriation of (contested) space. In the case of Istria, we could add that heritage becomes a medium for the (public) expression of silenced memories, a kind of cry from the mute presence of the silenced minority.

The Italians speak of a lost paradise, and the self-perception of the *esuli* is based on their encounter with barbaric Slavs and the Italian role of western civilizer or native (Ballinger 2003: 168–206). The Italians who stayed also have similar nostalgic memories of the "good old days," materialized in the urban landscape, which for them symbolizes Italian heritage and identity before the complete visual, ethnic, linguistic, and economic turnabout after World War II. Livio, an Italian immigrant from the Croat part of Istria, gives a nostalgic description of the landscape that reflects the degradation of prudent farming in contrast with the postwar socialist miscomprehension of agricultural activities:

> It's sad walking around Istria nowadays because everything is so neglected; in the past the forests were like parks, everything was raked clean . . . Then all this was abandoned; there wasn't any point anyway as these products had no value. The olive oil was worthless, only in recent decades has it begun to have value. The quality of the wine didn't matter, just the quantity. They cut down 100-year-old olive trees as the olives weren't even worth picking. They always looked after the flat in Manzioli's palace well [in Izola]; there were also inspections. But some people simply de-molished all these old houses on the inside, just so they could get a new flat and move. (note in field diary) (Hrobat Virloget 2020: 26)

We have already noticed that most Istrians were very critical of ag-ricultural activities being abandoned by the Yugoslav authorities, and were particularly disparaging of the "industrial" attitude of immigrants and the new authorities who "went to the fields with an accordion and flags!" We know that, especially in Yugoslavia's early years, the main emphasis was on industrialization and farming was deliberately discrim-inated against. In the new Yugoslav discourse, the countryside had to be urbanized and industrialized, farming land was neglected, rural areas were emptied of their population, and in light of the new faith in devel-opment and modernity everything that smacked of the past was aban-doned (Fakin Bajec 2011: 187–215). However, the question is whether the process to industrialize rural areas was intensive in Istria. Mila Orlić (2019: 581) makes the interesting observation that the communist pol-iticians noticed the imitation of the Soviet model was most ineffective particularly in agricultural policies, as is recorded in the case of Buje in the Croat part of Istria.

On the other hand, the above testimony clearly manifests nostalgia for feelings of homeliness that are materialized in idyllic images of the landscape. Researchers observe that nostalgia is filled with values and is often the consequence of changes or fear of them. The past is considered to be harmonic and idyllic, in contrast to the present, which is seen in a more or less negative light (Koskinen-Koivisto 2017).

The memories of Istrian Italians are filled with idyllic images of the past (urban) environment, destroyed by the flood of immigrants, and the exodus that severed all social ties. Ornella said "pre-exodus" Koper was "like an extended family" (Hrobat Virloget 2020: 26). Nostalgic memories of the bygone (interrupted) feelings of homeliness that mate-rialize in the idyllic images of towns correspond with Bryan S. Turner's (1987) interpretation of nostalgia founded on the "division between lost golden times and a sense of being at home against the coldness of the foreignness of today's world" (Koskinen-Koivisto 2017: 16). As has already been said, foreignness in this context stems from feelings of being a foreigner despite having stayed at home in the same, yet drastically changed town (Hrobat Virloget 2015a: 164–76).

What Is Heritage for the Different Communities Present in Istria? Conflicting Discourses

So what is heritage for the different groups of people living in Istria? The older Italian inhabitants of the Istrian towns have nostalgic memories of idyllic times surrounded by Venetian heritage and social networks within the same ethnic community, prior to the general mass invasion of "foreigners." We have seen that the immigrants from the southern republics of the former Yugoslavia are attached to the environment they have built with their own hands, so they describe themselves as "foreigners on their own turf." In a similar way it appears that the people who came from Slovenia's interior are also attached to the heritage constructed after the war. Especially judging by the furious reactions to the recent demolition of modernist buildings, like the Janko Premrl Vojko School in Koper's historic center, which was built after the war (Čebron Lipovec 2015: 194). However, in the case of these demolitions, conservator Neža Čebron Lipovec wonders why no mass protests were organized against them, especially if her hypothesis that modernist postwar architecture represents the basis for the identity of the postwar immigrant community holds true. Judging by the public memory-telling events, which were however not attended by immigrants from the southern republics of the former Yugoslavia, it could be said that the postwar community does care for this architecture (Čebron Lipovec 2015). Perhaps we should also ask ourselves whether this is a case of "heritage imposed on them" "top-down," which they do not recognize as really being their own heritage (Habinc 2020; see also de Certeau 1990; Hafstein 2018: 35), despite their rootlessness in space, or in this space in which they have only recently put down roots. There are also examples of revalorization or efforts to preserve the prewar urban heritage proposed by immigrants themselves, which all shows that nothing is as simple as appears at first glance.

These different evaluations of heritage by different communities in the same space clearly display competing discourses, as no space containing social interaction is ever homogeneous or harmonic, as "national" heritage would like to illustrate. This is why Laurajane Smith (2006) talks about a hegemonic or authorized and alternative, marginal, silent, silenced, subordinate heritage discourse, which in the case of Istria can be attributed to non-dominant groups—the Italian group and groups of people from the southern republics of the former Yugoslavia. The relationship between both discourses problematizes the instruments for decision-making and control, appropriation, ownership and use of culture, and favoring selected cultural areas and practices as models, and so forth. The polyphony and frequent cacophony of definitions of heritage, pervaded by politics and economics, is indicated with the concept of "dissonant heritage," which sets contentiousness and competition in the forefront as important characteristics of contemporary interpretations of heritage (Tunbridge and Ashworth 1996; Slavec Gradišnik 2014: 10–11; Habinc 2020).

This competitiveness and contentious nature of heritage discourse is commonplace in Istrian society, which consists of people from "all over." This was particularly evident at the public discussion that accompanied the renovation of the so-called Benečanka—one of the most representative palaces in Piran, located on the main square Tartinijev trg (Čebron Lipovec 2021: 24–25).[15] Prior to this event there had been a heated debate in the media, so Piran's conservators from the Institute for the Protection of Cultural Heritage organized a public discussion. Most of Piran's present-day inhabitants, who immigrated here after World War II, expressed considerable opposition to the authoritative decision by Piran's Institute for the Protection of Cultural Heritage to change the façade's color from the red they were accustomed to, to the original beige color. The palace was painted red when they arrived and the immigrants lived with this color for over seventy years. Meanwhile, a minor portion of Piran's population from the Italian national community greeted the authoritative change of color from red to beige—the color they knew before the town was overrun by immigrants—with enthusiasm. As an Italian lady commented during the public discussion, the violent appropriation of heritage—in this case through the façade color—leaves deep traumas in its wake.

> It feels like violence when the color you're used to is changed; you were born with this color. But look, the same thing happened at the end of the 1950s when they changed the color. Many suffered when the façade colors were changed because of the toponymy that no longer exists and was original, Veneto-Istrian, and so on. [Congratulations to the professional approach.] You can't distort things; you can't make politics out of color.

Contemporary conservation work demands a participative approach and the observance of multivocality in the evaluation of heritage, especially in such cases of contentious heritage (Čebron Lipovec 2015: 189–196; 2021). Heritage and memory are a complex and lasting process of negotiations and struggles for what to remember and what to forget, what to preserve and what to reject (Harrison et al. 2008: 8), so neither the choice of color nor letting a building decay are innocent decisions. In contrast to the statement "you can't make politics out of color," we can say that every decision or failure to reach a decision on heritage is a reflection of the current ideology, politics and dominant collective memory. Unlike the conventional, dominant heritage discourse, which allows the Venetian heritage to decay and does not connect it with Italian identity, this particular professional decision gave a voice to those who remain silent in contemporary Istrian society—the Italians. However, we must not forget that immigrants from the southern republics of the former Yugoslavia who arrived later are even more voiceless. Not only do they not have constitutional rights but are excluded from all these competing discourses as absent, "foreigners," "others," despite the fact that they perceive themselves as "foreigners on their own turf."

On (Dis)Continuity, Revitalization, and the Divisive and Cohesive Role of Immaterial Heritage

In addition to the general state of neglect of urban heritage, it is possible to observe a break with local tradition in many places in Istria. This was often caused by an interruption in continuity of settlement. Some local feast days have been discontinued, especially the celebrations known as *šagre*—village or town festivities linked to the local patron saint (Hrobat Virloget and Kavrečič 2019: 114–17). We have already seen how the Yugoslav regime initially clamped down on church celebrations, which was one of the reasons why Italians felt even more under threat. As Michela, an Italian Istrian from the hinterland of Koper said, all the saints died in Yugoslavia—not only in the toponyms but also in celebrations:

> [Speaking about St. Brigid as patroness:] Of course, they're not saints because in Yugoslavia, in Croatia, the saints died. There could be no saints, for us they were always Santa Brigida and San Colombano. Now the sign reads Brida. . . . In Slovene. And Kolomban. But in Italian, it's Santa Brigida and San Colombano. . . . With Yugoslavia, everything went to *ramengo* (ruin) [speaking about the church celebrations].

In contemporary ethnology, feasts are no longer understood to be only symbolic acts that bring together members of a homogeneous community and tell us about the community's values. According to agency theory, they also reveal power relations as the sources for which they compete and which are used in different ways by different groups (Habinc 2009: 32). It is known that after World War II in Slovenia, in places like Brežice, the church-going community no longer celebrated feasts publicly, remaining only inside churches. For the first few years after the war, the Church's public activity on Catholic feast days continued to be strongly present. In Brežice, where like in Istrian towns following the war the prewar population fell considerably relative to the number of immigrants from Slovenia and the former Yugoslavia, feast days were a connection with the past, a rare island of familiarity with which the "old inhabitants of Brežice" could identify in the flood of immigrants and new feasts (Habinc 2009: 32, 35). As was shown when we discussed the causes of the exodus, for most Italian-speaking Istrians the celebration of Church feasts under the postwar regime represented not only continuity with the past, but also acquired a powerful ethnic or national emotional component. That is why we can understand why nowadays many members of the Italian minority who stayed in Istria express outrage at the contempt Yugoslav politics had for Christian tradition.

The exodus cut deeply into many traditions, especially in the domain of immaterial heritage. Many people say the exodus brought an end to the annual church celebrations (*šagre*) in some towns and villages. Bruno and Ivana say the main reason these celebrations ceased is that villages in the immediate hinterland of Koper emptied as people left to fill the emptied town of Koper. "It was like this: the people from the village went to Izola, Koper, Trieste, Italy. Left, right? So the village was left empty." And as they describe, the immigrants, the *forešti* (foreigners) "from further south" were not interested in restoring them:

> Look, they organized this now. Once my daughter wanted to organize a *šagra*. A *šagra di fažuleti* [village runner bean festival]. But the population's all mixed up there. They'd already put up posters, you know. Signs saying there'll be a *šagra* up in Manžan. Where we live or up in the village, I don't know. But it came to nothing. . . . They didn't do anything. . . . There was nothing, we say *forešti*. They showed no interest.

There are also other reports of immigrants showing no interest in continuing traditions, like the lady from Zabavlje in Istria who blames the uninterested immigrants for the end of commemorations in the village. She blames all immigrants, regardless of their ethnicity:

> [Speaking about the World War II commemorations that are no longer held:] Yes it's a shame. We could still have them. Money's a problem here because everything costs something. There are other people in the village now, few natives, they've come from elsewhere. They're all OK, they've

adapted, but they still don't feel what I do living here (Hrobat Virloget and Kavrečič 2019: 115).[16]

It would be illusory to say that the *šagre* are no longer held purely because the population has changed. However, the conversations indicate that migrations played a considerable role in bringing an end to tradition. Of course, it is also necessary to take into consideration the general change in lifestyle as *šagre* are no longer the only source of entertainment for young people as they were in the past. The new villagers live according to the principles of contemporary consumerist and individualist society and do not make much effort to take part in village life. The villages are increasingly becoming dormitory settlements (Hrobat Virloget and Kavrečič 2019: 118). There is also the effect of secularization—if only we think of the contrast between the present-day St. George's day *šagra* in Piran and the celebration recorded on film in 1943, when an endless procession wound its way through the streets of Piran (*Le feste* 1943). The St. George's day *šagra* in Piran is an example of the revival of a tradition that was no longer practiced, as it was only recently restored as part of the salt festival, when the people of Piran left the town to spend several months living on the salt pans in Sečovlje/Sicciole. A conversation with the organizers and participant observation revealed that only a very small minority identifies with the feast—the Italian community and some enthusiastic immigrants from Slovenia. Most of Piran's inhabitants—most of them immigrants from the former Yugoslavia—do not identify with the feast, at least judging by the very small number of participants (Hrobat Virloget 2014). Irena Weber (2006: 72) also finds that Piran's inhabitants do not identify with the municipal feast—the St. Georges' day *šagra*. She finds that the European Heritage Days are more successful in bringing the town's inhabitants together as the organizers surpass ethnic divisions and include all groups—also in terms of social class and age.

Similarly, attempts were made some years ago to revive the traditional pilgrimage by boat from Piran to Our Lady in Strunjano, as the parish priest in Piran described. Unfortunately, the revival was not successful because they could not find enough boat owners. Again, we can see that the people who now live by the sea do not live with it as many had to grow accustomed to it. This is most evident nowadays in fishing tradition, which was mostly interrupted by the exodus or was reestablished with the help of immigrants, especially in Izola, where many fishermen are said to have come from the Croat part of Istria and Dalmatia. It is clear from accounts that the vast majority of fishermen moved out with the exodus. The rare Italian fishermen who stayed introduced farmers from the hinterland of Koper to the local fishing tradition (Menih 2011: 131–37). When the student Artur Steffe was researching fishing tradition, he was told that around fifty fishing families were active in Koper before the war. Only a handful remained following the exodus (Menih 2011: 132; Steffe 2020: 19). In fact, it was his great-grandfather who taught the immigrants how to fish, after his optant family returned due to the terrible conditions in the Italian refugee centers. The other natives did not want to share their skills with the new arrivals.

> So very few fishermen remained in Koper after the war and the Yugoslav authorities began granting fishing concessions. The bay known as Škocjanski Zatok was leased to fishing families. The fishermen belonged to a cooperative, which gave each fisherman a part of the "maritime field" in the bay. My grandpa said that after the war these concessions were granted to farmers from the village of Bertoki. But they had neither boats nor any previous fishing experience. So what happened? Those three remaining fishing families from Koper didn't want to show them how to fish, but my grandpa quickly realized he had no other option than to try, as he had to work to earn a living for his family. That's why he helped these farmers and was like a kind of advisor who helped them learn how to fish. This is how my grandfather became popular and was able to further develop his activity. (Menih 2011: 132–33)

In the first part of the book when we discussed conflicting memories, we showed that fishing tradition, together with aspirations to own the sea and the traditions connected with it, became one of the contested heritages. Both sides—Slovenian and Italian—attempt to prove their primacy by claiming tradition within nationalistic and ethnic discourses. Slovenian discourse has been dominated in recent decades by the opinion that the home of "true" Slovene fishing is the Slovene national community around Trieste and not the "Slovenian" coast (Ballinger 2006a; Rogelja and Janko Spreizer 2017: 50–60).

Tectonic demographic changes in Istria are also reflected in culinary culture. Kristina vividly describes how the mass immigration of people from the southern republics of the former Yugoslavia to Izola meant fish were replaced by *čevapčiči* (skinless meat sausages from the Balkans): "The Bosnians began arriving after the Slovenian interest in this coastal region cooled down a little. This was again connected with the construction industry. Not so much families, but just men. I say that was when fish were replaced by čevapčiči."

Even nowadays, *čevapčiči* is the most widespread dish at the so-called traditional *šagras* in Istria. This was characteristic of all public and private events in the time of (post)socialist Yugoslavia (Habinc 2014: 121; Hrobat Virloget and Kavrečič 2019: 113), and the situation has remained this way to this day although proponents of "authenticity" in tourism scoff at it (Sedmak 2012). Knowing that tradition is changeable, fictitious, revived, and forgotten again, in constant dependence on the requirements of modernity, it would be pointless to condemn this "import" as a terrible contamination (Dei 2002: 32; Mugnaini 2004; Bausinger 2004). *Čevapčiči* could easily be compared with the discourses concerning the *burek*, another dish from the "south," in which Jernej Mlekuž (2008; Janović 2008) sees otherness, Balkanness, and orientality, yet the *burek* is "foreign, yet ours." This again reflects the cultural distinction between "us versus them or the natives versus the immigrants" (Mlekuž 2008). The search for a "lost identity" in Istria, which we discussed in connection with the region's name, is also reflected in traditions. An example of this is the contemporary popularization of the Šavrini (inhabitants of the interior part of Slovenian Istria called Šavrinija; see chapter 1), who are sometimes included in the *šagre* and are like a cheap demonstration of what life was once like (Hrobat Virloget and Kavrečič 2019: 114). Tradition is not something that people passively accept from the past and that has always existed, but it is a vision or perception of what the past was for them. It is therefore an interpretation of the past using strict contemporary criteria (Mugnaini 2004; Lenclud 2004: 131). The Šavrini and the "Šavrinization" of Istria that is so popular nowadays involves a form of made-up identity that emerged in the 1990s, as a result of the Slovenization and nationalization of Istria after Slovenia became independent and the region was divided between Croatia and Slovenia. Later, it became an expression of rural identity in opposition to the coastal towns (Brumen 2000: 404; Baskar 2002: 130). Present-day "Šavrinization" may be seen as a façade erected by the tourist industry and a superregional depiction of "the nostalgic search for lost time and an authentic lifestyle," mythical traditions, uprooted in the modern-day globalized world (Ledinek Lozej and Rogelja 2012: 544–45).

In contemporary studies of tradition and feasts, ethnologists investigate how these do or do not contribute to forming a social group and social relations (Habinc 2009). Tradition can operate as a group-creating medium as it strengthens the feeling of belonging and mobilizes the individual in the community (Fakin Bajec 2011: 287–91; Poljak Istenič 2012: 88). Participation and sharing common traditions in a group enables members to feel they are part of the group. For example, when a bride who has come from elsewhere takes part in family rituals, her new family includes her traditional way of preparing dishes, thereby integrating her into the family circle. By recognizing the group's tradition, we confirm its identity and show the desire to become members of this group (Mugnaini 2004; Hrobat Virloget 2014). Tradition that accepts "others" into its framework shows integrative power. Although we have so far being talking more about symbolic borders in Istrian society, it is also possible to detect the opposite, the breaking down of social borders through tradition. A nice example of this is when the Italians who stayed showed their acceptance of the first immigrants by allowing them to participate in their traditional Venetian-style carnival celebration in Koper. This was experienced by Lucija who came here when the Italian language was still predominant:

> L: I was still a child at the time—I was six. I know that, I have vivid childhood memories of the carnival. People used to go from house to house, knocking, and I can clearly remember that they also entered our flat in Koper. But they were very nice Venetian masks. I remember their *bautas* [traditional Venetian masks]; I can remember the swishing of those dark blue-violet silk skirts . . . I can remember they had white stockings, crocheted with tassels—a child notices things like that—and that they came, and that they sang, and that Mum was pleased to see them, but my father stood to one side with a serious look on his face; he didn't smile at all. . . . And I also know that there was later a procession, and that I sang with all my heart *Carneval, carneval non sta a ander via, te daremo, te daremo un bel capotto!* [Carnival, carnival, don't go away, we'll give you a nice cloak] And that we then burned it where the marketplace is now . . .
> K: And immigrants, like yourselves, did you join in the carnival? Was everyone together or not?
> L: Yes, yes. Well, not my father. He was a representative of the new authorities, I don't know. Or simply because my father's a little less outgoing. I know our mother was there, I know I was there, as were the children from our house and the surroundings. I can't remember there being . . . And we all sang.

Similar observations were made in village carnivals elsewhere. If the carnival procession passes through parts of the village inhabited by new immigrants, it shows them it is accepting them in its community. However, the opposite can also occur when the community displays its aversion to the immigrants by not including them in its carnival customs and village processions. This is their way of showing that they do not accept the immigrants as members of their community (Hrobat Virloget, Kastelic, and Kavrečič 2012: 54–57). By including the immigrants in the carnival celebrations and visiting their homes, the natives have shown

Figure 3.7. Carnival procession through the streets of Koper/Capodistria, 1960 (Privat archive Zdenko Bombek)

that they accept them as part of their own community. According to some accounts, dances held in Koper also helped integration by bringing together different ethnic groups. They were organized at locations such as the Italian *Circolo* (Italian club) or the Slovene Hotel Triglav. All linguistic barriers were said to fall at these events, as described by people at the "Telling the Town's Story" events (Čebron Lipovec 2015: 201). Mario and Stanka said ethnicity was of no importance whatsoever at these evening dances. However, caution is necessary when interpreting these stories for we know that memories may be tinged with nostalgia, creating an illusion of the harmonious "good old days," purified of any conflicts (Brumen 2000):

> S: Elsewhere too, but other people also went. It wasn't specified, Italians here, Slovenes there. When someone came here, they gave a ticket, and I'll give you a ticket for the *Circolo* . . .
> M: We danced in the Triglav. Hotel Triglav was where they sell those phones . . . There was a glass hall. Where all the bars are. They built that after the war. There were dances here and there. Then there was the Galeb, Riva restaurant, and there was joy.
> K: And these people, would you call them Bosnians, did they also dance there?
> S: Some were still learning, others already knew how to dance . . .
> N: But they came to these parties?
> S: Yes, yes, they did.

Heritage as a Tool of Slovenization

We may study the cohesive or divisive social role of heritage, but its national aspect is also interesting. We know that heritage is a selective tradition and a discursive practice, which gives the "imagined community" (Anderson 1983) cultural meanings, and brings individuals together in the broader national narrative (Hall 2008). Heritage, therefore, functions very effectively as an ideological memory apparatus (Guillaume 1980; Jeudy 1990: 17; Candau 2005: 119). Its characteristic feature is that it expresses national interests and anticipates cultural homogeneity, but this is also a problem because we rarely come across culturally uniform communities (L. Smith 2006; Jezernik 2005; Harrison et al. 2008: 7). Even folklore in the hands of politics can be an excellent tool for nationalizing society and its territory, as shown by Kristina, a Slovene immigrant in Istria who was active in politics until recently. As she explains, already in the early years in Istria, the tradition of "national" folklore was used to Slovenize the multicultural society, which was already crumbling as a result of the exodus.

> K: Last time you also mentioned the folklore group you belonged to. And you said it was a Slovenizing element.
> K: Yes, now, I wasn't aware of this back then, but certainly after this territory was annexed to Yugoslavia, efforts were definitely made to establish Slovene culture. I realized this in two ways; first, there were many school celebrations. Then there was a television program called *Pokaži, kar znaš* [Show what you can do]. . . . Yes, perhaps this was also a way of spreading Slovene culture. Folklore was visible and therefore attractive. I think the folklore group that was organized and led by Ms. Marolt; now France Marolt and his wife can take much credit for the preservation of Slovene folklore. Well, Ms. Tončka Marolt attended the group that met once a week in Izola. With my schoolmates, we had this folklore group. We had the original Gorenjska [region in northern Slovenia] costumes. Back then we wanted to introduce this Slovene folklore into the mixed environment. It was popular. . . . I think this was done for political reasons, to preserve Slovene culture.

As she mentions the use of the Gorenjska regional costume in the region of Primorska, I should draw attention to the role of the so-called national costume, which was used in the 1870s by the bourgeoisie as a special way of displaying Slovene identity. Since then it has been preserved at all levels of society. After World War II, it appeared primarily in folkloric events. The national costume is an artificial phenomenon that was created with the clear intent to display Slovene national awareness. The costume does not resemble the nineteenth-century peasant dress, neither in terms of function nor in terms of form (Makarovič 1972; Knific 2003; Baš 2007: 357). It is therefore a typical expression of so-called folklorism, when folklore is removed from its native environment, thereby changing its function and its symbolic and social significance. The original connected meaning is transferred from the local to a broader, regional, or national level. "Folklorism" therefore denotes an incorrect, second-rate folklore, "applied folklore," "second-hand popular culture," a counterfeit or banalization "when we pretend to be doing something," and evoke new forms of expression through old forms. In selecting the past, we refer to tradition, uniqueness, originality, and typicality (Stanonik 1990: 32–34; Bogataj 1992: 16; Bausinger 2004: 158; Stanonik, Terseglav, and Slavec Gradišnik 2007; Poljak Istenič 2013: 141–46). Although after World War II, "Slovene dances" and the national costume became widespread in Slovenia, in the Istrian context, we could recognize an attempt to introduce "Slovene culture" to the contested multiethnic environment. The same has already been observed in the case of architecture, which is considered the main ideological language of power (Čebron Lipovec 2012: 29; 2018; 2019).

As has already been shown, it was necessary to re-establish the Slovenian school system in Istria, which had been abolished under fascism. People also had to be taught the standard Slovene language. Istrians had not been taught official Slovene in schools, and this frequently led to misunderstandings between older Istrians who spoke the Istrian dialect—which had many Italian words—and the immigrants who spoke official Slovene. Istrians were often discriminated against as a result (Brumen 2000: 402; Buić 2011: 7). Various conversations indicate a disdainful attitude toward the Istrian dialect. In those years, this was certainly not a problem only in Istria, but the Istrians felt this as a collision between the Istrian and Slovene identities. This is what Rožana Koštial, a campaigner for the Istrian dialect and folklore specialist, had to say at the roundtable discussion on Istria's name on 27 November 2019: "As a teacher, they threatened to fire me because I sometimes allowed pupils to speak in dialect, for example, on sports days."

Comments by Slovenian interlocutors from Istria show that immigrants—probably the educated ones in particular—had a superior attitude toward natives who spoke the Istrian dialect. This was also the case elsewhere. A Slovene Istrian resident of the nursing home in Koper talked about this: "The new arrivals looked down on the locals. Whoever spoke Italian was usually considered an enemy. The locals felt humiliated, inferior" (note in field diary). As has been shown, the immigrants may accept the inferior role of "outsiders" attributed to them by the natives (Elias and Scotson 1994), but the roles may also be reversed

(Čapo Žmegač 2002). For example, the Croats from Srem considered themselves to be more "Croat" although they immigrated to Croatia from outside, and they tried to prove this by reinventing "national" traditions (Čapo Žmegač 2002). A similar phenomenon may be observed in Istria, where Slovene immigrants evidently felt more Slovene than the local Istrians—as can be seen from their contemptuous attitude toward Istrians who spoke in dialect and the efforts they made for "proper" official Slovene to be spoken. The comments show that the dialect is seen as a second-class language, while pride is felt at the spreading of the official language through cultural institutions. For example, the importance of Radio Koper as a "cradle of proper Slovene" was emphasized at the first "Telling the Town's Story" gathering by one of Radio Koper's first presenters, an immigrant from Slovenia's interior (Čebron Lipovec 2015; Hrobat Virloget 2015b: 545).

> So, back then Radio Koper was the only cultural institution in the whole of Primorska and all . . . Our voice was even heard in Trieste. And that was the only source, or I can say cradle, of Slovene back then. Because the Primorska dialect was still spoken everywhere, which is not a bad thing, but proper Slovene could only be heard on Radio Koper. Then in the theater, but that came later.

Like in the case of the population exchange between Greece and Turkey after 1923, when schools and the Church were instrumental in establishing national awareness among Orthodox immigrants from Turkey (Tanc 2001), in Istria a similar role was played by the school and media in spreading "proper" official Slovene. My conversation with Roza, a Slovene language teacher from Ljubljana who was sent to Istria in the early 1950s, clearly shows that teachers from Primorska were sent to Ljubljana because they did not have sufficient knowledge of the official language. This was due to awareness that language is one of the foundation stones of national identification:

> An inspector for the Slovene language came down from Ljubljana and said to me: "You know what? She teaches history," he said, "but everything positive that you do with your language she destroys. Because she still speaks the language so poorly. She should sort this out once and for all; she should go up there and study history at the pedagogical high school."

When asked which language dominated when she arrived in Izola in 1959, Roza says it was the dialect, while official Slovene was hardly heard. "It sounded a lot like Italian. Yes, yes, not only Italian, but it sounded Italian. And also other, Slovene, dialects. So there wasn't much proper, official Slovene."

There was a process similar to the one that took place under fascism when names were Italianized—but in the opposite direction, as the local dialectal names were changed into official Slovene names. Even nowadays Istrians deride this, as is evident in the following commentaries:

> A: Why the moron in Ljubljana, writes surnames in German . . . For me he wrote Celestin.
> B: They made me into Amelija . . .
> C: I'm Mariano, but officially I'm Marian.
> B: And Karl? Carlo.

So, as Istrian writers describe, people are again caught up in forced national identifications, when national and political systems do not allow fluid, hybrid, and undefinable ethnic identities.

How to Coexist with a Negative Legacy from the Past?

During the twentieth century, urban communities in the former Yugoslavia, and indeed in all of Eastern and Central Europe, experienced an almost complete change from heterogenic, multiethnic to more or less "uninational" and "uniform" communities. The new urban population in communist states was affected by the hegemonic discourse of new nation-states, which altered urban history using ideology, in keeping with their own national, uniform vision of the past (Ruble 2003; Sezneva 2003). Most governments or countries that expelled populations or transferred them elsewhere kept the presence of the previous inhabitants quiet as far as possible, together with everything that could serve as a reminder of their former presence. History was either rewritten or silenced. New historical discourses justifying their expulsion were written *post festum*. Even following the democratization of Central and Eastern Europe after 1989, it was necessary to find new arguments to preserve the fragile stability and avoid demands for restitution, compensation, the right to return, and reflection on the responsibility of previous governments for the population movements (Bazin and Perron 2018: 30–31; see Halicka 2018).

In Istria, silencing and masking the past was much harder because not all the Italian inhabitants left—roughly 10 percent of them remained and acquired national rights. However, the Slovenization of Istria is still very obvious. Even in discussions on Istria's name, sensitivity for the

Italian community in the region was rarely felt. This is why many are vocally in favor of the name Slovenian Istria. It is also evident in everyday political speeches and commemorations—as we have been able to see—that there is not much interest in Italian-Slovenian multiculturalism. Usually there is only talk of Slovenian Primorska, the Slovenian antifascist struggle, and so on. My Italian interlocutors were hurt, for example, when the adjective "Slovenian" replaced "Italian" at an anniversary celebration of Izola's oldest school. As Ornella comments, "They say, Venetian, *izolski* (from Izola), *koprski* (from Koper), *piranski* (from Piran), but you never hear the word Italians!" This is what Silvano Sau, an Italian politician from Izola, had to say about the unappeased memory in Istria when discussing the great difference between the legal and the actual protection of the Italian national community:

> Kemperle: Why? Is the Slovenian majority afraid of the Italian minority?
> Sau: That's an interesting question. It seems irrational because 3,000 people, including babies, cannot inspire fear in two million people. The answer lies elsewhere. The Italian minority feels isolated, but others consider it to be a part of unappeased memory. Like a disruptive element in an area that would otherwise be entirely Slovene. (Kemperle 1997)

The anthropologist Daša Ličen, a native of Piran, made the (unpublished) comment that it is actually not the number of Italians that is perceived as a threat but the Italian discourse, which states that Istria belongs to them, and is still very present in the region of Trieste. Such words are not hollow but may have practical consequences, and that is what Slovenians are afraid of. Interestingly, the idea of the minority threatening the majority is also voiced by educated people such as Tone, a university professor who came to Istria from Slovenia's interior as a young man:

> But I asked myself a few years ago, why are my passport and other documents also in Italian; after all I'm Slovene and officials must see me as such, but I present myself as someone with two identities when I go abroad. Sometimes the majority is also sensitive, as the minority often fails to hear it if it speaks in its mother tongue. It's not simple. After all, it's very hard to organize study in a foreign language at university.

If I continue with my own experience from university: the struggle to use Italian in the officially bilingual environment takes place on a day-to-day basis. This pain of acknowledging the "other's" rights can often be sensed among intellectuals and professionals, who should be examples of intercultural tolerance and coexistence. For example, the

Italian community was hurt by the following comment made in a documentary on Slovenian national television RTV Slo (Novljan 2017): "In the Istrian coastal towns of Koper, Izola, and Piran, the Romance element is present in the language as the towns were once inhabited by a Romance-language-speaking population, while the hinterland was populated by Slavs." They felt hurt by the statement because they interpreted it as a denial of the existence of the Italian community in contemporary Istrian towns. The event highlights how we must be attentive and sensitive in our choice of words when dealing with something in a multiethnic society. Something that may not seem at all problematic to someone can hurt someone else.

This almost unnatural endeavor for the Slovene language in an officially declared bilingual area also become apparent among ethnologists at a roundtable discussion entitled "Why Don't We Hear Each Other? The Relationship between the Minorities, the 'Native' and the 'Majority' Nations."[17] When the speaker Isabella Flego, a representative of the Italian minority, commented that it would be right if she heard Italian greetings in the Italian school in Koper, and not Slovene as is the custom, she caused a great stir. Demanding Italian be spoken in Slovenia, in an area where the use of a minority language is set down by law, is considered an offense, and we Slovenians again refer to victimization and the inferior rights of the Slovene minority in Italy (Hrobat Virloget 2017b: 23). Such discourse always ends in Slovene victimization and the collective criminalization of "others." There is never any critical self-reflection about the role of perpetrator. Always the black and white dichotomy of victims and perpetrators, the good and the bad, winners and losers (Baussant and Foscarini 2017: 22–23). This is how the weight of the difficult and unprocessed past continues to haunt our present and our future.

Answering my question about coexistence and multiculturalism, Giulio, an Italian politician, commented, "This coexistence is only changing in one direction. I already told you earlier, coexistence is important as long as it is lived in the same way by both sides." As Stuart Hall argues, in today's multicultural societies, both postcolonial and other countries should revise their mainstream versions of heritage, rewrite the margins into the center, and include "their" histories in "our" history (Hall 2008: 225), regardless of whether the "others" were colonized or were the colonizer.

Finally, we may ask ourselves the rather naive question: how can a society with such conflicting memories, burdensome pasts, and contested heritages find a way to coexist? A precondition would probably be to listen to the "other" with empathy and consider one's own responsibility for the events that continue to burden us today (Assman 2007, 2010). This is how Ornella, an Italian from Koper, describes the need for each side to recognize its own share of responsibility: one side should admit to fascism and the other responsibility for the exodus, both without any accusations.

> I was traveling in Dalmatia. . . . I visited an island and said: "Look at the nice houses they built." It was an Italian concentration camp. I felt so ashamed . . . I walked down those streets and even felt too ashamed to speak Italian. And every person I met, to every person I spoke with I said: I'm sorry, I'm ashamed. . . . And when Tito spoke, I wept like crazy. But he was my idol. . . . Yes, because he spoke about fraternity—"we're all equal." And he, when he said, "we, brothers" . . . Someone who belongs to a minority feels they're being helped, protected. Even if it turns out they're never actually protected in reality. . . . But this coexistence [It. *convivenza*] will be possible when each one of us will say "We've made a mistake." . . . I admit to fascism and have said sorry countless times; it hurts me when I see what it's done. But the other side must also admit to wrongdoings. We have to admit and without any insults! We must speak without hurting each other!

How can we coexist with so much negative legacy from the past (Wahnich 2011; Baussant and Foscarini 2017)? The Jewish philosopher Jacques Derrida (2014: 20) said we have to coexist, with both the living and the dead, with our past and the past of those who are no longer here. "Acknowledgement, if it exists, must acknowledge what is difficult to acknowledge; and forgiveness, if it exists, must forgive the unforgivable—in other words do the impossible. If this was a requirement for coexistence we would have to do the impossible" (Derrida 2014: 16).

Are we as society mature enough for this today?

Notes

1. See the section on the exodus and immigration in numbers.
2. Gottscheers are the German settlers of the Kočevje region of Slovenia. When this territory was annexed to Italy during World War II, propaganda and Nazi ideology prevailed and they were mostly resettled to Lower Styria, which was annexed to the Reich.
3. In 2012 and 2013, seven public discussions were held that ended with an exhibition. The aim of these evenings was to understand the town "from the bottom up," to hear personal memories and stories from Koper's past. As in most public cultural events, it again turned out that the people who came were mainly Slovenians and Italians, while the voice of most of the working-class people who come from other republics of the former Yugoslavia was absent. Although they were present at events that were

connected with them, for example, when the subject was the Tomos factory and the Port of Koper, they did not say much in public (Čebron Lipovec 2015).

4. The interview was carried out in the course of the academic year 2016/2017 by Nikita Meden and Boris Meglič as part of the course entitled Practical Work in Heritage at the Faculty of Humanities of the University of Primorska.

5. The study was carried out in the Croat part of Istria, but it can be applied to the Slovenian side, where I often heard Istrians speaking about "hybridity," as was shown in the first part of the book.

6. The "erased" is a term for people living in Slovenia, mostly from other former Yugoslav republics, who were left without a legal status at the time of independence in 1991.

7. The interview was carried out by the pupil Klemen Baronik as part of a practical assignment at the grammar school in Piran, in cooperation with the Faculty of Humanities of the University of Primorska. I was his (external) mentor.

8. The interview was carried out by Klemen Baronik.

9. This comparison will be undertaken in project J5-2571, financed by the Slovenian Research Agency and led by Aleksej Kalc: "Migrations and Social Changes in a Comparative Perspective: The Case of Western Slovenia after World War II."

10. The interview was carried out in the course of the academic year 2016/17 by Nikita Meden and Boris Meglič as part of the course entitled Practical Work in Heritage, at the Faculty of Humanities of the University of Primorska.

11. From the discussion that followed a viewing of the film *Tujec na svojem* (A Foreigner on One's Own Turf, 2015) as part of the European Ethnology course at the Faculty of Humanities of the University of Primorska, 7 April 2021.

12. The interview was carried out in the academic year 2016/17 by Nenad Smajila as part of the Practical work in heritage course at the Faculty of Humanities of the University of Primorska.

13. Foreign or migrant workers, especially in West Germany between 1955 and 1973, on a formal guest worker program (*Gastarbeiterprogramm*).

14. A photograph of this graffiti is on the cover of the book by Hrobat Virloget et al. (2016).

15. Thanks to Neža Čebron Lipovec for the discussion and its content. As conservator and heritage specialist she brought my attention to it and provided me with recordings.

16. The interview was carried out by Jaka Godejša who studied Tourism at the University of Primorska, as part of a project entitled "Turizmo Ištriano" under the mentorship of Metod Šuligoj.

17. Dolenjske Toplice, 9–11 November 2014.

Conclusion

Let the Silence Speak!

The book's aim was to give people a voice. The people who were silenced, marginalized, on the fringes of both national discourses—Slovenian and Italian. Their memories do not belong anywhere; do not fit into either of the two national collective memories. And that is why they remained mute, inaudible, silenced. But Istria itself is crying out for their memories. Istria, which still cannot find a firm identity, not even in its own name; where the emptiness is calling out for us to listen to it; where there are people and yet it feels like something is missing. Bonds, rooted in a place.

Let us have no more illusions, Istria—at least its towns—lost the population that once made up its majority. It was replaced by a different population, which is still looking for its roots in this region of severed ties.

This book is an attempt to fill this void and give a voice to the people who experienced it—because they were never heard. Literature has described how Istria was contested by various nations. Memories have been studied near the frontiers, the official memory, of course, but we have never heard the voices of the people who struggled to survive in the grip of various national policies and ideologies and also actively resisted them. Again, we came up against the so greatly extolled national identity, which constricts and constrains all the people at its margins, where it was never "pure," just as no culture is "pure." Time and again, we hear the stories of people who either adapt or resist each new national system, and whose identities cannot be bundled into just one national category. National ideas, which were so progressive when they emerged, have become cumbersome, suffocating and the origin of numerous conflicts. In Istria too, they have sealed the fate of thousands of people, both those who left and those who stayed.

This book has spoken about this using their voices. Above all the voices of those who stayed and those who came. The voice of those who left has been heard—despite a decades-long silence—and uncritically accepted as the basis of Italian national discourse. Meanwhile, those who stayed have not been heard. Both in the Italian discourse, which hardly knows about them, as if those who stayed were not "proper" Italians, and in the Slovenian discourse, where those who experienced the exodus were not allowed to be heard. And also, those who came, because their experience is not consistent with what the Slovenian national discourse claims: this is Slovenian, they all left voluntarily. Is it possible that 90 percent of the people leave voluntarily? Neither is it appropriate to say there was mass immigration to Istria—why mass immigration if "we've always been here?" But it was not so. Yes, almost the entire Italian population left—voluntarily, according to the Slovenian discourse. However, some of them nevertheless decided to stay—about ten percent—and only they can say something about voluntariness.

The people have shown that it was not as voluntary as some would like to believe. When you live in constant fear of what will happen, the fear that someone will again come knocking at the door, in the day-to-day collective condemnation of the detested fascists. It is true—legally and formally the decision was voluntary, and yet these people were pushed into making these "voluntary" decisions.

On the other hand, there is no need to idealize the coexistence in Istria, especially not after twenty years of fascist violence. The tables turned, the master became the subordinate, while the slave or *sc'avo* became the master. Many people did not like this, especially those unused to multicultural coexistence on an everyday basis. Again fear—fear of the "Slavs," fear of the unknown, fear of the political system that confiscated property and give it to other, poorer people. This was how an Italian living in a villa could suddenly find himself living in just one room in his own home, the rest of which he had to hand over to others less fortunate than himself. The economic situation was also difficult, the dependency on Trieste, which stayed on the other side of the border. And there was fear of the extent to which they would still be able to be Italian, and many other things besides, many complex, intertwined reasons that pushed people to make "voluntary" decisions, the vast majority to leave while a minority (the brave?) remained. They stayed and adapted to the new system, regardless of how harsh it was: in the end, they adapted to it, learned the new language, and accepted their new "housemates." Memories speak of this and of much else besides—the memories of the Italians who stayed, and also the Slovene Istrians who experienced these things. When asked about the reasons for the exodus, not one person gave a clear unambiguous answer—there is simply not just one reason. But after all that has been heard, it will probably be difficult to continue talking about a "voluntary" decision, as for many people it simply was not.

As the Istrian Italian politician Silvano Sau put it, memory in Istria is unappeased (Kemperle 1997)—unappeased because of the weight of fascism and unappeased because of the weight of the exodus. Neither the former nor the latter has been discussed sufficiently, and this is why we continue to be haunted by the past. Perhaps someone might say I am imagining things as a researcher. That they are all at peace with each other and living in harmony, but I still dare say this: Anyone who fails to clear up their past will find it hard to live at ease in the present and the future. As we have heard in the book, it is time to talk, to listen to one another, to delve into our memories—those that remain silenced—and our responsibilities. There is no victim and no perpetrator, the roles are intertwined and everyone must assume their share of responsibility. To live with one's own dead, Derrida (2014: 20) would say. We could add: and with those who left. Or as the psychoanalyst Pavel Fonda would say, create a space for memory in which each nation will keep its disgraces, the crimes it has committed, so it can slowly come to terms with them, and gradually integrate them into grieving processes, above the negative aspects of our self-image. These spaces of shame and pain could save what is authentically human in us, to enable true, sincere encounters between different groups (Fonda 2009: 131). To live with one's past, to disclose it, and say "sorry"—both sides. This is what should be done in Istria, and not just by the Istrians—actually, this applies to them the least—but above all by politicians on both sides of the border. Like what the two presidents attempted to do by honoring both *lieux de mémoire*, and yet this irritated some people. Let us at last recognize that both sides have the right to mourn. Even if you are on the side of the perpetrator the sadness is real. Let us have respect for one another's memory. It is not necessary that they agree, but they can at least hear each other.

If this book helps achieve this, then that is no small thing. Many life stories will yet be published; many people will still have much to say, to criticize, to add. And rightly so! May the voices be heard, and may they drown out the silence into which they have been thrust by the national collective memory. If this book helps people begin to hear each other, then it has accomplished its purpose. The silence has spoken.

References

Accati, Luisa. 2009. "Žrtve in krvniki med pravičnostjo in nekaznivostjo." In *Fojbe: Primer psihopatološke recepcije zgodovine,* ed. Luisa Accati and Renate Cogoy, 185–218. Ljubljana: Krtina (Transl. from *Das Unheimliche in der Geschichte. Die Foibe. Beiträge zur Pschopathologie historischer Rezeption.* 2007. Berlin: Trafo).

Allcock, John B. 2000. *Explaining Yugoslavia.* London, New York: Hurst, Columbia University Press.

Althounian, Janine. 2005. *L'intradisible: Deuil, mémoire, transmission.* Paris: Dunod.

Altin, Roberta, and Nadka Badurina. 2018. "Divided Memories: Istrian Exodus in the Urban Space of Trieste." In *Memory, Identity, Culture II: Collection of Essays,* ed. Tatjana Kuharenkova, Irina Novikova, and Ivars Orehovs, 184–200. Riga: University of Latvia.

Anderson, Benedict. 1983. *Immagined Communities: Reflections on the Origins and Spread of Nationalism.* London: Verso.

Argenti Tremul, Alessandra. 2016. "Odnos uprave Slovenskega Primorja (Cona B STO) do italijanskega prebivalstva: Koper 1945–1957." Ph.D. dissertation. Koper: University of Primorska, Faculty of Humanities.

Arthurs, Joshua. 2010. "Fascism as Heritage in Contemporary Italy." In *Italy Today: The Sick Man of Europe,* ed. Anrea Mammone and Giuseppe A. Veltri, 114–27. London: Routledge.

Assmann, Aleida. 2007. "Europe: A Community of Memory?" *GHI Bulletin* 40: 11–25.

———. 2010. "From Collective Violence to the Common Future: Four Models for Dealing with the Traumatic Past." In *Conflict, Memory Transfers and the Reshaping of Europe,* ed. Helena Gonçalves da Silva, 14–22. Newcastle upon Tyne: Cambridge Scholars Publishing.

Audenino, Patrizia. 2015. *La casa perduta: La memoria dei profughi nell'Europa del Novecento.* Rome: Studi Storici Carocci.

Babelič, Janja. 2018. "Problem odtujenih umetniških del in primer slik iz mest Slovenske Istre ter njihove restitucije: poskus celostne obravnave problema odtujevanja kulturne dediščine." Master's thesis. Ljubljana: University of Ljubljana, Faculty of Arts.

Ballinger, Pamela. 2003. *History in Exile: Memory and Identity at the Borders of the Balkans*. Princeton, NJ: Princeton University Press.

———. 2004. "Exhumed histories: Trieste and the politics of (exclusive) victimhood. *Journal of Southern Europe and the Balkans Online* 6:2: 145–59.

———. 2006a. "Lines in the Water, Peoples on the Map: Maritime Museums and the Representation of Cultural Boundaries in the Upper Adriatic." *Narodna umjetnost* 43(1): 15–39.

———. 2006b. "Opting for Identity: The Politics of International Refugee Relief in Venezia-Giulia, 1948-1952." *Acta Histriae* 14(1): 115–40.

———. 2012. "Entangled or 'Extruded' Histories? Displacement, National Refugees, and Repatriation after the Second World War." *Journal of Refugee Studies* 25(3): 366–86.

———. 2015. "Remapping the Istrian Exodus: New Interpretive Frameworks." In *At Home but Foreigners: Population Transfers in 20th Century Istria*, ed. Katja Hrobat Virloget, Catherine Gousseff, and Gustavo Corni, 71–94. Koper: Univerzitetna založba Annales.

Baltić, Admir, and Dijana Harčević Ćatić, dir. 2015. *Tujec na svojem*. Film. Koper: Kulturno in športno društvo Behar.

Barth, Fredrik. 1969. *Ethnic Groups and Boundaries: The Social Organization of Culture Difference*. Bergen: Universitets-forlaget, George Allen & Unwin.

Bartulović, Alenka. 2013. *"Nismo vaši!" Antinacionalizem v povojnem Sarajevu*. Ljubljana: Znanstvena založba Filozofske fakultete.

Baš, Angelos. 2007. "Narodna noša." In *Leksikon etnologije Slovencev*, ed. Angelos Baš, 357. Ljubljana: Mladinska založba.

Baskar, Bojan. 2002. *Dvoumni Mediteran: študije o regionalnem prekrivanju na vzhodnojadranskem območju*. Koper: ZRS Koper and Zgodovinsko društvo za južno Primorsko.

———. 2010. "'That Most Beautiful Part of Italy': Memories of Fascist Empire-Building in the Adriatic." In *Mediterranean Frontiers: Borders, Conflict and Memory in a Transnational World*, ed. Dimitar Bechev and Kalypso Nikolaidis, 109–28. London: Tauris Academic Studies.

———. 2014. "Alpe antropologov: Od evolucije k zgodovini." In *Alpske skupnosti: okolje, prebivalstvo in družbena struktura*, ed. Pier Paolo Viazzo, 435–56. Ljubljana: Studia Humanitatis.

Bausinger, Hermann. 2004. "Per una critica alle critiche del folklorismo." In *Oltre il folklore: Tradizioni popolari e antropologia nella società contemporanea*, ed. Pietro Clemente and Fabio Mugnaini, 145–59. Rome: Carocci editore.

Baussant, Michèle. 2002. *Pieds-noirs: Mémoires d'exils*. Paris: Stock.

———. 2019. *(Re)commencements, d'une rive d'autre: Habilitation à diriger des recherches, dossier de synthèse*. Nanterre: Université Paris Nanterre, Institut des Sciences Sociales du Politique.

Baussant, Michèle, and Giorgia Foscarini. 2017. "Memories at Stake." *Ethnologies* 39(2): 17–30.

Bazin, Anne, and Catherine Perron. 2018. "Methodological Considerations in Addressing the Issue of Forced Migrations, Lost Territories and Related

Politics of History: A Comparative Approach." In *How to Address the Loss? Forced Migrations, Lost Territories and the Politics of History. A Comparative Approach in Europe and at Europe's Margins in the Twentieth Century*, ed. Anne Bazin and Cathrine Perron, 11–36. Brussels: P.I.E Peter Lang.

Behar, Ruth. 1996. *The Vulnerable Observer: Anthropology that Breaks Your Heart*. Boston, MA: Beacon Press.

Beltram, Julij. 1986. *Pomlad v Istri: istrsko okrožje cone B Svobodnega tržaškega ozemlja 1947–1952*. Koper: Založba Lipa and Založništvo Tržaškega tiska.

Bertucelli, Lorenzo, and Mila Orlić, ed. 2008. *Una storia balcanica: Fascismo, comunismo e nazionalismo nella Jugoslavia del Novecento*. Verona: Ombre corte.

Bjork, James. 2008. *Neither German nor Pole: Catholicism and National Indifference in a Central European Borderland*. Ann Arbor: University of Michigan Press.

Bjork, James, Tomasz Kamusella, Timothy Wilson, and Anna Novikov, ed. 2016. *Creating Nationality in Central Europe, 1880–1950: Modernity, Violence and Belonging in Upper Silesia*. London: Routledge.

Blasina, Paolo. 1993. *Vescovo e clero nella diocesi di Trieste-Capodistria 1938–1945*. Trieste: Istituto regionale per la storia del movimento di liberazione nel Friuli-Venezia Giulia.

Blok, Anton, and Henk Driessen. 1984. "Mediterranean Agro-Towns as a Form of Cultural Dominance (With Special Refference to Sicily and Andalusia)." *Ethnologia Europea* 14(2): 111–24.

Bogataj, Janez. 1992. *Sto srečanj z dediščino*. Ljubljana: Prešernova družba.

Bonin, Zdenka. 2004. "Življenje v Coni B Tržaškega svobodnega ozemlja." In *Cona B tržaškega svobodnega ozemlja: zbornik ob 50-letnici priključitve cone B STO Jugoslaviji / Almanacco per il cinquantesimo dell'annessione alla Jugoslavia della zona B del TLT*, ed. Zdenka Bonin, 9–58. Koper: Pokrajinski arhiv.

Branc, Eva. 2015. "Katja Hrobat Virloget: 'Ali bo sobivanje v Istri strpno.'" *Regional*, 27 April. Retrieved 3 November 2022 from https://www.regionalobala.si/novica/katja-hrobat-virloget-ne-vem-ali-bo-sobivanje-v-istri-kdaj-strpno.

Brate, Tadej. 2007. *Parenzana: železnica za vse večne čase*. Ljubljana: Kmečki glas.

Brown, Keith S. 2001. "Beyond Ethnicity: The Politics of Urban Nostalgia in Modern Macedonia." *Journal of Mediterranean Studies* 11(2): 417–42.

Brumen, Borut. 2000. *Sv. Peter in njegovi časi: socialni spomini, časi in identitete v istrski vasi Sv. Peter*. Ljubljana: *Cf.

———. 2001. "Avant, on était tous simplement des Istriens: L'émergence de nouveaux repères identitaires dans un village frontalier de Slovénie." In *Limites floues, frontières vives: des variations culturelles en France et en Europe*, collection Ethnologie de la France, Cahier 17, ed. Christinan Bromberger and Alain Morel, 343–59. Paris: Maison des sciences de l'homme.

Buić, Mirna. 2011. "'Šrajati' ali govoriti: jezikovne ideologije in govorne prakse dveh generacij v Izoli." *Glasnik Slovenskega etnološkega društva* 51(3/4): 5–13.

————. 2017. "Krepitev aktivne participacije narodnih skupnosti narodov ne-kdanje SFRJ v slovenski Istri." In *Nemi spomini: manjšine med obrobjem in ospredjem*, Knjižnica Glasnika Slovenskega etnološkega društva 51, ed. Saša Poljak Istenič, Mateja Habinc, and Katja Hrobat Virloget, 57-70. Ljubljana: Slovensko etnološko društvo.

Candau, Joël. 2005. *Anthropologie de le mémoire*. Paris: Armand Colin.

Čapo Žmegač, Jasna. 2002. *Srijemski Hrvati: etnološka studija migracije, identifikacije i interakcije*. Zagreb: Duriex.

————. 2007. *Strangers Either Way: The Lives of Croatian Refugees in Their New Home*. New York: Berghahn.

————. 2010. "Refugees, Co-Ethnic Migrants, and Diaspora: Blurring the Categories." In *Co-Ethnic Migrations Compared: Central and Eastern European Contexts*, ed. Jasna Čapo Žmegač, Christian Voß, and Klaus Roth, 177-94. Berlin: Verlag Otto Sagner.

Čapo, Jasna. 2015a. "Population Movements as Instances of ‹Co-ethnic› Encounters: A Critique." In *At Home but Foreigners: Population Transfers in 20th Century Istria*, ed. Katja Hrobat Virloget, Catherine Gousseff, and Gustavo Corni, 209-22. Koper: Univerzitetna založba Annales.

————. 2015b. "Prijepori oko naslijeđa prošlosti i memorija u Hrvatskoj: znanstveno-popularna publikacija pod pritiskom ideologija." *Studia ethnolgica Croatica* 27(1): 105-29.

————. 2019. *Dva doma: hrvatska radna migracija u Njemačku kao transnacionalni fenomen*. Zagreb: Durieux.

Carmichael, Cathie. 2002. *Ethnic Cleansing in the Balkans: Nationalism and the Destruction of Tradition*. London: Routledge.

Castelli, Lucia. 2018. *Italiani d'Istria: chi partì e chi rimase: Storie orali e ritratti fotografici raccolti tra Pirano e Fossoli*. Mantova: Sometti.

Čebron Lipovec, Neža. 2012. "Building the Brave New World in a Contested Land: Mihevc in Koper." In *45+: Post-War Modern Architecture in Europe*, ed. Stephanie Herold and Biljana Stefanovska, 25-36. Berlin: Universitätsverlag der Technischen Universität.

————. 2015. "'I'm Telling the Story of the Town': Places in a Contested Space." In *At Home but Foreigners: Population Transfers in 20th Century Istria*, ed. Katja Hrobat Virloget, Catherine Gousseff, and Gustavo Corni, 189-208. Koper: Univerzitetna založba Annales.

————. 2018. "Izgradnja slovenskih obalnih mest v času po drugi svetovni vojni: Primer mesta Koper." Ph.D. dissertation. Koper: Unviersity of Primorska, Faculty of Humanities.

————. 2019. "Post-War Urbanism along the Contested Border: Some Observations on Koper/Capodistria and Trieste/Trst." *Dve domovini* 49: 199-220.

————. 2021. Etnografske metode in ohranjanje stavbne dediščine. *Glasnik Slovenskega etnološkega društva* 61(1): 17-29.

Čebron Lipovec, Neža, Katja Hrobat Virloget, and Andrej Preložnik. 2017. "Heroes We Love . . . Or Not?" In *Heroes We Love: Ideology, Identity and*

Socialist Art in New Europe, ed. Simona Vidmar, 274–88. Maribor: Umet-
nostna galerija.

Čepič, Zdenko, and Dušan Nećak. 1979. *Zgodovina Slovencev.* Ljubljana: Cankarjeva založba.

Cernaz, Alberto. 2008. "La Città: Speciale odonimi." *La città, Foglio della Comunità italiana di Capodistria 13 (26).* 13 (26).

Cerutti, Simona. 2012. Étrangers: Étude d›une condition d›incertitude dan
sune société d›Ancien Régime. Paris: Bayard.

Cipek, Tihomir. 2009. "Sjećanje na 1945: čuvanje I brisanje. O snazi obitelj-
skih narativa." In *Kultura sjećanja: 1945. Povijesni lomovi i svladanje prošlosti*, ed. Sulejman Bosto and Tihomir Cipek, 155–65. Zagreb: Disput.

Cogoy, Renate. 2009. "Uvod." In *Fojbe: Primer psihopatološke recepcije zgodovine*, ed. Luisa Accati and Renate Cogoy, 7–22. Ljubljana: Krtina (Transl.
from *Das Unheimliche in der Geschichte. Die Foibe. Beiträge zur Pschopathologie historischer Rezeption.* 2007. Berlin: Trafo).

Colella, Amedeo. 1958. *L'esodo dalle terre adriatiche: rilevazioni statistiche.*
Rome: Opera per l'assistenza ai profughi giuliani e dalmati.

Colummi, Cristiana, Liliana Ferrari, Annamaria Brondani, and Giovanni Mic-
coli. 1980. *Storia di un esodo: Istria 1945–1956.* Trieste: Istituto regionale
per la storia del movimento di liberazione nel Friuli Venezia Giulia.

Confino, Alon. 1997. "Memory and Cultural History: Problems of Method."
The American Historical Review 102(5): 1386–403.

Corin, Ellen. 2007. "Personal Travel through Otherness." In *The Shadow Side of
Fieldwork: Exploring the Blurred Borders between Ethnography and Life*, ed.
Athena McLean and Annette Leibing, 239–61. Malden, MA: Blackwell
Publishing.

Corni, Gustavo. 2018. "Private versus Public: The Memorialization of the Ex-
odus of the Istro-Dalmatians, 1945–2015." In *How to Address the Loss?
Forced Migrations, Lost Territories and the Politics of History: A Comparative
Approach in Europe and at Europe's Margins in the Twentieth Century*, ed.
Anne Bazin and Catherine Perron, 57–78. Brussels: P.I.E Peter Lang.

Cunja, Leander. 2004. Škofije na Morganovi liniji. Koper: Lipa and Krajevna
skupnost.

———. 2020. "Scofie: Albaro Vescovà sulla Linea Morgan." In *Fuori dai confini: Memorie di un bambino sulla Linea Morgan*, Silvio Pecchiari Pečarič,
169–79. Trieste: Battello.

Czerwiński, Maciej. 2013. "Breme (post)komunizma: hrvatski i poljski kul-
turni kodovi." In *Komparativni postsocijalizam: slavenska iskustva*, ed. Maša
Kolanović, 47–80. Zagreb: FF Press.

D'Alessio, Vanni. 2006. "Istrians, Identifications and the Habsburg Legacy: Perspectives on Identities in Istria." *Acta Histriae* 14(1): 15–39.

———. 2008. "Dall'Impero d'Austria al Regno d'Italia: Lingua, stato e na-
zionalizzazione in Istria." In *Una storia balcanica: Fascismo, comunismo e
nazinalismo nella Jugoslavia del Novecento*, ed. Lorenzo Bertucelli and Mila
Orlić, 31–71. Verona: Ombre corte.

———. 2012. "Ponad egzodusa i fojbi nova talijanska literatura o 'istočnoj granici.'" *Časopis za povijest Zapadne Hrvatske* 6 and 7: 55-75.

"Dall'Istria alla Jugoslavia." n.d. Istituto piemontese per la storia della reistenza e della società contemporanea. I luoghi dell'esodo in Piemonte. Le parole dell'esodo. Retrieved 28 October 2022 from http://intranet.istoreto.it/esodo/parola.asp?id_parola=9.

de Certeau, Michel. 1987. *La Faiblesse de croire*. Paris: Seuil.

———. 1990. *L'invention du quotidien: Arts de faire*. Paris: Gallimard.

Dei, Fabio. 2002. *Beethoven e le mondine*. Rome: Meltemi.

Del Boca, Angelo. 2005. *Italiani, brava gente?* Vicenza: Neri Pozza.

Derrida, Jacques. 2014. *Le dernier des Juifs*. Paris: Éditions Galilée.

Dosse, Florence. 1993. *Les héritiers de silence: Enfants d'appelés en Algérie*. Paris: Stock.

Dota, Franco. 2010. *Zaraćeno poraće: konfliktni i konkurentski narativi o stradanju i iseljevanju Talijana iz Istre*. Zagreb: Srednja Evropa.

Elias, Norbert, and John L. Scotson. 1994. *The Established and the Outsiders: A Sociological Enquiry into Community Problems*, 2nd ed. London: SAGE.

Eriksen, Thlland Eriksen. 1995. *Small Places, Large Issues: An Introduction to Social and Cultural Anthropology*. London: Pluto.

Erzar, Tomaž. 2017. *Dolga pot odpuščanja*. Ljubljana: Družina.

Fabietti, Ugo, and Vicenzo Matera. 1999. *Memorie e identità*. Rome: Meltemi.

Fakin Bajec, Jasna. 2011. *Procesi ustvarjanja kulturne dediščine: Kraševci med tradicijo in izzivi sodobne družbe*. Ljubljana: Založba ZRC.

Fakin, Jasna, and Katja Jerman. 2004. "Istrski begunci: gradivo in raziskovalni nastavki." *Traditiones* 33(1): 117–42.

Figes, Orlando. 2009. *Šepetalci: zasebno življenje v Stalinovi Rusiji*. Ljubljana: Modrijan (Transl. from *The Whisperers: Private Life in Stalin's Russia*. 2007. New York: Metropolitan Books).

Fikfak, Jurij. 2009. "Cultural and Social Representations on the Border: From Disagreement to Coexistence." *Human Affairs* 19(4): 350–62.

Focardi, Filippo. 2020. *Nel cantiere della memoria: Fascismo, Resistenza, Shoah, Foibe*. Rome: Viella.

Fonda, Pavel. 2009. "Nedomačni notranji tujec." In *Fojbe: Primer psihopatološke recepcije zgodovine,* ed. Luisa Accati and Renate Cogoy, 101–33. Ljubljana: Krtina [Transl. from *Das Unheimliche in der Geschichte. Die Foibe. Beiträge zur Pschopathologie historischer Rezeption*. 2007. Berlin: Trafo].

Fornasin, Alessio, and Marianna Zacchigna 2007. "L'esodo dal Capodistriano nel secondo dopoguerra: Nuove indagini quantitative." In *Dopoguerra di confine: Povojni čas ob meji*, ed. Tulia Catalan, Giulio Mellinato, Pio Nodari, Raoul Pupo, Marta Verginella, Franco Cecotti, 575–88. Trieste: Istituto regionale per la storia del movimento di liberazione nel Friuli Venezia Giulia, Università di Trieste and Regione autonoma Friuli Venezia Giulia.

"Forum Tomizza: Short Take." n.d. *Forum Tomizza*. Retrieved 4 November 2022 from https://www.forumtomizza.com/hr/forum-tomizza-malo-povijesti/188/.

"Fulvio Tomizza." n.d. *Forum Tomizza.* Retrieved 4 November 2022 from https://www.forumtomizza.com/hr/fulvio-tomizza/229/.

Franzinetti, Guido. 2006. "The Rediscovery of the Istrian *Foibe." Jahrbücher für Geschichte und Kultur Südosteuropas* 8: 85–98.

Gams, Ivan. 1991. "Analiza imen za obalno regijo." *Annales, anali Koprskega primorja in bližnjih pokrajin* 1(1): 7–11.

Gellner, Ernest. 1983. *Nations and Nationalism.* Ithaca, NY: Cornell University Press.

"Giorno del ricordo." 2021. *Wikipedia.* Retrieved 5 November 2022 from https://it.wikipedia.org/wiki/Giorno_del_ricordo.

Gombač, Jure. 2005. *Ezuli ali optanti? Zgodovinski primer v luči sodobne teorije.* Ljubljana: Založba ZRC.

———. 2015. "Some New Findings on Masssive Post-War Population Movement from Present-Day Slovenian Istria." In *At Home but Foreigners: Population Transfers in 20th Century Istria*, ed. Katja Hrobat Virloget, Catherine Gousseff, and Gustavo Corni, 119–28. Koper: Univerzitetna založba Annales.

Gostečnik, Christian. 2008. *Relacijska paradigma in travma.* Ljubljana: Brat Frančišek.

Graziosi, Andrea. 2001. *Guerra e rivoluzione in Europa: 1905–1956.* Bologna: Il Mulino.

Gregorovich, Nevia. 2009. "Parenzo, a scuola dal 1953 al 1956." *L'Arena di Pola* 3307: 5. Retrieved 28 October 2022 from http://www.arenadipola.com/articoli/6448.

Gross, Jan T. 2012. *Neighbors: The Destruction of the Jewish Community in Jedwabne, Poland.* Princeton, NJ: Princeton University Press.

Guštin, Damijan, and Nevenka Troha, ed. 2004. *Neupogljivi zakon Rima: fašizem in osvobodilni boj primorskih Slovencev 1941–1943: dokumenti = La legge inflessibile di Roma: il fascismo e la lotta di liberazione degli sloveni nella Venezia Giulia 1941–1943: documenti.* Ljubljana: Društvo piscev zgodovine NOB.

Guillaume, Marc. 1980. *La politique du patrimoine.* Paris: Galilée.

Habinc, Mateja. 2009. "Prazniki in tvorjenje skupnosti." *Glasnik Slovenskega etnološkega druša* 49(1/2): 30–37.

———. 2014. "Intangible Culture as Tradition: The Cows' Ball, the Village Serenade and the Country Wedding in Bohinj." *Narodna umjetnost: hrvatski časopis za etnologiju i folkloristiku* 51(1): 113–29.

———. 2020. "Dediščina skupnega: skupnost in dediščina." *Glasnik Slovenskega etnološkega društva* 60(2): 70–81.

Hafstein, Valdimar Tr. 2018. *Making Intangible Heritage: El Condor Pasa and Other Stories from UNESCO.* Bloomington: Indiana University Press.

Hage, Ghassan. 1997. "At Home in the Entrails of the West: Multiculturalism, Ethnic Food and Migrant Home-Building." In *Home/World: Space, Community and Marginality in Sidney's West*, ed. Helen Grace, Ghassan Hage, Lesley Johnson, Julie Langsworth, Michael Symonds, 99–153. Annandale: Pluto.

Halbwachs, Maurice. 1925. *Les cadres sociaux de la mémoire*. Paris: Librairie Félix Alcan.

———. 1971. *La topographie légendaire des évangelis en Terre sainte: Etude de mémoire collective*. Paris: Presses Universitaires de France.

———. 2001. *Kolektivni spomin*. Ljubljana: Studia humanitatis (Transl. from *Les cadres sociaux de la mémoire*. 1952. Paris: Presses Universitaires de France).

Halicka, Beata. 2018. "The Kresy in Polish Memory: Between a Lost Arcadia and the Bloodlands of East-Central Europe." In *How to Address the Loss? Forced Migrations, Lost Territories and the Politics of History: A Comparative Approach in Europe and at Europe's Margins in the Twentieth Century*, ed. Anne Bazin and Catherine Perron, 107–30. Brussels: P.I.E Peter Lang.

Hall, Stuart. 2008. "Whose Heritage? Un-settling 'The Heritage,' Reimagining the Post-Nation." In *The Heritage Reader*, ed. Graham Fairclough, Rodney Harrison, John Schofield, John H. Jameson, Jr., 219–28. London: Routledge.

Han, Diego. 2014. "Roberto Spazzali. Radio Venezia Giulia. Informazione, propaganda e intelligence nella 'guerra fredda' adriatica (1945–1954), Gorizia: Editrice Goriziana, 2013, 234 str." *Histria: godišnjak Istarskog povijesnog društva* 4(4): 252–58.

Harrison, Rodney, Graham Fairclough, John H. Jameson Jr., and John Schofield Harrison. 2008. "Introduction." In *The Heritage Reader*, ed. Graham Fairclough, Rodney Harrison, John Schofield, John H. Jameson, Jr., 1–12. London: Routledge.

Harvey, David C. 2001. "Heritage Pasts and Heritage Presents: Temporality, Meaning and the Scope of Heritage Studies." *International Journal of Heritage Studies* 7(4): 319–38.

Hirschon, Renée. 1989. *Heirs of the Greek Catastrophe: The Social Life of Asia Minor Refugees in Pireus*. Oxford: Clarendon Press.

Hladnik-Milharčič, Ervin. 2008. "Mediteran je oljka in ovca: od tega dvojega lahko živiš vse življenje." *Dnevnik*, 9 August. Retrieved 3 November 2022 from https://www.dnevnik.si/339533.

Hobsbawm, Eric J. 1996. "Introduction: Inventing Traditions." In *The Invention of Tradition*, ed. Erik J. Hobsbawm and Terence Ranger, 1–14. Cambridge: Cambridge University Press.

Horvat, Marjan. 2010. "Dogodek v posebnem mestu." *Mladina*, 15 July. Retrieved 17 September 2019 from https://www.mladina.si/51160/dogodek-v-posebnem-mestu/.

Hostnik, Majda. 2002. "Kdor ga je bral, je strpen." *Dnevnik*, 13 May. Retrieved 3 November 2022 from https://www.dnevnik.si/23136.

Hrobat Virloget, Katja. 2014. "Nesnovna dediščina Istre: avtentičnosti, razmerja moči in ustvarjanje vezi." In *Interpretacije dediščine*, Knjižnica Glasnika Slovenskega etnološkega društva 48, ed. Tatjana Dolžan Eržen, Ingrid Slavec Gradišnik, and Nadja Valentinčič Furlan, 226–41, 286–87. Ljubljana: Slovensko etnološko društvo.

————. 2015a. "The Burden of the Past: Silenced and Divided Memories of the Post-war Istrian Society." In *At Home but Foreigners: Population Transfers in 20th Century Istria*, ed. Katja Hrobat Virloget, Catherine Gousseff, and Gustavo Corni, 159–88. Koper: Univerzitetna založba Annales.

————. 2015b. "Breme preteklosti: Spomini na sobivanje in migracije v slovenski Istri po drugi svetovni vojni." *Acta Histriae* 23(3): 531–54.

————. 2017a. "'Istrian Exodus': Between Official and Alternative Memories, between Conflict and Reconciliation." *Ethnologies* 39(2): 31–50.

————. 2017b. "Slišati 'drugega' med nami: o spominih etničnih Italijanov v Istri in o medetničnih odnosih." In *Nemi spomini: manjšine med obrobjem in ospredjem*, Knjižnica Glasnika Slovenskega etnološkega društva 51, ed. Saša Poljak Istenič, Mateja Habinc and Katja Hrobat Virloget, 13–31. Ljubljana: Slovensko etnološko društvo.

————. 2019. "The 'Istrian Exodus' and the Istrian Society that Followed It." *Dve domovini* 49: 163–80.

————. 2020. "Urban Heritage between Silenced Memories and 'Rootless' Inhabitants: The Case of the Adriatic coast in Slovenia." In *The Routledge Handbook of Memory and Place*, ed. Sarah de Nardi, Hilary Orange, Steven High, and Eerika Koiskinen-Koivisto, 22–30. Abingdon: Routledge.

————. 2021. "'Better Be Quiet.' Silence in Memories of 'Istrian Exodus,' National Heroes and Beliefs." *Cultural Analysis* 19(1): 7–23.

Hrobat Virloget, Katja, and Neža Čebron Lipovec 2017. "Heroes We Love? Monuments to the National Liberation Movement in Istria between Memories, Care, and Collective Silence." *Studia ethnologica Croatica* 29(1): 45–71.

Hrobat Virloget, Katja, Catherine Gousseff, and Gustavo Corni, eds. 2015. *At Home but Foreigners: Population Transfers in 20th Century Istria*. Koper: Univerzitetna založba Annales.

Hrobat Virloget, Katja, Emilija Kastelic, and Petra Kavrečič. 2012. "Sodobne 'tradicionalne' prireditve v severni Istri s stališča predstavitve dediščine." In *Istrski praznik: preteklost, sedanjost, avtentičnost: šagre in ljudski prazniki v severni Istri*, ed. Aleksander Panjek, 54–74. Koper: Univerza na Primorskem, Znanstveno-raziskovalno središče, Univerzitetna založba Annales.

Hrobat Virloget, Katja, and Petra Kavrečič. 2019. "Traditional Festivities in North Istria in Terms of Authenticity and (Dis)Continuity." *Academica Turistica: Tourism & Innovation Journal* 12(2): 109–20.

Hrobat Virloget, Katja, and Janez Logar 2020. "Kaj sporoča molk? Poskus interdisciplinarne etnološke in psihoterapevtske interpretacije (po)vojnih spominov na primeru Primorske." In *Mikro in makro: pristopi in prispevki k humanističnim vedam ob dvajsetletnici UP Fakultete za humanistične študije: 1. knjiga*, ed. Irena Lazar, Aleksander Panjek, and Jonatan Vinkler, 257–74. Koper: Založba Univerze na Primorskem.

Hrobat Virloget, Katja, Saša Poljak Istenič, Neža Čebron Lipovec, and Mateja Habinc. 2016. "Abandoned Spaces, Mute Memories: On Marginalized Inhabitants in the Urban Centres of Slovenia." *Glasnik Etnografskog instituta* 64(1): 77–90.

"Il piacere di leggere." 2008. Estratto dal libro: CAP XVII – PRIMUM VIVERE. InCamper no. 124: 111. Retrieved 28 October 2022 from http://www.incamper.org/public/numeri/124/113.pdf

Ingold, Tim. 2018. *Anthropology and/as Education.* London: Routledge.

Ivelja, Ranka. 2004. "Porta mi le rokavice, prosim!" *Dnevnik,* 14 February. Retrieved 8 August 2019 from https://www.dnevnik.si/73905.

Ivelja, Ranka, and Blaž Petkovič. 2010. "Tržaško srečanje korak k spravi: trije predsedniki skupaj položili venec pred simbol slovenstva." *Dnevnik*, 14 July. Retrieved 17 September 2019 from https://www.dnevnik.si/1042373760.

Janović, Nikola. 2008. "Jernej Mlekuž, Burek.si?! Koncepti/recepti. Studia Humanitatis (Varia), Ljubljana, 2008, 202 p. Review." *Dve domovini* 28: 169–71.

Jerman, Katja. 2008. "Dve Gorici – eno mesto: konstrukcija urbanega." Ph.D. dissertation. Ljubljana: University of Ljubljana, Faculty of Arts.

Jeudy, Henri Pierre, ed. 1990. *Patrimoines en folie.* Paris: Ed. de la MSH.

Jezernik, Božidar. 2005. "Preteklost in dediščina." In *Dediščina v očeh znanosti*, Zbirka Županičeva kjižica 12, ed. Jože Hudales and Nataša Visočnik, 11-24. Ljubljana: Filozofska fakulteta, Oddelek za etnologijo in kulturno antropologijo.

———. 2013. "Politika praznovanja." In *Politika praznovanja: prazniki in oblikovanje skupnosti na Slovenskem*, Županičeva knjižnica 37, ed. Ingrid Slavec Gradišnik, Mitja Velikonja and Božidar Jezernik, 7-16. Ljubljana: Znanstvena založba Filozofske fakultete.

Judson, Pieter M. 2006. *Guardians of the Nation: Activists on the Language Frontiers of Imperial Austria.* Cambridge, MA: Harvard University Press.

Judt, Tony. 2005. *Postwar: A History of Europe Since 1945.* New York: Penguin.

Juri, Aurelio. 2020. "Pahor k bazoviški fojbi?" *Dnevnik*, 27 June, 11.

Juri, Franco. 2010. *Vrnitev v Las Hurdes: vojne, ljubezni, črne štorklje in oddaljeni Istrani.* Ljubljana: Založba Sanje.

Jurić Pahor, Marija. 2004. "Neizgubljivi čas: travma fašizma in nacionalsocializma v luči nuje po 'obdobju latence' in transgeneracijske transmisije." *Razprave in gradivo* 44: 38–64.

Kacin Wohinz, Milica. 1998. "Zgodovinski oris." In *Tigrova sled: pričevanje o uporu primorskih ljudi pod fašizmom,* ed. Lida Turk and Dorče Sardoč, 5-24. Gorica: Sklad Dorče Sardoč.

Kacin Wohinz, Milica, and Nevenka Troha, eds. 2001. *Slovensko-italijanski odnosi 1880-1956, poročilo slovensko-italijanske zgodovinsko-kulturne komisije, I rapporti italo-sloveni 1880–1956, Relazione della commissione storico-culturale italo-slovena, Slovene-Italian Relations 1880–1956: Report of the Slovene-Italian Historical and Cultural Commission.* Ljubljana: Nova revija. Retrieved October 2022 from file:///C:/Users/Katja/Downloads/slo-ita-odnosi-1880-1956_2000.pdf.

Kacin Wohinz, Milica, and Marta Verginella 2008. *Primorski upor fašizmu: 1920–1941.* Ljubljana: Društvo Slovenska matica.

Kalc, Aleksej. 2019. "The Other Side of the 'Istrian Exodus': Immigration and Social Restoration in Slovenian Coastal Towns in the 1950s." *Dve domovini* 49: 145–62.

Kavrečič, Petra. 2008. "Italijanska narodna skupnost v Republiki Sloveniji in primerjava nekaterih aspektov pravne zaščite in pravic s slovensko manjšino v Italiji." In *Pre-misliti manjšino: pogledi reprezentativnih predstavnikov Slovencev v Italiji in pravno-politični okvir*, ed. Gorazd Bajc, Devan Jagodic, Borut Klabjan, Maja Mezgec, Zaira Vidau, and Luisa Vigini, 221–45, 297–99. Koper-Trieste: Univerza na Primorskem, Znanstveno-raziskovalno središče, Založba Annales and Slovenski raziskovalni inštitut.

———. 2017. "'Sacro pellegrinaggio': Visits to World War I Memorials on the Soča/Isonzo Front in the Interwar Period." *Etnološka tribina: godišnjak Hrvatskog etnološkog društva* 47(40): 141–60.

Kemperle, Marjan. 1997. "Čigav odposlanec je manjšina? Pogovor s Silvanom Sauom." In *Zbornik Primorske: 50 let*, ed. Slobodan Valentinčič, 86. Koper: Primorske novice.

Kersten, Krystyna. 2001. "Forced Migration and the Transformation of Polish Society." In *Redrawing Nations: Ethnic Cleansing in East-Central Europe, 1944–1948*, ed. Philipp Ther and Ana Siljak, 75–86. Oxford: Rowman & Littlefield Publishers.

Kidron, Carol A. 2009. "Toward an Ethnography of Silence: The Lived Presence of the Past in the Everyday Life of Holocaust Trauma Survivors and Their Descendants in Israel." *Current Anthropology* 50(1): 5–27.

King, Jeremy. 2002. *Budweisers into Czechs and Germans: A Local History of Bohemian Politics, 1848–1948*. Princeton, NJ: Princeton University Press.

Klabjan, Borut. 2010. "Nation and Commemoration in the Adriatic: The Commemoration of the Italian Unknown Soldier in a Multinational Area: The Case of the Former Austrian Littoral." *Acta Histriae* 18(3): 399–424.

———. 2012. "'Partizanska pokrajina': partizanski spomeniki in komemoriranje partizanov na Tržaškem. *Acta Histriae* 20(4): 669–92.

Knez, Kristjan. 2013a. "Editoriale. Emozioni e riflessioni." *Il Trillo*, November–December 12a, 1–2.

———2013b. "Commozioni, riflessioni e tanti applausi. 'Magazzino 18': I commenti di chi ha visto il spettacolo." *Il Trillo*, November–December 12a, 10–13.

Knific, Bojan. 2003. "Vprašanje narodne noše na Slovenskem: njen razvoj od srede 19. stoletja do 2. svetovne vojne." *Etnolog* 16: 435–68.

Koskinen-Koivisto, E. 2017. "Negotiating the Past at the Kitchen Table: Nostalgia as a Narrative Strategy in an Intergenerational Context." *Journal of Finnish Studies* 19(2): 7–23.

Kosmač, Miha. 2015. "'Botherhood and Unity': Yugoslav Authorities' Attitude toward the Population in the Northern Adriatic, 1945 to 1948." In *At Home but Foreigners: Population Transfers in 20th Century Istria*, ed. Katja Hrobat Virloget, Catherine Gousseff, and Gustavo Corni, 95–118. Koper: Univerzitetna založba Annales.

————. 2017. *"Etnično homogena Evropa": preselitve prebivalstva v Istri in Sudetih 1945–1948*. Koper: Znanstveno-raziskovalno središče, Založba Annales.

Kostov, Ekaterina. 2005. "Izseljevanje prebivalcev iz nekdanjega okraja Koper: Cone B Svobodnega Tržaškega ozemlja." *Borec* 57 (621–625): 46–98.

Kralj, Ana. 2008. *Nepovabljeni: globalizacija, nacionalizem in migracije*. Koper: Univerza na Primorskem, Znanstveno-raziskovalno središče; Založba Annales and Zgodovinsko društvo za južno Primorsko.

Kralj, Ana, and Tanja Rener. 2010. "Meja kot razlika, metafora in diskurz." *Teorija in praksa* 47 2/3): 509–32.

Kržišnik-Bukić, Vera. 2014. "Albanci, Bošnjaki, Črnogorci, Hrvati, Makedonci in Srbi kot neustavne narodne manjšine v Republiki Sloveniji na začetku 21. stoletja." In *Kdo so narodne manjšine v Sloveniji*, ed. Vera Kržišnik-Bukić, 151–78. Ljubljana: Zveza zvez kulturnih društev narodov in narodnosti nekdanje SFRJ v Sloveniji.

Lapierre, Nicole. 1989. *Le silence de la mémoire: A la recherche des Juifs de Plock*. Paris: Plon.

Lavabre, Marie-Claire. 2007. "Paradigmes de la mémoire." *Transcontinentales: Sociétés, idéologies, système mondial* 5: 139–47.

Lavrenčič, Leo. 2012. "Demografska slika italijanske manjšine v Kopru po poteku roka za izselitev leta 1956." *Acta Histriae* 20(3): 505–532.

Ledinek Lozej, Špela, and Nataša Rogelja. 2012. "Šavrinka, Šavrini in Šavrinija v etnografiji in literaturi." *Slavistična revija* 60(3): 537–47.

Le feste per il 600° anniversario dell'apParisione di s. Giorgio a Pirano. 1943. The copy of a film recorded on 16 mm tape, kept by Paolo Venier, Triest.

Lenclud, Gerard. 2004. "La tradizione non è più quella d'un tempo." In *Oltre il folklore: Tradizioni popolari e antropologia nella società contemporanea*, ed. Pietro Clemente and Fabio Mugnaini, 123–133. Rome: Carocci.

Lesjak, Miran. 2020. "Intervju: Jože Pirjevec." *Dnevnik, Objektiv*, 11 July, 8–12.

Levi, Primo. (1986) 2003. *Potopljeni in rešeni*. Ljubljana: Studia humanitatis.

Ličen, Daša. 2018. "Reinventing Habsburg Cuisine in Twenty-First Century Trieste." *Folklore: Electronic Journal of Folklore* 71: 37–54.

Lichterman, Paul. 2017. "Interpretive Reflexivity in Ethnography." *Ethnography* 18(1): 34–45.

Lorenci, Gloria. 2020. "(Intervju) S psihiatrom Željkom Ćurićem o tem, kako doživljamo krizo in samoizolacijo: komu je najtežje in zakaj?" *Večer*, 4 April. Retrieved 3 November 2022 from https://vecer.com/v-soboto/intervju-s-psihiatrom-zeljkom-curicem-o-tem-kako-dozivljamo-krizo-in-sam oizolacijo-komu-je-najtezje-in-zakaj--10152744.

Lowenthal, David. 1985. *The Past Is a Foreign Country*. New York: Cambridge University Press.

Makarovič, Maria. 1972. "Narodna noša." *Slovenski etnograf* 23/24: 53–70.

Makuc, Neva. 2015. "Sclavi, Schiavi in podobni izrazi v miselnem svetu novoveških italijanskih avtorjev." In *Škrabčev zbornik 8*, ed. Danila Zuljan Kumar and Helena Dobrovoljc, 165–76. Nova Gorica: Založba Univerze v Novi Gorici.

Masero, Monica. 2017. "The Wisdom of the Body and Couple Therapy: A Sensorimotor Psychotherapy Perspective; An Interview with Pat Ogden." *Australian and New Zealand Journal of Family Therapy* 38(4): 657–68.

Mazower, Mark. 2010. *L'Impero di Hitler: Come i nazisti governavano l'Europa occupata.* Milano: Mondadori.

Mazzini, Miha. 2020. "Miha Mazzini: zagrenjena psiha teh nesrečnikov hoče vse stlačiti v blato." *Siol plus,* 2 April. Retrieved 3 November 2022 from https://siol.net/siol-plus/kolumne/miha-mazzini-zagrenjena-psiha-teh-nesrecnikov-hoce-vse-stlaciti-v-blato-522218.

Mekina, Igor. 2021. „Priključitev Primorske domovini, še en praznik, s katerega so Janšo pregnali praporji z rdečimi zvezdami." *Insajder,* 15 September. Retrieved 5 November from https://insajder.com/slovenija/prikljucitev-primorske-domovini-se-en-praznik-s-katerega-so-janso-pregnali-praporji-z.

Menih, Kristina. 2011. *Koprčani.* Piran: Mediteranum.

Mežnarič, Silva. 1986. *"Bosanci": a kuda idu Slovenci nedeljom?* Ljubljana: Republiška konferenca ZSMS, Univerzitetna konferenca ZSMS.

Milani Kruljac, Nelida. 2011. *Skrajni rob grebena.* Ljubljana: Društvo 2000 and C KUD AAC Zrakogled.

———. 2015. *Vojne zgodbe.* Koper: Unione Italiana.

Miletta Mattiuz, Olinto, and Guido Rumici. 2008. *Chiudere il cerchio: Memorie giuliano-dalmate. Vol. 1, Dall'inizio del Novecento al Secondo conflitto mondiale.* Gorizia: Associazione nazionale Venezia Giulia e Dalmazia Comitato provinciale di Gorizia and Mailing List Histria.

Miletto, Enrico. 2007. *Istria allo specchio: Storie e voci di una terra di confine.* Milan: Franco Angeli.

Miličić, Budimir. 1985. *Radnička klasa Sarajeva 1919–1941.* Sarajevo: Institut za istoriju u Sarajevu.

Milošević, Orban. 2020. "Kako so blokirali denarce Socialistične federativne EU." *Dnevnik, Objektiv,* 21 November, 13.

Mlekuž, Jernej. 2008. *Burek.si?! Koncepti/recepti.* Ljubljana: Studia Humanitatis.

Monica, Luciano. 1991. *La scuola italiana in Jugoslavia: Storia, attualità e prospettive.* Trieste-Rovigno: Unione Italiana-Fiume and Università popolare di Trieste.

Mori, Anna Maria, and Nelida Milani Kruljac. 2012. *L'anima altrove.* Milan: Rizzoli.

Mrđenović, Marko. n.d. "Claudio Ugussi, omaggio a un grande autore." *La voce del popolo.* Retrieved 4 November 2022 from http://www.editfiume.info/archivio/lavoce/2012/121217/cultura.htm.

Mugnaini, Fabio. 2004. "Introduzione: Le tradizioni di domani." In *Oltre il folklore: Tradizioni popolari e antropologia nella società contemporanea,* ed. Pietro Clemente and Fabio Mugnaini, 11–72. Rome: Carocci editore.

Muršič, Rajko. 1999. "Postmodernity, Postmodernism and Postmodern Anthropology: Circling around Decentredness." In *MESS: Mediterranean Ethno-*

logical Summer School, Vol. 3, Piran/Pirano, Slovenia 1997 and 1998, ed. Zmago Šmitek and Rajsko Muršič, 11–27. Ljubljana: Filozofska fakulteta.

"Nelida Milani e la memoria tagliata." 2017. *Punto e a capo MMC RTV SLO*, radio broadcast, 13 April, 25. Retrieved 5 November from https://4d.rtvslo.si/arhiv/punto-e-a-capo/174465868.

Nemec, Gloria. 1998. *Un paese perfetto: Storia e memoria di una comunità in esilio: Grisignana d'Istria (1930–1960)*. Trieste-Gorizia: Istituto regionale per la cultura istriana and Libreria editrice goriziana.

———. 2012a. *Nascita di una minoranza. Istria 1947–1965: Storia e memoria degli italiani rimasti nell'area istro-quarnerina*. Fiume; Trieste; Rovigno: Unione italiana, Università popolare, Università degli studi, Dipartimento studi umanistici and Centro di ricerche storiche.

———. 2012b. "Processi di formazione della minoranza italiana, memorie e interpretazioni sul tema delle opzioni." Časopis za povijest Zapadne Hrvatske 6 and 7: 179–209.

———. 2015. "The Hardest Years: Private Stories and Public Acknowledgment in the Recollections of Istrian Italians, either Exiled or Stayed Behind." In *At Home but Foreigners: Population Transfers in 20th Century Istria*, ed. Katja Hrobat Virloget, Catherine Gousseff, and Gustavo Corni, 145–58. Koper: Univerzitetna založba Annales.

Nikočević, Lidija. 2003. "Negotiating Borders: Myth, Rhetoric, and Political Relations." *Focaal* 41: 95–105.

———. 2011. *Valiže & deštini: Istra izvan Istre – L'Istria fuori dall'Istria – Istri out of Istria*. Pazin: Istarska županija.

"Nino e i suoi ricordi di Giusterna." 2009. *La città* 14 (29): 23–29.

Novljan, Neva. 2017. "Primorska narečna skupina, 1/3. Dokumentarna oddaja Slovenska narečja." *RTV Slovenija*, 28 January. Retrieved 4 November 2022 from https://4d.rtvslo.si/arhiv/dokumentarni-filmi-in-oddaje-kulturno-umetniski-program/174451674.

Nora, Pierre. 1984. *Les Liéux de mémoire, tome 1: la Republique*. Paris: Gallimard.

———. 1986. *Les Liéux de mémoire, tome 2: la Nation*. Paris: Gallimard.

———. 1993. *Les Liéux de mémoire, tome 3: les France*. Paris: Gallimard.

Orlić, Mila. 2012. "Javni diskursi, nacionalne memorije i historiografija na sjevernojadranskom prostoru." Časopis za povijest Zapadne Hrvatske 6 and 7: 12–22.

———. 2015. "Se la memoria (non) mi inganna . . . L'Italia e il 'confine orientale': Riflessioni sulla storia e sul suo uso pubblico." *Acta Histriae* 23(3): 475–88.

———. 2019. "Né italiani né slavi: State- e nation-building jugoslavo nel secondo dopoguerra in Istria." *Contemporanea* 22(4): 561–84.

Orlić, Olga. 2008. "Mnogoznačje istarskog multikulturalizma." *Etnološka tribina* 31(38): 39–59.

Pahor, Špela. 2007. *Srečanja v Piranu: življenjske pripovedi prebivalcev Pirana*. Piran: Mediteranum.

————. 2011. *Srečanja v Piranu 2: življenjske pripovedi prebivalcev Pirana*. Piran: Mediteranum.

————. 2014. *Srečanja v Piranu 3: življenjske pripovedi prebivalcev Pirana*. Piran: Mediteranum.

Panjek, Aleksander. 2011. *Tržaška obnova: ekonomske in migracijske politike na Svobodem tržaškem ozemlju*. Koper: Univerza na Primorskem; Znanstveno-raziskovalno središče and Univerzitetna založba Annales; Zgodovinsko društvo za južno Primorsko.

Passerini, Luisa. 2008. *Ustna zgodovina, spol in utopija: izbrani spisi*. Ljubljana: Studia humanitatis.

Pavone, Claudio. 1992. *Una guerra civile: Saggio sulla moralita nella Resistenza*. Milan: Bollati Boringhieri.

Pecchiari Pečarič, Silvio. 2020. *Fuori dai confini: Memorie di un bambino sulla Linea Morgan*. Trieste: Battello.

Pečenko, Valentin. 2020. *Sto let od koroškega plebiscita*. Ljubljana: RTV Slovenija. Retrieved 5 November 2022 from https://365.rtvslo.si/arhiv/dokumentarni-filmi-in-oddaje-kulturno-umetniski-program/174724467.

Pelc, Stanko. 2018. "Marginality and Sustainability." In *Nature, Tourism and Ethnicity as Drivers of (De)Marginalization: Insights to Marginality from Perspective of Sustainability and Development,* ed. Stanko Pelc and Miha Koderman, 31–42. Cham: Springer.

Pelikan, Egon. 2002. *Tajno delovanje primorske duhovščine pod fašizmom: primorski krščanski socialci med Vatikanom, fašistično Italijo in slovensko katoliško desnico – zgodovinsko ozadje romana Kaplan Martin Čedermac*. Ljubljana: Nova revija.

Perron, Catherine. 2017. "'Voyages des racines' et mémoire de la Heimat perdue dans la littérature allemande post unification." *Ethnologies* 39(2): 143–66.

Perrot, Martyne. 1987. "La part maudite de l'ethnologie: Le journal de terrain." In *Anthropologie sociale et Ethnologie de la France: Colloque du Centre d'ethnologie française et de Musée national des arts et traditions populaires, Nov. 1987*, II. Communications, n.p., 1–7. Paris. Retrieved 28 October 2022 from https://core.ac.uk/download/pdf/47810423.pdf.

Petrovec, Janko. 2020. "Srečanje med slovenskim in italijanskim predsednikom prva novica italijanskih medijev." *MMC RTV Slovenija*, 14 July. Retrieved 4 November 2022 from https://www.rtvslo.si/svet/evropa/srecanje-med-slovenskim-in-italijanskim-predsednikom-prva-novica-italijanskih-medijev/530671.

Piko-Rustja, Martina. 2012. "Slovenska ledinska in hišna imena v Unescovem seznamu nesnovne dediščine v Avstriji." *Traditiones* 41(2): 213–26.

Pirjevec, Jože. 1982. "La fase finale della violenza fascista: i retroscena del processo Tomažič." *Qualestoria: bollettino dell'istituto regionale per la storia del movimento di liberazione nel Friuli-Venezia Giulia* 10(2): 75–94.

————. 2000. *"Trst je naš!" Boj Slovencev za morje (1848–1954)*. Ljubljana: Nova Revija.

———. 2009. *Foibe: una storia d'Italia.* Torino: Einaudi.

———. 2012. "Fojbe: katera resnica?" In *Fojbe*, ed. Tine Logar, 1–241. Ljubljana: Cankarjeva založba.

Pletikosić, Ivica. 2002. "'Čišćenje' v Piranu (1945–1948)." *Acta Histriae* 10(2): 465–92.

Poljak Istenič, Saša. 2012. "Aspects of Tradition." *Traditiones* 41(2): 77–89

———. 2013, *Tradicija v sodobnosti: Janče – zeleni prag Ljubljane.* Ljubljana: Inštitut za slovensko narodopisje, Založba ZRC.

Portelli, Alessandro. 1997. *The Battle of Valle Giulia: Oral History and the Art of Dialogue.* Madison: University of Wisconsin Press.

———. 2016. "Allessandro Porteli: Speaking of Oral History." Filmed 28 April 2016, Canada's History, 8:23. Retrieved 4 November 2022 from https://www.youtube.com/watch?v=vEToq3T_LZQ.

Promitzer, Christian, Hermanik Klaus-Jürgen, and Eduard Staudinger 2009. *(Hidden) Minorities: Language and Ethnic Identity between Central Europe and the Balkans.* Vienna: Lit Verlag.

Pupo, Raoul. 2000. "L'esodo degli Italiani da Zara, da Fiume e dall'Istria: un quadro fattuale." In *Esodi: Trasferimenti forzati di popolazione nel Novecento europeo*, Quaderni di Clio – Istituto Regionale per la Cultura Istriana, ed. Marina Cattaruzza, Marco Dogo, and Raoul Pupo, 183–208. Napoli: Edizioni Scientifiche Italiane.

———. 2005. *Il lungo esodo. Istria: Le persecuzioni, le foibe, l'esilio.* Milan: Rizzoli.

———. 2015. "Italian Historiography on the Istrian Exodus: Topics and Perspectives." In *At Home but Foreigners: Population Transfers in 20th Century Istria*, ed. Katja Hrobat Virloget, Catherine Gousseff, and Gustavo Corni, 25–47. Koper: Univerzitetna založba Annales.

———. 2021. *Adriatico amarissimo: Una lunga storia di violenza.* Bari: Laterza.

Pupo, Raoul, and Aleksander Panjek. 2004. "Riflessioni sulle migrazioni ai confine italo-jugoslavi (1918–60): identità, politica e metodo." In *Oltre l'Italia e l'Europa = Beyond Italy and Europe: ricerche sui movimenti migratori e sullo spazio multiculturale : Atti del Convegno internazionale . . . Mobilità geografica in Italia: caratteristiche e tendenze, differenze regionali e processi di territorializzazione nella nuova società multiculturale, Trieste, 14–17 marzo 2002 e del VI Colloquio italoromeno di geografia umana ed economica, Il Friuli Venezia Giulia come regione di transito e insediamento di immigrati romeni, Trieste, 13–16 marzo 2002,* ed. Carlo Donato, Pio Nodari, and Aleksander Panjek, 343–60. Trieste: Edizioni Università di Trieste.

Purini, Piero. 2010. *Metamorfosi ethniche: I cambiamenti di pololazioe a Trieste, Gorizia, Fiume e in Istria (1914–1975).* Udine: Kappa Vu.

Purini, Piero, and Wu Ming. 2014. "Quello che Cristicchi dimentica: Magazzino 18, gli 'Italiani brava gente' e le vere larghe intese." *Giap*, 24 February. Retrieved 4 November 2022 from https://www.wumingfoundation.com/giap/2014/02/quello-che-cristicchi-dimentica-di-dire-magazzino-18-gli-italiani-brava-gente-e-le-vere-larghe-intese/.

"Radio Koper praznuje 70 let". 2019. *Regional Obala*, 22. May. Retrieved 26 October 2022 from https://www.regionalobala.si/novica/radio-koper-praz nuje-70-let-se-vedno-je-pomemben-gradnik-primorske-identitete#.

Radošević, Milan. 2011. "Franko Dota, Zaraćeno poraće: konfliktni i konku-rentski narativi o stradanju i iseljavanju Talijana Istre, Zagreb: Srednja Europa, 2010., 149 str." *Histria: godišnjak Istarskog povijesnog društva* 1(1): 242–46.

Rakovac, Milan. 1983. *"Riva i druži" ili, caco su nassa dizza.* Zagreb: Globus.

Ramšak, Jure. 2015. *Ab initio: moderne ideologije in izgradnja novega urbanega prostora: zgodovina, arhitektura in perspektiva kulturnega turizma v Novi Gorici in Raši.* Koper: Univerzitetna založba Annales.

Reinisch, Jessica, and Elizabeth White, eds. 2001. *The Disentanglement of Populations. Migration, Expulsion and Displacement in Postwar Europe, 1944– 49.* Hampshire: Palgrave Macmillan.

Renan, Ernest. 1998. *Che cos'è una nazione e altri saggi.* Rome: Donzelli.

Rihtman Auguštin, Dunja. 2001. *Etnologija i etnomit.* Zagreb: Naklada Publica.

Rijavec, Jani. 2020. "Meja na Goriškem: življenje in pogledi ljudi ob meji v 2. polovici 20. stoletja." Master's thesis. Koper: University of Primorska, Faculty of Humanities.

Rodman, Margaret C. 1992. "Empowering Place: Multilocality and Multivoca-lity." *American Anthropologist, New Series* 94(3): 640–56.

Rogelja, Nataša, and Alenka Janko Spreizer. 2017. *Fish on the Move: Fishing between Discourses and Borders in the Northern Adriatic.* Cham: Springer.

Rogoznica, Deborah. 2011. *Iz kapitalizma v socializem: gospodarstvo cone B Svobodnega tržaškega ozemlja 1947–1954.* Koper: Pokrajinski arhiv.

Rožac Darovec, Vida. 2012. "'Po svobodi je v vas pršu hudič!': pomen ustne zgodovine za razkrivanje mitoloških struktur v preteklosti na primeru spo-minjanja Rakitljanov." *Acta Histriae* 20(4): 693–700.

Ruble, Blair A. 2003. "Living Together: The City, Contested Identity, and De-mocratic Transitions." In *Composing Urban History and the Constitution of Civic Identites*, ed. John Czaplicka and Blair A. Ruble, 1–21. Baltimore, MD; Washington, DC: Johns Hopkins University Press and Woodrow Wilson Center Press.

Sansone, Caterina, and Alessandro Tota. 2012. *Palachinche.* Rome: Fandango Libri.

Sanzin, David. 2015. *Zaščiteni!?: manjšine in njihove pravice.* Trieste: Slovenska kulturno-gospodarska zveza.

Šaunik, Tomaž J. 2001. "Nikoli končana zgodba. Ponovno oživljanje zahtev italijanskih optantov najbrž ne bo imelo resnejših posledic. Je pa napoved novih zahtev, ki jih bodo še postavljali ‹Staroavstrijci.'" *Mladina*, 6 August. Retrieved 4 Novemeber 2022 from https://www.mladina.si/93725/ nikoli-koncana-zgodba/.

Scounti, Ahmed. 2009. "The Authentic Illusion: Humanity's Intangible Cul-tural Heritage, the Moroccan Experience." In *Intangible Heritage*, ed. Lau-rajane Smith and Natsuko Akagawa, 74–92. London: Routledge.

Sedmak, Gorazd. 2012. "Podlage in smernice za trženje šager in ljudskih praznikov." In *Istrski praznik: preteklost, sedanjost, avtentičnost: šagre in ljudski prazniki v severni Istri*, ed. Aleksander Panjek, 76–87. Koper: Univerza na Primorskem, Znanstveno-raziskovalno središče, Univerzitetna založba Annales.

Sezneva, Olga. 2003. "The Dual History: Politics of the Past in Kaliningrad, Former Koenigsberg." In *Composing Urban History and the Constitution of Civic Identites*, ed. John Czaplicka and Blair A. Ruble, 58–85. Baltimore, MD; Washington, DC: Johns Hopkins University Press and Woodrow Wilson Center Press.

Simić, Andrei. 1973. *The Peasant Urbanities: A Study of Rural-Urban Mobility in Serbia*. New York: Seminar.

Širca, Majda. 2020. *Požig*. Ljubljana: RTV Slovenija.

Širok, Kaja. 2007. "Manifestacija ljudske volje: spomini na Gorico v letu 1946." *Kronika* 55(2): 369–84.

———. 2009. "Kolektivno spominjanje in kolektivna pozaba v obmejnem prostoru: Spomini na Gorico 1943–1947." Ph.D. dissertation. University of Nova Gorica.

Slavec Gradišnik, Ingrid. 2000. *Etnologija na Slovenskem*. Ljubljana: Založba ZRC, ZRC SAZU.

———. 2014. "V objemih dediščin." V *Interpretacije dediščine*, Knjižnica Glasnika Slovenskega etnološkega društva 48, ed. Tatjana Dolžan Eržen, Ingrid Slavec Gradišnik, and Nadja Valentinčič Furlan, 8–25. Ljubljana: Slovensko etnološko društvo.

Smith, Andrea. 2006. *Colonial Memory and Postcolonial Europe*. Bloomington: Indiana University Press.

Smith, Laurajane. 2006. *Uses of Heritage*. London: Routledge.

Spalová, Barbora. 2017. "Remembering the German Past in the Czech Lands: A Key Moment Between Communicative and Cultural Memory." *History and Anthropology* 28(1): 84–109.

Spazzali, Roberto. 2013. *Radio Venezia Giulia: Informazione, propaganda e intelligence nella "guerra fredda" adriatica (1945–1954)*. Gorizia: Editrice Goriziana.

Stanonik, Marija. 1990. "O folklorizmu na splošno." *Glasnik Slovenskega etnološkega društva* 30(1–4): 20–42.

Stanonik, Marija, Marko Terseglav, and Ingrid Slavec Gradišnik. 2007. "Folklorizem." In *Slovenski etnološki leksikon*, ed. Angelos Baš, 131–32. Ljubljana: Mladinska knjiga.

Štefančič, Marcel. 2010. "Piran-Pirano: Goran Vojnović, 2010." *Mladina*, 7 October. Retrieved 4 November 2022 from https://www.mladina .si/51962/piran-pirano/.

Steffe, Artur. 2020. "Dediščina ribištva v luči demografskih sprememb na območju Kopra: tematska pot nekdanjih ribiških pristanišč." Thesis, bachelor's degree, University of Primorska, Faculty of Humanities, Anthropology and Cultural Studies.

Strčić, Petar. 2001. "Ekzodus Hrvata iz Istre i drugih hrvatskih krajeva između 1918 i 1958. godine kao politička, nacionalna i gospodarska pojava." In *Talijanska uprava na hrvatskom prostoru i ekzodus Hrvata*, ed. Marino Manin, 19–60. Zagreb: Hrvatski institut za povijest and Društvo Egzodus istarskih Hrvata.

Šuklje, Borut. 2019. "Zaplet ob kosilu v rimski palači Chigi." *Primorske novice*, 15 February. Retrieved 4 November 2022 from http://www.pri morske.si/mnenja/kolumne/regionalni-horizonti/zaplet-ob-kosilu-v-rim ski-palaci-chigi.

Šuligoj, Boris. 2016. "Množično dokazujejo, da so bili politični preganjanci." *Delo*, 17 March. Retrieved 4 November 2022 from https://www.delo.si/ novice/slovenija/mnozicno-dokazujejo-da-so-bili-politicni-preganjanci .html.

Tanc, Barbaros. 2001. "Where Local Trumps National: Christian Orthodox and Muslim Refugees since Lausanne." *Balcanologie* 5 (1–2). https://doi .org/10.4000/balkanologie.732.

Ther, Philipp. 2001. "A Century of Forced Migration: The Origins and Consequences of 'Ethnic Cleansing.'" In *Redrawing Nations: Ethnic Cleansing in East-Central Europe, 1944–1948*, ed. Philipp Ther and Ana Siljak, 43–74. Oxford: Rowman & Littlefield Publishers.

Titl, Julij. 1961. *Populacijske spremembe v Koprskem primorju: koprski okraj bivše cone B*. Koper: J. Titl.

Todorović, Suzana. 2016. *Narečje v Kopru, Izoli in Piranu*. Koper: Libris.

Tomizza, Fulvio. 1980. *Boljše življenje*. Koper: Lipa.

———. 1989. *Materada*. Koper: Lipa.

———. 2015. *Zlo pride s severa: roman o škofu Vergeriju*. Ljubljana: Beletrina.

Troha, Nevenka. 1997. "STO – Svobodno tržaško ozemlje." In *Zbornik Primorske – 50 let*, ed. Slobodan Valentinčič, 56–60. Koper: Primorske novice.

———. 1998. *Politika slovensko-italijanskega bratstva (Slovansko-italijanska antifašistična unija v coni A Julijske krajine v včasu od osvoboditve do uveljavitve mirovne pogodbe)*. Ljubljana: Arhiv Republike Slovenije.

———. 2000. "Preselitve v Julijski krajini po drugi svetovni vojni." *Prispevki za novejšo zgodovino* 40(1): 255–68.

———. 2002. "Italijanska narodnostna skupnost v Sloveniji med letoma 1954 in 1990." *Zgodovinski časopis* 56(3/4): 447–64.

———. 2006. "Osimo in manjšine." In *Osimska meja: jugoslovansko-italijanska pogajanja in razmejitev leta 1975*, ed. Jože Pirjevec, Borut Klabjan, and Gorazd Bajc, 137–49, 333–35. Koper: Univerza na Primorskem, Znanstveno-raziskovalno središče, Založba Annales and Zgodovinsko društvo za južno Primorsko.

———. 2010. "Odseljevanje in prebegi Slovencev z območja, ki je bilo z Mirovno pogodbo z Italijo priključeno k Ljudski republiki Sloveniji." In *Migracije in slovenski prostor od antike do danes*, Zbirka Zgodovinskega časopisa 39, ed. Peter Štih and Bojan Balkovec, 432–46. Ljubljana: Zveza zgodovinskih društev Slovenije.

———. 2019. "Nekaj utrinkov iz političnega življenja na Svobodnem tržaškem ozemlju (1947–1954)." *Kronika* 76(3): 677–92.

Tucovič, Vladka. 2012. "Slovenska Istra: pokrajina na slovenskem literarnem zemljevidu." *Slavistika v regijah: slovenski slavistični kongres,* ed. Boža Krakar Vogel, 52–57. Ljubljana: Zveza društev Slavistično društvo Slovenije and Znanstvena založba Filozofske fakultete.

———. 2013. "Istra v sodobni slovenski književnosti." Ph.D. dissertation. Ljubljana: University of Ljubljana, Faculty of Arts.

Tunbridge, John E., and Gregory J. Ashworth. 1996. *Dissonant Heritage: The Management of the Past as a Resource in Conflict.* Chichester: Wiley.

Turner, Bryan S. 1987. "Note on Nostalgia." *Theory, Culture and Society* 4(1): 147–56.

Ugussi, Claudio. 1991. *La città divisa.* Udine: Campanotto Editore.

———. 2002. *Podijeljeni grad.* Zagreb: Durieux.

Van Boeschoten, Riki. 2005. "'Little Moscow' and the Greek Civil War: Memories of Violence, Local Identities and Cultural Practices in a Greek Mountain Community." In *Memory and World War II,* ed. Francesca Cappeletto, 39–65. Oxford: Berg.

Van de Port, Mattijs. 1999. "'It Takes a Serb to Know a Serb': Uncovering the Roots of Obstinate Otherness." *Critique of Anthropology* 19(1): 7–30.

Van de Port, Mattijs, and Birgit Meyer. 2018. "Introduction. Heritage Dynamics: Politics of Authentication, Aesthetics of Persuasion and the Cultural Production of the Real." In *Sense and Essence: Heritage and the Cultural Construction of the Real,* ed. Mattijs van de Port and Birgit Meyer, 1–39. New York: Berghahn.

Van der Kolk, Bessel. 2014. *The Body Keeps the Score. Mind, Brain and Body in the Transformation of Trauma.* London et al.: Penguin Books.

Van Ginderachter, Maarten, and Jon Fox, eds. 2019. *National Indifference and the History of Nationalism in Modern Europe.* London: Routledge.

Várdy, Steven Béla, and T. Hunt Tooley. 2003. "Introduction: Ethnic Cleansing in History." In *Ethnic Cleansing in Twentieth-Century Europe,* ed. Steven Béla Várdy, T. Hunt Tooley, and Agnes Huszar Várdy, 9–14. Boulder, CO: Columbia University Press.

Verginella, Marta. 1995. "Poraženi zmagovalci: slovenska pričevanja o osvobodilnem gibanju na Tržaškem." In *Ljudje v vojni: druga svetovna vojna v Trsteu in na Primorskem,* ed. Marta Verginella, Sandi Volk, and Katja Colja, 13–52. Koper: Zgodovinsko društvo za južno Primorsko.

———. 1996. *Ekonomija odrešenja in preživetja, odnos do življenja in smrti na tržaškem podeželju.* Knjižnica Annales 14. Koper: Zgodovinsko društvo za južno Primorsko and Znanstveno raziskovalno središče Republike Slovenije.

———. 2000. "L'esodo istriano nella storiografia a slovena." In *Esodi – Trasferimenti forzati di popolazione nel Novecento europeo,* Quaderni di Clio – Istituto Regionale per la Cultura Istriana, ed. Marina Cattaruzza, Marco Dogo and Raoul Pupo, 269–77. Naples: Edizioni Scientifiche Italiane.

————. 2009. "Med zgodovino in spominom. Fojbe v praksi določanja itali-jansko-slovenske meje." In *Fojbe: Primer psihopatološke recepcije zgodovine*, ed. Luisa Accati and Renate Cogoy, 23–72 (Transl. from *Das Unheimliche in der Geschichte. Die Foibe. Beiträge zur Pschopathologie historischer Rezeption*. 2007. Berlin: Trafo).

————. 2010. "Zgodovinjenje slovensko-italijanske meje in obmejnega prostora." *Acta Histriae* 18(1/2): 207–16.

————. 2015. "Writing Historiography on Migrations at the Meeting Point of Nations in the Northern Adriatic." In *At Home but Foreigners: Population Transfers in 20th Century Istria*, ed. Katja Hrobat Virloget, Catherine Gousseff, and Gustavo Corni, 49–70. Koper: Univerzitetna založba Annales.

————. 2017 „O zgodovinjenju dihotomije mesta in podeželja." *Acta Histriae* 25(3): 457–72.

Veschambre, Vincent. 2008. *Traces et mémoires urbaines: Enjeux sociaux de la patrimonilasation et de la démolition*. Rennes: PED.

Vidmar, F. U. 2009. "Radio Koper-Capodistria." *Istrapedia: Istarska internetska enciklopedija*. Retrieved 5 November 2022 from https://www.istrapedia. hr/hr/natuknice/883/radio-koper-capodistria.

Vojnović, Goran. 2020. "Velik korak za diplomacijo." *Dnevnik, Objektiv*, 11 July, 7.

————. 2010. *Piran/Pirano*. Film, 101 min. Franci Zajc, Arsmedia.

Volk, Sandi. 2003. *Istra v Trstu: naselitev istrskih in dalmatinskih ezulov in nacionalna bonifikacija na Tržaškem 1954–1966*. Koper: Univerza na Primorskem; Znanstveno-raziskovalno središče and Zgodovinsko društvo za južno Primorsko.

————. 2004. *Esuli a Trieste: Bonifica nazionale e rafforzamento dell'italianità sul confine orientale*. Udine: Kappa Vu.

Wahnich, Sophie. 2011. "L'impossible patrimoine négatif." *Les cahiers Irice* 1(7): 47–62.

Wajnryb, Ruth. 2001. *The Silence: How Tragedy Shapes Talk*. Crows Nest, Australia: Allen & Unwin.

Weber, Irena. 2006. *Vključenost prebivalcev mesta Piran v življenje mesta in njihov odnos do razvoja in prenove starega mestnega jedra: rezultati antropološke terenske raziskave*. Research report (unpublished). Piran: Municipality.

Werner, Michael, and Bénédicte Zimmermann. 2006. "Beyond Comparison: Histoire Croisée and the Challenge of Reflexivity." *History and Theory* 45(1): 30–50.

Wieviorka, Michel. 2004. "Mémoire, identité et histoire*.*" *Pour* 181: 89–93.

Wolff, Larry. 2001. *Venice and the Slavs: The Discovery of Dalmatia in the Age of Enlightment*. Standford, CA: Standford University Press.

————. 2021. *Inventing Eastern Europe: The Map of Civilization on the Mind of the Enlightenment*. Stanford, CA: Stanford University Press.

Zahra, Tara. 2008. *Kidnapped Souls: National Indifference and the Battle for Children in the Bohemian Lands, 1900–1948*. Ithaca, NY: Cornell University Press.

————. 2010. "Imagined Non-Communities: National Indifference as a Category of Analysis." *Slavic Review* 69(1): 93–119.

Žerjavić, Vladimir. 1993. "Doseljevanja i iseljevanja s područja Istre, Reke i Zadra u razdobju 1910–1971." *Društvena istraživanja* 2(4–5): 631–56.

Židov, Nena. 2019. "Nacionalni in globalni seznami nesnovne kulturne dediščine in Unescova Konvencija (2003)." In *Nesnovna dediščina med prakso in registri: 15. vzporednice med slovensko in hrvaško etnologijo*, Knjižica Glasnika Slovenskega entološkega društva 53, ed. Ana Svetel and Tihana Petrović Leš, 12–25. Ljubljana-Zagreb: Slovensko etnološko društvo and Hrvaško etnološko društvo.

Zorn, Jelka, and Uršula Lipovec Čebron. 2008. *Once upon an Erasure: From Citizens to Illegal Residents in Republic of Slovenia*. Ljubljana: Študentska založba.

Index

Milton Keynes UK
Ingram Content Group UK Ltd.
UKHW051923140823
426877UK00006B/262